Crime Prevention and Community Safety

Longman Criminology Series

Series Editor: Tim Newburn

Titles in the series:

Ian Brownlee, *Community Punishment: A Critical Introduction*
Adam Crawford, *Crime Prevention and Community Safety: Politics, Policies and Practices*

Crime Prevention and Community Safety
Politics, Policies and Practices

Adam Crawford

LONGMAN
London and New York

Addison Wesley Longman Limited
Edinburgh Gate,
Harlow,
Essex CM20 2JE,
United Kingdom
and Associated Companies throughout the world

First published 1998

ISBN 0-582-29457-6 PPR

Visit Addison Wesley Longman on the world wide web at http://www.awl-he.com

British Library Cataloguing-in-Publication Data

A catalogue record for this book is available from the British Library

Set by 35 in 10/12pt New Baskerville

Printed in Great Britain by Henry Ling Ltd., at the Dorset Press, Dorchester, Dorset.

Contents

List of Figures   vii
Series Editor's Preface   viii
Acknowledgements   x
Dedication   xii

Introduction   1

**1 Conceptualising Crime Prevention and
      Community Safety**   5
   The purposes and uses of classification   6
   Defining crime prevention: its conceptual boundaries   8
   Classifying types of crime prevention   13
   Victim-oriented prevention   22
   Identifying the actors   25
   Conclusions   27

2 The British Experience   29
   A brief history of crime prevention   29
   Recent central government initiatives   35
   The police   42
   The probation service   45
   Local government   47
   The voluntary sector and NACRO   49
   Crime Concern and the private sector   50
   The Safer Cities Programme   52
   New Labour, new era?   58
   Conclusions   62

3 Situational and Environmental Strategies   65
   Situational prevention defined   66
   The theoretical background   68

Rational choice theory   70
'Designing out' crime   74
Routine-activity theory   78
Displacement – the Achilles heel?   80
Some case studies   84
Offender-oriented situational prevention   85
Community-oriented and estate-based situational
    prevention   90
Victim-oriented situational prevention   94
Some conclusions by way of a critical assessment   98

4 **Social and Communal Strategies**   103
Assumptions within social crime prevention   104
Broad social policies   108
Young people and criminality prevention   109
Case studies of youth prevention   116
Criminality prevention – some issues   119
Community-focused preventive measures   124
Community crime prevention case studies   140
A critique of community crime prevention   155
Conclusions   160

5 **Implementation and the Partnership Approach**   161
Planning and information-gathering   162
The 'partnership' approach   169
Some further issues   179
Making sense of 'partnerships'   184
Community participation and involvement   186
Commercial sector involvement   187
Conclusions   192

6 **Evaluating Crime Prevention and Community Safety**   196
Outcome evaluation   197
Process evaluation   206
Replication   208
Displacement   209
Redefining success and failure   214
Conclusions   215

7 **Some Comparative Experiences**   218
Sweden – a national strategy   219
France – social crime prevention   220
The Netherlands – a culture of tolerance?   229
Japan – a culture of informal control?   235
Conclusions   242

8 **The Politics of Crime Prevention and
   Community Safety**   245
   Responsibilisation strategies   247
   The reinvention of government?   252
   Risk, governmentality and power – the 'new penology'?   255
   Whither the state?   258
   Future visions   260
   Conclusions   269

   Suggestions for Further Reading   272
   Bibliography   275
   Index   299

List of Figures

Figure 1.1 An Audience/Target Two-Dimensional
            Typology of Crime Prevention   16

Figure 1.2 A Process/Target Two-Dimensional
            Typology of Crime Prevention   19

Figure 2.1 Morgan's Recommended Structure   39

Figure 2.2 The Structure of the Safer Cities
            Programme in Phase 2   54

Figure 3.1 Stages of Decision-Making   74

Figure 5.1 The Prisoners' Dilemma   189

Figure 5.2 Individual Preferences in the Prisoners'
            Dilemma   189

Figure 6.1 The Classic Experimental Design   198

Figure 6.2 The Realist Experimental Design   204

Series Editor's Preface

Our society appears to be increasingly preoccupied with crime and with criminal justice. Despite increasing affluence in the post-war period, crime has continued to rise – often at an alarming rate. Moreover, the pace of general social change at the end of the twentieth century is extraordinary, leaving many feeling insecure. High rates of crime, high levels of fear of crime, and no simple solutions in sight, have helped to keep criminal justice high on the political agenda.

Partly reflecting this state of affairs, the study of crime and criminal justice is burgeoning. There are now a large number of well-established postgraduate courses, new ones starting all the time, and undergraduate criminology and criminal justice degrees are also now appearing regularly. Though increasing numbers of individual textbooks are being written and published, the breadth of criminology makes the subject difficult to encompass in a satisfactory manner within a single text.

The aim of this series as a whole is to provide a broad and thorough introduction to criminology. Each book covers a particular area of the subject, takes the reader through the key debates, considers both policy and politics and, where appropriate, also looks to likely future developments in the area. The aim is that each text should be theoretically-informed, accessibly written, attractively produced, competitively priced, with a full guide to further reading for students wishing to pursue the subject further. Whilst each book in the series is designed to be read as an introduction to one particular area, the Longman Criminology Series has also been designed with overall coherence in mind.

In this book, Adam Crawford examines the dramatic growth of crime prevention and community safety. Given the context of rising crime and fear of crime mentioned above, it is perhaps not surprising that techniques and strategies which are aimed at preventing crime, or alleviating its effects, have become a central concern of government – both national and local. Politicians are under immense pressure to be seen to be 'tackling crime' and, as a consequence, crime preventing has often been presented as the new panacea within criminal justice. Enormous claims, for example, have been made on behalf of new technologies such as closed-circuit television and yet rigorous evaluation of the impact of such schemes is still largely absent. Moreover, despite the profile of crime prevention, it is still the poor relation of criminal justice in terms of expenditure.

Security and safety, as Adam Crawford argues, involve normative and not just technological and administrative questions. He shows how so much of what is written about crime prevention or community safety lacks clarity and consistency, and all too often is inadequate in its discussion of the wider social implications of new initiatives and programmes. He steers the reader through these complex debates, helps make sense of the confusion that still abounds, provides and challenging theoretical examination of the 'shift to prevention', and argues that we must not lose sight of the importance of seeing and treating *security* as a 'public good'. This is an important book which will be of great interest to students of criminology and related subjects, and to all those working in the field of community safety.

Tim Newburn
London, June 1998

Acknowledgements

The timing of this book has been both fortuitous and problematic for me as author. The election of the new Labour government in May 1997, when I was halfway through the completion of this book, posed plenty of new challenges. At the same time, it has allowed me to take stock of, and consider, what has come to constitute a major reinvigoration of crime prevention and community safety in Britain. This was made all the more evident given the new government's decision that law and order, in general, and community safety, in particular, are to be key areas of initial government policy against which they are to be judged. The flurry of consultation documents, policy proposals and Green and White Papers which emerged in the autumn of 1997 made keeping track of unfolding developments particularly difficult as some of the detail changed through the twists and turns of the policy process. I have tried to keep abreast of developments up to and including the publication of the Crime and Disorder Bill which brought together the government's programme in this area. To my knowledge the discussions in this book are accurate up to January 1998. While particular elements of the Crime and Disorder Bill may be amended slightly in its passage through Parliament, the size of the government's majority should ensure that the general thrust of the policy is likely to remain unchanged. As a consequence, the timing of this book has allowed me to look both to the history and future prospects of crime prevention and community safety in Britain with some confidence – which could not have been the case a year earlier.

In writing this book I have received considerable support and assistance from many people. I should like to thank Ian Brownlee, David Wall and Jill Enterkin for their many helpful comments and suggestions on sections of the book as it emerged. Particular thanks go to Clive Walker who, as Director of the Centre for Criminal Justice Studies, has been supportive throughout. Tim Hope has been a continual source of ideas and collegial support. Furthermore, I have benefited from discussions with many community safety practitioners over recent years, both in this country and abroad, who have been given the challenging task of translating the fine-sounding ideals of crime prevention into muddy practice, often with one hand tied behind their back by the stringencies of managerialist auditing. In particular, I should like to thank Cath Mahoney, Andy Mills, Alison Taylor and Karen Evans for sharing their experiences and insights. In relation to the comparative experiences, outlined in Chapter 7, I have benefited considerably from discussions with Antoine Garapon, Jean-Pierre Bonafé-Schmitt, Jacques Faget, Anne Wyvekens, Jeanne de Calan and Satoshi Minoura, among others.

I should like to acknowledge my gratitude to Tim Newburn, as series editor, for suggesting this project to me in the first place and for his comments and support throughout. Thanks to all the secretarial staff in the Law Department for keeping me on my toes and for the occasional nice word. I am indebted to Dave for the various 'world tours' that he has taken me on from the relative safety of numerous bars across the UK – the gigs almost seemed real! I am grateful to Phil, Ian and Kieran for encouragement and a stabilising influence. Apologies to Alex that there are no pictures in this book, but thanks for keeping me sane and for showing me how a 'real' book can be finished in a day. Finally, there cannot be many people blessed with a companion who will willingly(?) give up another weekend to read yet another chapter of yet another book and not only to correct the odd(!) grammatical and typographical error but also to question, with seeming ease, the philosophical foundations of an argument with which I have toiled for hours or merely to add with a smile: 'Couldn't you have said that more simply?' To Susan, for all of that and much, much more besides, a million thanks are not enough.

Adam Crawford
Centre for Criminal Justice Studies
University of Leeds

For Susan and Alex

Introduction

Currently, there are more than 5 million recorded crimes per annum in England and Wales. This represents more than a doubling of the official crime rate since 1979 and a tenfold increase on the 1950 figure. While the findings of the periodic British Crime Surveys suggest a less steep rise in crime, they also point to a much larger 'dark figure' of crime missed by recorded statistics. According to the latest British Crime Survey, crimes against individuals, such as theft, burglary and assault, have increased by 73 per cent between 1981 and 1995 to 19 million in England and Wales alone (Mirrlees-Black *et al.* 1996). Despite the massive investment by successive governments in 'law and order' – through considerable legislative changes and a cost of the criminal justice system to the Treasury which exceeds £10 billion – we appear to be 'losing the fight against crime'. The traditional institutions of policing, prosecution and punishment appear powerless to make a significant impact. Against this background, concerns about personal security have become an increasingly powerful dynamic in social life, influencing what people do, where they live, as well as whether, where, and when they go out. In these conditions the private security industry has mushroomed. And yet, as opinion polls continue to remind us, we are becoming more, rather than less, fearful of criminal victimisation.

For many politicians, policy-makers, professionals and academics 'crime prevention' and 'community safety' represent the new panaceas to the ills of criminal justice. And yet, few of the implications of this 'major shift in paradigm' appear to have been considered. Exactly what 'crime prevention' or 'community safety' mean or entail is neither self-evident nor uncontested. In the search for practical solutions to immediate problems we have tended to become blind to the more enduring political, cultural, ethical and social issues. The appropriateness, effectiveness and efficacy of particular strategies should be, but all too often are not, the subject of considerable normative and empirical debate. Every lock, security device, CCTV camera, neighbourhood watch scheme, community initiative, parenting class or youth leisure policy launched in the name of crime prevention, carries deep philosophical and political assumptions, commitments to particular models of social explanation and implications for social relations. In this book, I aim to open up the subject of crime prevention and community safety to a wider and more critical glare. The intention is to provide the reader with tools for understanding, contextualising and evaluating both the general move towards prevention and the nature of specific strategies undertaken.

The sub-title of this book indicates something about the approach that will be adopted to the study of crime prevention.[1] First, crime prevention will be studied and analysed as essentially political in nature and not merely as a rational form of technology nor as a disinterested science, the application of which is value-free. The arguments that follow will seek to show that crime prevention poses fundamental political questions about the nature of the society that we are in the process of constructing and social relations therein. It is not the intention of this book to provide a clear or consistent definition of what crime prevention is by specifying tasks, techniques and/or technologies (although the relative value of different definitional typologies will be considered in Chapter 1). However, a variety of different types of intervention will be considered and assessed throughout. A particular emphasis will be placed on the social embeddedness of crime prevention as a political and organisational ideology. Hence, an important task of the book is to uncover the political assumptions that lie behind and infuse given preventive strategies and implementation structures.

The second element implicit in the sub-title concerns the complex inter-relationships between the three levels of analysis identified: *politics* – i.e. a body of ideas and conceptualisations which seeks to influence the art and craft of government; *policies* – i.e. formal governmental and organisational strategies; and *practices* – i.e. institutional actions, day-to-day operations and routine activities in fields of crime control and prevention. The arguments that follow do not take for granted any simple top–down implementation of ideas into practices, but rather seek to problematise the interconnections between these levels of analysis. It might seem preferable to insert a fourth level of analysis, that of criminology or 'criminological knowledge' – i.e. a body or cluster of ideas and explanations which seeks to make sense of crime as a phenomenon and societal reactions to it – as distinct from 'politics'. Political and academic ideas do have different referents, legitimating techniques, rituals and audiences. Furthermore, the means through which one passes into and influences the other are complex. Nevertheless, their separateness is too often overplayed. The politics and power of what passes for 'criminological knowledge' is increasingly apparent (see Garland 1992, 1994; Young 1994). So much so that it almost seems unnecessary to disconnect them and to accord them a misleading distinctiveness.

There is a strong tendency in conventional crime prevention literature, given the significant pragmatic, practical and 'professional' focus of crime prevention, to exclude discussions of the politics of crime prevention, or even to acknowledge its relevance and existence. Crime prevention is often seen as a series of administrative techniques or value-neutral tools. And yet all crime prevention measures, either explicitly or implicitly, embody understandings and assumptions about the causes of crime, the nature of human behaviour and social relations. Nearly all criminological theories are to some extent theories about the prevention of crime.

The approach advocated here is one which seeks to demonstrate the complexity of relationships between politics – and the criminological knowledge infused therein – policies and practices. The book attempts to identify the ways in which policy debates inform, and are informed by, a broader politics of crime control. Furthermore, it seeks to highlight the ways in which policies are shaped by, and in turn shape, existing practices and the institutions to which they give rise. It also gives a significant emphasis to the social consequences of certain policies, both intended and unintended.

Crime prevention is itself ill-defined. Its boundaries, terms of reference and defining characteristics are all the subject of debate and contention. As befits a growing area of academic policy and practical interest and research, crime prevention has produced a profusion of terms, concepts and approaches with their own accompanying lexicon. Consequently, Chapter 1 begins with an examination of the definitional boundaries of crime prevention and some of the debates to which they give rise. The chapter includes an overview of some of the most important attempts to categorise different types of crime prevention. In order to assist the reader in charting a way through the salient terminology, some of the key terms are defined and distinguished. Some of the central theoretical questions which re-emerge throughout the book are introduced and their relevance explained. Chapter 1 can be used as a general reference and guide to be (re)turned to for assistance when reading the subsequent chapters. Chapter 2 charts the recent renaissance of interest in crime prevention in England and Wales. It outlines and seeks to assess some of the key recent policy and institutional developments, both at the level of central government and locally based initiatives. While the potential preventive effect of the criminal justice system, as currently constituted, together with the debates to which these issues give rise are noted, it is not the intention of this book to rehearse arguments about rehabilitation, reform, deterrence or incapacitation through punishments. Rather the focus is on developments and debates at and beyond the frontiers of the formal criminal justice system.

Chapters 3 and 4 consider some of the different crime prevention strategies, drawing on experiences from the UK and the USA. Chapter 3 focuses on situational approaches to crime prevention, while Chapter 4 examines social crime prevention, targeted both at individuals and communities. Both chapters include theoretical discussions supplemented by descriptions of notable case studies and their empirical research evaluations. The implications of each approach are considered, as are some of the vexed issues to which they give rise. Chapter 5 considers the implementation processes of crime prevention initiatives as essential elements in determining their outcome. In particular, the nature of the collection of local information to inform prevention projects, crime data analysis, public consultation and the structure of local 'partnerships' between the relevant agencies are all examined. Chapter 6 considers the process of evaluating crime prevention initiatives. It poses the question, how do we know what works, when and for whom? In so doing, the chapter considers methodological issues associated with different models of evaluation and different sources of data.

Most of the examples and issues referenced in the discussions are drawn from the recent Anglo-American experiences. However, a central contention of this book is that modes of crime control are infused with political and cultural artefacts. Much of the crime prevention literature which has sought to bring together the experiences of various countries has paid scant regard to important cultural and socio-political differences (Clarke 1992; Graham and Bennett 1995). Rather like butterfly collectors, the authors of such books have assembled an array of different models with no understanding of the divergent habitats from which each has been plucked. As Nelken rightly warns, 'many claims about . . . crime control which purport to be universal in fact take their sense and limits of applicability from such cultural connections' (1994a: 221). Consequently, Chapter 7 seeks to consider a wider horizon by looking at the way in which some other societies have interpreted and developed crime prevention. It is anticipated that this wider canvas permits us to begin to discern the ways in which culture can inform us about modes of crime control. By way of conclusion, Chapter 8 considers the wider social implications of the contemporary 'shift to prevention'. It raises a number of questions about the politics of crime prevention and control, as well as about the appropriate allocation of responsibility for personal and communal security. In so doing, it identifies a number of possible 'future visions' of crime prevention and community safety.

Note

1. Here as elsewhere in this book, the term 'crime prevention' is used as a generic category to include 'community safety' programmes, although conceptual debates about the relationship between these two terms are considered in Chapter 1.

Conceptualising Crime Prevention and Community Safety

The dramatic growth, in the last two decades, of crime prevention and community safety as terms around which policy initiatives, practices and intellectual debates cluster is a notable feature of crime control at the end of the millennium. It constitutes what one leading British commentator described as a 'major shift in paradigm' (Tuck 1988). Nevertheless, crime prevention and community safety remain in their infancy. They do not represent a definable set of techniques or established strategies, nor are they ideologically unproblematic. Rather, they are concepts struggling to establish themselves in a context of uncertain debate and fluctuating policy agendas.

The purpose of this chapter is to sketch out and assess some of the most prominent attempts to define and classify what is meant by crime prevention. Such a detour is a necessary first step for a number of specific reasons. The first is simply to introduce the reader to some of the various terminology used in debates about crime prevention and to map out the congruity and variance between concepts used. Academic researchers and practitioners involved in crime prevention have begun to develop a whole lexicon of terms and ideas, all of which carry their own particular meanings. It is hoped that, as a consequence of this initial excursion, the reader can begin to build a conceptual map of the terrain out of which crime prevention politics, policies and practices are formulated and promoted. The second, and more fundamental, aim is to expose some of the assumptions which lie, sometimes hidden, behind the use of particular concepts and terms. Ideas about what is 'appropriate' crime prevention carry with them ideological and political baggage. As a consequence, they need to be extensively stripped and searched for their unspoken presuppositions. Following from this, the third aim is to begin to specify some of the questions which the reader should ask about certain strategies, courses of action and initiatives. In sum, this chapter aims to equip the reader with a toolkit full of concepts and questions with which to explore the domain of crime prevention, so that the reader can identify and understand the connections and divergences between the terms and their use, as well as begin to question the political assumptions and strategies which underpin them.

The purposes and uses of classification

Crime prevention is a concept of almost unending elasticity. As Harvey *et al.* suggest, there are effectively no boundaries to crime prevention work (1989: 85). Proponents and practitioners subsume widely divergent practices under the heading of 'crime prevention' and 'community safety'. At one extreme, crime prevention can be very narrowly defined in terms of physical security techniques or apparatuses. It may refer in a limited sense to the latest technological wizardry. At the other extreme, it can be, and often is, extended to encompass any interventions which are perceived to have some beneficial impact on the physical or social world, however defined and for whomsoever. In part, this stems from the fact that genuine crime prevention is inherently very difficult to assess, as it involves securing a 'non-event'. Crime prevention, in part, is activity which results in inactivity: a 'non-crime'. This begs the question, how do we know when a crime has been prevented? The concept 'crime' as a generic term is also itself the subject of fierce definitional debates. As a social construct 'crime' is not static but culturally informed. New crimes may emerge (some potentially unforeseeable, albeit that little criminological attention is given to the prediction of future crimes), some previously tolerated activities may be accorded the status of 'crime', while the social meaning of older crimes may change. This raises the questions: what activity are we seeking to prevent, and how may that activity be viewed in the future? Prevention presupposes certain elements of prediction, itself an uncomfortable task. Furthermore, the relationship between a preventive activity and the desired outcome – the 'non-crime' – is far from direct or simple. The potential influences on crimes and their prevention are extensive. Hence, the very subject matter of crime prevention is itself problematic.

Nevertheless, we can begin to strip down crime prevention work into some of its key component parts by asking a series of inter-related questions about any given intervention or activity:

1. What intervention or activity is proposed?
2. To whom or what is it directed?
3. What is the intended outcome of the intervention or activity?
4. What is it about the intervention or activity which it is believed will lead to a certain outcome?
5. Under what conditions or in which contexts will the activity produce the desired outcome?
6. What intervention or activity is actually delivered?

7. Under what conditions or in what contexts is the intervention or activity actually delivered?
8. What outcomes result from the intervention or activity?
9. How is the outcome evaluated or measured?
10. What is the relative social value of the various outcomes?

Together, these questions highlight a number of issues which often remain submerged or ignored in discussions about crime prevention. Questions 1 and 2 are reasonably straightforward in that they ask us to identify the intervention and its intended focus or audience. As we shall see, it is in response to these two questions that much of the conceptualisation to date has been focused. Questions 3 to 5, however, require us to specify *aims*, how they relate to desired *outcomes*, and the *mechanisms* used to secure them (Pawson and Tilley 1994). What is the ultimate objective of the activity? What is its intended impact? And how is this supposed or intended to come about? All of this necessitates rendering explicit theoretical presuppositions and underlying hypotheses. All crime prevention measures embody assumptions or theories about the causes of crime: what it is about a given intervention which leads to it having particular preventive outcomes. And yet the causes of crimes are neither settled nor uncontentious, but rather the subject of intense debate, competing theories and explanations, as well as conflicting evidence. We should be cautious of politicians, policy-makers and academics who proclaim a naïveté or lack of interest in respect of aetiology: understandings of, or knowledge about, the causes of crime. Aspects of the design, implementation and analysis of a mode of crime prevention work carry with them commitments to particular models of social explanation and human nature. Furthermore, Question 5 recognises that all interventions will not have the same effects in different contexts. Hence, there is a need for a degree of context specificity or, at the very least, context sensitivity. Therefore, it is not just a question of what works? – i.e. which mechanisms produce what outcomes? – but what works where and for whom? – i.e. under what conditions or in which context?

Questions 6 and 7 require us to interrogate the implementation process. Hence, we need to know about the *process* and *outcome*, as well as the impact of the former on the latter. Many crime prevention projects have failed not necessarily because the idea was a bad one but because it was never properly implemented. Once again, the process will have implications for any assessment of the social and organisational context. Finally, Questions 8 and 9 demand clarity as regards the means through which data is collected concerning the outcomes or effectiveness and how this is measured. Collectively, they pose the question: how do we know when a crime – or the harm and damage associated with it – has been prevented? Therefore they raise methodological issues about whether something 'works'. More fundamentally, they also raise philosophical questions about the limits of our knowledge and how we come to know things.

Methodological principles carry epistemological assumptions about the theory of how things come to be known. Consequently, they have implications for the methods used to gather knowledge in order to evaluate 'success'. These and related issues will be considered in more detail in Chapter 6. Finally, Question 10 forces us to relate the measured outcomes to normative issues about the appropriateness of the measures taken. Here we are asked to consider the social value of the consequences, whether intended or not, of preventive actions and their overall contribution to notions such as the 'general good' or 'social justice'.

Collectively, these questions identify three broad levels at which to analyse crime prevention: *theory, implementation* and *evaluation*. Each of these introduces further contentious conceptual and definitional issues. These will be examined in their own right throughout this book: theoretical issues will be the primary focus of Chapters 3 and 4, implementation issues are examined in Chapter 5, while evaluation and measurement questions are raised in Chapters 6 and 8.

Defining crime prevention: its conceptual boundaries

Crime prevention lies somewhere between the narrow craft of 'policing' and the elephantine and somewhat amorphous processes of 'social control'. The debates as to precisely where along this path crime prevention should be situated are reflected in the complex history of activity associated with the term and its organisational location. As we shall see in Chapter 2, the narrow interpretation of crime prevention, until recently, has occupied the ascendancy in large part because of its traditional association with the work of the police.

The first issue that is raised in attempts to define crime prevention is where to draw its boundaries. This brings us directly to the heart of Question 3 (above): should crime prevention be restricted to measures, the intended outcomes of which relate only *directly* to the reduction of criminal events? Or should it be sufficiently encompassing to include activity which may impact directly on 'quality of life' issues, such as the 'fear of crime', but which may have only an *indirect* impact on crime? This tension between a narrow and broad definition is reflected in most of the conceptual and practical debates about what crime prevention is, whose responsibility it is and how it should be conducted.

'Crime prevention' and 'community safety'

For crime prevention practitioners, this polarised conflict tends to be reproduced in, and coalesce around, an explicitly terminological debate, one which – as we shall see – is also mirrored in theoretical debates. Here the arguments revolve around the distinction between 'crime prevention' and 'community safety'. More recently, the latter has found favour among many practitioners engaged in delivering local crime prevention initiatives. This has been particularly true of those operating outside of the police, although increasingly the police are also beginning to adopt the term. 'Community safety' is the preferred term for many precisely because it reflects a broader approach to crime prevention and, hence, its evaluation (see Osborn and Bright 1989; AMA 1990). Through reference to the term 'safety' it encompasses not just crime, narrowly defined, but also the much wider physical and social impact of crime and the anxieties to which it gives rise.

Furthermore, the term 'community safety' suggests a break with traditional assumptions about crime prevention as a narrow specialism. Proponents of such a terminological distinction argue that crime is intrinsically related to wider social problems. Crime compounds and is compounded by other forms of social disadvantage (Young 1988, 1992). Crime is rarely the only problem within a community, particularly high crime communities, and hence measures to address crime also need to address these wider issues. Furthermore, crime rarely has a simplistic or monocausal explanation. Crime is not caused in the deterministic sense that A + B = Crime. Rather, crime is the outcome of a variety of influencing factors and conditions which are overlaid on each other. This is embodied in the principle of 'multiple aetiology' (Young 1992: 30) as opposed to any idea of 'monocausal explanations'. The diversity and range of severity of acts which constitute 'crimes' only serve to compound this.

The term 'community safety' is seen by practitioners to be preferable for another reason. Implicitly, it stresses the idea that action to prevent crime should be *local*. The notion of 'community', here, appeals both to a decentralised (or 'bottom-up') understanding of policy-making and to collective, not just individual, experiences. 'Community' is seen as a locus of informal social control and as constituting an important force in reducing crime. It is simultaneously a target of, and a resource for, crime prevention (to which I return in Chapter 4). Furthermore, the argument here is that the control of crime should reflect the nature of the phenomenon itself. Since a considerable degree of crime, particularly that which has a significant direct impact on people's everyday lives, is local in nature, it follows that crime prevention should reflect this through a 'community' or neighbourhood focus.

In keeping with this broader understanding, a further attraction of the term 'community safety' is that it has come to imply the need for interventions to be delivered through a 'partnership' approach, drawing together a variety of relevant organisations – in the public, voluntary and private sectors – as well as community groups. As we shall see throughout the book and most notably in Chapter 5, this has become a dominant aspect of recent policy. It is premised on the belief that social reactions to crime, as far as possible, should reflect the nature of the phenomenon itself, which as we have noted has a 'multiple aetiology'. A multi-agency or 'partnership' approach is favoured in that it affords an holistic approach to crime which is problem-oriented rather than organisationally led.

The Home Office's Standing Conference on Crime Prevention (Morgan 1991) strongly endorsed such an understanding. Consequently, it played a crucial role in the promotion of 'community safety' as an appropriate alternative term. It came to the view that the 'term "*crime prevention*" is often narrowly interpreted and this reinforces the view that it is solely the responsibility of the police' (Morgan 1991: 13, emphasis in original). Instead they advocated the use of the term '*community safety*' as it is open to wider interpretation which could encourage 'greater participation from all sections of the community in the fight against crime' (*ibid.*). Hence, 'community safety', it is argued, incorporates and encompasses a greater diversity of activity and people (both professional and lay) which itself, it is believed, will assist in the reduction of crime. The Report deliberately sought to include wider social processes in the prevention of crime and its effects. Here, community safety comes close to forms of urban regeneration and community development.

Others, however, have warned of the dangers of turning crime prevention into a 'catch all' category by forever stretching its boundaries. The concern is that it will lose any sense of specificity and become virtually meaningless in its desire to be all encompassing (Ekblom 1994; Gilling 1996a). However, rather than trying to resolve this conceptual debate in one way or the other, we should recognise that the issues which it references constitute the very fabric of crime prevention work. Consequently, these tensions re-emerge throughout the ensuing discussions. However, I will continue to use the term 'crime prevention' as a generic one, rather than as something which excludes, or defines itself in contradistinction to, 'community safety'.

In an attempt to give a certain degree of clarity to a broad meaning of crime prevention, van Dijk proposes a definition of crime prevention as:

> the total of all policies, measures and techniques, outside the boundaries of the criminal justice system, aiming at the reduction of the various kinds of damage caused by acts defined as criminal by the state.
>
> (1990: 205)

This is a useful definition in that it takes the formal criminal justice system as a key element in the construction of crime prevention. It seeks to specify 'crime' as an act which is so labelled by the state, through the processes of criminalisation, and juxtaposes 'prevention' against the activities of formal criminal justice. As a definition it is sufficiently broad to encompass strategies to address the harm and damage which may arise as a result of crime. It covers fear-reduction programmes, as well as policies which seek to give assistance to the victims of crimes, as they address the damaging results of criminality. Understandably, van Dijk's definition seeks to focus attention on informal strategies outside of the criminal justice system. However, in doing so, he unnecessarily and falsely rigidifies the distinction between what is 'inside' and 'outside' the 'boundaries of the criminal justice system'. These boundaries are neither clearly demarcated nor static. They change over time and place. For example, when is a social worker or a doctor part of the criminal justice system? Is a police officer always within the system? In practice there is often an overlap between interventions which fall under the headings of 'criminal justice' and 'crime prevention'. Much that takes place within, or at the boundaries of, the criminal justice system is concerned with the prevention of future crimes by means of its perceived 'rehabilitative' or 'deterrent' effect. Some initiatives, particularly those aimed at juveniles, deliberately take their referrals both from those who have broken the law and those who may be 'at risk' of offending or 'getting into trouble'. Such initiatives blur the boundaries of what constitutes the criminal justice system. As we shall see in Chapter 5, this blurring is further complicated by the dominant 'partnership' approach to crime prevention, whereby a variety of agencies, many of which are not traditionally associated with criminal justice, are brought together to develop collaborative policies and practice. Furthermore, the criminal justice system itself is an historically contingent and (arbitrary) social construct, which has arisen more through competition between professional groups and agencies in pursuit of their own claims to specialist expertise and legitimacy than any rational strategic plan (Garland 1990).

Fear of crime

The perceived appropriateness of the term 'community safety', with its broader social referents, has marched hand-in-hand with, and been fuelled by, debates about the 'fear of crime'. The recent elevated concern with 'fear of crime' is largely associated with the growth of victimisation surveys as an instrument of criminological research and criminal justice policy. Surveys have revealed the apparent increasing concern about crime among the public (Hough and Mayhew 1983; Mayhew *et al.* 1994). Of greater significance has been the finding that this anxiety leads to changes in individual behaviour patterns, such as not going out alone at certain times or avoiding certain places or people, which itself may have an adverse impact on community life and processes of informal social control (Lewis and Salem 1986; Skogan 1990b). On the assumption that victimisation surveys offer researchers a means of objectively measuring risk, 'fear has generally come to be treated as predominantly a function of risk' (Sparks 1992: 120). Consequently, much debate has focused on the relationship between fear and the risk of victimisation.

The social and spatial patterning of levels of fear revealed by local crime surveys broadly maps the distribution of victimisation (see Jones *et al.* 1986). However, the literature has also identified a weak correlation between 'fear of crime' (as reported in survey findings) and the risk of victimisation, most notably among women, the elderly and people living in low crime, rural or suburban areas (Skogan and Maxfield 1981; Hough and Mayhew 1983). This has led some commentators to identify 'the apparent paradox that those who are most fearful are least often victims' (Mayhew and Hough 1988: 16). One American commentator, after reviewing the available empirical evidence, concluded that, 'there has been no convincing evidence that criminal victimisation produces greater fear of crime than does the lack of being victimised' (Rifai 1982: 193). Despite the theoretical and methodological objections that could be raised against such an assertion (see Crawford *et al.* 1990; Sparks 1992; Walklate 1997), this 'apparent paradox' has taken centre stage in debates about fear of crime. Moreover, the fear of crime has come to be seen as analytically separate from the problem of crime itself.

Hence, as the authors of the first British Crime Survey noted, 'fear of crime appears to be a serious problem which needs to be tackled separately from the incidence of crime' (Hough and Mayhew 1983: 26). As a consequence, people's fears have come to be seen as deserving specific policy attention almost irrespective of issues about the incidence of crime. Reducing, or at least addressing, people's fear of crime has become a major policy goal in and of itself (Home Office 1989). It is this ambiguous relationship between fear and crime which the term 'community safety' captures by incorporating them both under one broad heading. Moreover, there is an important paradox in the connection between 'community safety' or 'crime prevention' and 'fear of crime'. Policies addressed at the first two may actually serve to increase the latter by reminding people of their vulnerability. Fear, after all, is an incentive for crime prevention, one which commercial interests are willing to exploit. However, whether preventive activity actually reduces fear is itself a more complex matter (Brantingham and Brantingham 1997). The desire for security and the absence of fear may be insatiable and unattainable, as the quest itself fuels anxiety. This serves to remind us that the growth of crime prevention may be a symptom of a much deeper sense of insecurity. However, it is apparent that crime prevention and fear of crime are both part of a dynamic, if volatile, relationship.

'Strategy' and 'structure'

A further useful distinction in terminology, often found in the literature as well as in crime prevention practice, is that between crime prevention 'strategy' and 'structure'. This references the earlier distinction between 'theory' and 'implementation' as levels of analysis. 'Strategy' refers to a systematic and coherent set of methods for attaining given ends. It specifies the measures which collectively form part of an overall and long-term 'strategic' approach, rather than a case-by-case *ad hoc* approach. 'Structure', by contrast, refers to an institutional configuration through which policy-making and service delivery are arranged. It identifies the processes and organisational arrangements which need to be in place in order to deliver the 'strategy'. The distinction between the two highlights the different levels at which problems and 'failures' can occur. For example, the lack of a strategy or the existence of one which is internally contradictory will give rise to certain difficulties regardless of the structures put in place, and vice versa. Furthermore, it suggests an appropriate sequential progression. It suggests that the structure should be dependent on the nature of the strategy envisaged and, hence, that the strategy should precede the structure and inform it. Finally, this implies a vision of crime prevention as occupying and performing a broad social role as well as having long-term implications which need to be grasped rather than buried under the weight of 'scientific' technologies. The very idea of a strategy suggests that piecemeal and *ad hoc* developments are insufficient to address this social role of crime prevention.

However, there is a potential tension between the terminological emphasis on 'strategy' and 'structure' and the earlier noted concept of 'community safety', partly because the former terms are often understood as referring to or implying central or national coherence. The importance of developing strategic and structured approaches to crime prevention has to confront the need to take account of and respond to local contexts and variations in crime conditions. Consequently, one of the key issues in crime prevention is the appropriate balance of responsibilities and powers between central government and agencies, on the one hand, and local areas or communities, on the other. This gives rise to questions about what is appropriate information about a locality – its social, economic and cultural context and the nature of its crime problem – as well as how best to gather it (which will be considered in Chapter 6). The very notion of 'implementation' suggests the imposition of a pre-established model or set of mechanisms on an area. Should strategies and structure precede or follow an assessment of the local problems and conditions or even emerge out of a responsive dialogue with them? If the latter, can they really be referred to as 'strategy' and 'structure' or are we talking about something more adaptable and flexible? Furthermore, this raises the question whether crime prevention measures are area specific. If so, the question whether we can transfer the lessons or 'good practice' from one area to the next becomes inherently problematic.

Classifying types of crime prevention

The most significant attempts to conceptualise and classify types of crime prevention have focused on specifying the two concerns raised by Questions 1 and 2 (above). These are, first, the nature of the measure itself and the processes or structures that it seeks to alter and, second, the intended target audience for the measure, or to whom it is addressed.

With this in mind, one of the earliest recent attempts to define crime prevention was that offered by Lejins (1967) who developed a threefold typology, differentiating between the techniques employed in various crime prevention activities:

- punitive prevention, or deterrence
- corrective prevention, or the elimination of crimogenic social conditions
- mechanical prevention, or measures to reduce criminal opportunities.

What is important here is that Lejins, unlike van Dijk, does not exclude the formal criminal justice system but begins to broaden the field of enquiry beyond its 'deterrent effect', which has been the dominant understanding of crime prevention since the early nineteenth century (see Chapter 2). Lejins began tentatively to point towards forms of proactive prevention which were either concerned with social conditions or physical opportunities. What is more, this early definition captured (and helped reproduce) the essential problematic which remains at the heart of crime prevention theory today: namely the tension between reducing opportunities through situational measures and social modes of intervention.

The public health analogy

It was the definition offered by Canadian criminologists, Brantingham and Faust (1976) which began to sharpen the conceptual focus. This emerged in the mid-1970s at the time when a renewed interest in prevention was enthusing much practice. Like so much criminology before, it drew its inspiration from medicine and the natural sciences. They distinguish between primary, secondary and tertiary crime prevention, drawing on the medical and public health analogy. The dependent variable is the principal population target at which the initiative is aimed. *Primary* prevention is work directed at general populations and may involve interventions into the social and physical environment. Such interventions are aimed at addressing potentially crimogenic factors before the onset of the problem, such as 'good citizenship' classes in school curricula. *Secondary* prevention involves work with 'at risk' groups of potential offenders: those who have been identified because of some predispositional factor. This may be their age group, where they live, their life-style, their socio-economic circumstances or some other diagnostic predictor of risk. As a consequence, the target audience is deemed to be more prone to criminality and therefore worthy of special attention. *Tertiary* prevention includes strategies targeted at known offenders in order to reduce further crimes or the harm associated with them. This will often occur within the criminal justice system as a part of the sentencing process, but may also be an aspect of voluntary aftercare.

In essence, Brantingham and Faust's typology revolves around the nature of the relationship between the intended audience and the form of intervention offered. Hence, primary prevention is aimed at a general population about whom no assumptions as to their criminality are presupposed. Secondary prevention, on the other hand, assumes the audience to be 'at risk' in some way or other, while tertiary prevention is focused on foreshortening, reducing or limiting the criminality of those already presupposed to be criminal. In so doing, the public health analogy assists in characterising elements in the targeting of preventive measures. It is useful in framing the lens of crime prevention. It forces us to consider at what level the supposed target of a given intervention is set. It does not require us to choose whether something is 'inside' or 'outside' of the criminal justice system and does not need to fall back on arbitrary professional boundaries. As a conceptual framework it allows sufficient flexibility to capture the diverse and fused nature of crime prevention.

However, it tells us little about the nature of the activity itself. It lacks clarity as to the different types of potential targets and it lacks sufficient understanding of the different philosophical, ideological and political assumptions about crime on which different crime prevention initiatives are premised. Furthermore, it only begins to specify the audience or target. It requires additional dimensions. One way to develop on the public health analogy is to distinguish more clearly between the targets of prevention either as potential victims or as potential criminals. These constitute important and yet analytically separate targets of crime prevention to whom divergent messages and measures are aimed. To this end, van Dijk and de Waard (1991) propose a two-dimensional approach, which builds on to the public health analogy a distinction between situational, offender-oriented and victim-oriented measures. Thus, for example, in relation to secondary prevention 'at risk' can mean 'a place at risk of being the site of crime', 'a person at risk of being the victim of crime', or 'a person at risk of engaging in criminal activity'.

Significantly, this two-dimensional model accords an important place to the different and specific preventive measures targeted at victims. The distinction between primary, secondary and tertiary victim-oriented crime prevention is useful in that it clarifies the criteria on which the success of an initiative should be judged (this is considered in detail in Chapter 6). Specifically, some measures seek to lower average victimisation risks (primary prevention), others attempt to reduce the level of special risks (secondary prevention), while still others try to prevent the risk of repeat victimisation to those who have already suffered as victims of a particular crime (tertiary prevention). The impact of any intervention, not only on the targeted group, but also on other groups in the population, will be an important factor in determining its empirical success and wider policy ramifications.

This is useful but begins to confuse the audience with the nature of the intervention. What is more, it fails to identify audiences which are

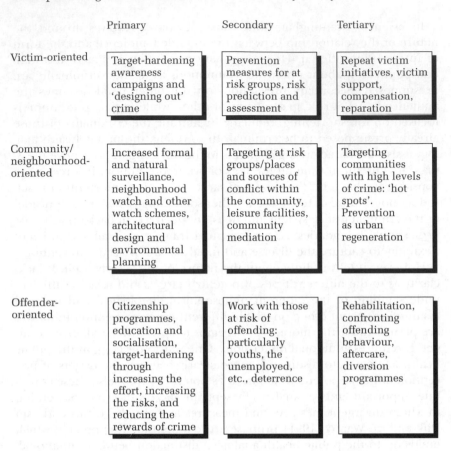

	Primary	Secondary	Tertiary
Victim-oriented	Target-hardening awareness campaigns and 'designing out' crime	Prevention measures for at risk groups, risk prediction and assessment	Repeat victim initiatives, victim support, compensation, reparation
Community/ neighbourhood-oriented	Increased formal and natural surveillance, neighbourhood watch and other watch schemes, architectural design and environmental planning	Targeting at risk groups/places and sources of conflict within the community, leisure facilities, community mediation	Targeting communities with high levels of crime: 'hot spots'. Prevention as urban regeneration
Offender-oriented	Citizenship programmes, education and socialisation, target-hardening through increasing the effort, increasing the risks, and reducing the rewards of crime	Work with those at risk of offending: particularly youths, the unemployed, etc., deterrence	Rehabilitation, confronting offending behaviour, aftercare, diversion programmes

Figure 1.1   An Audience/Target Two-Dimensional Typology of Crime Prevention

collectivities or groups, rather than individuals. Rosenbaum (1988a) addresses this by focusing on the unit to be protected by the preventive measures. In this he identifies three fields of potential victims in relation to: personal protection, household protection and neighbourhood protection.

Hence, if we suspend issues about the nature of the intervention for a moment (to which I return below) and instead focus on the intended target and audience, we can build an alternative two-dimensional set of typologies along the lines identified in Figure 1.1.

The introduction of community-oriented intervention allows for measures which may involve physical or social strategies, which are not reducible to individuals. Social groups, organisations, associations and communities represent collectivities which involve different decision-making processes from, and assert different pressures over, individuals. As a consequence, they constitute fundamentally different audiences for crime prevention (either as potential offenders or victims) which require a different message. Organisations and groups think and act in different ways. Furthermore, there are targets of crime prevention which bypass human beings themselves and are concerned only with 'places', with the modification, planning or design of the built environment and which have implications for the area or neighbourhood. However, this does conflate community as both the potential 'victim' of crime and as the potential generator of crimogenic conditions. This is not particularly problematic given that research generally shows that areas and communities with high concentrations of offenders also suffer from high levels of victimisation. In fact, conflating the two potentially allows areas and communities to be targeted for crime prevention interventions on the basis of the dual needs of potential offenders and victims, and hence in a way which is neither divisive nor contentious by avoiding charges of favouritism or stigmatisation.

Situational and social prevention

The most enduring distinction between types of crime prevention measures is that between 'social' and 'situational' approaches. This distinction revolves around the nature of the processes which a crime prevention measure seeks to affect. Social crime prevention is concerned with affecting social processes. It is primarily concerned with 'measures aimed at tackling the root causes of crime and the dispositions of individuals to offend' (Graham and Bennett 1995). It is sometimes seen as synonymous with an individual offender-oriented approach in that it seeks to explain and address the social causes of offending behaviour which are seen to lie in the social and economic environment – for instance, unfavourable living conditions, relative deprivation, the development of non-conforming subcultures, social disorganisation and so on. And yet there are clearly aspects of social crime prevention which address victims' and potential victims' needs and concerns, such as interventions which seek to enhance the capacity of communities to reduce crime or the fear of crime by increasing their ability to exert informal social control. Some commentators have sought to emphasise the differences within the broad umbrella of 'social' crime prevention by identifying two subcategories: 'developmental' and 'community' crime prevention (Tonry and Farrington 1995a). The former refers to interventions designed to prevent the development of criminal potential in individuals, particularly targeting risk factors identified by human development and 'criminal careers' studies (Farrington 1994). This is also referred to in the literature as 'criminality prevention', as it seeks to address the factors in an individual which may predispose them towards a criminal motivation. By contrast, 'community' prevention, as the name suggests, is concerned with alterations to the social conditions that influence offending in community settings. This subcategorisation will be followed loosely in the more in-depth analysis in Chapter 4.

The development of a situational approach to crime prevention is very much associated with work emanating from the Home Office in the early 1980s, which advocated an 'opportunity reduction' model (Clarke 1980a, 1980b; Clarke and Mayhew 1980; Heal and Laycock 1986). Broadly speaking, situational crime prevention involves the management, design or manipulation of the immediate physical environment so as to reduce the opportunities for specific crimes. Prevention is to be achieved through measures which alter the situational or spatial characteristics of the environment in order to make offending harder or increase the likelihood of detection. It is often referred to as 'physical' crime prevention. The most obvious form that this takes is 'target-hardening' whereby the opportunities for attaining the potential object of crime are made harder or less attractive through physical barriers or alterations. In some cases this may even involve 'target removal' whereby the object is removed altogether.

Clearly some crime prevention measures do not fit neatly into this dichotomy of situational and social type, but rather combine certain elements of each. Some commentators have suggested that this points to a lack of value and utility in such a conceptual distinction (Forrester *et al.* 1990: 47). Ekblom, for example, suggests this is a 'conceptually rather sloppy approach' as some 'situational or physical methods rely on social processes to work and vice versa' (1994: 190). In support of this, he identifies examples, such as physical improvements to the environment to facilitate social surveillance and the use of social policy to improve the physical conditions of housing in order to improve parenting. As with any 'ideal type' these categories do not reflect reality perfectly but nevertheless are useful tools in making sense of reality. More importantly, by its focus – on the type of processes that measures seek to alter, be they situational or social – this conceptual distinction explicitly recognises and embodies different assumptions about *what causes crime*. While social crime prevention is premised on an understanding that crime is the product of complex social, economic and cultural processes, situational crime prevention presupposes that crime is opportunistic and can be controlled through the modification of the physical environment. Hence, as a system of classification, despite its 'sloppiness', it serves a useful function in helping to specify the theoretical underpinnings of given crime prevention measures. For this reason, it constitutes the framework for the fuller examination of case studies, issues and implications in Chapters 3 and 4.

By overlaying the public health analogy – of primary, secondary and tertiary crime prevention – on top of the situational and social distinction we can build another useful two-dimensional set of typologies of crime prevention (see Figure 1.2). This combines a focus on the target audience with a specification of the processes to be affected by the measure, and hence some understanding of the causes of crime.

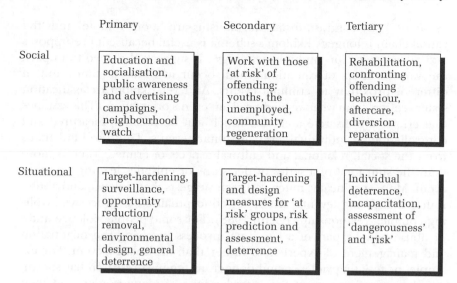

	Primary	Secondary	Tertiary
Social	Education and socialisation, public awareness and advertising campaigns, neighbourhood watch	Work with those 'at risk' of offending: youths, the unemployed, community regeneration	Rehabilitation, confronting offending behaviour, aftercare, diversion reparation
Situational	Target-hardening, surveillance, opportunity reduction/ removal, environmental design, general deterrence	Target-hardening and design measures for 'at risk' groups, risk prediction and assessment, deterrence	Individual deterrence, incapacitation, assessment of 'dangerousness' and 'risk'

Figure 1.2   A Process/Target Two-Dimensional Typology of Crime Prevention

Proximal and distal mechanisms

Ekblom offers a somewhat different definition of crime prevention as 'the intervention in mechanisms that cause criminal events' (1994: 194). Here, mechanisms are always causal, in that they are 'linked together in chains of cause and effect'. These are interpreted broadly to include any process or condition which by its presence, absence or particular state affects the probability of a criminal event occurring, either by itself or in conjunction with other mechanisms. By 'intervention', Ekblom refers to 'action prior to the criminal event that interrupts a chain of cause and effect which would otherwise have ultimately led to the event' (*ibid.*). This definition is useful because it requires us to explain both why criminal events occur and why certain interventions are believed to prevent criminal events from occurring. Hence, it seeks to render theories about crime and its causation explicit. This is important precisely because so much crime prevention currently lacks any theoretical dimension. Young, for instance, has accused much of the work associated with the revival of interest in crime prevention of ushering in a 'silent revolution' in thinking, which he terms 'administrative criminology' in that it is premised on a 'lack of interest in aetiology' (1986: 9–10).

Ekblom goes on to distinguish between causal mechanisms which are 'proximal' and those which are 'distal'. The distinction between the two lies in the proximity or distance at which a mechanism seeks to interrupt the 'chain of causation'. So that, 'proximal mechanisms are directly linked to the event in question, and generally close in time and space' (Ekblom

1994: 195). By contrast, distal mechanisms are 'more remote' and 'the causal chain is longer'. Ekblom's schema is useful because it presupposes and allows space for 'multiple aetiology'. It suggests the need to unpack the various layers of causation which occur at different times and in different proximity to criminal events. And yet Ekblom's classification system suffers from what we might call an 'events orientation'. This assumes that crimes are discrete incidents which can be isolated, measured and controlled at an individual level, as solitary events. To do so blinkers us from the social, relational and cultural aspects of crime. Crime is more than the sum total of a series of decisions or episodes leading up to an event. More specifically, much research suggests that violence and abuse, rather than being 'events' are better conceptualised as processes involving complex relationships (Genn 1988). For some people violence and/ or abuse may be part of a continual process involving the negotiation and management of experiences rather than an isolated event. For example, negotiating violence and danger, as feminist research has shown, may be a routine part of the everyday lives of many women and men (Stanko 1988, 1990). In these situations violence may form part of a continuum of experience which is not exceptional but routine, and which affects its meaning (see Kelly 1988). While this may seem less problematic in relation to some other crimes such as burglary, even here an 'events orientation' misses complex features of the crime. These have been exposed by local crime surveys which show that much crime is highly localised, creating a social relationship between offender and victim by their shared locality (Jones *et al.* 1986; Crawford *et al.* 1990). More recently, an 'events-orientation' has been further undermined by repeat victimisation research which shows that burglaries may not be discrete incidents but rather may have wider referents (see Farrell 1992; Farrell and Pease 1993). Hence, we need to understand crime as the product of relationships rather than individual incidents. These are different levels of analysis: not, as Ekblom suggests, merely points along a continuum.

A second problem with Ekblom's classification system is that it implicitly over-prioritises proximity by suggesting that 'inescapably, the chain connects up to influence the events only via the proximal causes' (Ekblom 1994: 195). This approach starts from the incident and then moves backwards rather than being an understanding which starts from the broader social structure and underlying relationships within which incidents arise. The core concerns are the surface incidents rather than the context within which they are set. Combined with the prevalent 'events orientation', the focus is heavily on symptoms rather than deep causes. Furthermore, despite his desire to expose the theoretical underpinnings of given measures by identifying the specific chains of causation, Ekblom marginalises the politics of crime prevention through his 'mechanistic' approach. The political nature of choices as to where, when, against whom and in what ways to intervene, as well as with what implications, is distinctly absent from his schema. Rather like cogs in a machine with explicit functions to perform, crime prevention mechanisms are cleansed of any commitment to, or alignment with, political modes of social explanation.

Political models of crime prevention

Some commentators have sought to make political perspectives the defining characteristic of differences between crime prevention strategies. Iadicola (1986) for instance identifies three models of crime prevention aimed at communities and neighbourhoods, each emphasising a commitment to different political ideologies. The first, a *conservative* model, is focused on victimisation deterrence, primarily through opportunity reduction, protection and surveillance. This model shares much in common with situational crime prevention. It is 'conservative' because its founding principles are concerned with the *control* of crime control and it adheres to a narrow definition of conventional crime. Its assumptions about human behaviour suggest that crime is ultimately connected to choice within a framework of incentives and disincentives (or deterrents). Its policies tend towards the social exclusion of offenders and other social groups, either by keeping them out of certain areas or through incarceration. Furthermore, the public in their local communities are seen as playing an auxiliary role in support of official policing as extensions or supplements to the established law enforcement agencies. As such, it tends to complement punitive policies and rhetoric.

Iadicola's second model, *liberal* crime prevention, sees crime as a social problem. Crime evidences itself in pathological behaviour which requires correcting, often in relation to individuals. The sources of such pathological behaviour may lie in a lack of opportunities, a mismatch between cultural goals and institutional means of achieving them, social disorganisation or the lack of social control (be it because of inadequate parenting or whatever). The aim of crime prevention in this model should be to identify risk factors in individuals, families and communities and to seek to correct them. Consequently, this perspective is associated with social crime prevention strategies, particularly those aimed at early intervention with 'at risk' groups. Hence, it tends to underlie much offender-oriented crime prevention thinking in relation to juveniles. The approach principally focuses on the allocation of resources and institutional reform targeted at those individuals who are exposed to, or express, single or multiple risk factors.

Finally, *radical* crime prevention is concerned with community control and social change. It sees crime and disorder as arenas of political struggle, whereby crime is the product of social divisions and inequalities. These are structural features of the society in which we live which produce themselves around social divisions of class, gender and ethnicity. Here, rather than focusing on crime control or the correction of pathological individuals or communities, the 'radical' approach shifts attention to economic inequalities, social exclusion and political marginalisation. Under this model, the criminal justice system should appropriately centre on 'crimes of the powerful'. The aim is the reduction of power differences and inequalities coupled with community empowerment. Hence, this model is part of a transformative project which seeks to challenge the *status quo*.

Iadicola's schema makes an important initial attempt to specify the politics of crime prevention. It forces us, rightly, to interrogate the underlying assumptions on which crime prevention strategies are premised. However, this typology suggests a coherency of strategy which, on closer examination, these political perspectives do not deserve. It fails to identify the connections between, and inconsistencies within, political programmes. Furthermore, it fails to identify the very 'radical' nature of recent New Right programmes and neo-liberal ideology which draw together notions of choice, self-help, responsibility, community empowerment, anti-statism and punitiveness (albeit in sometimes antagonistic relations) as something transformatory which blurs and cuts across the three models that Iadicola suggests. While it is important to recognise the differences between measures, it would be wrong to associate them with particular political programmes in either a narrow or simplistic fashion. The danger is that in highlighting the politics of crime prevention as his starting point, Iadicola confuses and simplifies the alliances and connections between political programmes and specific crime prevention strategies.

Victim-oriented prevention

For many commentators crime prevention is synonymous with measures aimed at offenders or potential offenders. Partly, this has been a product of the traditional association between crime prevention and the criminal justice system. One of the most interesting recent developments in crime prevention has been to conceptualise it as connected to victim support or assistance, and hence to target victims or potential victims as the recipients of preventive measures. This understanding is implicit in van Dijk's (1990) conceptualisation of crime prevention referred to earlier.

The renaissance of crime prevention has coincided with a growth of interest in the victims of crime, their individual and social characteristics and needs (Walklate 1991). Hence, one of the central aspects of the revival of interest in crime prevention has been the identification of potential victims as the targets of preventive attention. Potential victims have been increasingly exhorted to take responsibility for their own safety and to adopt appropriate measures to prevent crime and to protect themselves from risks. The two-dimensional typology developed in Figure 1.1 serves to clarify the levels at which potential victims (as well as offenders) can be the target of preventive measures. The general public is the focus of primary victim-oriented prevention, for example, as in national awareness campaigns, good quality street lighting in cities and the required installation of steering column locks in cars. Secondary victim-oriented prevention focuses on those at particular risk of certain types of victimisation. Insurance companies may foster the production of categories of 'at risk' populations and promote secondary crime prevention among potential victims by offering financial incentives through the cost and availability of insurance cover. Hence, insurance companies will often cut the cost of premiums where certain crime prevention devices are in operation, for example, burglar alarms and locks for domestic burglary, CCTV cameras for commercial premises and so on. Secondary victim-oriented prevention offers particular opportunities in using risk assessment methods to target advice and interventions and encouraging insurance to be more discriminating in the terms of cover. Finally, tertiary victim-oriented prevention targets those who have already been the victims of a particular crime. For example, initiatives run by the police may seek to offer a domestic security 'upgrading', including a check on existing arrangements and/or the provision of new locks, bolts and so on, to those who have already reported a burglary. Similarly, 'scene of crime' police officers may offer preventive advice. Under the heading of tertiary victim-oriented crime prevention, van Dijk (1990: 210) includes more general assistance to victims, whether it be legal, emotional or financial, such as that provided by organisations like Victim Support. This he justifies on the basis that such activities seek to minimise the harm done by a crime, regardless of its impact on the chances or impact of any future revictimisation. It is in relation to tertiary victim-oriented crime prevention that the growing research into repeat victimisation offers some insights.

Repeat victimisation

One of the most significant developments within the growing victimological literature has been to recognise the importance of the phenomenon of repeat or multiple victimisation. Sparks' (1981) pioneering work used early victimisation survey findings to show that certain groups of people suffer disproportionately large amounts of crime. Subsequent victim survey research has only served to confirm the significance of such repeat victimisation. Consequently, understanding the reasons for repeat victimisation, its extent and its implications for crime prevention and our knowledge about the distribution of crime, have become pressing issues of criminological concern (Farrell 1992, 1995). Criminologists have become increasingly aware that repeat victimisation of people and places represents a significant proportion of all victimisation (Genn 1988; Forrester *et al.* 1988; Farrell and Pease 1993). On the basis of victimisation survey findings, Farrell estimates that the 2 or 3 per cent of respondents who are the most victimised commonly report between a quarter and a third of all incidents (1995: 470). The conclusion to be drawn is that a relatively small proportion of the population experiences a disproportionate amount of crime.

Traditionally the extent of repeat victimisation has been underestimated. This is due in part to a statistical bias when interpreting crime rates which has prioritised a focus on the *incidence of victimisation*: in other words the number of crimes per head of population over a specific period of time. This results in a 'quantitative' moral bias, whereby public discussion about the crime rate is premised on the axiom that *more* crime always reflects a social evil, while less crime is indicative of greater social well-being (Barr and Pease 1990; Hope 1995b). This has tended only to be further broken down and analysed in terms of *victim prevalence*, i.e. the proportion of victims in the population (the rate at which victims are found within a group of people). It is only more recently that criminologists have begun to consider the question of *victim concentration*, i.e. the number of crimes per victim (the rate at which people are victimised). Importantly, the interaction between victim prevalence and victim concentration opens up relational criteria obscured by the quantitative bias of traditional crime statistics, most notably the issue of equity and the distribution of victimisation within the population. It is only when we begin to focus on such issues that what becomes clear is that inequality is the defining characteristic of the distribution of victimisation (Trickett *et al.* 1992; Ellingworth *et al.* 1995). Crime is not evenly distributed throughout the population. It tends to be concentrated both socially and spatially. Within this, repeat victimisation is a significant factor in skewing crime data, be it from official statistics or victimisation surveys.

The insights provided by research into repeat victimisation have a number of important implications. First, victimisation may itself be a good predictor of future victimisation. Second, if this is assumed it follows that preventing revictimisation should prevent a significant proportion of all offences. The obvious message for crime prevention is that to link it with victim assistance, after victimisation, through the provision of victim-oriented interventions offers considerable potential. Forrester *et al.* thus suggest that: 'To acknowledge that the best predictor of the next victimisation is the last victimisation is to acknowledge that victim support and crime prevention are two sides of the same coin' (1990: 45).

Furthermore, using victimisation as a basis for crime prevention offers a particularly attractive means of targeting need. For not only does repeat victimisation target individual need, it also tends to target communal need, given that repeat victimisation is disproportionately concentrated in high crime areas (Trickett *et al.* 1992, 1995). If victimisation is itself a predictor of future victimisation then crime prevention aimed at victims will, most likely, focus energies where the need is greatest. This may help address the problem, raised earlier, that too often crime prevention 'does best in the areas that need it least' (Buerger 1994a: 411). If victimisation is a reasonable predictor of future 'repeat' victimisation, it will help to shift the supply of resources closer to demand. Thus, repeat victimisation potentially offers simultaneously a socially just and efficient means of targeting crime prevention.

Furthermore, targeting the victims of crime for tertiary preventive assistance carries a number of additional attractions. First, such an approach is likely to be attractive to the victims of crime themselves, who often feel not only the subject of victimisation but also let down or abandoned by the criminal justice system (Newburn and Merry 1990). There is a growing recognition that victims are neglected within the criminal justice process (Shapland *et al.* 1985). Consequently, there has been considerable concern to address victims' needs and rights (Miers 1992), as represented for example by the Victim's Charter (Home Office 1990a). This in turn makes crime prevention which follows victimisation an attractive approach for policy-makers.

Second, it removes difficult and divisive choices about who should be the targets of prevention. Identifying specific social groups or places for assistance can lead to claims of special preference or favouritism, may result in those people or places becoming the targets of criminal attention and can lead to the stigmatisation of those groups or places as 'crime ridden'. The fact of having been victimised presents a relatively uncontentious basis for the special attention accorded by crime prevention. It identifies the most vulnerable social groups without having to identify those groups as such (Forrester *et al.* 1990: 3).

Finally, as Farrell and Pease (1993) argue, the rate at which victimisation occurs potentially allows the providers of crime prevention a realistic pace to which to respond. As such it may provide a way of progressively 'drip-feeding' crime prevention into an area (Forrester *et al.* 1990). Crime prevention following victimisation affords a constant, and yet relatively minor, effort in contrast to many short-term 'saturation' projects. Case studies of repeat victimisation targeted crime prevention will be considered in more detail in Chapter 3.

As a consequence, victim-oriented prevention schemes have been promoted by researchers and policy-makers alike (see National Board for Crime Prevention 1994), some of which will be considered in Chapter 3. However, our understanding of repeat victimisation remains incomplete. For example, the fact that repeat victims are to be found in communities with high concentrations of victims can be interpreted as evidence that communities are high crime communities because they contain high risk, repeat victims or that repeat victims are high risk precisely because they live in particular communities. Furthermore, the implications of victim-oriented approaches to crime prevention raise a number of problematic social issues, which will be examined in Chapter 8.

Identifying the actors

As I have argued throughout this chapter, crime prevention strategies need to be based on wide-ranging theories. These theories need to address the causes of crime as well as the interactions between key actors in certain situations and over time. It is worth briefly considering a couple of attempts to specify the nature of these interactions.

Cohen and Felson's (1979) 'routine activities' theory offers one such model. It identifies elements and audiences in the specification of strategies which can be adapted to specific types of crime in different places. Cohen and Felson suggest that crime is patterned by the convergence of people and things over space and time. They identify three key variables, the absence or presence of which impacts on the likelihood of crime:

- the presence of likely offenders
- the presence of suitable targets
- the absence of capable guardians against crime or the existence of inadequate surveillance.

Hence, routine activities which bring together all these in the same place at the same time are crimogenic. Prevention, by contrast, should seek to affect change on one or more of these levels to reduce the likelihood of crime. This theoretical frame is sufficiently flexible to allow different levels of analysis for different types of crime. This can encourage the construction of tailored crime prevention strategies (see further Chapter 3). However, this framework itself embodies theoretical assumptions about causation. It assumes an opportunistic understanding of crime in which potential offenders are 'amoral calculators' of profit and loss. There is no space for wider social factors.

Young, by contrast, constructs a wider framework in which he identifies a number of relationships, all of which need to be better understood in order to target strategic prevention against specific forms of criminality. This, he suggests, needs to acknowledge 'the *form* of crime, the social context of crime, the shape of crime, its trajectory through time and its enactment in space' (1992: 26, emphasis in original). He offers the image of a 'square of crime', in which the four corners constitute definitional elements of crime: victims, offenders, formal social control (the state) and informal social control (the community). Here, 'formal social control' refers to the activities of state agencies such as the police, probation service and other organisations incorporated into crime prevention partnerships. 'Informal social control' relates to the role of the public, as individuals or in communities, neighbourhoods and associations. This element recognises the potential of the public as agents of social control, be it as 'guardians against crime' as envisaged within Cohen and Felson's framework or in some other capacity. Crime is the product of social relationships between each of these four points on the 'square' (Young 1992: 27). The nature of the relationships will vary with different types of crime. Again, this is a useful schema in that it requires us to ask how a given crime prevention strategy seeks to affect each of these elements. It provides a valuable framework within which to ask aetiological questions and to propose preventive solutions. Both of the above theoretical frameworks allow crime prevention methods to be classified and analysed according to which elements, or conjunction of elements, they seek to alter or affect.

Conclusions

Definitions of crime prevention, its boundaries and appropriate conceptualisations, remain the subject of intense debate and considerable academic interest. They embody assumptions about the causes of crime, the nature of social relations and principles of justice. At the same time they connect with, and are promoted by, political strategies and ideological perspectives. In this context 'crime prevention' and 'community safety' can become metaphors for a variety of other, much wider questions about social order.

In this chapter I have not defined crime prevention conclusively, but have tried to identify some of the terminological controversies and vexed issues which constitute crime prevention politics, policies and practices, thereby opening up the key conceptual debates. I have also attempted to provide the reader with a number of questions and to outline the main ways in which crime prevention strategies and claims can be interrogated. The danger inherent in the kinds of classification and conceptualisation presented in this chapter is that they can present rigid dichotomies. This can have two implications. First, it can ignore the overlaps and linkages between different measures. The real world does not divide up neatly into typologies. Second, it can encourage a sense that all interventions under one heading embody the same assumptions or political affiliations. The different classification systems presented are by no means watertight. They act as levers into the debates that follow, rather than as pieces of a jigsaw which need only be assembled together for the sake of completeness.

What is more, we need to be aware of the often unspoken assumptions and the silences that crime prevention embodies. The institutional growth of crime prevention (the subject of Chapter 2) has served to ignore or marginalise certain issues. The focus on 'community safety' and 'fear reduction' as aspects of crime prevention have tended to orient attention towards public displays of unruly behaviour and away from offending which takes place in 'private spheres', behind peoples' backs or which involve a less visible and more indirect relationship between offender and victim. For instance, the gendered nature of crime often gets lost from the crime prevention literature. The fact that crime is primarily a young male activity is largely absent from understandings of crime prevention. Perversely, this has occurred at the same time as a greater awareness about issues of gender within both criminology and the criminal justice system. Similarly, there is less discussion of fraud and corporate criminality – despite the considerable harm they cause – as compared with minor acts of incivility, such as begging. Again, this appears to have occurred in the face of the growing recognition of corporate criminality and its consequences.

There is a danger that as a subdiscipline of criminology, crime prevention studies may reproduce and serve to accentuate many of the historical flaws of criminology. For, like the discipline of criminology, it is oriented towards both a 'scientific' – often technological – project and an institutional task (Garland 1994). These two elements sometimes compete and sometimes converge. Institutional practices and concerns fuse with aetiological questions. And yet this relationship is particularly acute in relation to the study of crime prevention given its significant pragmatic, policy-oriented and administrative focus. As we shall see in Chapter 2, the historical genesis of modern crime prevention is rooted in the perceived failure of the 'science of criminology' and our inability to 'know' offenders and reform offending behaviour. It is concerned, moreover, with an institutional field where theoretical issues are shunned in favour of practice and administrative efficiency. But this does not mean the absence of theoretical presuppositions: merely that the desire to *manage* has eclipsed the desire to *know*. And yet, embedded in all crime prevention strategies, however commonsensical they may appear at first sight, are powerful claims to 'science'. Moreover, as we have seen, this 'science' now encompasses objects of knowledge hitherto largely disregarded within mainstream criminology: the victim – or at least categories of potential victims – and the community. Crime prevention, like criminology, as an emergent discipline attempts to use science and technology in the service of control and management. In this, the relationship between theory and practice is a complex and dynamic one. Furthermore, those who articulate and promote crime prevention work in their claims to 'science' deploy important strategies of power. Technological 'know-how' in the crime prevention field is not a value-neutral discipline but rather embodies vexed ethical, social and political questions. It is with these concerns in mind and with the conceptual tools available to us, that we can now embark on an examination of the emergent policies and institutional fields which constitute the recent history of crime prevention in England and Wales.

Chapter 2

The British Experience

The definitional difficulties associated with the term 'crime prevention', as reviewed in the previous chapter, make an assessment of its policy developments and institutional effects somewhat problematic. In this chapter I confine myself to an overview of the developments in Britain that have explicitly used or been advanced under the banner of 'crime prevention' or its sibling, 'community safety'. The chapter begins with a brief historical account of the institutional transformation of crime prevention with the establishment of the 'new police' in the early part of the nineteenth century, before going on to consider the rebirth of crime prevention over the last 30 years. Key government policy initiatives are outlined and assessed, as are the recent national and local developments within relevant organisations, including the police, the probation service, local government and the voluntary and private sectors. Particular consideration is given to the contribution of the Safer Cities Projects as the 'flagship' of recent Conservative governments. The chapter concludes with a critical assessment of the prospects for crime prevention under the programme of the new Labour government.

A brief history of crime prevention

Weatheritt suggests that 'two histories of crime prevention can be written' (1986: 49). These two histories reflect a considerable gulf between official rhetoric and institutional practice. The first history, she suggests, is to be found in official reports and mission statements in which crime prevention is held up as being the primary aim of policing, the promotion of which is facilitated by designated institutions and action. From this account, the history of crime prevention is an encouraging one, in which crime prevention not only receives strong rhetorical support, but also appears to rest on a sound base of institutional deliberation and activity. The other history of crime prevention, however,

> goes behind the statements of intention to look at how far and in what ways preventive objectives have become part of day-to-day policing . . . on what crime prevention officers do and how useful and effective this is . . . On these criteria, the achievements are less impressive . . . Whatever the expressed commitment of senior police officers and successive governments to the view that prevention is the primary objective of policing, the crime prevention job remains an activity performed on the sidelines while the main action takes place elsewhere.
>
> (Weatheritt 1986: 49)

Implicit in this insight is the notion that an understanding of crime prevention is intrinsically linked to the history of modern policing. This is so for two reasons. First, for most of the past two centuries the police have claimed 'crime prevention' to be a central element of their function. Second, the development of modern policing has fundamentally transformed what is meant by 'crime prevention' as well as the involvement of other agencies and the public in the prevention process. With the birth of the 'new police' in 1829 our conception of policing – and hence crime prevention – has become particularly narrow in focus. Where once it referred to a whole array of strategies for regulating and managing populations through a political economy, by means of economic, social and cultural policy, over time it has become synonymous with 'what the police actually do'. As a consequence, *policing* has become conflated with *the police* (Reiner 1992).

Key architects of the 'new police', namely Peel and the first two Metropolitan Police Commissioners, Rowan and Mayne, sought to foster a distinctive image of policing. This was primarily concerned with a quest for legitimacy, given the hostile reception that the 'new police' received in the early and mid-nineteenth century. At its core, alongside the imagery of the 'citizen in uniform', lay crime prevention as a pre-eminent function of policing. This was made clear in the Metropolitan Police Act 1829 and in the instructions to the first new recruits who were informed that, 'the principal object to be obtained is the prevention of crime. To this great end every effort of the police is to be directed' (cited in Emsley 1983: 66). The form of 'prevention' that the Peelian legacy envisaged was of a highly visible presence of uniformed patrol officers, minimally armed and relying on limited legal powers approximating those of the citizenry. The preventive effects were believed to derive from the authority and order that such a form of policing would bring. This Reiner has called the 'scarecrow' function of regular uniformed patrols (1992: 99). They were genuinely intended to represent a 'bureaucracy of official morality' (Storch 1975: 61) which shone out through their symbolic uniforms. And yet, this legacy was forged out of social and political conflict, related to quests for legitimacy, more so than on the basis of concerns about effectiveness or cost, which were subsequently to undermine it. These conflicts impacted on the meaning and place of crime prevention as advocated by proponents such as Peel. There was an ever-present danger that the more proactive forms of prevention could become linked with intrusive forms of surveillance associated with Continental policing, particularly in France (Emsley 1983). 'Surveillance' carried connotations of government spies and secret police which the architects of the 'new police' were keen to avoid. Policing was to be preventive without being threatening. Hence, within the police the notion of 'prevention' was borne in a limited guise. Crime prevention was deemed to derive from the perceived 'deterrent effect' of conspicuous uniformed officers. The Peelian vision of the centrality of such prevention to modern policing declined with the 'grudging acceptance' and greater social integration of the police throughout the ensuing century.

A number of inter-related reasons for the decline and residualisation of the role of crime prevention within policing can be identified. First, many of those outside London were unconvinced by it, because it appeared either inefficient or alien. Steedman, for example, notes that in Victorian England a prominent view outside London was that 'a paid constable on the Metropolitan model would give rise to a great deal of "unnecessary lounging", and such men would be "forever watching and suspecting"' (1984: 18). As the 'new police' spread out from the metropolis, the preventive element often became diluted.

Second, the Peelian model was rather costly, particularly for provincial areas with large distances and dispersed populations to cover.

Third, the 'grudging acceptance' of policing in many working class communities remained precarious. It was also the subject of continual and fragile, local renegotiation by both police and public. Hence, a delicate balance endured, more so in some areas than others, which proactive preventive policing – particularly of a kind which might conjure up images of sinister surveillance or the insidious collection of information – could easily undermine.

Fourth, with the growth of the 'science of criminology' (Garland 1994) in the latter part of the nineteenth century a greater emphasis was accorded to the measurement, differentiation and categorisation of activities, in relation both to those of 'criminals' and of criminal justice agents. Against the background of a statistical explosion whereby measurement indicated social value, crime prevention lost out. There was little to show for the success of crime prevention. The police could not easily measure a 'non-crime'.

Fifth, the location of the task of prevention within the organisational hierarchy of the police remained an ambiguous one. As a generic function of policing, prevention through patrol beat work has always been regarded as 'an apprenticeship through which all police officers must pass, but seldom wish to stay in or return to, and most patrolling constables are young and inexperienced' (Reiner 1992: 98). On the other hand, as a specialist function it has never held a particularly high status. It has tended to be viewed as 'a sort of pre-retirement course for experienced but tired detectives' (Harvey *et al.* 1989: 88).

Sixth, the growth of a police organisational sub-culture which emphasised 'action' (Reiner 1992) also served to devalue preventive work and laud crime detection.

Finally, the Peelian legacy embodied a contradictory logic. While its philosophy lay in notions of prevention, it sought simultaneously the specialisation, bureaucratisation and professionalisation of the police, all of which pulled policing in other directions, often into new technologies and specialist tasks and off the streets. After the initial hostility met by the establishment of the new police, their historic quest for legitimacy became bound up with appropriate symbols of 'modernisation' and 'professionalisation'. These often referenced claims to rational management and effectiveness, which tended to cluster around detection rather than prevention and to push the organisation into the ever greater specialisation of tasks and functions.

Crime prevention gradually slipped from its central place and was subsequently pushed to the margins of institutional public policing. Despite an enduring breadth of 'service' functions, law enforcement and order maintenance soon became established as the core activities of police officers. Crime prevention became increasingly defined in terms of the 'deterrent effect' of the criminal justice system as a whole. Hence, as has often been noted, crime prevention has become a core activity of no one single organisation, and yet a peripheral concern of many.

The recent renaissance of crime prevention

Until relatively recently, therefore, crime prevention was understood as a by-product of the formal system of policing, prosecution and punishment, by virtue of its 'deterrent effect'. However, over the past three decades, in Britain as in other parts of the world, there has been a dramatic expansion of interest and activity under the banner of 'crime prevention' and 'community safety'. Crime prevention has now moved to centre stage, combining a 'partnership' or 'inter-agency' approach with appeals to revive some sense of local 'community'. It has even acquired an international status, as recognised by the unanimous resolution of the United Nations Congress on the Prevention of Crime and the Treatment of Offenders, in August 1990. The resolution declared crime prevention not simply to be a matter for the police but must:

> bring together those with responsibility for planning and development, for family, health, employment and training, housing and social services, leisure activities, schools, the police, and the justice system, in order to deal with the conditions that generate crime.
>
> (United Nations 1991)

This statement reflects a shift from prevention as deterrence to prevention through proactive interventions into factors which influence crime.

In Britain it was in the late 1950s and early 1960s that the incipient traces of a re-renewed interest in crime prevention can first be detected. However, it was not until 1963 that institutional change began to take effect. In that year the Home Office established a National Crime Prevention Centre in Stafford. Soon thereafter, the Home Office set up the Cornish Committee on the Prevention and Detection of Crime, which reached a number of important recommendations. It proposed the training of specialised police officers in crime prevention skills (Home Office 1965). These officers would become the identified 'experts' in preventive technologies located in specialist Crime Prevention Departments. It also recommended the setting up of 'crime prevention panels' by the police in order to form wider networks within communities and encourage support for crime prevention within given localities. Further, the Cornish Report recommended the establishment of a Home Office Standing Committee on Crime Prevention, incorporating the Association of Chief Police Officers (ACPO) among its key members. The general viewpoint of the Cornish Committee was to emphasise a professional and specialist approach towards crime prevention and the provision of publicity and advice material used by the police.

The Cornish Report's attempts to stimulate crime prevention were largely overtaken by events which conspired to reinforce the centrality of reactive policing, notably the expansion in the use of information technology and patrolling in vehicles. These served to reduce the contact between the police and public. Furthermore, the organisational imperatives which had for long marginalised crime prevention within policing were always likely to undermine the intentions of the Report.

Nevertheless, a number of inter-related developments which have contributed to the recent renaissance of crime prevention in Britain have become increasingly evident. First, there has been a growing strain on the criminal justice system, evidenced by the increasing rate of recorded crime and the numbers of people passing through the system. The UK witnessed a doubling of the rate of recorded crime in the years between 1979 and 1990. This exerted considerable new pressures on the various criminal justice institutions, whereby overload has combined with a crisis of efficiency. For example, the police clear up rates have fallen to approximately one in four recorded crimes; the courts have become increasingly overloaded; and the penal system has experienced increases to the prison population to peaks, currently over 61 000 in England and Wales, which not so long ago were deemed 'unacceptable' in a civilised society. Recent Home Office projections suggest this trend is set to continue to a prison population of an estimated 82 800 by the year 2005 (White and Powar 1998).

Second, the above combined with and fuelled the increased politicisation of crime, particularly after the 1979 general election at which the incoming Thatcher government had made crime a high profile element of its campaign. Crime surveys and opinion polls have repeatedly shown the deep-seated concerns and fears about crime held by most people (Hough and Mayhew 1983). Crime is often identified as one of the principal anxieties which most worries the public, second only to unemployment (see Crawford *et al.* 1990; Hough 1995). Furthermore, the vast majority of people now feel that the likelihood of becoming a victim of crime has increased over recent years. There has also been a growing awareness of the extensive social and economic effects of crime. Estimated business losses from crime are £5–10 billion a year and the value of property stolen in recorded burglaries and thefts alone in England and Wales in 1992 was approximately £4 billion (Crime Concern 1994a).

Third, traditional modes of crime control have come to represent an increasing financial burden on the public purse. In the 1994/5 financial year the operating cost of the criminal justice system was more than £10 billion (Home Office 1995a). Indirect social and health costs considerably add to this bill.

Fourth, there has been a growing realisation – encouraged by the findings of victimisation surveys – that most crimes are never reported to the police, and hence are unaffected by the reactive policies of the criminal justice system. The discovery of a considerable 'dark figure of crime' has highlighted the fact that for most offenders and victims the formal criminal justice system is largely irrelevant. By conservative estimates fewer than 50 per cent of crimes are reported to the police and only 3 per cent result in a caution or conviction (Home Office 1995b). Thus, only a small percentage of crime is dealt with by the criminal justice system and hence any capacity to prevent crime through a 'deterrent effect' is severely limited.

Fifth, it has become increasingly recognised that the formal processes of criminal justice – through the detection, apprehension, prosecution, sentencing and punishment of offenders – have only a limited effect in controlling crime. By contrast, academics and practitioners increasingly began to highlight the importance of mechanisms of informal social control and early intervention in the reduction of crime. It increasingly became clear that informal social controls are more influential in regulating conduct than formal measures. Research findings have reinforced this message, identifying the limited effectiveness of policing (Clarke and Hough 1980, 1984) and imprisonment (Broady 1976). This dispirited outlook has connected with a much wider crisis of confidence in the effectiveness of criminal justice, captured in Martinson's (1974) infamous phrase, 'nothing works'. With the collapse of the 'rehabilitative ideal' there emerged what one commentator has called a 'crisis of penological modernism' (Garland 1990: 7).

Sixth, what is more, this crisis of confidence has not been restricted to those within the criminal justice complex. It has affected the wider public, whose attitudes towards the criminal justice system appeared to be becoming more critical and less deferential (Skogan 1990a).

Seventh, the 'nothing works' pessimism has precipitated a criminological shift in focus away from the offender as the object of knowledge towards the offence – its situational and spatial characteristics – as well as the place and role of the victim. This has encouraged Home Office researchers to suggest that a considerable amount of crime is casual and opportunistic – hence preventable through opportunity reduction strategies (Mayhew *et al.* 1976b).

As a consequence, a new prominence began to be accorded to crime prevention, with its appeals to informal control and wider responsibility. However, the question of whose responsibility for what tasks? is a problematic one for crime prevention, which is in danger of being everyone's responsibility and yet simultaneously no one's in particular. It raises issues about organisational competence for a broad range of services which may impact, either directly or indirectly, on the 'crime problem', as well as about the appropriateness of the private sector and the public. Moreover, the emergence of crime prevention arose in the context of a politics of failure. It had its roots in a fundamental – if implicit – critique of the modern criminal justice system, which was perceived to have failed in its own terms, lost direction and become an increasingly crippling financial burden. Instead of reliance on specialist public agencies – such as the police, courts and correctional institutions – to solve the crime problems alone, crime is increasingly seen as a problem within society which needs to be dealt with or managed by reducing crime promoting conditions. Rather than supplanting 'informal' sources of authority in society, the role of public agencies should be to support and enhance them.

Recent central government initiatives

In 1980, these developing ideas found resonance in the Gladstone Report. It sketched out a methodology for crime prevention which was both problem-oriented and project-focused (Gladstone 1980). It involved four stages:

- a thorough analysis of the crime problem, 'high crime' area, or situation in which the offence occurs, in order to establish the conditions that need to be met for the offence(s) to be committed
- the identification of measures which would make it more difficult or impossible to fulfil these conditions
- the assessment of the practicability, likely effectiveness, and cost of each measure
- the selection of the most promising measures.

Subsequent practice has added two further stages to this methodology:

- an implementation process
- the subsequent monitoring and evaluation of the initiatives undertaken.

This collective method has largely set the agenda ever since. It was put into practice in high profile Home Office projects which have emphasised the importance of the 'quality' and extent of policy implementation (Hope and Murphy 1983; Hope 1985). It embodies an implicit situational – offence focused – orientation and in so doing reinforced the earlier Cornish Report's approach. This methodology and situational bias was developed and entrenched with the establishment of the Crime Prevention Unit (CPU) in the Home Office in 1983. Its work was heavily influenced by Ron Clarke's intellectual legacy. He had previously been head of the Research and Planning Unit at the Home Office and had pioneered and promoted a situational approach to crime prevention (see Chapter 3). According to Tilley, the 'role of the CPU from the outset was to light fires, to provoke crime prevention activity as and where it could' (1993a: 43). This it has sought to do largely through demonstration projects, which are then evaluated and the findings published, with the aim of disseminating good practice. As a result, in the years since its establishment the CPU has managed to produce a wealth of research reports which acts as a useful reference point and resource for practitioners.

Furthermore, in 1983 the Home Office Standing Conference on Crime Prevention – originally established following the Cornish Report – was reorganised and strengthened by a Home Office Minister taking the chair. This was followed by the issuing of inter-departmental circular 8/1984 which has become a crucially symbolic milestone in the renaissance of crime prevention. The circular declared:

> A primary objective of the police has always been the prevention of crime. However, since some of the factors affecting crime lie outside the control or direct influence of the police, crime prevention can not be left to them alone. Every individual citizen and all those agencies whose policies and practices can influence the extent of crime should make their contribution. Preventing crime is a task for the whole community.

This message has been reiterated in the ensuing years, with an ever-increasing crescendo. The Home Office followed up circular 8/1984 by setting up an inter-departmental Ministerial Group on Crime Prevention which led to two important seminars, the first of which was chaired by the Prime Minister, Margaret Thatcher. The inter-Ministerial Group was given the responsibility for ensuring that central government departments operate in partnership to achieve more effective co-ordination.

Central government policy became clearly fixed around the idea of a 'partnership' approach, the implications of which are considered in detail in Chapter 5. However, for the moment we can note that government policy, while lucid about the principle of 'partnerships', was highly ambiguous about the appropriate distribution of responsibilities associated with partnerships. There was no significant guidance on leadership or the allocation of roles. Hence, vexed questions about the nature and shape of collaborative relations remained unanswered. The question of leadership remained a controversial issue: one which the Home Office sought to duck by suggesting that the notion of identifying a single lead agency was anachronistic to a genuine partnership approach. Despite a certain veracity in this argument, in practice it tended to result in leadership falling back on to the police. Furthermore, no new resources were forthcoming. It was the government's view that crime prevention could be supported through existing programmes and resources.

The late 1980s saw a number of loosely connected central government initiatives to promote the model of crime prevention which it had been developing. In 1986 the experimental Five Towns Initiative was established which acted as a precursor for the more extensive Safer Cities Programme launched in 1988 which took centre place as the medium through which the crime prevention message was to be delivered. In the same year the government set up Crime Concern to focus on private sector involvement. Both these developments will be considered in greater detail later in this chapter.

The Home Office returned to, and reinforced, the message spelt out in circular 8/1984 by issuing a follow-up circular 44/1990 entitled 'Crime Prevention – The Success of the Partnership Approach'. Again this was sent out to local authority chief executives, chief police and probation officers and other relevant agencies. This time, however, the circular was accompanied by a Home Office compiled 'good practice booklet' (Home Office 1990a). This identified six headings: structure, leadership, information, identity, durability and resources. It suggested that these are all 'necessary elements' for any effective crime prevention project. In support of this, it offered a number of specific examples of existing 'good practice'. Interestingly, omitted from this list is any reference to monitoring and evaluation or training needs.

The Morgan Report

The Home Office then charged the Standing Conference on Crime Prevention chaired by James Morgan with the responsibility for reviewing the development of crime prevention since the 1984 circular and making recommendations for the future. The 1990 circular had called on all those involved in crime prevention and community safety to review their activities. It also requested them to submit documentation about the nature and extent of local crime prevention work in which they were engaged, to the Standing Committee. The Morgan working group's terms of reference were to:

consider and monitor the progress made in the local delivery of crime
prevention through the multi-agency or partnership approach, in the
light of the guidance in the booklet 'Partnership in Crime Prevention'
[which accompanied circular 44/90].

(Morgan 1991: 10)

The Standing Conference's subsequent report represents an important
milestone in the development of crime prevention through a 'partnership' approach in Britain and acted to stimulate further activity. The
principal recommendations of the report include:

- local authorities should be given 'statutory responsibility', working
  with the police, for development and stimulation of community
  safety and crime prevention
- where possible 'a co-ordinator with administrative support' should
  be appointed to the local authority structure
- particular attention should be given to issues of young people and
  crime in local partnerships
- chief constables should nominate for each local authority area the
  'most senior local operational officer' in order to promote
  coterminous boundaries
- particular attention should be given to make the 'best use of the
  resource represented by voluntary effort'
- more attention should be given to 'involving business as a partner
  instead of regarding it solely as a possible source of funds'
- government should examine 'how far the strong focus needed at
  the centre can be provided' by strengthening existing
  organisations or creating new ones
- a need to develop 'a clear statement of crime prevention training
  needs and an action plan to meet those needs'
- 'central government should provide a community safety impact
  statement for all new legislation and major policy initiatives'.

In the Report's recommendations a clear three-tiered structure (see
Figure 2.1) of responsibility begins to emerge, which in some ways
parallels the French experience (see Chapter 7). At the national level are
institutions – namely an inter-ministerial committee and an independent
'standing conference' – primarily charged with co-ordination functions.
The Report proposed that the former be given the task of monitoring
the impact of new legislation or policy initiatives on crime prevention
and co-ordinating the activity of government departments. The latter's
functions were to include monitoring future progress; developing a
code of practice; developing and promoting quality standards for crime
prevention activity; developing and implementing a national training
strategy; directing research on the uses of resources, planning, monitoring and evaluation; providing a national forum to oversee and report on
developments; and identifying problems and issues, initiating discussion
and action to resolve them.

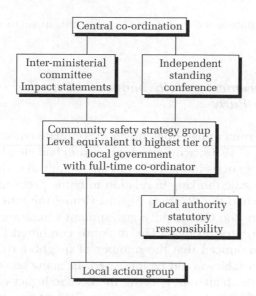

Figure 2.1   Morgan's recommended structure

At the intermediary level, equivalent to the highest tier of local government, the Morgan Report recommended the role of a Community Safety Strategy Group with a full-time co-ordinator. It recommended that this group be given the task to formalise a joint commitment to crime prevention; formulate overall policy objectives for the strategy based on analysis of local problems; identify the responsibilities of different departments and organisations; assess the resource implications; monitor progress, partly by receiving progress reports about more local activities; and produce an annual publication reporting on progress and setting targets for the following year.

Finally, at the local level the Report recommended the establishment of Local Action Groups. These groups would be responsible for assessing the nature of the crime problem locally; formulating objectives and a strategic plan for community safety within the local area; consulting local organisations and communities about the strategy; appointing either topic-based groups or neighbourhood-based groups to plan and implement the detail of the strategic plan; and monitoring, reviewing and reporting publicly on progress.

What Morgan's proposals embody – which had been sorely lacking from much central government thinking – is a coherent structure in which the distribution of responsibilities between the parties is made clear and rendered comprehensible. As we shall see, central government developments up to 1997 had been anything but coherent, and responsibility all but clearly distributed. However, the Morgan Report largely fell on deaf ears, primarily because the government was vehemently opposed to key elements of the recommendations – notably the proposal for a statutory duty for local authorities in relation to community safety.

Central government activity bequeathed by the Conservative Party

While the government had done much to stimulate enthusiasm in crime prevention in the 1980s, activity and innovation had clearly shifted to the realm of local agencies in the 1990s. In an attempt to revitalise what had become rather stale thinking in relation to crime prevention, the Home Secretary launched the 'Partners Against Crime' initiative in September 1994. Even here the Conservative government's initiative seemed to reflect the bankruptcy of ideas. The initiative combined three elements. First, it was announced that the number of neighbourhood constables and special constables would be increased. In many senses, special constables constitute an attempt to revive the Peelian legacy of visible patrols through the reliance on ordinary civilians. Volunteers operate in their own neighbourhood to which they bring a visible police presence, but do so at relatively little cost to the taxpayer. They constitute part of a much wider process of voluntarisation and civilianisation within policing generally (Gill and Mawby 1990). The Conservative government's aim was to double the 1990 figure of 15 000 to 30 000 special constables. To this end, the Home Office set up a Working Party to consider all aspects of the special constabulary, including ways of achieving its expansion (Southgate *et al.* 1995). Second, it was announced that in collaboration with Crime Concern the number of neighbourhood watch schemes would be increased by 50 per cent from its 1994 figure of 130 000 schemes covering 5 million households. Third, in order to re-energise the neighbourhood watch idea it was proclaimed that schemes were to be encouraged to include patrols of active citizens, who would 'walk with a purpose' in their local areas. 'Street watches' are intended to take the watch idea of using 'eyes and ears' of the local population out into the street in a supposedly structured and organised way. Street-watch members are ordinary citizens with no police powers. The idea is that if they notice anything suspicious, they are supposed to report it to the police. This is the kind of 'voluntary collective action' which the Home Secretary had declared to be the mainstay of civil society (Howard 1994). However, this proposal received a mixed response, particularly from the police themselves. Consequently, the proposal was revisited and any reference to the idea of 'patrols' was removed in order to avoid the notion that this merely represented 'policing on the cheap'. Furthermore, the proposal also raised concerns about the growing spectre of vigilantism (*Guardian* 21.6.1993). This episode exposes crucial ambiguities in the idea of devolving responsibility for crime control to the public. It also represented a watermark in that government seemed to have become trapped in the logic of its own limited vision: all it seemed capable of proposing was more of the same.

The situational and technological focus of much government inspired crime prevention also prevailed. Towards the end of 1995 the government announced the establishment of a special fund, known as the 'CCTV Challenge Competition', to encourage local authorities to set up and part fund surveillance schemes. Administered by the Home Office, this fund supports bids to resource the installation of CCTV cameras. As part of this programme £15 million was to be made available in the financial year 1996/7, with the intention to help provide up to 10 000 more CCTV cameras in high streets and other places over the ensuing three years (Home Office 1995c). In the three years to the end of 1997 the Home Office and local authorities collectively invested £120 million in CCTV systems (*Guardian* 9.1.1998).

One structural innovation introduced was the announcement in November 1995 by the Home Secretary of the establishment of a National Crime Prevention Agency. Its tasks are to focus and co-ordinate the national agenda (discussing new ways to reduce crime), to disseminate good practice and to develop strategies for preventing and reducing crime. Based at Easingwold, North Yorkshire, alongside the new police crime prevention training centre, the Agency replaces the National Board for Crime Prevention. It brings together the Home Office, the Police, Crime Concern and a number of individuals from business, the media and academia, although interestingly no representative of local government. The government announced that: 'We will commission the Agency to set and publish targets for reducing certain types of crime and report back on progress' (Citizens Charter 1996: 36). It was proclaimed that the initial targets would cover vehicle crime and retail crime. More bold proposals concerned the possibility of establishing a national crime prevention database for practitioners and the setting up of a 'Futures Group' to examine possible future trends within crime prevention.

The National Agency is not an independent body, separate from government. It is organisationally located within the Home Office and has a non-executive function. It is a pale imitation of the type of body envisaged by the Morgan Report. It does not have the agenda-setting powers of comparable national organisations in other European countries such as Sweden, France and The Netherlands (see Chapter 7). And yet it does have the potential to reinvigorate government thinking and to take a more prominent role in encouraging the formulation of a national crime prevention strategy.

Having considered the recent evolution, as well as the *ad hoc* and piecemeal nature of crime prevention at government level under Conservative leadership, let us now consider the changes and developments within some of the relevant organisations before returning to consider the implications of the new Labour government elected in May 1997.

The police

Two particular developments have undermined the traditional Peelian assumptions about crime prevention within the police. The first is the increased realisation that uniform foot patrols are not an effective form of crime prevention. This culminated in the Home Office research study by Clarke and Hough (1984). Drawing on comparative data, the authors persuasively argued that police patrols could not possibly be an effective means of preventing crime. They concluded that on average, by their estimation, a patrol officer in London could expect to pass within 100 yards of a burglary in progress once every eight years and even then they would probably not even know that a crime was being committed. As one of the authors later commented, 'the weight of research evidence is that further expenditure on conventional deterrent strategies will secure only small gains at the margin' (Hough 1987: 73). This confirmed what many had come to suspect and shattered any residual belief that the generic tasks of policing had a significant preventive effect.

The second development was the introduction of new technologies – particularly cars, communication systems and computerisation – and associated organisational restructuring which further destroyed the centrality of foot patrols. The most symbolic and notable development was the introduction of a system of 'unit beat policing'. This reduced the number of foot patrol officers and transferred them into panda cars, assigning to them a more reactive crime fighting role as opposed to the less conflictual, public interactions and service functions that foot patrolling enabled. This became known as 'fire-brigade' policing, with its emphasis on instant response. While often blamed for the destruction of police–public relations (Manwaring-White 1983), 'unit beat policing' was in reality the product of much deeper organisational antagonisms and a part of much wider trends. The reorganisation brought about by 'unit beat policing' represented a significant shift towards specialisation within the patrol function itself. One of the consequences of these developments was that 'crime prevention' as a specialism became increasingly defined in contrast to mainstream reactive policing. Crime prevention became 'pre-emptive' and 'proactive', through the use of surveillance, low level information gathering and police data to target particular locations, problems or people. What is clear, as Reiner suggests, is that 'the pursuit of greater effectiveness has meant a proliferation of specialist and plain-clothed units, reversing the original strategy of Peel, Rowan and Mayne' (1992: 100).

Moreover, the division of labour for the crime prevention function and its location within the police organisation served to constrain the nature of the activities pursued in the name of crime prevention work. The increasing specialisation of crime prevention and the reduced emphasis on foot patrols produced a crucial dilemma, one which was not lost on the Cornish Committee. The dilemma was that of identifying designated specialist officers to perform what had been seen as a primary objective of the organisation as a whole. The Cornish Committee had been clear in stating that the specialism should not be taken to imply any reduction in the responsibility of other officers in respect of general crime prevention, albeit that this was exactly what occurred over the ensuing years. By the mid-1980s crime prevention officers comprised on average 0.5 per cent of force strength (Weatheritt 1986). Harvey *et al.* have highlighted the absurdity of the prevailing organisational location of crime prevention within policing:

> In short, the precise leadership role of the police in crime prevention is obscure, and assigning some police officers to be crime prevention officers is perverse if the prevention of crime is a primary aim of the organisation as a whole.
>
> (1989: 63)

The specialisation of the crime prevention function within the police resulted in its 'ghettoisation'.

A further dilemma arose out of the realisation that while foot patrols are not directly an effective way of preventing or detecting crime, they are both generally liked by the public – with an impact on levels of fear of crime (Bennett 1991) – and may be a central element in sustaining police legitimacy (Kinsey *et al.* 1986). Consequently, despite the fact that 'unit beat policing' only had a short history, policing initiatives have invariably returned to the problem of the visible public presence of the police officer as a *sine qua non* of preventive policing, by way of a variety of forms of organisational readjustment including 'community policing', 'problem-oriented policing' and 'sector policing'.

The 1970s and 1980s also saw police force organisation reinforce the distinction between crime detection and crime prevention by situating responsibility for crime prevention often in Community Affairs and analogous departments. Some commentators (Harvey *et al.* 1989; Pease 1994) have been highly critical of such organisational arrangements, which leave most operational detectives believing that crime prevention has nothing to do with them. Rather, it is suggested that crime prevention should be located within and inform Criminal Investigation Departments. More recently, there has been a growing recognition that all police officers can contribute to a broader conception of crime prevention. Consequently, some police forces have sought organisational reorganisations in order to reintegrate crime prevention within mainstream policing. For some, this has involved greater organisational support and training in crime prevention for all officers. Elsewhere has seen the transfer of crime prevention out of Community Affairs departments and into newly formulated Crime Management departments. One of the dangers of such an approach is that this may entrench an organisational contrast between crime prevention and community affairs, with the potential result of further narrowing the definition of crime prevention and restricting it to technological and security hardware with little wider social focus. Other initiatives have involved the redefinition of the line command structure for all crime management matters, and encouraged a greater awareness of crime prevention among rank and file officers through training (Johnston *et al.* 1993). Increasingly, the analysis of local crime data is being used to inform policing strategies with a preventive focus. There has clearly been a move away from the idea that day-to-day crime prevention advice can only be offered by designated staff in a specialist department.

Nevertheless, the work of Crime Prevention Officers tends to have a narrow technical focus and is primarily concerned with physical security (Johnston *et al.* 1993). Advice to crime prevention panels, often chaired by police officers, constitutes an established area of police work. A more recent area of 'expertise' which the police have consolidated and extended is in relation to the 'secured by design' programme and the appointment of Police Architectural Liaison Officers. Under these schemes police forces have issued written guidance and trained officers to advise on the principles of crime prevention through environmental design. The service is offered to architects, planners and developers to encourage and enable them to construct environments which avoid obvious security problems.

Since 1988 the Audit Commission has had a considerable influence over policing policy, not merely in its implementation but also in its interpretation. Set up in 1982, it has encouraged the spread of 'new public management' reforms within local authorities and allied public sector organisations such as the police. It has acted as a catalyst in promoting objective-driven performance and the quest for 'value for money'. This has had implications for crime prevention as it has other areas of policing. In its report *Helping with Enquiries: Tackling Crime Effectively*, the Audit Commission (1993) directly touched on the contradictory role and place of prevention in policing. It recommended a form of proactive crime prevention integrated into the heart of policing operations. It advanced an intelligence-led crime management approach to policing, in which crime pattern analysis and information gathering are used to target offenders and high crime areas. This strategy is based explicitly on the proposition that a small proportion of offenders commit a large amount of crime and that they can be better targeted. More problematically, it also assumes the greater use of surveillance, undercover work, police informants and other forms of covert tactics. As we have seen, these do not have a strong tradition in British policing precisely because of the vexed questions such practices raise for legality and legitimacy (Maguire and John 1996). It also suggests that resources and manpower can be moved unproblematically away from other aspects of traditional policing and result in more effective crime prevention. The Audit Commission conclude their report by stating that 'the police can help to prevent crime and raise clear-up rates significantly, which itself will help to deter would-be criminals' (1993). The report develops a sophisticated and coherent case for the approach advanced which is already influencing practice.

However, rather than resolve the dilemmas around the place of crime prevention within policing it may merely serve to promote a new form of specialisation.

Furthermore, its recommendations touch on a further tension exposed by crime prevention within the police: namely whether the police can act alone in the prevention of crime. The idea of any measurement of police performance linked to crime rates presupposes a 'police solution' to crime. While this has been the traditional assumption underpinning key aspects of police legitimacy, it would appear to fly in the face of the new-found emphasis on partnerships in crime prevention. The new version of crime prevention or community safety, with its multi-agency focus – unlike its Peelian ancestor – is premised on the recognition that the police alone cannot prevent crime, the conditions for which lie beyond their reach.

What this review shows is that despite the various attempts to reintegrate crime prevention into mainstream policing there remain a number of unresolved structural and organisational tensions concerning the legitimacy and effectiveness of policing strategies. These in turn give rise to a considerable degree of varied practice across the 43 police forces in England and Wales. These tensions have been rearticulated recently in a Her Majesty's Inspectorate of Constabulary report, following its thematic inspection of crime prevention in the police (HMIC 1998). The report concludes that although most forces are committed to crime prevention, few are implementing the practical, well thought-out solutions needed. It calls for improvements to the national framework, particularly on co-ordination and training, and further development of the national 'key objectives' for policing to reflect crime prevention priorities. At the national level ACPO has sought to respond to this deficit by issuing a national strategy on crime prevention and establishing working parties to attain seven key objectives in an attempt to promote and co-ordinate developments (ACPO 1996). The strategy document, entitled *Towards 2000 – A Crime Prevention Strategy for the Millennium*, encourages 'a recognition by every policeman and woman that crime prevention is an integral part of mainstream policing, rather than a purely specialised, peripheral function' (*ibid.*). What this means in practice is much more complex and contradictory.

The probation service

Circular 8/1984 had urged the probation service to join the new co-ordinated approach to crime prevention. This was followed up in 1984 by the Home Office's 'Statement of National Objectives and Priorities' for the probation service which encouraged the service to contribute beyond individual work with offenders. It declared that: 'The probation service can make a unique contribution [to crime prevention] in providing a link between the offence and the offender, and in the wider social context in which offending takes place and in which preventive action has to be taken if results are to be achieved' (Home Office 1984). A report of the Central Council of Probation Committees (CCPC 1987) responded that: 'The probation service has always been concerned with crime prevention and that a widening of its boundary to participate in community focused crime prevention projects and activities would be a legitimate development.' In 1987 the Association of Chief Officers of Probation (ACOP) established a national committee on crime prevention. It subsequently published a document summarising the various contributions that the service can make to crime prevention (ACOP 1988). Consequently, following government's lead, probation managers are increasingly taking crime prevention seriously, albeit primarily at the level of sharing information with other agencies (ACOP 1993). Nevertheless, by the time of the Home Office's *Three Year Plan for the Probation Service, 1993–96* the aim of 'reducing and preventing crime and the fear of crime by working in partnership with others' had been accorded the special place of the first operational goal (Home Office 1992a: 12).

And yet what is meant by crime prevention in probation circles and the role of the probation service therein remains extremely vague. Furthermore, the nature of actual probation practice and the service's contribution to crime prevention is geographically variable (Geraghty 1991). It remains unclear whether the probation service has anything worthwhile to offer situational crime prevention – despite attempts to do so (see Laycock and Pease 1985) – and to what extent it is worth significantly getting involved in primary or secondary prevention, beyond public relations exercises. There is considerable current ambiguity as to what the probation service's response to crime prevention should be, particularly in the realm of its relations to the 'community' – itself a problematic concept for probation work (Sampson and Smith 1992) – and to victims of crime. One school of thought is that the probation service cannot afford to sit on the sidelines while others hitch themselves to the crime prevention/community safety wagon. Another perspective suggests that, as crime prevention addresses the impact of crime on victims and the fear of crime for ordinary people, it offers an important means of organisational legitimation in a period of rapid change and turmoil for the service. A third approach is that any contribution of the probation service should be limited to the field of social crime prevention based on probation officers' existing work with offenders (NAPO 1984).

All three of these perspectives recognise that central government's exhortation to the probation service to join the crime prevention bandwagon have come at a time of heightened political debate and uncertainty about the future role of the service. The collapse of the 'rehabilitative ideal', combined with 18 years of a government openly hostile to the traditional social work basis and individual offender focus of probation work, has left the service defensive and cautious. Nevertheless, some probation managers have embraced the new rhetoric of crime prevention as it represents 'a major opportunity to present some traditional probation service objectives in a way which commands widespread public support' (Bryant 1989: 15). Others have seen involvement in crime prevention and community safety initiatives as potentially a more secure premise from which to articulate a distinct probation identity and set of values for the future, in direct contrast to the government's attempts at a 'coercive tilt' to the service (Nellis 1995: 33–5).

Local government

Local government has seen a significant shift in attitudes towards crime prevention over the last 15 years. In the early 1980s there was little acceptance of any significant responsibility for crime prevention in local government. Now, however, there is a high level of recognition that crime prevention – or 'community safety' as it is more frequently referred to in local government circles – is a crucial issue for local authorities. The beginnings of this shift can be traced back to the establishment of local authority 'community safety teams' in metropolitan areas, most notably the Greater London Council (before its abolition in the mid-1980s), Birmingham, Hammersmith and Fulham and Islington. Between 1985 and 1994 the government encouraged local authorities in England to fund physical and social improvements to unpopular housing estates through the Estate Action programme. The crime prevention implications of architectural design have been extended beyond problem estates to the general fabric of city architecture – as witnessed by a Department of Environment circular (5/1994) sent out to local authority chief executives on 'planning out crime'.

A recent survey showed that of the 71 per cent that responded, 9 out of 10 authorities across the country recognise community safety as a policy area (LGMB 1996). Over half have published policy statements or aims and objectives and over half have a separate identified budget for community safety. The survey also discovered a 'high level of activity in most local authorities on community safety' (LGMB 1996: 1), notably in the larger urban areas.

The debate over the appropriate co-ordinating responsibility for local crime prevention and the role of local authorities did not disappear with the Conservative government's response to the Morgan Report recommendations. In 1996 the combined might of the joint local authority associations[1] and the Local Government Management Board (LGMB) pooled their energies to raise the issue of local government's proper role in community safety. As a means of developing political momentum in the run-up to the 1997 general election, they published four important documents: a survey of activities, a 'position statement', a manifesto and a guide to good practice. The community safety position statement entitled *Crime – The Local Solution* had a simple message: 'Local Authorities should be given statutory responsibility for preparing and monitoring the implementation of a community safety plan for their local area, in consultation with a range of local agencies' (ADC 1996: 1). This argument received support from a wide variety of sources including the Cassels Report on *The Role and Responsibilities of the Police*, published in March 1996, which had been the product of an independent inquiry set up by the Police Foundation and the Policy Studies Institute. The Audit Commission (1996) also appeared to arrive at a very similar conclusion, albeit starting from a concern with the costs of youth crime and youth justice. As with the Morgan Report, the Local Government Association's argument was premised on the belief that local government is the only strategically placed organisation which has sufficient leverage over diverse areas of policy such as housing, planning, education, social services, leisure, and so on, all of which have a community safety dimension. This, it was argued, puts them in a position to draw in other agencies (AMA 1990: 22). It is argued that by giving local authorities the leadership role in coordinating local work, community safety will be accorded greater long-term and strategic oversight, commitment and funding. This would allow for a significant element of durability which is currently lacking. Furthermore, local authorities would connect local community safety directly to the local democratic structure, and hence enhance its legitimacy. This, as Morgan had argued, can act to enhance a sense of 'local ownership' and increase the profile of community safety. In sum, an increasingly growing lobby has argued that local government is best placed to intervene both effectively and democratically, an argument endorsed by both the Labour and the Liberal Democrat Parties at the 1997 general election in their manifestos (Labour Party 1997; Liberal Democrat Party 1997).

The LGMB survey of community safety activities in local government also showed that a considerable amount of activity was already taking place within local authorities. The survey found that almost two-fifths of local authorities in England and Wales have appointed community safety officers (LGMB 1996). This figure is higher in metropolitan areas: approximately three-fifths. Traditionally, local authority involvement in crime prevention has been restricted to work on council run housing estates, often in collaboration with the voluntary sector. More recently, this has broadened to include activities in town centre security, environmental design, young people and crime and support for crime prevention by the voluntary sector. Town centre initiatives principally revolve around the installation and use of CCTV cameras which, as we have seen, has been strongly promoted by the government.

In their 'manifesto', the local authority associations call for local authorities to be given a new power to promote and co-ordinate community safety, supported by a new duty to prepare and publish an annual

Community Safety Plan to be deposited with the Home Secretary (ACC 1997a). As some commentators have suggested these Community Safety Plans could be prepared alongside and help inform police authorities' annual plans as required by the Police and Magistrates' Courts Act 1994 (Morgan and Newburn 1997). However, some police commentators have seen this as constituting a site of potential conflict (Povey 1997). The local authority associations, in rearticulating the Morgan Report's findings, deliberately sought to raise community safety as a political issue in the 1997 general election campaign and to encourage the Labour Party to adopt its detailed policies (to which I return later).

The voluntary sector and NACRO

Outside of government the National Association for the Care and Reset-tlement of Offenders (NACRO) has a long and distinguished record in promoting and realising innovative crime prevention. NACRO developed its track record of pioneering work with the establishment in 1979 of its Crime Prevention Unit and then a year later with the launch of its influ-ential Safe Neighbourhoods Unit (SNU). Much of NACRO's work has focused on high crime public sector housing estates. It has acted as an important antidote to much of the central government initiated work with its situational focus. NACRO has instead sought to highlight the complementary importance of long-term social crime prevention (some of the more notable examples of which will be considered in more detail in Chapter 4). Over the years NACRO has developed a loose methodo-logy which largely comprises the following:

- consultation with residents and local staff
- local analysis of crime to specify the action to be taken and a plan drawn up
- working in conjunction with local councils and the police
- involving local residents in elements of decentralised management
- oversight by a multi-agency steering committee
- usually, initiatives that embrace a multi-focus approach which seeks to tackle the multiple problems within an area through a combination of situational and social interventions
- an emphasis on 'quality of life' issues for residents which extend beyond 'crime', narrowly defined
- an evaluation of the impact of the intervention which allows for collecting evidence from a variety of sources, not least the residents themselves.

On the basis of its work (Bright and Petterssen 1984), SNU has come to advocate good, localised and locally accountable management as the key to community safety (Bright 1991: 76–7). In this it echoes the lessons of the Priority Estates Projects (PEP) which initially had been set up in 1979 with funding from the Department of Environment (DoE) as a 'sticking plaster' over some of the most unpopular, marginal and run-down council estates (Power 1984; Rock 1988; Foster and Hope 1993; Power and Tunstall 1995). And yet they have provided a rich source of material on the benefits and difficulties associated with management focused initiatives. NACRO has also promoted the importance of resources to support tenant management initiatives, address design problems and provide facilities for young people. In 1993 SNU prepared an important report for the DoE entitled *Crime Prevention on Council Estates*, which sought to draw together the lessons of the developments throughout the 1980s (DoE 1993). The report advocates the importance of high quality evaluation, even if this has been beyond the resources of many of the initiatives they have supported. In line with earlier work, the report promotes a framework for evaluating crime prevention initiatives, including an assessment of costs and benefits which extends beyond monetary matters and includes 'quality of life' issues (see Chapter 6).

Crime concern and the private sector

The government has encouraged the private sector to take on board greater responsibility for crime prevention. It has sought to provoke businesses to address concerns about their own security and that of their employees, as well as to engage in and support initiatives which impact on the security of their local community. The *Practical Ways to Crack Crime* handbook has a particular section addressed to private businesses (Home Office 1991). The government has also encouraged the establishment of various 'Business Watch' schemes. Most significantly, Crime Concern was set up as a charity by the Home Office in May 1988 with the explicit aims to promote crime prevention partnerships and encourage the involvement of the commercial sector. It has sought to stimulate the development of local crime prevention activity and to encourage good practice through initiatives such as neighbourhood watch and Crime Prevention Panels. Other work includes consultancy services for local agencies and support for local partnerships. It is a national organisation which raises funds and provides assistance on a consultancy basis to local 'partnerships'. As well as the money it raises itself to pay for its activities and the 100 or so staff it employs, the Home Office provides an annual grant of £750 000. Its aim is to act as an 'independent' catalyst to local activity and to disseminate 'good practice' in the field of crime prevention. Crime Concern has also been involved in the management of 14 Safer Cities Projects. In the intervening years since its establishment, Crime Concern has firmly marked itself as a major player in the spread of community-based and inter-agency crime prevention.

Crime Concern organises local and national events, including the national neighbourhood watch conference. Together with the Prudential Corporation in 1993, Crime Concern launched a five-year strategy costing about £1.5 million to develop Youth Action Groups in secondary schools across the country. These aim to tackle problems of bullying, vandalism, graffiti, personal safety and drug abuse, and to increase young people's interest in crime prevention and encourage a sense of social responsibility. By 1997 there were some 640 of these groups in existence. In keeping with its catalytic role, Crime Concern in association with the Confederation of British Industry (CBI) launched a 'Business and Crime Initiative' which resulted in the publication of best practice guides for both large companies and small businesses. Architects and builders, encouraged by schemes such as 'secured by design', have been keen to take account of domestic security in building or renovating residential property. The Institute of Housing and the Royal Institute of British Architects have worked collaboratively with Crime Concern in this regard. Furthermore, insurance companies have not been slow to appreciate the implications of crime prevention for insurance cover, particularly for people in high risk areas.

Probably the biggest growth area has been in the installation and use of CCTV cameras both to protect private businesses and survey public places. As already suggested, this is an area in which government promotion has featured strongly, but also where private companies have taken the initiative, particularly in large shopping malls. For example, in 1995 Marks and Spencer announced it was committing most of its £30 million budget for security improvements on CCTV (*Guardian* 21.9.1995). More generally, the private sector has been quick to exploit the opportunities presented by the expanding 'market' in crime prevention. The past 25 years have seen a boom in the security industry as crime prevention technology has become commodified. The annual turnover of the private security industry in 1994 was estimated to be a staggering £2.8 billion according to the British Security Industry Association (Jones and Newburn 1995: 226). The number of people employed in the private security industry in a policing capacity has also outgrown the number of public police officers. One estimate suggests that by the end of 1994 some 7850 firms were employing more than 162 000 people. This compares with 142 000 people employed within the public police (cited in Gallagher 1995: 23).

However, the recent history of corporate sponsorship in relation to community safety initiatives has been less successful (Bright 1991). Nevertheless, certain companies are willing to contribute to local or national initiatives primarily for public relations reasons. There are organisations such as 'Business in the Community' which aim to encourage 'partnerships' in key areas of concern and to promote an ideology of corporate community investment in the UK, along the lines of the United Ways initiative in the USA. At one level, private sector involvement has raised the issue of how further to encourage opportunities for crime prevention by structuring specific incentives (Pease 1996). At another level, it raises two fundamental issues. The first concerns the implications of private sector involvement in local community safety partnerships (see Chapter 5). The second relates to the nature of appropriate 'private' and 'public' responsibilities for crime prevention and the role of the state, private companies, communities and individuals (to which I return in Chapter 8).

The Safer Cities Programme

The Safer Cities Programme extended the earlier Five Towns Initiative which had run for 18 months from early 1986. It was announced in March 1988 as part of Action for Cities, which was principally concerned with urban regeneration. In the first phase local measures against crime and the fear of crime were introduced in three waves (1988, 1989 and 1991). It was believed that three years funding would allow for a more effective process of foundation-building than the 18 months allowed for by the Five Towns Initiative. In the first phase, the Safer Cities Programme provided Home Office pump-priming funding for a local co-ordinator, assistant co-ordinator and personal assistant, supported by a multi-agency steering committee – with representatives drawn from relevant public, private and voluntary sector agencies – to run grant funds to support local crime prevention activities in the designated Safer City areas.[2] The first phase projects were given a sum of £250 000 each per annum (in addition to the salaries of staff and their office costs). The money was hoped to 'lever' in other local funds (Tilley 1992: 2). The stated aims of the Safer Cities Programme were: (a) to reduce crime; (b) to lessen the fear of crime; and (c) to create safer cities where economic enterprise and community life can flourish. The latter aim reflected the government's ideological preference for urban regeneration by means of stimulating an 'enterprise culture' (Keat and Abercrombie 1991). Surprisingly, despite the short-term nature of the funding, longer term strategy development was not one of the explicit aims of Safer Cities.

An integral element in the Safer Cities framework was the role of the multi-agency steering committee. Through this, the programme dovetailed the promotion of crime prevention with a partnership approach. The steering committees' terms of reference were primarily: (a) to act as a focus for the local multi-agency crime prevention partnership; (b) to set priorities for the project and oversee the implementation of community safety measures, acting for the benefit of the project area as a whole; and (c) to facilitate contact and co-operation between local agencies and interests. The intention was for the steering committees to accommodate and balance the relevant public, private and voluntary sector interests and to develop a clear role, which was more than just a 'grant giver' or 'rubber stamp'.

By the end of the first phase in 1995 the programme had extended to cover 20 cities and claimed to have initiated more than 3600 crime prevention and community safety schemes at a cost of £22 million, plus £8 million in administration. Domestic burglary schemes were typical of the type of activities supported. In the first phase some 300 schemes were targeted on domestic burglary. Most involved improving the physical security of homes, some on an individual basis, others on whole estates. According to Home Office research there was good evidence, from both surveys and recorded crime, that Safer Cities schemes reduced the risk of burglary (Ekblom et al. 1997). For example, in areas with a 'high' risk of burglaries – i.e. ten recorded incidents per 1000 households per year – Safer Cities action of 'average' intensity – i.e. £3.57 worth of action per household per year – was followed by a 10 per cent drop in risk. There was evidence of displacement to other areas. The research also found evidence of the diffusion of benefit, the preventive effect reaching beyond the intended boundaries of the schemes. This, they suggest, seems to mitigate displacement where action was more intensive. Furthermore, burglary action in an area appeared to deflect away displacement coming from neighbouring burglary schemes, and also to protect against 'crime switch' from other offences into burglary. Crime switch from burglary to other property offences occurred only when burglary action was of low intensity. At higher intensities, the risk of other property crime decreased too.

The 1992 Conservative Manifesto promised another 40 new Safer Cities projects as part of what became known as 'phase two'. The DoE took over the funding of the Safer Cities Programme as part of the Single Regeneration Budget (SRB).[3] They stopped at 32 new projects. The new projects have been and are managed by 'independent' organisations through a competitive tendering process. The principal management occurs through NACRO, Crime Concern and the Society of Voluntary Associates (SOVA). In each of the second phase areas an average of £100 000 has been made available, and project running costs are funded centrally (see Figure 2.2). After the end of the second phase initiatives, future funding is to be through the general SRB. This means the loss of Safer Cities as a distinct crime prevention entity. However, now that crime prevention has become inscribed within the bidding criteria of mainstream and large-scale policy initiatives such the SRB, it has become a defining part of the much wider process of urban regeneration. According to the Conservative government, in the first three phases of SRB funding 63 per cent of funded areas included a crime prevention element (Widdecombe 1997). This raises fundamental questions about the future shape of crime prevention and its relationship to social policy more generally.

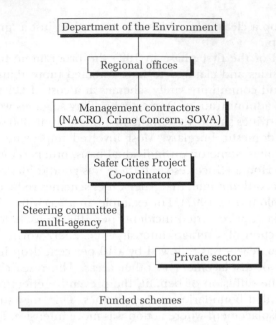

Figure 2.2   The structure of the Safer Cities Programme in phase 2

Some criticisms of the Safer Cities structure

Leaving aside the problems of multi-agency 'partnerships' more generally (see Chapter 5), the Safer Cities Programme has a number of serious
flaws. First, it has suffered from a very real 'democratic deficit'. From the
outset the Safer Cities Programme was designed by the Conservative
government to parallel rather than supplement or enhance the work
of local authorities. In this regard, the structure of the Safer Cities
Programme embodied the government's antipathy towards the power of
local authorities. In doing so, it circumvented existing structures of local
democratic accountability. This, King rightly saw as illustrative of the way
in which government 'constructs the crime problem and ways of controlling and preventing crime very much in its own image' (1991: 107). In
the 1980s and early 1990s the Safer Cities Programme became a potent
vehicle for disseminating the Conservative government's own ideology.
The response of the Conservative government to any subsequent proposals to increase the responsibility of local authorities in the field of
crime prevention has been unequivocally dismissive (Home Office 1992b:
1–2). Most notable was the key recommendation of the Report from Standing Conference on Crime Prevention set up by the government itself,
that 'local authorities, working in conjunction with the police, should
have clear statutory responsibility for the development and stimulation
of community safety and crime prevention programmes' (Morgan 1991:
29, para. 6.9). In so doing, they supported the Association of Metropolitan Authorities' (AMA) position and recognised that without such a

statutory responsibility the role that local authorities could have played in crime prevention has been inhibited and compromised. Furthermore, they went on to argue that,

> the absence of elected members from crime prevention structures may have the effect of marginalising crime prevention from local political issues. Any meaningful local structure for crime prevention must relate to the local democratic structure.
>
> (Morgan 1991: 20)

The Report also recommended that a code of practice for local authorities be established in order to encourage the spread of crime prevention partnerships. However, these sentiments did not accord with Conservative government ideology, which was set against local authority ownership of crime prevention and sought to 'leapfrog' established local government administrative structures. Consequently, the government's curt response to the Report was to disband the Standing Conference (replacing it with a National Board for Crime Prevention) and to ignore many of their conclusions (Home Office 1992b, 1993).

There was no requirement imposed on Safer Cities by central government to show that they had any kind of local mandate from the local population or that there were explicit lines of representation in terms of those incorporated on to the steering committees. This stands in contrast to the experiences of other countries where either the community safety body is accountable to the local democratic structure – as in France – or there are formal requirements to establish a local mandate as a prerequisite for receiving government funds – as in New Zealand where prospective safer community councils are required to produce a 'profile' of their locality, a 'mandate' demonstrating the incorporation of appropriate groups and a 'plan' of action (see New Zealand Crime Prevention Unit 1994a, 1994b). It is argued that such formal processes act as important legitimating devices as well as ways in which a sense of local vision, limited consensus and ownership are constructed.

Second, the Safer Cities model appears to have been dropped into a 'policy vacuum'. Contrary to King's (1991) early assessment of the Safer Cities Programme, the problem was often not a matter of too much central government steering but rather a lack of guidance or even facilitative advice on the basis of what was happening elsewhere. It is certainly true, as King notes, that the structure of the Programme reflected its own ideological approach to crime prevention. Furthermore, it is also correct that government exercised considerable control over certain aspects of the programme, particularly in the early days. Initially, for example, the maximum sum that local steering groups were able to approve without formal Home Office consent was £500. This was increased to £2000, but nevertheless applications for larger grants still had to be passed for approval to the Home Office/DoE, as did the names of co-ordinators and steering committee members prior to their appointment. However, a central ethos of the Safer Cities Programme involved the view that it would be improper to impose a universal blueprint upon communities. Needless to say, the local nature of a given crime problem requires important sensitivity to the specific nature of the locality. However, in many senses this was taken to an extreme resulting in the partial abdication of responsibility by central government for guidance or enhancement. Constrained by the limited nature of the funding provided, Safer Cities projects were genuinely caught in a situation of responsibility with very little power. In many senses the Safer City Programme was founded on uncertainty and produced considerable diversity of outcomes. This lack of guidance and facilitation was compounded by the fact that the Home Office and Crime Prevention Unit were unaccustomed to a direct service delivery function (Tilley 1993a).

Furthermore, there has been little guidance on the problematic relationship with non-Safer Cities Programmes. On the basis of the evidence collected by the Standing Conference on Crime Prevention about the local delivery of crime prevention up to the end of 1990, the Morgan Report claimed that:

> There is a confusion at local level about the various centrally funded
> schemes with a crime prevention element and concern about potential
> over-lap and duplication of effort. What is clearly perceived at a local level
> is a tendency for government departments to promote *ad hoc* initiatives,
> often implemented without proper consultation either with other
> government departments or with the local authorities.
>
> (Morgan 1991: 26)

Moreover, the Metropolitan Police in their submission to the Standing Conference stated that:

> there is a lack of co-ordination between individual Government departments
> in the planning and implementation of crime prevention activity . . . There is
> a real danger that, without strategic co-operation centrally, the impact of
> central Government crime prevention resources will be greatly reduced.
>
> (cited in Morgan 1991: 26)

Third, this translates into a wider lack of strategic foresight, which has been most notable in relation to succession strategies. Despite the fact that it has long been known that all Safer Cities projects were, and are, only short-term funding initiatives, central government and the Home Office failed to provide any significant advice to project workers as to how they might exit the Safer Cities funding phase and what, if anything, they might leave behind. There was also a paucity of evaluation of the benefits or pitfalls of different strategies and models developed by the earliest projects. If the Safer Cities Programme really conformed to a 'quasi-research project', as Tilley suggests (1993a: 55), it should have had integral strategic aspects of evaluation inscribed into its structure. Much of the monitoring and evaluation conducted for central government was more concerned with financial accounting purposes than with the assessment of the impact, outcome or effectiveness of given projects or initiatives. Instead, the evaluation research that was conducted was often conceived after the event, completed too late to inform the development of the programme and primarily concerned with short-term measurement rather than long-term strategy design (see Chapter 6). For example, by the time of the end of the funding for the first wave of the second-phase projects in early 1997, there was no substantial advice or models of assistance for steering committee members and project workers to consider. This was symptomatic of the much wider lack of evaluation of government-initiative programmes.

Fourth, the whole model has suffered from a short-term project-orientation approach to crime prevention. The finite life of Safer Cities projects and the issue of continuity have been constant problems. In common with the vast majority of British crime prevention developments, Safer Cities is time-limited and project-oriented rather than programme-driven (King 1988). Despite the intentions of many Safer Cities projects to try to establish a broad-based, long-term approach to crime prevention, the funding structure and institutional framework have only served to undermine this. As a consequence, many more situational crime prevention schemes were implemented in the Safer Cities Programme than other types of crime prevention activity (Sutton 1996: 13).

Fifth, the lack of sufficient resources and funds for what are after all city-wide projects has meant it has been difficult for projects to effect significant change within their locality. It has often left co-ordinators and steering committees in the unenviable position of turning down funds for innovative local projects. Often it is less the case that there are not enough innovative ideas and projects coming through but rather that there is no durable and long-term funding to sustain them beyond an initial phase.

Finally, there have been concerns over the implications of the contracted-out management in the second phase. While the intention had been to use the expertise of organisations such as NACRO, Crime Concern and SOVA, there have been some uncertainties as to whether this may have injected a further element of competition into what is supposed to be a 'partnership' process. This competitive edge can be exacerbated by the non-coterminous boundaries of many criminal justice agencies which means that some organisations may be working with more than one 'manager', or may be forced to prioritise one set of relations against another. This concern is one of the issues which the second-phase programme evaluators have been asked to assess.

In the light of nearly ten years' experience of the Safer Cities Programme, it would be inaccurate to conclude, as King (1991) does, that it merely constitutes a powerful vehicle for disseminating into practice a Conservative ideological vision. The relationship between ideology, policy and practice is more complex than that. As we have seen, on closer

examination its development has been haphazard, ambiguous, geographically variable and lacking in a significant strategic vision. The real policy-
making functions of Safer Cities projects, and the diversity of schemes
assisted, increasingly became apparent, albeit that they were essentially
dealing with 'drops' in the proverbial 'ocean'. And yet it would be wrong
to suggest, as Tilley implies, that the Safer Cities story is essentially one
of 'accidental contingencies' developed through the 'exploitation of
opportunity' (1993a: 55). It was infused with ideological prejudices and
inclinations, but not necessarily ones that pulled in the same direction
at the same time. The hostility towards local authorities, the preference
for short-term, situational interventions, the emphasis on enterprise and
the involvement of the private sector, the prioritisation of monitoring
through financial accounting rather than evaluation research – the measurement of 'outputs' rather than 'outcomes' – are all key aspects of how the
programme unfolded. However, these were neither part of a consistent
vision nor were they implemented coherently.

New Labour, new era?

In the months after the election of the Labour government in May 1997
a flurry of activity occurred which breathed new life into community safety
and crime prevention. In its manifesto the Labour Party (1997) had firmly
committed itself to introducing the recommendations of the Morgan
Report regarding the creation of a statutory duty for local authorities.
This has manifested itself as the Crime and Disorder Bill, published on 2
December 1997. However, there have been some changes to the nature
and scope of the duty from that proposed by Morgan and the LGA, largely
in response to concerns expressed by the police. The government proposes that the new statutory duty will be placed simultaneously on local
authorities (at both district and unitary authority levels) *and the police* to
develop, co-ordinate and promote local 'community safety partnerships'
(Home Office 1997a). This avoids the notion of a 'lead agency' with sole
responsibility in that the duty will be shared. Thus the local authority
and police will be charged with the responsibility to produce a joint crime
audit; to consult and involve other local agencies (including the probation service, the health service, local schools and education institutions,
the CPS and youth services), as well as local businesses, voluntary organisations and the residential community; and to produce and publish a
'community safety strategy'. According to clause 6 of the Bill, a number
of steps must be fulfilled before the formulation of the strategy. The duty
requires the responsible authorities to:

- conduct a review of the levels and patterns of crime and disorder
  in the area
- prepare an analysis of the levels and patterns of crime and
  disorder in the area

- publish a report of that analysis
- obtain the views on that report of people and organisations in the area whether by holding meetings or otherwise.

In formulating the strategy, regard should be given to the crime data analysis and the views obtained. It is proposed that the strategies will include long and short-term targets for crime and disorder reduction and timescales for each element of the plan. It is also envisaged that the local authority and police will consult with the other partners annually on progress towards the targets and from time to time revisit the basic process of joint audit to produce a new strategy. It is hoped that the equal responsibility given to the role of the police will ensure complementarity between a local 'community safety strategy' and 'policing plan' as required of the police under the Police and Magistrates' Courts Act 1994. It is envisaged that the Home Secretary will have a power to call for a report from the 'leadership group' (the local authority and police) as to how the joint duty is being discharged.

It is unclear, as yet, how prescriptive the new government will be as to the structure and membership of the partnership bodies to be set up or reconfigured in order to implement the proposed statutory duty. The intention of the government appears to be to encourage the development of community safety partnerships where currently they do not exist, rather than to transform practice where it is already established. It is also unclear what role the National Crime Prevention Agency will play in relation to the local developments which will inevitably be spawned by the new duty. Some commentators see it as too closely associated with the previous government to survive, while others believe that with an expanded remit (and membership) it is ideally placed to co-ordinate and lead national developments. There will clearly be no additional funds attached to the new duty.

Nevertheless, the statutory duty will add a powerful dynamic in promoting the expansion of community safety in Britain and entrenching a partnership approach to the delivery of crime prevention. This will be fuelled by the decision of the Audit Commission to embark on an extensive 18-month study of 'community safety', which it is anticipated will be published in the autumn of 1998. The Audit Commission will work alongside Her Majesty's Inspectorate of Constabulary who have just completed an HMIC thematic inspection of crime prevention in the police service (HMIC 1998). The subsequent Audit Commission report is likely to heavily influence the guidance which the Home Secretary has promised to provide in relation to the implementation of the new statutory duty under the Crime and Disorder Bill. Collectively these are likely to propel forwards and shape the future of community safety and crime prevention.

The new statutory duty to formulate and implement a 'community safety strategy' will also be supported by a general duty on local authorities to consider the likely effect of all its policies on the prevention of crime and disorder in their area. The legislation will create an 'Anti-Social Behaviour

Order' – originally referred to as a 'Community Safety Order' (Labour Party 1995; Home Office 1997f) – which will provide a civil remedy, for senior police officers and/or chief executives of a council, to restrain 'anti-social behaviour' by individuals or a group. Breach of the order may give rise to criminal prosecution punishable by imprisonment (up to six months before a magistrates' court and up to a maximum of five years before the Crown Court). Significant concern exists about the scope of the new order which is broadly defined, covering a wide range of non-criminal conduct (von Hirsch *et al.* 1995). Moreover, it potentially introduces criminal measures through the civil 'back door', where the standard of proof is reduced to the 'balance of probabilities'. It also transfers considerable judicial power – effectively the power to criminalise conduct – into the hands of local officials.

Alongside this, local authorities will have the power to order a curfew (not exceeding 90 days) for youths under ten years of age in a specific area following consultation with the police and local community (Home Office 1997b). The curfews will operate in relation to children in public places and not under the effective control of a responsible person aged 18 or over between specified hours (9pm and 6am). These orders will be enforced by the police, who would be expected to return a child breaking the curfew to his or her home and to the care of a responsible adult. If there is no responsible adult to take charge of the child, then under existing powers (section 46 of the Children Act 1989) the police will be able to remove the child to suitable accommodation if the child would otherwise be likely to suffer significant harm. In all cases where a curfew has been breached, the local authority will be required to visit the family within 48 hours to assess the need for support or intervention.

The new government also proposes to introduce a swathe of legislative changes to the youth justice system, the principal aim of which will be 'to prevent offending by children and young persons' (Home Office 1997e). This emphasis on prevention is strongly reinforced in relation to those children and young people who come into contact with the youth justice system as a consequence of their initial offending behaviour. Most notable among the proposed changes is a new system of police 'reprimand' and 'final warning' to replace cautions. This will be administered by the police where they decide it inappropriate to bring a young person before the courts. It will 'trigger a set of interventions unless local agencies considered this unnecessary' and will be recorded by the police in the same way as cautions.

The government's focus on youth offending is also articulated by its proposed duty on local authorities to ensure the availability of youth justice services, plus a duty on the police and probation service to co-operate in the discharge of the local authority's responsibility. This is strengthened by the requirement to establish Youth Offending Teams (YOTs) across the country which will bring together relevant local agencies in delivering community-based interventions to 'turn young offenders away from crime' (Home Office 1997d). It is envisaged that YOTs 'will bring together the experience and skills of relevant local agencies to address the causes of a young person's offending . . . and so reduce the risk of reoffending' (Home Office 1997e: para. 8.13). As well as carrying out considerable pre-court work, YOTs will be charged with the responsibility of supervising the proposed 'action plan' orders and 'reparation' orders – both of which are intended to reduce reoffending through targeted action to confront a youth's offending behaviour – which the Crime and Disorder Bill introduces as new sentences of the court for young offenders.

The government also intends to introduce a 'parenting order' on the parent or guardian of a young offender, a child who is subject to a 'child safety order' or a child who is not attending school regularly. Such parents will be required to attend parental training in the form of counselling and guidance sessions to control the criminal behaviour of their children. For those parents who 'wilfully neglect their parental responsibilities, the courts will be able to require them, for example, to ensure that their child is home by a certain time at night, or is escorted to and from school by an adult' (Home Office 1997b: 5).

Clearly the thrust of the proposed reforms to the youth justice system is earlier intervention, which places considerable emphasis on the prevention of further offending among those already drawn into the criminal justice 'net'. Moreover, if YOTs are effectively implemented they will go a long way towards institutionalising a multi-agency response to crime. Nevertheless, much of the focus remains on the criminal justice process. The sections of the Bill which deal with preventing youth crime prefer to offer broad intentions – such as placing a statutory duty on youth justice agencies to have regard to the need to prevent offending by young people – supported by non-statutory objectives, rather than targeted proposals. This may represent a missed opportunity by the government to dramatically shift the focus of youth justice away from a deterrent paradigm towards a preventive one.

Nevertheless, the Crime and Disorder Bill will undoubtedly reinvigorate community safety in Britain and will entrench a partnership approach to the delivery of crime prevention. In this sense it will extend themes which had become dominant but which lacked national coherence and guidance. As such it represents a 'great leap forward', rather than a 'new departure'. However, the danger is that behind the various 'community safety' and 'protection' orders envisaged by the new government lurks a penal response. It is unclear to what extent these proposals will actually fuel the prison population – which has continued to rise under the new government – rather than reduce it. Clearly, the discretion of the police and the courts will be sharply curtailed. Hence, the central question is to what extent the new government will concentrate effort on the second half of its famous catchphrase, 'tough on crime, tough on the causes of crime', or whether it will continue to be swept along by the momentum of 'punitive populism' bequeathed by the Conservative Home Secretary, Michael Howard.

Conclusions

As we approach the end of the millennium, we appear to be witnessing a growing focus on the prevention of crime. There seems to be a political and academic consensus that greater attention needs to be paid to the role of informal social control in producing and sustaining order. As a consequence, it seems to be accepted in theory, if not in practice, that the role of the formal criminal justice system should be to support and enhance such informal control systems, as opposed to undermining or supplanting them. An emergent methodology about implementation and evaluation has developed. There appears now to be an acceptance of a 'partnership' approach to crime prevention as offering the most effective and constructive approach. Crime prevention and policing broadly understood have become pluralised: dispersed throughout the social fabric. Now diverse agencies, organisations and various community groups have become deeply implicated in the task of crime control. It is no longer solely the responsibility of the police or central government but of us all. Significant shifts have occurred, as organisations which some 15 years ago saw crime issues as 'none of their business' are now promoting the importance that they attribute to their own role in crime prevention. What is perhaps most remarkable is the way in which, in such a short space of time, organisations and groups have accepted and, in some cases, even sought a greater involvement in the provision of their own and others' security.

While the recent renaissance in crime prevention has produced a flurry of policy interventions and activity at local and national levels, generally this has lacked coherence and strategic vision. Britain does not yet have a national crime prevention strategy as such and there has been a distinct lack of co-ordination between government departments in the setting of priorities and the distribution of responsibilities. No organisation has been charged with duties and given sufficient powers to assess the crime prevention implications of new legislation or policy initiatives or ensure coherency and consistency across government departments. As a consequence, government interventions have been piecemeal and somewhat contradictory. In part, this has been due to an uncertainty as to the appropriate relationship between central steering and local delivery as well as the ideological ambiguities presented by certain aspects of crime prevention. A key difficulty for successive Conservative governments was the appropriate structure through which to promote crime prevention, given its antipathy towards local government. It is as if ministers were more comfortable with national media campaigns – such as the 'together we will crack crime' campaigns – which speak directly to individuals. The catchphrase 'local solutions to local problems' accords to an important dynamic in crime. However, it has almost become a mantra in the crime prevention field which government has used to absolve itself of responsibility for constructive leadership. While local crime problems

require locally delivered solutions, the challenge for central government is to facilitate local initiatives and commitment within a national
strategy which accords a place to the wider social implications of crime
prevention.

Those structures which have been established appear to have reached
a crucial stage in their development, in which they have either run out of
steam – as with the Safer Cities Programme – or are uncertain as to how
far they should be taking on board the responsibility for crime control
and prevention or passing it on to the public (and thus doing themselves
out of a role, or at least transforming it). For example, local authorities,
like that in Sedgefield, have set up their own uniformed 'Community
Force' to patrol the streets on a 24-hour basis. Similarly, the police now
ask themselves whether they should authorise certain local groups to police
their own areas. Hence, rather than constituting an easy solution to the
crime problem, crime prevention has opened up a new Pandora's box of
questions about appropriate roles, responsibilities and legitimacy.

There is a distinct ambivalence about crime prevention; it is much
lauded but less often practised. For example, despite the heavy financial
burden of the criminal justice system, relatively little money is allocated
to crime prevention. In the financial year 1993/4 government expenditure on crime prevention in its widest sense was £241 million (Home Office
1995b: 73), of which 72 per cent was spent by the DoE as part of urban
and estate regeneration programmes. The Home Office spent only an
estimated £13.1 million. This amounts to just over 1 per cent of the criminal justice budget being allocated to crime prevention.

Garland has provided a potential explanation for this state of affairs.
He suggests that there are 'two contrasting visions at work in contemporary criminal justice – the passionate, morally toned desire to punish and
the administrative, rationalistic, normalizing concern to manage' (1990:
180). The latter is epitomised by concerns over crime prevention. These
two visions are present within the processes of criminal justice and are
frequently expressed in conflicts within contemporary crime control and
penal policy and practice. As a consequence, official criminology is increasingly ambiguous and polarised. Garland calls these two voices within
official criminology a 'criminology of the self' and a 'criminology of the
other'. The former is invoked to 'routinize crime, allay disproportionate
fears and promote preventive action'; the latter is concerned to 'demonize
the criminal, to excite popular fears and hostilities, and to promote support for state punishment' (1996: 461). More importantly, we see within
these tensions, simultaneously, a recognition of the limitations of traditional criminal justice – police, prosecution and punishment – only for
them, subsequently, to be discounted or ignored in other fields. This
dualistic denial and recognition of the state's own capacity for effective
action in crime control is founded in 'the political *ambivalence* which
results from a state confronted by its own limitations' (Garland 1996:
462, emphasis in original).

While it is clear that crime prevention has become confirmed as having a major new place within the criminal justice complex, fundamental uncertainties remain about the future strategy and structure of crime prevention in Britain. Ambiguities in policy and practice represent important dynamics in the unfolding shape of, and volatile spaces within, crime control and prevention.

Notes

1. This united position statement brought together the various local government associations incorporating the Association of District Councils (ADC), the Association of County Councils (ACC) and the Association of Metropolitan Authorities (AMA).

2. Here as throughout, the terminology reflects that generally used in government discourse: 'programme' refers to the overall Safer Cities approach and delivery mechanisms, 'project' refers to each of the Safer Cities areas and components, and the terms 'scheme' or 'initiative' are used to refer to the funded local arrangements.

3. The Single Regeneration Budget has brought together the various existing forms of government funding for urban regeneration – including City Challenge and the Urban Programme – under one programme. The programme is administered through a new structure of regional government offices and is premised on a competitive 'challenge' model of fund allocation.

Chapter 3

Situational and Environmental Strategies

Situational crime prevention has become a major force in policy and research since the early 1980s. Primarily focused around the work of the Home Office, it has enjoyed a period of considerable political success and influence in the UK. As in the USA and Australia, this status coincided with a political, as well as an academic, shift. The installation of governments committed to a neo-liberal ideology – emphasising the free market, a minimal state and individual free choice and responsibility – dovetailed with and promoted criminological ideas which shared the same basic presuppositions. As a consequence, the spread of situational crime prevention needs to be understood as connected to the political programmes with which it is aligned (O'Malley 1992). It represents less the discovery of a 'good idea' than the coming together of a constellation of ideological, political and social forces.

In this chapter I begin by outlining the defining characteristics of a situational approach to crime prevention and assessing the theoretical framework and assumptions on which it is premised. This includes an examination of the specific development of crime prevention through environmental design as well as broader situational strategies. In so doing, I seek to expose and highlight the claims about human behaviour, decision-making processes and social relations which such an approach embodies. In reviewing the theoretical foundations of a situational approach, the political assumptions and implications that it incorporates are discussed and evaluated. I then consider some of the critical issues associated with a situational approach, most notably whether such initiatives merely displace crimes to other places and targets. The chapter then outlines and reviews a number of high-profile case studies of situational and environmental crime prevention in practice. This includes both individual and neighbourhood-based interventions. Particular consideration is given to schemes which target the victims of crime in order to prevent 'repeat victimisation'. The chapter concludes with some general observations about the potentially problematic implications of situational approaches.

Situational prevention defined

The development of a situational approach to crime prevention, its theoretical premise and empirical research base, is closely associated with the work of the Home Office Research and Planning Unit in the late 1970s and early 1980s, particularly that of Ron Clarke. In criminological terms, situational crime prevention represents a shift towards:

- the prioritisation of the *control* of crime, through practical yet limited policy-oriented measures
- an emphasis on alterations to the *physical* environment
- the significance of processes of *informal* social control
- the *offence* rather than the offender as the primary focus of attention.

Earlier criminologists, notably those associated with the Chicago School and subsequent British Areal studies, had identified the importance of informal control and the environment in the understanding of crime (see Chapter 4). However, they had focused on the relationship between offenders and their environment, both physical and social. Consequently, their concern lay in the study of areas with high offender density. Situational approaches are part of a renewed interest in the crimogenic character of the environment. Unlike earlier work they converge on the nature of the relationship between offences (crimes) and areas (places). Areas with high incidents of crime, it is suggested, are not necessarily areas with high offender density: city centres, particularly shopping districts, are the most obvious example.

Hough and colleagues define situational crime prevention as:

(i)   measures directed at highly specific forms of crime;
(ii) which involve the management, design or manipulation of the immediate environment in which these crimes occur;
(iii) in as systematic and permanent a way as possible;
(iv) so as to reduce the opportunities for these crimes;
(v)   as perceived by a broad range of potential offenders.

(1980: 1)

Within this schema, opportunity reduction can take three inter-related and sometimes overlapping forms (see Clarke 1992), by:

- *increasing the effort* involved in crime by making the targets of crime harder to get at or otherwise hindering the commission of crime
- *increasing the risks*, whether real or perceived, of detection and apprehension
- *reducing the rewards* of crime. In some cases this may involve removing the targets of crime altogether.

Let us consider each of these in turn. First, strategies designed to *increase the effort* of criminality are often referred to as forms of 'target-hardening'.

This involves the introduction of physical barriers to protect property including locks, bars, screens, fences and other forms of alteration to the physical environment or surroundings which render specific crimes more difficult to commit. The target of the offence – be it a person or an object – is often surrounded by some form of physical protection. Two diverse examples serve to illustrate the variety of ways that opportunity reduction may be translated into practice. The first is the introduction of 'sleeping policemen' (humps) in the road to slow down traffic, and hence reduce speeding. It is harder to speed down a road with humps in it without damaging the car's suspension. A second example is the replacement of glass beer mugs with plastic ones in public houses and bars. The implication here is that if a fight occurs it is harder for anyone to do significant harm to others.

Second, situational crime prevention initiatives which seek to *increase the risks* of detection tend to involve either the introduction of heightened forms of surveillance or screening. Screening may include the monitoring of entry and exit or merchanise tagging. Surveillance may occur by means of technology such as security CCTV cameras or burglar (and other forms of) alarms. The latter can increase surveillance by drawing attention to an incident. It may also act to increase the effort, for example, by requiring a burglar first to disable an alarm system. As with alarms, allied approaches can try to capitalise on civilian or 'natural' surveillance. For example, 'natural' surveillance can be used in the design of environments so that places and things are potentially observable to others. This underlies ideas about 'defensible space', 'designing out' crime and improved street lighting. Other types of formal and informal surveillance include the use of individuals as guardians in key locations, for example, employees in shops, concierges guarding entrances to residential and business premises, park keepers and guards on train station platforms. Rather like neighbourhood watch, however, these forms of intervention fit more readily within the category of social crime prevention as they seek to affect *social* relations through human rather than *physical* alterations – albeit often in combination with technological alterations. For example, concierges may use CCTV cameras, as well as act as informal guardians and conflict mediators themselves.

Third, situational strategies that involve *reducing the rewards* of crime often overlap with either of the above strategies, so that, for example, property marking will both increase the likelihood of detection and decrease the sale value of a stolen article on the black market. The potential likelihood of a stolen item being traced will reduce its value. In some cases, reducing the rewards may entail the removal of the target of offending altogether. The substitution of coin-operated fuel meters in domestic premises and the replacement of coin-operated telephones with ones operated by swipe cards are both examples of target removal, as are removable car radios.

Collectively strategies which reduce the rewards and those which increase the risk are concerned with altering or modifying the costs and benefits of offending. The success of situational crime prevention, therefore, depends on the extent to which potential offenders are affected by situational modifications such that they are perceived as adversely influencing the ease, risk and rewards of committing offences.

In relation to the two-dimensional typology – which combines the public health analogy (of primary, secondary and tertiary prevention) with a focus on either offender, victim or community-oriented strategies – most situational interventions into the built environment constitute forms of primary prevention, in that they apply potentially to the whole population. Yet it is only once we consider the different types of audiences to which preventive measures are addressed – offender, victim or community – that a more complex picture emerges. Situational prevention is primary prevention in so far as it seeks to influence potential offending behaviour. Thus, it constitutes an example of primary offender-oriented prevention. And yet situational prevention not only seeks to affect the behaviour of potential offenders. It may be targeted at victims, be they potential victims, those particularly 'at risk' of victimisation because of their work, life-style or where they live, or even those who have just been victims of crime. This last category of prevention which seeks to reduce 'repeat victimisation', by target-hardening measures for example, is an illustration of where primary offender-oriented prevention and tertiary victim-oriented prevention overlap. Victims may be the initial recipients of the preventive action and yet that action may seek to affect the decision-making processes of all potential offenders.

Situational crime prevention may also make assumptions about, or seek to alter, communal processes of informal social control. Hence, situational measures may have a community or neighbourhood focus. For example, housing may be designed to promote social interaction between residents, to facilitate community surveillance or to support the socialisation of children. Alterations to the physical environment may enhance the desirability of residential areas, counteract stigmatisation by making the place look more appealing and encourage greater community spirit. In these instances, situational interventions are addressed not just to individuals but whole neighbourhoods. As such, they seek to effect communal or social processes. Consequently, to label situational crime prevention merely as primary offender-oriented prevention is to miss many of the subtleties of the messages which situational alterations carry, as well as the processes they seek to affect.

The theoretical background

Of the many measures which are included within situational crime prevention, few have been explicitly developed with reference to the theoretical framework within which they are set. Situational crime prevention has largely been driven by practical considerations. This has led some proponents to seek to develop the conceptual thinking behind situational crime prevention measures in order to provide 'a more scientific framework for some practical and common sense thinking about how to deal with crime' (Clarke 1995: 93). Despite its diversity and practical focus, situational crime prevention embodies a number of clear theoretical hypotheses:

- a belief that situational features are more susceptible to change than any others which may influence crime and, therefore, constitute the more appropriate targets of policy
- an assumption that much crime is opportunistic
- a belief in human choice in the criminal act, premised on a 'rational choice' model of human behaviour
- an advocacy of deterrence, with a relative emphasis on the certainty of detection rather than the severity of punishment.

One of the central attractions of situational measures is their apparent simplicity and their capacity to provide what appear to be realistic solutions to specific kinds of offending in a variety of different contexts. They are not concerned with inculcating a permanent disposition not to offend, but rather are focused on short-term reductions of opportunities at particular times and places. Situational crime prevention is a pragmatic response to crime in that it focuses on what can most easily be achieved. Situational features, unlike social factors, it is believed, are eminently manipulable. Spatial, design and environmental factors can more easily be modified than can offenders.

There is also an optimism within situational crime prevention which directly confronts the pessimism of the 'nothing works' era. While liberal and predispositional theories of crime appeared to be either unproven or impracticable, as James Q. Wilson so forcefully argued in *Thinking About Crime* (1975), situational measures offer some practical signs of hope. This sense was captured by Marvin Wolfgang in his comment that: 'If we have little effect in making people more honest and loving we can at least make stealing more difficult and increase the risk of getting caught and punished' (cited in Young 1986: 9). The implication, for proponents of situational crime prevention, is that even if it could be shown that social causes do play a part in crime, generally they are not amenable to change. For example, we cannot manipulate social factors such as gender, age, race or class through obvious policy interventions, albeit that they are significant in the distribution of offending (Wilson 1975). Hence, situational crime prevention is grounded in the same kind of 'realism' that James Q. Wilson stressed through his emphasis on 'moderate expectations' and 'marginal gains' rather than 'utopian goals':

  The demand for causal solutions is, whether intended or not, a way of deferring any action and criticizing any policy. It is a cast of mind that

> inevitably detracts attention from those few things that governments can do reasonably well and draws attention toward those many things it cannot do at all.
>
> (1975: xv)

It is also, therefore, a limited vision: it is uninterested in addressing the 'root causes' of offending and is only concerned with controlling or managing the symptoms of crime.

The contention that a considerable element of crime is opportunistic and susceptible to variations in opportunities grew steadily throughout the 1970s (Mayhew *et al.* 1976b). This view was supported by research findings, notably some prominent research based on interviews with residential burglars (Brantingham and Brantingham 1975; Bennett and Wright 1984). These suggested that the avoidance of risk plays an important part in the decision-making processes through which burglars choose which properties to burgle and at what times. Consequently, from within this perspective, crime rates are seen as the product of fluctuations in opportunities and incentives. Rising crime is explained by the increased opportunities for crime, whether they be as a consequence of the increase in targets – particularly with the proliferation of consumer goods such as hi-fi's, televisions and cars – or the decrease in control over targets and hence their increased vulnerability – such as the breakdown of community and the increased crime provoking dynamics produced by the urban environment.

Rational choice theory

At the heart of situational crime prevention is a rational choice theory of human decision-making. Rational choice theory connects with a wider renewed interest within criminology in neo-classical understandings of crime. Following Beccaria and Bentham this neo-classicism emphasises the rationality and voluntary thought processes of individuals in the commission of crime. It conceptualises the decision-making process on which choices – as to whether or not to engage in criminal activity at any given moment – are premised, as the product of calculation on the basis of the relative balance between the perceived risks and effort involved as against the potential rewards offered. Here, the potential criminal is perceived as a self-maximising decision maker who carefully calculates the advantages and disadvantages associated with certain activities. Prevention therefore is aimed at altering that decision-making process in order to increase the risks or effort involved in the commission of a crime and decrease any rewards associated with it.

On the one hand, the formulation of rational choice theory has developed from a perceived need to validate and assist situational crime prevention practice. On the other, the revival of neo-classicism is premised on a critique and rejection of the 'dispositional bias' of mainstream criminology, whereby theories have sought to show how some people are born with or come to acquire a criminal 'disposition' (Clarke 1980a: 136). In its place, rational choice theory offers an economic model of crime, analogous to a cost-benefit analysis of choice. According to Gary Becker, in a significant contribution to the revival of a neo-classical model, someone commits a crime,

> if the expected utility to him [*sic*] exceeds the utility he could get by using his time and other resources at other activities. Some persons become 'criminals', therefore, not because their basic motivation differs from that of other persons, but because their benefits and costs differ.
>
> (Becker 1968: 169)

Here, the focus shifts from the individual to the nature of the costs and benefits, as well as how they express themselves in the context or situation in which a crime occurs. The traditional 'conservative' approach had been to increase costs by increasing sentences: in other words, the severity of punishments. However, as victimisation surveys have repeatedly shown, most offences are never reported, let alone the offenders apprehended or convicted. Hence, as Wilson (1975) argued, the key to addressing crime is not more draconian punishments, but rather lies in increasing the certainty of detection and punishment through greater surveillance, informal control and effective policing. In practice, control strategies have focused on increasing the 'cost' of crime rather than increasing the relative 'benefit' of lawful activity.

In its extreme form, crime is seen as the product of market-based decisions rather like any other commodity-exchange process along the lines depicted by the neo-conservative commentator Ernest van den Haag, who suggested that:

> The number of persons engaged in any activity, lawful or not, depends on the comparative net advantage they expect. Thus, the number of practising dentists, grocers, drug dealers, or burglars depends on the net advantage which these practitioners expect their occupations to yield compared to other occupations available to them.
>
> (1982: 1025)

This represented an attempt to express a neo-classical, utilitarian philosophy in mathematical terms. Criminal behaviour is assumed to be like other transactions in the market place. More recently, this model of decision-making has been adapted to understand the behaviour of potential victims.

Situational crime prevention thus makes certain assumptions about offenders and potential victims. They are viewed as 'rational choice' actors who weigh up the potential gains, risks and costs before committing an offence or taking crime preventive measures. In this, offenders are abstracted from their social or structural context. In O'Malley's (1992) words, they become the 'abstract and universal abiographical' individual, the 'homo economicus' of classical economics translated into neo-conservative thinking about crime. There is no concern for 'knowing' about the attributes of individual offenders. Such questions are banished alongside the relevancy of social conditions for any understanding of criminality. Through the manipulation of situational factors, biographical-causal theories of crime are marginalised. Correctionalism is rejected as the focus of concern is shifted to situations rather than individuals or groups. As O'Malley suggests 'not only is the knowledge of the criminal disarticulated from a critique of society, but in turn, both of these may be disarticulated from the reaction to the offender' (1992: 265).

In this abstract model of decision-making, individuals appear logically capable of voluntary choice, free to act in a rational self-interested fashion, be they potential offenders or victims. So that the potential victim, for example, is seen as 'free' to make choices whether or not to install target-hardening measures and to manage their personal safety. There is no conception of the uneven social distribution of crime which undermines any notion of formal equality in matters of victimisation.

The notion of choice carries with it responsibility. Victimisation, thus envisaged, becomes the outcome of rational choices for which the victim bears ultimate responsibility. Within situational crime prevention discourse, victims have become responsible for their own safety and security. Situational crime prevention shifts responsibility for crime control away from the state and on to individuals (Crawford 1997a). In this, it constitutes 'the displacement of socialized risk management with privatized prudentialism' (O'Malley 1992: 263). What is more, responsibility carries with it blame for failure, such that it heralds a rearticulation of the criteria of failure and success.

The important point to note is the convergence between the theoretical assumptions which underlie situational crime prevention and neo-liberal political ideology of the type embraced by the Thatcher and Reagan administrations, as well as by their successors (see Levitas 1986). Rational choice theory combines classical economics and the 'marketisation of crime' with notions of autonomy, choice and responsibility in the management of risk. And yet, as O'Malley rightly notes, 'situational crime prevention is by no means *necessarily* associated with neo-conservatism' (1992: 267, emphasis in original). However, the alignment of the two helps to explain the attraction and proliferation of situational crime prevention at a particular historic juncture.

More specific criticisms of rational choice theory relate to particular implications of the assumptions about offenders and their behaviour. Most notably, the extent to which offenders actually make rational decisions of the type envisaged by the theory is the subject of considerable controversy (Trasler 1986). The 'rational' model is particularly suspect given the expressive or compulsive nature of some crime. Situational measures have tended to be oriented towards property crimes – particularly less serious ones – but are seen to have less value in relation to crimes of violence which would appear to be less susceptible to suppression. The image of the self-maximising decision-maker, who carefully calculates the net advantages and disadvantages of certain activities, does not fit the impulsive, reckless, opportunistic and ill-considered nature of much criminality, particularly that associated with young offenders. The market model does not fit most ordinary crime in that although there is a supply of victims there is no demand for victims to be victimised. The great variety of behaviours which fall under the heading of crime raise problems for what appears to be an inflexible and overly abstract model of human decision-making.

There is a question mark beside the validity of much empirical research used to support the rational choice theory, particularly in so far as it relies on the testimonies of convicted offenders. A number of methodological problems arise in relation to such interview data, most notably the concerns that, first, *convicted* offenders are more liable to be 'career criminals' – exactly the type of person most likely to conform to the rational choice model – and second, in explaining their offending, they are more likely to rationalise events in the light of hindsight. Other sources of research information are required to help validate the claims of situational crime prevention.

In defence of the theory behind situational crime prevention, Clarke and colleagues have long argued that the rational choice model is not a 'general theory of crime' but rather an 'organising perspective' or 'blueprint' from which theories for specific crimes may be developed (Clarke and Cornish 1985: 163). In the light of some of the criticisms of rational choice theory, Clarke has reworked his earlier 'simple choice' model (Clarke 1980a) and substituted in its place a model of 'limited rationality' (Cornish and Clarke 1986a, 1986b, 1990; Clarke and Cornish 1985). Here, concepts are expressed, not as static mathematical terms but in the form of fluid 'decision diagrams'. Although premised on the economic model of perceptions of risk, effort and reward, greater weight is given in this later version to non-instrumental motives for crime and the 'limited' nature of the rational processes involved. Choices are seen as constrained by limits of time and ability as well as by the availability of relevant information. Offenders may have a limited capacity to acquire and process information and then to weigh the risks against the potential benefits. Within this model due emphasis is given to the belief that explanations of criminal choices need to be crime specific in focus, particularly as crimes serve different purposes, the situational context of decision-making is different and the information available will vary. Finally, it asserts the need for a fundamental distinction between 'criminal involvement' (or criminality) and 'criminal events' (or crimes). This differentiation is somewhat analogous to Ekblom's (1994) distinction between 'proximal' and 'distal' mechanisms, but sees them as wholly separate phenomena for which different explanatory frameworks are required.

'Criminal involvement' refers to the 'processes through which individuals choose to become initially involved in particular forms of crime, to continue and to desist' (Clarke 1995: 98). The decision processes at each of these stages, Clarke argues, are influenced by a different set of factors, are dependent on their own special categories of information and need to be modelled separately. 'Event decisions', on the other hand, are usually shorter and require more circumscribed information which relates to the immediate circumstances and situations. This model specifies four stages of decision-making: three relating to criminal involvement and one relating to the criminal event, as shown in Figure 3.1. It is only the fourth stage of decision-making at which situational crime prevention intervenes.

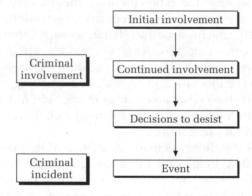

Figure 3.1   Stages of decision-making

This model of 'limited rationality' offers a more complex, sophisticated and specific means of analysing measures to address proximal circumstances. However, its fundamental organising framework remains trapped in the analytic embrace of the abstract rational choice actor, regardless of how limited or fluid this should be interpreted. It also remains aligned to neo-liberal political strategies, given the nature of the concepts it deploys.

'Designing out' crime

In addition to the development of rational choice theory, situational crime prevention has emerged through a number of practical and theoretical developments in relation to the design of the physical environment. These separate but related strands actually preceded situational crime prevention theory by some years. There are a number of particular developments with their own slightly different traditions which are worth considering in some detail, as they inform some of the case studies to be examined later.

'Defensible space'

First, drawing on Jane Jacobs' (1961) powerful critique of postwar urban planning, Oscar Newman (1972), an American commentator on architecture, identified a link between architectural design and crime rates in residential areas. This, he argued, exists over and above other contributing factors. The creation of designs which are least likely to promote or encourage criminality, he argued, would constitute an effective form of crime prevention. To this end, Newman developed and elaborated the notion of 'defensible space'. This he defined as:

> a model for residential environments which inhibits crime by creating the physical expression of a social fabric that defends itself . . . 'Defensible space' is a surrogate term for the range of mechanisms – real and symbolic barriers, strongly defined areas of influence, and improved opportunities for surveillance – that combine to bring an environment under the control of its residents.
>
> (1972: 3)

Newman argued that architectural design can release the latent sense of territoriality and community among inhabitants, so that these become accepted parts of residents' assumption of responsibility for preserving a safe and well-maintained living environment. He argued that by dividing spaces in and around residential buildings into small areas over which individual residents have some functional control, a form of local social control would be generated. Newman identified four key constituents of good design to encourage social control networks:

- *Territoriality*: entails the definition of space which demarcates areas of control, through the subdivision of places into 'zones of territorial influence'. A part of this is clearly demarcating space as public or private. This acts to discourage outsiders from entering and encourage residents to defend their areas
- *Surveillance*: the design of buildings so as to allow and enable easy observation of territorial areas. This provides residents and their agents opportunities for surveillance
- *Image*: the design of buildings to avoid the stigma of particularity and the suggestion of vulnerability, particularly apparent in public housing estates
- *Environment*: the juxtaposition of public housing with 'safe zones' in adjacent areas and, conversely, the location of developments away from areas that provide a continued threat.

Newman argued that the nature of many large mass-housing projects of the postwar period have squeezed out important social processes which prevent or lessen the likelihood of crime. In their place 'indefensible spaces' have proliferated. These include walkways, underpasses, lifts, stairwells, long dark corridors and easy access to the public. They constitute 'confused' and 'anonymous' areas which belong to and are cared for by no one. Smaller units over which householders could survey and supervise and be seen to be responsible could engender a sense of ownership and community spirit – and thus revive important processes of control.

Newman failed to identify clearly the processes by which residents come to define space as their territory and act to defend it (Merry 1981: 398). Hillier and Hanson (1984) have suggested that, contrary to defensible space theory, the segregation of residential areas may encourage crime because of the lack of pedestrian flow. Mawby (1977) suggests that in over-simplifying the nature of crime and the qualities of defensible space, Newman overlooks the fact that his four key constituents may contain contradictions within themselves, and might include elements which threaten security as well as enhance it. Most notably, Newman has been accused of architectural determinism. This charge appears justified, given his failure to consider the role of social variables and behaviour both directly and in mediating the effects of architectural features (Mayhew 1979). For example, Merry makes the obvious yet important point that: 'Spaces may be defensible but not defended if the social apparatus for effective defence is lacking' (1981: 419). Newman's failure to acknowledge the importance of the 'offender rate', rather than merely offence rates across different estates, is also problematic (Mawby 1977). Nevertheless, Newman did later modify his thesis to accord greater weight to the social characteristics of the resident population and as a stronger predictor of crime rates than architectural design (1976: 20).

Related to 'defensible space' theory has been the looser array of design practices which cluster under the heading of 'crime prevention through environmental design' (CPTED). Associated with the work of Jeffery (1971), this encompasses a broader set of techniques and extends beyond residential contexts. It applies notions of environmental change through the application of territoriality to domestic, school and commercial sites. The US federal government sponsored an extensive multi-million dollar programme of action research undertaken by the Westinghouse Corporation to implement the ideas behind CPTED. However, the results of the project were a 'total failure', as recognised by Jeffery himself (Jeffery and Zahm 1993: 329). Despite continuing to attract federal funds criminological research interest in the USA has since declined. The failure of the lavishly funded CPTED projects in the 1970s appears to have held back American interest in situational crime prevention. Some commentators have suggested that CPTED was misconceived in that it tried to extend the defensible space concept outside of residential contexts to places where 'territorial' behaviour is much less 'natural' (Clarke 1995: 97).

Design disadvantagement

While the impact of CPTED and 'defensible space' declined in the 1980s in the US, it received an important revival in the UK through the work of Alice Coleman. In her book *Utopia on Trial* (Coleman 1985) she develops

Newman's ideas about defensible space in the context of the British housing estates. Like Newman and Jacobs before her, Coleman's target is what she identifies as the failed 'Utopias' of modern urban architecture, most notably large-scale, often high-rise, public sector housing estates. She advances a 'design disadvantagement' theory, in which situational and dispositional aspects of crime are identified, not as mutually independent, but as 'two sides of the same coin' (Coleman 1989). In developing this theory she identifies a number of 'design disadvantages', such as overhead walkways, large numbers of storeys and multiple access and entry points, and so on, the presence or absence of which collectively constitute a 'design disadvantagement score'. She argues that there is a direct correlation between design variables and crime. Using a number of indicators of anti-social behaviour she claims empirical support for her thesis from the study of many public sector housing estates. Crudely put, the worse the design, the worse the crime problem. Unlike Newman she seeks to explain the processes through which design affects crime. She suggests that design encourages an environment in which crime is a 'learned response':

> Architectural situations that are highly vulnerable to crime can teach
> children to adopt criminal decisions, and this learned disposition can then
> cause them to see all situational weaknesses as rational opportunities for
> crime.
>
> (Coleman 1989: 109–10)

More specifically, poor physical design causes social breakdown by the processes of destroying community, letting in outsiders at will and preventing an effective response. Here the boundaries between situational crime prevention and community crime prevention (the subject of Chapter 4) are blurred, as design is seen as a means of allowing 'natural' processes of community interaction and surveillance to be revived.

Coleman's proposed solution is to redesign the current flaws on housing estates so as to remove or lessen the impact of design disadvantages. Hence, each disadvantage has its own crime prevention antidote. Coleman has been criticised for her methodology in attempting to quantify social breakdown and in over-interpreting her own empirical data in her conclusions (Smith 1986). While it is generally accepted that the design of mass public housing of the kind criticised by Coleman encourages a sense of insecurity, it is more questionable whether, in itself, design directly generates crime. Like Newman, Coleman neglects important social processes such as the impact of local authority allocation policies, the social stigma attached to certain estates (Bottoms and Wiles 1986), social organisation and the character of management and supervision of rented housing estates (Power 1989). The problem with Coleman's arguments lies in the nature of the relationship between design and crime. She suggests that people commit anti-social behaviour because of design. A more persuasive argument is rather that 'certain designs are unpopular and hard to deal with as a result of which those *who have least ability to cope* are the most likely to be rehoused in the least popular blocks, where large scale communal design creates additional pressures' (Power 1989: 217, emphasis in original). Nevertheless, Coleman's work has an enduring legacy (Poyner and Webb 1992; Ekblom 1995) and has been widely recognised and endorsed by the British government (see DoE 1994). Together with the notions derived from CPTED and 'defensible space', Coleman's ideas have been promoted heavily by the Home Office Crime Prevention Centre and through the work of police crime prevention and architectural liaison officers.

Routine activity theory

More recently, routine activity theory has contributed to the growing theoretical underpinnings of situational crime prevention. The routine activity approach seeks to explain the supply of criminal opportunities. It began as a consideration only of 'direct-contact predatory violations' (Cohen and Felson 1979). Its focus is on criminal events rather than inclinations. The latter is not denied but rather the theory takes the supply of offenders as given. Criminal incidents are seen as physical acts in that they relate to objects with a position in time and space. The routine activity approach identifies three minimal elements for direct contact predatory crime: a likely offender, a suitable target and the absence of a capable guardian against crime. A 'likely offender' is anyone who for any reason might commit a crime. Consideration of how this likelihood might vary across the population or at different times is avoided, as to confront it would raise the taboo subject of criminal motivation. A 'suitable target' is an object or person likely to be taken or attacked by the offender. The definition of 'capable guardians' is deliberately encompassing in order to extend beyond the conventional focus of much criminology on the criminal justice system and its agents. For routine activity theory the most likely guardians against crime are not policemen but rather neighbours, friends and bystanders.

The city is seen to be a particularly crime stimulating environment in that its 'routine activities' bring together motivated offenders, vulnerable targets and inadequate surveillance. While it assumes, both unproblematically and unquestioningly, the existence of 'motivated offenders', routine activity is a causal theory in that it links changes in routine activities to changes in crime rates. Hence, Cohen and Felson (1979) explain the escalating burglary rate in the US after 1960 by reference to first, the increasing proportion of empty homes in the day – in part caused by the greater number of single person households and the expanded participation of women in the workplace – and second, the increased availability of valuable, lightweight portable electronic goods.

Felson (1995) has developed notions of 'guardians', who can discourage crime from occurring at specific times and places even by their simple presence. He identifies three types of guardians or supervisors, including those who keep watch over potential crime targets (referred to as 'guardians'), those who supervise potential offenders (termed 'handlers') and those who monitor places (referred to as 'managers'). Drawing on Clarke's (1992) differentiation between varying levels of responsibility for crime prevention, Felson suggests 'four steps of crime discouragement' relating to different levels of responsibility: personal, assigned, diffuse and general. *Personal* discouragement is the responsibility of family and friends; *assigned* discouragement is the responsibility of those employed to do so, such as a police officer; *diffuse* discouragement is the responsibility of those employed but not assigned that specific task, such a school teacher; and *general* discouragement is the responsibility of unpaid persons lacking a personal tie or designated occupational task, such as strangers and other citizens. Responsibility, Felson suggests, is an ordinal variable which decreases as one moves along a continuum from personal to general types. The probability and extent of intervention, as well as its perceived legitimacy *vis-à-vis* the offender also decreases from personal to general. Felson constructs a model of 12 types of crime discouragement by bringing together the four levels of responsibility with the three forms of 'supervisor' (and objects of supervision). The implicit question for crime prevention that Felson's analysis begs is how to increase responsibility for crime control at all levels. This has implications for both social and situational crime prevention, but has particular ramifications at the general level where there may be assumed to be a moral connotation: that not to accept general responsibility is to behave irresponsibly and hence to be implicated in blame. Here lies the theoretical justifications for the 'responsibilisation strategies' referred to earlier.

Routine activity theory is part of a broader convergence of ideas around the spatial and situational attributes of crimes and a number of commentators have sought to develop links between routine activities and Clarke's rational choice theory (Felson 1986; Clarke and Felson 1993). This has caused considerable preventive attention to be focused on the relationship between places – their design, environment and architecture – and crimes. It has caused commentators to ponder why certain places experience particularly high levels of criminal incidents and whether there is something about given places which attracts crime. This is exactly the question that Sherman and colleagues (1989) pose, working within a routine activities framework. Using 'police call data' – all telephone calls for police assistance – for Minneapolis for 1985–6, they discovered a considerable variation in the number of crimes which occur at specific micro-locations even within high crime areas. These they termed 'hot spots' of crime (Sherman *et al.* 1989; Sherman 1995). They go on to pose a number of questions which have considerable import for situational crime prevention:

Do places vary in their capacity to help *cause* crime, or merely in their frequency of *hosting* crime that was going to occur some place inevitably, regardless of the specific place? Are the routine activities of some hot spots criminogenic *generators* of crime, or merely more attractive *receptors* of crime?
(Sherman *et al.* 1989: 46, emphasis in original)

It is this 'generator' versus 'receptor' problem that lies at the heart of much debate about the relevance of situational crime prevention. For, while commentators such as Coleman, Newman and Jeffery have argued that the built environment actually generates crime, critiques suggest that the relevance of situational factors lies only in their capacity to play 'host' to crimes which would otherwise have occurred. This debate is far from being resolved either theoretically or empirically. And yet the essential practical attraction of modifications to situational characteristics of places, with which we started, has led to the skewing of policies in favour of them. Sherman *et al.* conclude their analysis with the observation that,

since the routine activities of places may be regulated far more easily than the routine activities of persons, a criminology of place would seem to offer substantial promise for public policy as well as theory.
(1989: 49)

What is notable about routine activity theory and rational choice theory is that they set out from the premise that crime is a usual and normal aspect of modern life. In contrast to earlier criminology, crime is understood as a series of events which require no particular motivation or pathology, but rather is seen as inscribed within the routines of contemporary social existence. Collectively, these theories represent what Garland has called 'the new criminologies of everyday life' (1996: 450), for which crime is seen as a risk to be calculated and hence avoided or managed, rather than a moral abnormality in need of explanation.

Displacement – the Achilles heel?

Given the focus of situational crime prevention on altering opportunities for crime in particular contexts, there is a danger that all that is being achieved is that offenders are being moved around without ever reducing crime. If offending is merely displaced elsewhere, then situational crime prevention would appear to offer little to policy-makers (Heal and Laycock 1986: 123–4). The issue of displacement therefore probably constitutes the most telling criticism for situational crime prevention, in that it addresses its own terms of reference and claims to success. Consequently, it has been the subject of much theoretical debate and empirical enquiry.

Bennett and Wright (1984) have argued that displacement is a 'short-term psychological process', which occurs when alternative offences are committed subsequent to an offender being prevented from offending against the original target. Displacement can take a number of different forms (see Reppetto 1976; Hakim and Rengert 1981):

- *spatial or geographic* displacement occurs where the same crime is committed in a different place
- *temporal* displacement involves the same crime being committed against the same target at a different time
- *tactical* displacement involves the same crime being committed against the same target but in a different way or by a different means
- *target* displacement is where the same type of crime is committed but a new target is selected in place of the original (for example a shift from robbing post offices to robbing banks)
- *type of crime* displacement occurs when there is a change in the nature of criminal activities from the type of crime originally intended (for example a shift from robbing post offices to street mugging).

Barr and Pease (1990: 279) suggest a further form of displacement which they call *perpetrator* displacement where a crime is so lucrative that new offenders fill a vacuum left by the removal of an existing perpetrator. The example they use is drug couriers where there appears to be an inexhaustible supply of new recruits. To complicate matters further, the above forms of displacement can occur simultaneously. The identification and operationalisation of the phenomenon of displacement constitutes a major problem for research. The failure to detect displacement does not necessarily mean that it does not exist. Hence, the implications of displacement for the evaluation of crime prevention initiatives are extensive (I return to this in Chapter 6).

Critics have tended to use displacement as a conventional stick with which to attack proponents of situational approaches. In so doing, however, they have tended to over-emphasise the extent of displacement and see its implications in an inherently negative vein. While there is a broad consensus that levels of displacement are a likely product of many situational initiatives (Cornish and Clarke 1986a), displacement is not inevitable. Displacement, like situational crime prevention, makes certain assumptions about crime. The first and most obvious is the assumption that the incentive to commit a crime is sufficiently strong to survive the initial thwarting of intention as presented by an effective situational crime prevention measure. This presupposes that the demand for crime is inelastic and that offenders are driven by irresistible pressures to commit crimes (Hesseling 1994). Second, it assumes that offenders are sufficiently adaptable and capable of committing a variety of crimes in a variety of places or at different times. This is sometimes referred to as the 'polymorphous or non-specialised nature of most offenders' (Gabor 1990: 44). Cornish and Clarke (1987) suggest that such conclusions are contingent on the belief that many, if not most, crimes are functionally equivalent to offenders. Instead, they claim that the willingness of an individual to substitute one offence for another depends on the extent to which the alternative corresponds with the offender's goals and abilities. If, on the contrary, offenders lack sufficient flexibility then crime is less likely to be displaced. Third, it assumes that the opportunity structure is comprised of an unlimited number of alternative targets. The accuracy of all of these assumptions will determine the actual extent of displacement in relation to given measures.

Rational choice theory allows for displacement 'but only to the extent that alternative crimes present similar rewards without unduly greater costs in terms of risks or effort' (Clarke 1992: 22). This suggests that displacement will be more limited than many commentators believe. Clarke has pointed out:

> The dispositional bias of criminological theory has tended to reinforce popular beliefs in the inevitability of displacement ('bad will out'). People find it hard to accept that the occurrence of actions with often momentous consequences for both the victim and the offender can turn on apparently trivial situational contingencies of opportunities or risks.
>
> (1983: 245)

Proponents of rational choice theory have advocated the need for an understanding of the 'choice structuring properties' (Cornish and Clarke 1987) of given crimes in order to assess the likelihood and implications of displacement. These are defined as,

> those properties of offences (such as type and amount of pay-off, perceived risk, skills needed, and so on) which are perceived by the offender as being especially salient to his or her goals, motives, experience, abilities, expertise, and preferences. Such properties provide a basis for selecting among alternative courses of action and, hence, effectively structure the offender's choice.
>
> (Cornish and Clarke 1987: 935)

The legitimate assumption here is that displacement will not be random but is likely to be structured, or clustered, by certain factors. However, in using a rational choice model, as a way of understanding displacement, the same objections and criticisms already rehearsed remain applicable. Choice remains wholly voluntaristic with no regard for wider social or psychological properties or processes which may influence such 'structuring'.

Routine activities theory suggests that crime cannot be displaced merely by displacing motivated offenders. The offenders must also be displaced to other places with suitable targets and weak guardianship. Nevertheless, in relation to many types of offences the reality is that there are a vast number of potential targets over which low levels of guardianship exist. And yet it seems probable that the more 'professional' the crime and the criminal, the greater the probability of displacement. This implies a theoretical conundrum for situational approaches: those most likely to conform to a rational choice model of behaviour – the self-maximising professional criminals – are exactly the group of offenders most likely to be displaced. Those least likely to conform to the rational choice model – the impulsive and reckless opportunists – are exactly those least likely to be displaced. Much of the research on displacement relies on interview data with convicted criminals which is subject to the same methodological flaws noted earlier.

However, there also tends to be a mistaken assumption that displacement is always a 'bad thing'. Following Barr and Pease (1990, 1992) it is important to differentiate between two kinds of displacement, with regard to their outcome:

- *malign* displacement involves a shift to more serious offences or to offences which will have worse consequences
- *benign* displacement occurs where a less serious offence or non-criminal act (often known as 'desistence') is committed or an act of similar seriousness is committed on a victim for whom, or in a place where, it has less serious consequences.

Hence, displacement is not necessarily an undesirable consequence of social intervention. Benign displacement may seek to deflect crime away from vulnerable social groups and into social spheres which limit or serve to redistribute the level or impact of victimisation. Displacement may be a legitimate policy choice. For example, the displacement of prostitutes from residential areas and into industrial estates or non-residential areas through the creation of 'zones of tolerance', in which prostitution is not prosecuted, may be considered to be a form of benign displacement. The new location is perceived to have a less harmful impact on the wider society and local community (see Lowman 1992; Matthews 1992a). Barr and Pease (1990) prefer the term 'deflection' to that of displacement precisely because it acknowledges that a crime has been prevented and does not imply anything about the extent to which crime may have moved elsewhere. They suggest that the basic error made in discussions about crime displacement is:

> to conceive of it as an explanation of change but not of the *status quo*...
> Crime patterns at any time are frozen displacement patterns. Displacement
> is but another placement . . . The distribution of crime can be likened to
> that of iron filings held in a magnetic field. Change the field and the filings
> are rearranged. As magnets create a force field so do policy and practice
> create a crime pattern. As we choose a field by positioning magnets, so do
> we 'choose' a crime pattern by selecting particular policies and practices.
>
> (1990: 281)

The importance of this insight is to understand patterns of criminal activity not as static, natural or immutable, but rather to see them as the outcome of conscious and unconscious decisions by the public, politicians and practitioners which are subject to alterations. Consequently, as Barr and Pease suggest, crime displacement should be conceived as a potential tool of crime control policy rather than as an unwanted constraint on crime prevention programmes (1990: 279). For even if the displacement effect of a given crime prevention measure is absolute – i.e. all intended crimes are displaced – then this poses the seldom asked question, 'If crime is not preventable, where, to whom and by what means should it take place?' As Barr and Pease note this is 'the placement question rather than the displacement question' (1992: 201). I return to consider some of the broader implications of this insight in Chapter 8.

There is also the potential for a 'diffusion of benefits' arising from situational measures, whereby the effects of a situational measure may extend beyond the targeted offences or areas, thus heralding more general benefits of crime reduction. This may be a process tantamount to the 'inverse' of displacement but which has, as yet, commanded little attention in research literature. The diffusion of benefits – otherwise referred to by some commentators as the 'halo' or 'free rider' effect – is concerned with the processes that spread the crime reduction benefits beyond its primary targets. It refers not merely to unforeseeable 'side effects' but to:

> the spread of the beneficial influence of an intervention beyond the places which are directly targeted, the individuals who are the subject of control, the crimes which are the focus of intervention or the time periods in which an intervention is brought.
>
> (Clarke and Weisburd 1994: 169)

Hence, it is important that the possibility of diffusion is taken into account when evaluating preventive measures in order that the full benefits and implications can be assessed.

Some case studies

What follows is a descriptive account of a number of case studies of situational crime prevention measures. They have been selected to give an overview of some of the recent research that has informed developments in the UK and the USA, as well as to illustrate and develop the earlier theoretical discussions by way of practical examples. The case studies by no means constitute an exhaustive list of developments but rather a suggestive one. The case studies are described with little attempt to evaluate them as such at this stage. Rather, it is for the reader to consider them in the light of the previous theoretical discussions and the critical commentary with which the chapter concludes. The reader is also directed to more detailed accounts and reviews of each case study. Finally, the research findings in each case study are the product of the methodology which gives rise to them. These debates are postponed until Chapter 6, where they are considered in some detail.

The case studies are collected together under three broad categories relating to the intended primary audience of the intervention. These reflect offender, community and victim-oriented approaches (as discussed in Chapter 1). These categories are by no means pure nor mutually exclusive, as many schemes involve the application of multiple measures targeted at different mechanisms, processes and audiences.

Offender-oriented situational prevention

The British gas suicide story

Barr and Pease note with irony that: 'Paradoxically the behaviour most intensively analysed by criminologists in relation to the displacement hypothesis is not a crime: it is suicide' (1992: 198). They are referring to the British experience of the detoxification of domestic gas during the 1960s and 1970s and its impact on suicide. In a retrospective evaluation Clarke and Mayhew (1988, 1989) have sought to highlight the criminological implications of the experience across England and Wales which saw the progressive removal of carbon monoxide from the public gas supply. Between 1963 and 1975, at a time when suicide continued to increase in most other European countries, the annual number of suicides in England and Wales declined from over 5700 to under 3700. During the same period of time, suicide by domestic gas went from a position in which it accounted for more than 40 per cent of all suicides to a situation in which it was all but eliminated as a means of committing suicide. Crucially, the figures suggest there was no significant increase in other forms of committing suicide: the implication was that few of those prevented from poisoning themselves with gas appear to have found other ways of killing themselves.

Clarke and Mayhew explain this last point by reference to 'choice structuring properties' associated with suicide through intoxication by gas. The use of domestic gas as a form of suicide, it was claimed, holds particular advantages – its ready availability in every home, its simplicity to use, its painlessness, its cleanliness (it left no marks or blood) and the fact that it is highly lethal – which are not all available in alternatives. Sleeping pills and other poisons, for instance, which are possibly the closest alternatives, were much less lethal.

The 'British gas suicide story' is often held up as an exemplar of successful situational prevention, particularly in regard to the question of displacement. Despite the fact that the interventions were not introduced for crime prevention reasons, the power of the example lies in the argument that if we can effect change in behaviour commonly regarded as deeply motivated, such as suicide, merely by altering the opportunities available, without significant displacement effects, then the potential applicability of appropriately tailored situational measures should be extensive, particularly with regard to less momentous and more opportunistic crimes. This example, Clarke and Mayhew suggest, 'furnishes clear proof' that the preventive gains of opportunity reduction need not be undermined by displacement. This, they claim, 'changes the balance of the argument about the value of situational measures. It is now more incumbent on the sceptic to show that displacement has defeated a crime prevention measure than for the advocate to prove beyond doubt that it has not' (1988: 104).

Some commentators have challenged the inference that the detoxification of gas supplies to domestic consumers in England and Wales accounts for the sharp decline in the suicide rate. Detoxification of gas in The Netherlands in the early 1960s appears to have had much less of an impact on the overall rate of suicide. This has lead some commentators to suggest that the decline in Britain may be the product of a particularly British phenomenon, be it a decrease in the propensity to commit suicide or the spread of services by the Samaritans, the organisation which provides confidential crisis intervention service by volunteers. Sainsbury (1986) has argued that towns whose gas supplies were detoxified later in the period had the same pattern of decline in suicides as towns detoxified earlier, with the implication that the reduction, at least in the earlier period, must have been caused by some other factor. In a reasonably convincing review, Clarke and Mayhew (1988, 1989) attempt to dismiss these and other hypotheses. However, there does remain the argument that even if this is an example of a successful, although unintentional, situational crime prevention measure, it has only a temporary effect. The current suicide rates, particularly for males, suggest that it was only a matter of time before the suicidally inclined found other methods and that the suicide rate reverted to its former level.

Motorcycle theft and helmet legislation

Like the 'gas suicide story' the case of motorcycle theft and helmet legislation was not introduced as a specific crime prevention measure: essentially it was motivated by concerns over safety. However, its implications have been assessed through retrospective evaluations (Mayhew *et al.* 1989). In West Germany (as it then was) legislation was passed in a number of phases such that by 1980 fines were introduced for motorcyclists who failed to comply with wearing helmets. Mayhew and colleagues suggest that a drop of more than 60 per cent in motorcycle thefts in West Germany in the years between 1980 and 1986 is attributable to the introduction of the motorcycle helmet legislation. The reason for this, they argue, is that potential offenders who engage in the opportunistic theft of motorcycles are likely to be deterred from committing the offence for fear of being observed for committing the less serious but more obvious offence of riding a motorcycle without a helmet and, possibly, suspected of stealing the motorcycle. While 'professional' criminals may take a helmet with them when going out to steal a motorcycle, the opportunist is unlikely to do so.

Mayhew and colleagues claim that similar results had been produced in The Netherlands and England in the early 1970s, albeit that no rigorous attempt was made to see whether any displacement occurred. In looking for displacement the authors concentrated on the rates of thefts of cars and bicycles on the assumption that these were the kinds of crimes that opportunistic thieves would turn to, given the restricted opportunities to commit motorcycle theft. They found that the reduction in the number of motorcycle thefts – about 100 000 fewer in 1986 than in 1980 – was 'by no means matched by an equivalent increase in either car or bike theft' (Mayhew *et al.* 1989: 5). Car thefts increased by only 6000 over the period, which was similar to the rise in the seven years prior to the introduction of the legislation in 1980. In relation to bicycle theft there was an overall reduction of over 50 000 thefts by the end of the seven year period. This, they claim, shows that 'opportunity-reducing measures are not inevitably undermined by displacement' (Mayhew *et al.* 1989: 6).

Gabor is critical of the conclusions that Mayhew and colleagues reach on the basis of their evidence, which he prefers to describe as 'somewhat more hazy' (1990: 64). He suggests that they accord insufficient significance to the fact that car thefts actually increased noticeably from 1980 until 1983 as did bicycle thefts between 1980 to 1982, at a time when motorcycle thefts began to decline. He concludes that 'it is conceivable that a fair amount of displacement occurred' (Gabor 1990: 65). Nevertheless, if we accept that displacement was limited to car or bicycle theft, the figures for the years 1983 to 1986 do suggest more convincing evidence of a real decline.

Steering column locks in cars

Mayhew *et al.* (1976a) have shown that the compulsory fitting of steering column locks to all cars in West Germany resulted in a reduction in the number of car thefts. This reduction appeared to be sustained over a period of at least a decade. The compulsory fitting of steering column locks to all new cars, as introduced through legislation in 1971 in the UK, also led to a reduction in the number of new cars stolen. However, there did appear to be a displacement to the theft of older vehicles – those without locks – in relation to which the risk almost doubled.

Significantly, this is an example of what we might call 'regressive displacement' whereby the cost is passed on to those already less able to pay or to look after themselves. In this instance the cost, through the increased risk of theft, was displaced on to those who could only afford to buy older, second-hand cars as opposed to new cars with built-in steering column locks. Interestingly, the introduction of early steering locks in the USA did not prove to be very successful as they were too easily defeated by offenders who discovered that they were highly vulnerable to slide hammers. Clarke and Harris (1992) have argued that a possible explanation for the apparent success of the steering locks in West Germany (apart from the possibility that the equipment itself was of a better quality) is due to the fact that the locks were made compulsory for all cars on the road at one stroke. As a result theft was reduced almost overnight.

CCTV in car parks

Poyner (1992) reports on a Home Office funded project which sought to address the problems of the theft of motor vehicles and thefts from motor vehicles in the University of Surrey parking lots, through the introduction of CCTV together with increased surveillance. A CCTV camera was installed on a tower overlooking the two largest parking lots and was able to scan the other two parking facilities. It was equipped with infrared sensing and loudspeakers through which the security guards could give warnings or provide information. The effects of CCTV appear to have been different in relation to the two types of crime considered. Theft *from* cars was a more frequent problem than the theft *of* cars and it was in relation to the former that the most significant effect was recorded. The number of thefts from vehicles dropped dramatically from 92 in the year when the camera was installed to 31 in the year following its introduction. The degree of reduction to theft of cars was much less certain. Poyner explains this by the fact that access to the campus was supervised by a manned security post and that this may well have reduced the risk of car theft. The CCTV camera assisted the security guards in the arrest of a number of offenders and was deemed to have acted as a deterrent for other potential offenders. Furthermore, Poyner suggests that, rather than displace crime, CCTV appears to have resulted in a diffusion of benefits:

> the fact that crime was reduced in a parking lot without the benefit of the surveillance system but close to areas with surveillance sheds doubt on the theory of displacement. Rather than displace crime to less well protected targets on the campus, the 'good effect' has spread out beyond the immediate area of application.
>
> (Poyner 1992: 182)

However, Poyner does warn that his findings suggest the need for crime-specific situational measures, given the different impact of the measures on the theft of cars and theft from cars.

Tilley's (1993b) overview of the installation of CCTV introduced by a number of Safer Cities projects generally supports Poyner's conclusions that schemes deploying CCTV have led to a reduction in various categories of car crime. However, Tilley raises a number of cautionary warnings in noting that:

- it is difficult to make a judgement about specifically how CCTV may result in a reduction in crime in particular contexts
- it is not possible to estimate the displacement of offences by place, type or time which may have occurred
- the effect of CCTV appears to be enhanced when it is installed alongside other complementary measures
- if and when the real potential of CCTV to lead to apprehension loses credibility among car criminals, the effect will begin to fade
- the effectiveness of technology such as CCTV is highly dependent on its use by security personnel.

In support of the latter point Tilley cites cases in which the CCTV was not monitored by security personnel.

There appears to be reasonably widespread support for CCTV from the media, the public and politicians (Honess and Charman 1992), albeit alongside concerns about civil liberties. Its spread has been dramatically encouraged and enhanced by various British government initiatives which have seen the introduction of CCTV to diverse areas of social life. Burrows (1980) concluded that the installation of CCTV in four London underground stations resulted in some spatial displacement of thefts and robberies to the 15 stations without CCTV in the same area. Moreover, displacement was particularly high in the seven closest stations to the target stations where CCTV had been installed. Brown (1995), in an evaluation of three case studies of CCTV in town centres, found that the deterrent effects may only be short-term. In relation to personal crime he concludes that: 'In large metropolitan areas, the cameras have had very little effect on overall levels of assaults and wounding, despite being used to prompt many arrests' (Brown 1995: vi). Consequently, he suggests that the strength of CCTV in town centres lies not in preventing offending through deterrence, but more in co-ordinating a quick response which may reduce the seriousness of an incident and in assisting the investigation and conviction processes. For a critical review of the wider implications of CCTV in public places see Davies (1996), Groombridge and Murji (1994), Norris and Armstrong (1997a, 1997b).

Preventing robberies of post offices

Ekblom (1988) evaluated the introduction of security screens in 1300 sub-post offices in London. The screens sought to provide physical security by forming a barrier between the cashier and the customer, and hence protecting the post office from robberies. The number of successful robberies decreased from 266 in 1982 to 21 in 1985. However, this was accompanied by an increase in the number of failed robbery attempts which was double the number of successful robberies. The failed attempts resulted from robbers switching to different methods, in most cases using firearms threats at the screen. The improvements to counter screens forced robbers to abandon their sledgehammers and rely on guns, which many already carried as a back-up. Ekblom observed that where there is a switch from sledgehammer to gun during the raid this is likely to result in a failed robbery, as 'the robbers will commence their firearms threat from a position of psychological disadvantage in a game where bluff is more important than actual use of weaponry' (1988: 40). This example illustrates the side-effects, often unintended, that situational interventions can produce.

Community-oriented and estate-based situational prevention

Residential security on a difficult-to-let estate

This project involved the physical improvement of residential security, along classic target-hardening lines, for an entire difficult-to-let estate, the Scotswood Estate, in the West End of Newcastle. Initiated in 1980, the project involved the installation of ground floor security devices so as to secure points of entry against burglary. No structural changes were made to the dwellings. The project did suffer from some implementation problems. The measures were thoroughly evaluated using monthly police statistics supplemented by a two-stage tenant survey, conducted both pre- and post-implementation of the security improvements (Allat 1984a, 1984b). The surveys sought to measure the effects on residents' perceptions of crime, their fear of crime and any alterations in behaviour. A control estate was also identified and monitored in the same way in order to assess the effects of outside influences and the implementation process. The control estate was similar with regard to design standards, amenities, number of dwellings, household structure and low reputation, as reflected in the absence of or short waiting lists for tenancies.

On the target estate the risk of burglary remained high but static for about a year. In contrast the burglary rate on the control estate increased. While attempted burglary declined on the target estate, other types of property crime increased. The results showed no real reduction in burglary on the target estate, but they did show a significant reduction in the fear of crime among the residents. However welcomed, whether the reduction in fear was due to the presence of the security devices themselves or the fact that something was seen to be done by the authorities was not clear (Allat 1984b: 181). By contrast, there was no significant change in the level of fear on the control estate.

The study identified some displacement of burglaries to two adjacent estates and in the pockets of private housing and other unprotected properties within the estate itself, where burglaries rose. However, comparison with the control estate, where burglaries also rose, suggested that the full extent of the increase on the adjacent estates and private properties could not be attributed solely to a displacement effect from the targeted areas. There was, however, according to the author of the research, 'a clearer displacement effect to other property crimes within the estate' (Allat 1984a: 113), those to which a frustrated burglar might turn.

Phone entry systems

On the South Acton Estate, in Ealing, over a period of time between 1980 and 1985 a number of physical improvements were made. The most prominent saw the installation of phone entry systems and garage security measures, in order to limit access and create more clearly defined 'defensible spaces'. However, these measures were not introduced throughout the estate but only on part of it. The evaluation of the impact of the measures was based on recorded crime statistics over the period of 1980 to 1986 (Osborn 1986). No increase in crime was detected in the part of the estate where the security improvements were introduced. In 1986 the burglary rate dropped by 50 per cent where the phone entry systems were in operation. Autocrime fell by 7 per cent where the garages were secured. However, this was mirrored by an opposite trend in the areas where security improvements were not introduced. This suggests there may have been evidence of displacement of burglary and car theft from areas secured to areas without security.

The Safe Neighbourhoods Unit (SNU) (1985) in a report entitled *After Entryphones* noted the importance of the social context in which entryphones and other physical improvements to blocks of flats are introduced. They identify a number of potential reasons for the apparent failure of many costly entryphone schemes including lack of consultation with residents, inadequate maintenance arrangements and inadequate assessment of the level of abuse and misuse, as well as the volume of traffic which the technology has to withstand. They also raise the possibility that fear of crime, particularly of incivilities, may be caused, often unwittingly, by strangers who may live in the block or whose access is authorised by someone living in the block. The implication is that target-hardening measures such as entryphone systems may encourage the assumption that crime is generated by strangers, and hence heighten fear when strangers appear to have penetrated the 'defended space' (see also SNU 1993).

Improved street lighting

Based on two projects in London, Painter (1988, 1989) has argued that improved lighting can have an immediate impact on pedestrians' and residents' experiences and perceptions of crime, particularly in relation to incidents of threatening, pestering and insulting behaviour and property crime. In one of the projects, one street was provided with improved lighting and the effects were evaluated by way of a before and after survey (1988). According to the survey data, Painter claimed that incidents of assault, autocrime and threats fell by 75 per cent in the six week period after the lighting improvements were installed. Impressive reductions in the level of fear of crime were recorded after the installation of the improved lighting, with most people interviewed believing that crime had been reduced. It was Painter's contention that improved street lighting had a number of positive effects including encouraging people to use the streets, reviving public spaces, encouraging informal surveillance by pedestrians and increasing the likelihood of victims or witnesses identifying offenders.

However, Painter offers little concrete evidence to support these assertions. Furthermore, the short timespan of the monitoring period in both projects leaves the value of the findings questionable, as there is no possibility of drawing conclusions about the longer-term effects of lighting on crime or the fear of crime. The positive reactions of pedestrians and residents may be as much a product of a response to an improvement in the area brought about by the lighting rather than any effect that the lighting may have either directly or indirectly on crime.

Other research suggests that while good street lighting contributes to the quality of urban life, 'better street lighting by itself has very little effect on crime' (Ramsay 1991: 24). Offenders appear not to be particularly influenced by lighting conditions. The findings of a major relighting scheme in the London Borough of Wandsworth seem to support these contentions. The authors summarised the evaluation research stating that: 'The principal conclusion is that no evidence could be found to support the hypothesis that improved street lighting reduces reported crime' (Atkins *et al.* 1991: 20). And yet it appears that the public has considerable faith in street lighting as a means of crime prevention, and it does seem to reduce the public's fear of crime. In line with Painter's findings, Atkins and colleagues found 'clear evidence that perceived safety of women when walking alone after dark had been improved in the treated area' (*ibid.*). It appears that while the evidence as to any long-term impact on crime is debatable, improved street lighting is a popular measure in itself.

'Designing out' kerb-crawling and prostitution in London

In the mid-1980s around the Finsbury Park area of north London, which had traditionally been associated with prostitutes and kerb-crawling, a multi-agency approach to policing prostitution was adopted. A central element of this approach was the introduction of an extensive programme of road closure in the area. The simple theory was that putting up barriers and closing streets to cars would reduce, if not remove, kerb-crawling, and hence prostitutes, from the area (see Matthews 1986, 1992a, 1992b). This was accompanied by the establishment of a 16 strong vice squad to police the area. The author of the research reports claims that:

within a relatively short period of time, a remarkable transformation occurred. Soliciting and kerb-crawling virtually disappeared, and the area was transformed from a noisy and hazardous 'red light' district into a relatively tranquil residential area.

(Matthews 1992b: 94)

Contrary to expectations the research uncovered very little evidence of displacement to adjacent neighbourhoods. Matthews concluded that prostitution is much more opportunistic than had previously been supposed, despite it being the 'oldest profession in the world'. Matthews speculated that the 200–300 or so 'away day' girls who had been travelling to London to practise prostitution simply abandoned an occupation to which they had been only marginally committed, as did members of an even larger group whose involvement was highly sporadic. In comparison, the 30 to 40 'hard core' prostitutes who had been working and living in the area were displaced into their homes using advertisements or began operating from a local public house.

Matthews reports a number of other significant benefits that resulted from the road closure programme, including an increased sense of security (particularly evident among the female residents of the area), a reduction in the volume of traffic and an improved relationship among the police, the public and the local authority (Matthews 1992b: 95). Significantly, there was a reduction in the number of crimes reported. In the 12 month period prior to the implementation of the road closure scheme, the number of crimes reported to the police in the area stood at 475. In the 12 months that followed implementation the total number of reported crimes decreased to 275. At the same time the number of serious crimes reduced by 50 per cent. Hence, the scheme seems to have produced a 'diffusion of benefits'. The supposition is that other crimes committed by prostitutes, pimps and clients or attracted by their presence in the area, including burglary and car theft, were reduced.

The replication of the Finsbury Park experience in Streatham, an area of south London, also found a reduction in the level of soliciting and kerb-crawling (Matthews 1993). Furthermore, lower levels of disorder were reported and there was a marked improvement in the overall quality of life for residents. However, the commitment to prostitution among the prostitutes working in Streatham was very different to that of the women in Finsbury Park and a much more considerable displacement effect was noted as prostitutes moved to adjoining areas (Matthews 1993: 29). Matthews claimed this constituted a form of 'benign' displacement as the prostitutes moved away from residential areas and into locations where the nuisance element was reduced and other negative effects minimised.

Lowman (1992), however, has reported a very different experience in Vancouver. He has questioned Matthews' methodology and hence his findings. His principal criticisms relate to the question of displacement. He suggests that from Matthews' study we do not actually know what happened to the prostitutes that were 'designed out' of Finsbury Park, or where they went. On the basis of the Vancouver experience he suggests that much displacement may have occurred into off street locations outside the targeted area – such as escort services, massage parlours and bars – and that canvassing prostitutes about their adjustments in response to the road barriers might have told us more about this process. Finally, he questions Matthews' failure to discuss the long-term effects of the measures implemented, suggesting that some displacement effects can take longer than 12 months to materialise. Lowman also cites an example from the Vancouver experience of how situational measures can have perverse unintended consequences. One result of the introduction of barriers in Vancouver, quite contrary to its intended purpose of 'designing out' kerb crawlers, was to enable prostitutes to sit on the bollards and proposition clients who had been forced to slow down!

Victim-oriented situational prevention

Kirkholt burglary project and the prevention of repeat victimisation

The most notable example of victim-led crime prevention was the Home Office funded anti-burglary demonstration project, on the Kirkholt housing estate in Rochdale in the mid-1980s (Forrester *et al.* 1988, 1990). The council run estate suffered from a particularly high level of crime, especially burglary. In 1985 about one in four properties were burgled. According to British Crime Survey findings Kirkholt should have had a 'medium' rate of burglary, given the housing type, as compared nationally. In fact, at the time, the rate of recorded burglaries on Kirkholt was double the figure for recorded and unrecorded burglaries in housing types at high risk. The researchers found that in 1986 the chance of being the victim of a second or repeat burglary was over four times as high as the likelihood of a first burglary. They deduced that 'a burglary flags the high probability of another burglary' (Pease 1991: 74). Consequently, the project concentrated preventive energies on previously victimised properties. The measures selected originated out of information collected through surveys of burglary victims and their neighbours on the estate, as well as interviews with convicted burglars from the Rochdale area (Forrester *et al.* 1988). It was believed that this information could provide guidance on where and when preventive action could be most effectively targeted.

The initiative involved a package of interventions, concentrating on previously victimised dwellings primarily by means of physical security improvements to properties in the immediate aftermath of a burglary. The measures implemented included:

- the installation of 'up-graded' security hardware, such as window locks and strengthened doors
- a scheme of property postcoding
- the removal of coin-fed gas and electricity meters from all the properties. These had been identified as particularly attractive to burglars
- 'cocoon' neighbourhood watch schemes set up around victimised properties. This involved the residents of the five or six homes around a previously victimised dwelling being enlisted and encouraged to keep a special watch on it
- 'community support' for burglary victims on the estate, whereby project workers visited victims' homes offering support and advice.

In sum, this package of measures incorporated elements of target-hardening, increased surveillance and target removal. As such, it incorporated both situational and social approaches, albeit with a heavy emphasis on the former.

Repeat burglary victimisation was found to have declined by 80 per cent during the seven months after implementation in comparison with the seven months prior to implementation. Within three years the level of burglary on the estate had been reduced to 25 per cent of its pre-implementation level. There was little or no evidence of displacement to other areas or other crime categories. On the contrary, other forms of acquisitive crime also showed a reduction in comparison with neighbouring areas. Hence, it has been claimed that as well as assisting victims of crime, the targeting of repeat victimisation may have a diffusion effect, in which benefits diffuse beyond the immediate recipient of assistance to those living elsewhere on the estate.

The disadvantage of a package of multiple measures such as that introduced on the Kirkholt estate is that the relative contribution of the various elements were not distinguishable. This raises particular problems with regard to any lessons to be drawn from such projects for future preventive action (see Chapter 6). The success of the Kirkholt project – particularly the diffusion effect – may well be explained less by the concentration on previously victimised dwellings and more by the removal of cash pre-payment fuel meters. It is clear that a large proportion of the reduction in burglary rates on the Kirkholt estate was attributable to the removal of the pre-payment meters. This is particularly pertinent given that the burglary rate on the Kirkholt estate was so high prior to the upgrading of household security. We also know that 49 per cent of the burglaries on the estate involved the loss of money from pre-payment fuel meters. While the exact contribution of their removal is unknown, it does raise questions about the possible transferability of the Kirkholt project mechanisms to residential areas without coin-operated fuel meters (SNU 1993; Crawford and Jones 1996), and its model as a successful repeat victimisation project.

The researchers failed sufficiently to describe or evaluate the wider contexts in which the changes were introduced, particularly the substantial programme of environmental improvements undertaken by the Housing Department at the same time. The effects of this programme may have had an impact on the estate's crime problems. Furthermore, the number of recorded burglaries began to rise quite sharply again in early 1990 and had returned to pre-1988 levels by early 1992, albeit not to the very high levels evident in 1987 (Osborn *et al.* 1994: 70). This would seem to question the capacity of situational interventions to have a durable impact.

Nevertheless, the Kirkholt approach to burglary prevention has rightly highlighted the potential of victim-led crime prevention. It has become a template of 'good practice' which subsequently has been replicated elsewhere (Tilley 1993c), almost to the point that it has now become the dominant model for burglary prevention. Similar patterns of repeat victimisation to those suggested by the Kirkholt findings have been shown to exist in other countries (Polvi *et al.* 1991). The Kirkholt project, particularly the targeting of prevention activity at repeat victimisation, has implications both for situational and social crime prevention. Some of the lessons have been adapted to other types of crime, including crimes against schools (Farrell and Pease 1993), racial attacks (Sampson and Phillips 1992, 1995), car crime (Anderson *et al.* 1995) and domestic violence (Lloyd *et al.* 1994). Repeat victimisation work has also had significant implications for police practice and advice following victimisation (see Tilley 1995).

Repeat victimisation and crime prevention considered

One of the most enduring messages of the Kirkholt project – in conjunction with the research on repeat victimisation (as discussed in Chapter 1) – is that it offers an important reconceptualisation of how best to target crime prevention activity. This warrants a consideration of some of the general issues to which it has given rise. One question that crime prevention aimed at repeat victimisation poses is, over what period the increased risk persists, or put the other way, how soon after the first victimisation should crime prevention be introduced? Research in Canada suggests that the period of greatest risk of repeat burglary is within six weeks of the first incident (Polvi *et al.* 1991). It was found that the risk of repeat victimisation returns to an average level and subsequently remains so once six months have passed. Analysis of the repeat burglaries within one month showed that half of the second victimisations occurred within seven days of the first (Polvi *et al.* 1991: 412). The implication is that very early crime prevention interventions are most likely to bring the desired preventive results.

A recent attempt to integrate such an approach into routine service delivery in relation to burglary and car crime was established in Huddersfield, in West Yorkshire (see Anderson *et al.* 1995). The project developed a three-tier grading of crime prevention response according to the number of previous victimisations (as recounted by the victim) from bronze through silver to gold. The components of the response varied from the simple property marking to security upgrading, through the focused patrolling of victimised places, to the loan of high technology measures such as vehicle tracking and silent alarms. Similarly, there was a grading of the crime detection response in relation to fingerprinting analysis and targeting previous offenders against the same property. This project has begun to show the way, particularly for the police, to integrate crime prevention into their mainstream response to incidents of crime. In so doing, it has re-awoken the Peelian legacy of crime prevention as a central component of policing and presented a considerable challenge to modern police forces.

However, there are a number of important reservations about the possible implications of victim-led crime prevention through a focus on repeat victimisation. The principal concern is that victim-led crime prevention may lead to 'victim blaming' whereby victims are blamed for their subsequent or repeat victimisation, as 'they had been warned'. Significantly, this may have implications for insurance. For if victimisation is an indicator of increased risk then insurance companies, most likely, will increase the premiums for insurance cover, attach stringent conditions as a requirement of future cover or simply refuse to renew insurance cover as 'too risky'. There is some evidence that this is already happening (see Association of London Authorities 1994). The implications are that those least able to afford the cost will increasingly be asked to pay, either directly or indirectly, or be written out of cover, as insurance companies attempt to protect their profit margins in an increasingly cut-throat market.

Criminologists are still unclear as to the exact causes of repeat victimisation. Hence, the most obvious and yet the most problematic question which still vexes criminologists is, why repeat victimisation occurs. Here, much research is still needed and for the moment we can only speculate. The following potential explanations have been offered in the case of burglary (see Farrell and Pease 1993; Farrell 1995). First, the same offender returns to the same location, perhaps because they know the contents, either what was left behind or in anticipation that the stolen goods have been replaced, because they know the layout of the dwelling and hence the exits, or for some other reason. There is some limited indirect research evidence that the same offender may be responsible for some repeat burglary (Anderson *et al.* 1995). Second, the original offender supplies information about the dwelling to others who are then attracted to it. Third, the characteristics of the house mark it out as highly attractive to potential offenders, leading to repeat victimisation connected only by the luring attributes of the target. In other words, an incidence of victimisation does not necessarily increase the likelihood of a repeat victimisation, but rather reflects the high prior probability of victimisation, which is merely confirmed by repeat victimisation. However, this explanation does not address the question of increasing and decreasing risk (or attractiveness), i.e. fluctuations in the probability of victimisation over time. Fourth, it may be that repeat victimisation is largely the product of victim concentration rather than the other way round. In other words, repeat victimisation may merely be an expression of a high crime area rather than a high crime area being a product of high numbers of repeat victims. In answering the question, do certain areas have high crime rates because more people are victimised or because there is more revictimisation of the same people? we may be looking through the wrong end of the telescope at the problem. Fifth, some commentators have suggested that some element of repeat victimisation may be the product of insurance fraud, as victims try to recoup their loss through insurance which they may not have had on the initial occasion of victimisation. Sixth, the data itself may be unreliable, it may be a product of the methodology itself, or it may be that in searching for explanations researchers have over-interpreted the data. Finally, of course, the answer may lie in a complex mix of all of the above.

Some conclusions by way of a critical assessment

Clearly, what the above review of some situational crime prevention case studies shows is that situational measures can be successful in reducing levels of crime. They can have an impact in relation to certain crimes, committed by certain criminals, in certain places, at certain times under given conditions. The exact nature of this impact remains open to question, as does the extent of displacement, as well as how these things can be appropriately measured and quantified (I return to this in Chapter 6). For the moment I wish to critically consider some of the implications of a situational approach.

It over-prioritises property crimes in public places: the concern is that by implication situational crime prevention tends to silence from the crime prevention agenda certain forms of criminality, most notably violent crimes which occur in private. Consequently, there is a tendency to ignore the gendered nature of much crime, a failing which is exacerbated by the lack of concern for 'biographical' details of offenders. Heal and Laycock (1986: 127) have suggested that because violent crimes are less common and are less likely to cluster in time or space, they are also less amenable to situational controls. While this may present practical problems in terms of violence in public places, it also confronts both theoretical and practical problems in relation to crime in private settings, particularly the home. In practice situational measures are harder to implement in private domains which often serve as a site of much violence (Gabor 1990: 68). The 'events orientation' of situational approaches has difficulties confronting the interpersonal nature of some crime. Situational notions of 'target-hardening', 'increasing surveillance' and 'reducing the rewards' of crime are distinctly less appropriate in private spheres.

It addresses symptoms and not causes: implicitly or explicitly situational crime prevention involves at least a rejection of, and some might say an assault on, the social causes of crime (O'Malley 1992). While theorists such as Clarke do leave space within their models for 'distal' understandings of why people get involved in criminality in the first place, situational crime prevention – with its policy-orientation – focuses on the practical and the achievable – which undoubtedly serves to marginalise causal explanations of crime, particularly those emphasising socio-economic factors. Situational prevention, therefore, heralds a shift to the control of crime rather than any attempt to understand its causes. This preoccupation with control and efficient management has been captured by Young's reference to situational crime prevention as part of a more general 'administrative criminology' (1986: 10) and by the association which Downes and Rock (1988) make with varieties of what they term 'control theory'. Situational crime prevention does not explain why people commit crime: in fact the thinking behind situational crime prevention actively shuns such an investigation. Situational crime prevention clearly represents an example of what Garland (1994) refers to as the 'governmental project' within criminology, its gaze firmly focused on the administrative task of crime control and management. As such it has connected with, and been promoted by, 'managerialist' concerns with efficiency, effectiveness and economy.

It is only ever temporary: the issue of displacement highlights the way in which situational crime prevention may only ever be temporary as crime is moved elsewhere. Technology and design may have 'habituation effects' – as the novelty wears off – the extent of which is rarely considered in evaluation but which will undermine its long-term effectiveness (Hough 1996: 68). There is another sense in which it is temporary: yesterday's situational prevention appears to become redundant soon after its implementation as the nature of crime and criminals change. Certainly, the security industry has a vested interest in the commodification of security in which the market is for ever developing and reproducing itself. To some it may appear as if offenders and security manufacturers are engaged in an escalating cycle of development and counter-development in which each seeks an advantage over the other. As a consequence, the nature of the target and its prevention appears to be continually changing. Moreover, security technology does not only ever serve a beneficial purpose. It can be a double-edged sword and can be used for criminal ends – such as the offenders who use security cameras to identify when their victims have left their properties before burglarising them and car thieves who copy car security signals to open them without setting off the alarm.

It may encourage a (blind) faith in technology which may be unwarranted: this 'undeserved' faith in the 'technological fix' is something we have already noted in relation to CCTV and street lighting. It is likely to be fuelled by powerful commercial interests in selling the latest technologies. This *faith* that situational measures 'work' may have unintended and unexpected outcomes. It may leave people more exposed or vulnerable as they alter their life-style accordingly; it may lead to raised expectations and greater cynicism when it does not work. This may actually serve to undermine the important role of the public in crime control (Shapland and Vagg 1988) by disempowering and undermining the human element. Technology is more likely to have enduring effects if it is conceived of as an enhancement of human activity rather than as a substitute for it.

There are other things which are more important than crime prevention: there is a concern that we may have rushed down the path of physical and technological crime prevention without thinking clearly about the social, cultural and ethical dimensions. Some commentators have suggested that through crime prevention, crime issues have been given undue prominence over other matters. For example, there is considerable debate between the relative merits of fire security as against crime prevention. While the former may have an overriding concern with allowing people to get out of premises, the latter is concerned with stopping people getting in to them. This is not to say that the interests of crime prevention and fire security are always mutually exclusive, but that with the prominence accorded to situational crime prevention, issues such as fire security in certain circumstances have been overlooked.

Surveillance can be highly intrusive: the proliferation of modes of 'natural' and 'unnatural' (i.e. technological) surveillance raises ethical and social issues. Surveillance may be unnecessarily intrusive into peoples' private lives and activities. There are many unanswered and ill-considered questions. What happens to the information collected? For what purposes should it be legitimately used? How should it be regulated? Who surveys the surveyors? The danger here is that situational crime prevention acts repressively, by subjecting ever greater populations to surveillance techniques which restrict freedoms (Downes and Rock 1988: 239). While the spectre of Big Brother may be too all-encompassing and instrumental, it should serve to remind us of the need to face the difficult issues that surveillance technologies pose.

It is socially divisive: there is a danger that in 'designing out' *crime* we are in fact actually 'designing out' *troublesome people* or, more specifically, 'designing out' *youths*. The logic of situational crime prevention, often, is to keep strangers out. Defensible space is premised on an understanding of the offender as an outsider (Currie 1988), a theme to which I return in the next chapter. As such, situational crime prevention inherently embodies the dynamics of social exclusion.

It may increase the social concentration of crime through displacement: if crime is significantly displaced and the central paradox of crime prevention remains unresolved – that there is an inverse relationship between preventive activity and need – it is likely that crime will be increasingly displaced on to those who (a) already suffer the most crime and (b) can least afford security measures. There is the increasing danger that ' "security differentials" become defining characteristics of wealth, power and status' (Crawford 1997a: 280–1).

It has adverse cultural implications: there is a concern that situational approaches breed a 'fortress mentality' which will lead people increasingly to retreat behind locked doors, grills and bars, and 'defensible spaces'. This will have wider implications for the nature of social relations. It may foster and encourage what Lasch has referred to as 'privatism', a form of introspective preoccupation with the safety and care of the self, resulting in forms of both social and spatial withdrawal (1980: 25). Perversely, this may actually serve to make people feel more, rather than, less fearful as the symbols of situational crime prevention – CCTV, security guards, alarms and locks – remind us of our own vulnerability and insecurity. The Cassels Committee recognised this paradox, stating that: 'the increased proliferation of security devices may themselves increase feelings of threat' (1994: 11). The available research evidence confirms this view (Rosenbaum 1988a: 330–9). If crime prevention through opportunity reduction becomes a fundamental part of everyday life – from turning on the burglar alarm through fastening the clamp on a wheel of the car to the physical make-up of the environmental landscape – it will only communicate to us how ephemeral and contingent security really is. The technology of situational security has an inbuilt dynamic for expansion as private companies seek more advanced technological wizardry in order to keep one step ahead of the tenacious criminal. The extensive amount of potential places, targets and victims to be secured, surveyed or guarded, further fuels this expansionist logic. In building visible barriers between people and retreating behind target-hardened premises we may actually be destroying the framework of culturally important interpersonal trust relations. Situational crime prevention by its nature is inscribed with distrust, whether appropriate or not.

I return to some of these issues in Chapter 8, but for the moment we can conclude by noting that over the past 200 years or so, one of the central tensions within criminological theory has been that between deterministic-(i.e. predispositional) and voluntaristic-(i.e. rational choice) based understandings of human behaviour. Situational crime prevention has not resolved this tension but represents a lurch towards one extreme polar position. Proponents of situational approaches, such as Clarke, would probably see this as an appropriate corrective to the excesses of the predispositional bias within dominant theory. To counteract this pro-situational argument by restating deterministic assumptions about what motivates offenders is to fail to grasp some of the important insights that situational crime prevention may have to offer.

Much of the debate between protagonists for and against situational approaches is merely about the degree of emphasis to be given to different factors. Hence, it would be wrong to throw out the situational 'baby' with the rational choice 'bath water'. Significantly, much contemporary social theory has begun to stress the dynamic relationship between broad social structures and the agency of human subjects. Structures do not exist outside of action, nor do they only constrain but also enable social action (see Giddens 1984, 1990; Bottoms and Wiles 1992). Environmental cues, spatial attributes and the routine manner in which social behaviour is patterned over time and space are all significant elements which construct the 'practical consciousness' within which human subjects largely act. Rather than accepting either voluntarism or determinism as the basis for crime preventive measures, there is a need to conceive of human behaviour as both dynamic and responsive in relation to varying situational and social contingencies. Hence, it is not a question of all or nothing. However, in the search for the appropriate degree of weight to be accorded to situational or social factors we should not lose sight of the more fundamental questions about the normative and social value of given measures.

Chapter 4

Social and Communal Strategies

For some considerable time, social policy has been seen to have implications for crime and its prevention. However, with the recent 'shift to a preventive paradigm' we have seen a greater awareness of the potential crimogenic or crime preventive effects of given social policies. The interrelationship between crime and social policies – such as urban policy, education policy, housing policy, family policy and employment policy – raises two fundamental questions. First, what are the consequences of given social policies for crime and its prevention? Itself the subject of heated political and ideological debate, this is rendered more problematic by the complex, indirect and mediated nature of any relationship between broad social policies and specific incidences of crime, as well as by the timespan over which given policies may have visible or tangible effects. The second and more troublesome question is whether social policies should be judged on the basis of their implications for crime. And if so, what weight should be accorded to such judgements and with what ramifications? Crime prevention will not, nor should, be the only criterion against which social policies are assessed. Social policies have value in their own right, regardless of their potential crimogenic consequences.

As we saw in Chapter 2, social crime prevention has faired less well than its situational cousin in the British context. Over the last two decades, situational initiatives have been the subject of substantial government funding and research, while dedicated social crime prevention has survived on poorly researched, piecemeal and usually 'one off' local projects. This has been no accident of history but the fruit of an alignment between the assumptions that underpin the divergent approaches and prevailing political programmes.

This chapter considers the theoretical assumptions that inform, and the strategies that seek to promote, social crime prevention. In contrast to the previous chapter, the focus here is on strategies aimed at *criminality prevention*, whereby the crimogenic causes and criminal predispositions of people, either as individuals or as group members, are the object of policy interventions. The chapter is divided into two sections. The first begins with an examination of individual, or 'developmental', social crime prevention, with an overview of primary social prevention and its focus on broad social policies, before a more detailed analysis of secondary social prevention, with its emphasis on identifying and targeting people 'at risk' of offending. Here, the focus is directed at youth crime in particular, as it is in relation to young people and their socialisation that most of the developmental prevention work has been targeted. This chapter does not, however, consider tertiary offender-oriented social prevention through strategies to reduce offending as a consequence of the detection of an identified offender by the criminal justice system. This is the domain of traditional texts on criminal justice, sentencing and punishment and is extensively covered elsewhere (see May and Vass 1996; Worral 1997; Brownlee 1998).

The second section, by contrast, focuses on community-based strategies, which seek to increase the crime preventive capacity of communities and groups. In both sections some of the assumptions and theories that underlie the various approaches will be considered. This is supplemented by an overview of a number of case studies and an analysis of some of the issues to which they give rise. As in the previous chapter, these case studies will be illustrative of divergent approaches, albeit that they often incorporate a diversity of measures which combine a variety of theoretically informed strategies.

Assumptions within social crime prevention

Social crime prevention embodies predispositional assumptions about what causes an individual to offend. It is concerned with preventing criminality or criminal propensities from developing within a person or group, rather than with preventing the opportunities for crime itself. Consequently, there is a considerable variety of predispositional theories drawing on sociological, psychological and even physiological insights. However, we can identify two broad ways of understanding some of these theories by juxtaposing those concerned with the restraints on, or controls over, offending (be they externally imposed or internalised by individuals) as against those which focus on the absence or presence of incentives to be law abiding. We can call these two approaches 'control theory' and 'stake in conformity', respectively.

Control theory

Hirschi (1969) outlined a 'control theory' in order to explain why people conform, rather than why they commit crime. He emphasised that crime needs no special motivation, as human beings are basically weak. Rather, he suggests, there is a need to explain why people do not commit crime. For him, the answer lay in social control. Through social bonds society encourages individuals to forego their selfish motivations and conform to rules. Without social bonds people would revert to pursuing their selfish interests and hence crime. Hirschi stressed four 'control' variables: attachment, commitment, involvement and belief. Each of these represents a significant social bond which encourages socialisation by inculcating values. The bond of 'attachment', for example, lies in the ongoing association that people have with conventional groups. For Hirschi, the two conventional institutions through which people form bonds with society are the family and the school.

More recently Gottfredson and Hirschi (1990) have argued that people vary not in motivation but rather in self-control. They suggest that self-control, internalised early in life, determines an individual's ability or inability to resist crime. Crime, for them, fulfils short-term gratification. By implication, the law abiding do not fall victim to these seductions of crime because of their internalised self-control, which allows them to resist the temptations offered by crime. Low self-control, they argue, arises from defective socialisation. Those who exhibit anti-social behaviour early in life are likely not to have received effective socialisation, thus identifying them as 'at risk' of offending. Families and schools are identified as the principal institutions through which effective or ineffective socialisation influences the propensities of young people to offend. As control implies prevention, supporting and strengthening these institutions of early socialisation become fundamental aspects of crime prevention.

On the basis of Gottfredson and Hirschi's control theory, institutions which fail adequately to socialise young people are placed under the spotlight of preventive attention. There is an assumption that *under*-socialisation produces crime. It presupposes that the offender is attached to values and norms which are at odds with the dominant law abiding culture. Consequently, it feeds recent arguments about the existence of an 'underclass' of people who are morally and culturally cut off from mainstream society (Murray 1994). This 'underclass' is perceived to be the product of pathological institutions – families and schools – whose failure to socialise and inculcate self-control has produced young people who are socially and morally disconnected from the rest of society.

There is no sense in Gottfredson and Hirschi's work that the bonds of 'attachment' to mainstream popular cultural values may themselves be crimogenic. Conventional values, in their thesis, are cleansed of any association with criminality. Hence, there is no space for an understanding that *over*-socialisation may result in crime. To do so might allow us to begin to theorise the attachment of criminal boys and young men to dominant masculine values. And yet 'control theory' fails to help us explain why criminal subcultures often mirror the values epitomised by mainstream culture. Control theory only allows us to blame and demonise the immediate socialising institutions, the school and the family (notably the 'lone mother') without critically examining the broader social and cultural framework in which they are set. It fails to engage with recent research which suggests that members of the so-called criminal 'underclass', far from being disconnected from prevailing cultural norms, are saturated with them. For example, Campbell (1993) has shown how young men involved in urban riots on some of Britain's peripheral housing estates in 1991 were not rejecting dominant male values derived from key institutions, such as the media and the police, but aping and reconfiguring them. Hence, the fascination among youths that engage in TWOCing ('taking a car without the owners consent') with fast performance cars, 'a quintissentially modern commodity with masculinised notions of power, flight and freedom' (Campbell 1996: 106), may be an important bond of attachment in relation to which control theory is silent.

'Stake in conformity'

An alternative theoretical premise to that of 'control' is one that emphasises the socio-economic opportunity structure in which individuals find themselves trying to live out the expectations, values and beliefs with which initial socialisation has provided them. Such an approach connects with Merton's (1938) theory of 'strain', which he suggested arises as a result of a disjuncture between the culturally defined aspirations which are held out to all and the 'limited legitimate opportunities' to fulfil these. The problem is that the opportunities – the means of achieving the cultural goals – are unequally distributed within the social structure. Criminality, thus understood, stems from alienation and a lack of opportunities as experienced by certain members of society.

Albert Cohen (1955) criticised the individualistic assumptions of Merton's strain theory. He argued that people do not jump from conformity into deviance alone, without 'a tentative, groping, advancing, backtracking, sounding-out process'. This he suggests is a collective 'subcultural' process, whereby groups of people together attempt to make sense of the world as they experience it. Subcultures may be understood as problem-solving devices as groups of people collectively attempt to reconcile and 'solve' the structural problems that confront them. Crime and delinquency represent one form of subcultural adaptation. Thus criminality can be understood as intimately connected to the development and maintenance of subcultures which sustain criminal activity. Cloward and Ohlin (1960) developed and extended Merton's ideas. For them, Merton had only explained why people violate the law, not why the 'strains' result in one deviant solution rather than another. By contrast, they asserted that delinquency is the product of the available illegitimate opportunities; these are inherently related to an individual's social and class position. Hence, while the middle class deviant may embezzle and defraud, the lower class deviant is more likely to rob and steal. They argued that deviant subcultures, as collective adaptations to the strains for status and goal fulfilment, are intimately shaped by the neighbourhood the deviants occupy.

The implications of these theoretical insights for crime prevention are twofold. The first relates to the opportunity structures, both legitimate and illegitimate, available to young people. The second relates to the treatment of delinquency at a group or 'community' level, in terms of understanding the local opportunity structures available and the subcultures which 'blocked opportunities' may foster. The relevance of this latter insight is developed later in this chapter in considering community-based crime prevention. However, while some initiatives concerned with addressing blocked opportunities may have a community focus, most do not.

Drawing together the above theoretical strands, it is argued that prevention should address any existing dissociation caused by creating forms of opportunities sufficient to provide marginalised people, youths in particular, with a 'stake in conformity'. This suggests the need to attempt to meet or at least cater for people's expectations of being able to fulfil a useful role in life and attain some of the dominant cultural goals cherished by society. The assumption behind this approach is that those who are provided with opportunities will be more likely to obtain meaningful roles in society, as a result of which they will develop a sense of fulfilment and usefulness that will translate into a greater sense of affiliation to the social order in which they find themselves.

A 'stake in conformity' requires the recognition of an individual's quest for status, fulfilment and private purpose:

> A legitimate identity among young people is most likely to occur if they
> have a stake in conformity; if, in other words, they develop a sense of
> competence, a sense of usefulness, a sense of belonging, and a sense that
> they have the power to affect their own destinies through conventional
> means.
>
> (Empey 1977: 1107)

The ideas of Cloward and Ohlin heavily influenced the Mobilisation for Youth (MFY) programme, begun in a large area of New York City's Lower East Side in 1962. MFY, as a classic 'stake in conformity' project, aimed to provide and create job opportunities and work training. It received considerable funding and was spread to other inner-city areas of America. Despite this, MFY produced little measurable success and along with similar 'welfarist' strategies, it has become associated with the 'aetiological crisis' of the 1960s – in both the USA and the UK – whereby crime soared *despite* an improvement in employment, housing and educational conditions. Social policies aimed at reducing inequality, it was argued most vehemently by Wilson (1975), appeared to have failed the prevention test. The paradox was a stark one: as poverty appeared to decrease in the 1960s so crime increased. Hence, Wilson argued there is little that social policy, with its blunt and inefficient governmental instruments, can or should do in relation to crime.

Broad social policies

Nevertheless, the relationship between social policies and crime is once again the subject of debate for at least two related reasons. First, currently dominant neo-liberal political thinking, rather than seeing social policy as a means of reducing crime, has come to identify it as the cause of contemporary social ills, including delinquency and disorder. According to neo-liberal commentators, such as Murray (1990) and Osborne and Gaebler (1992), the recent history of social policies in Western democracies – as typified by the 1960s welfare programmes – has ensured 'over-generous' welfare handouts which have fostered a 'culture of dependency'. 'Welfarist' social policies, it is argued, administered by an over-inflated state apparatus, are identified as the source of blame for social disintegration. On the back of this kind of political thinking, the role and reach of social policy have been significantly transformed and restricted by successive governments since the late 1970s. Second, despite the radical change in political direction inspired by neo-liberal ideas, the 1980s and 1990s have seen unparalleled rises in crime rates alongside *increases* in social inequality.

The complex relationship between broad social policies and crime has left this the subject of highly charged, often ill-informed, political debate. In this context it might seem appropriate for governments to attempt to anticipate and monitor the potential implications of given social policies. To this end, the Morgan Report recommended the introduction, by government, of crime prevention and community safety 'impact statements' for all new legislation and major policy initiatives (Morgan 1991: 35, para 6.41). This would encourage government to think and plan ahead. However, given the inherent tendency of policies to produce unintended, and sometimes unforseeable, consequences this assessment appropriately should be an ongoing process. The unintended consequences of legislation can have a significant impact on crime. For example, it appears that the introduction of Compulsory Competitive Tendering under the Housing Act 1993 has led to a reduction in 'preventive management' by public sector landlords and the Single Regeneration Budget has served to undermine the estate-based focus of successful projects such as the Priority Estates Projects. Both policies risk bypassing local communities and the benefits of estate-based intensive initiatives. The Education Act 1993, despite its intentions, has also produced a threefold increase in school exclusions (Bright 1997). Similarly, the budgetary constraints imposed on local authorities by a series of legislative changes has virtually destroyed the provision of youth services in many areas.

Young people and criminality prevention

Young people have been the focus of much social crime prevention for a number of reasons. First, a considerable amount of crime is committed by the young. It is estimated that people under the age of 21 are responsible for about half of all crimes committed (Home Office 1995b: 21). The peak age for male offending, according to criminal statistics, is 18. In 1994 two out of every five known offenders were under the age of 21 and a quarter were under 18. Hence, by focusing on young people, social crime prevention particularly targets prominent groups of potential offenders. Second, the dominant criminological view is that youth, for a variety of reasons, constitutes a period of transition, in which many young people engage in criminal and deviant activity, but that only a small percentage of them go on to develop 'criminal careers' (see Farrington 1994). Consequently, it is often assumed that it is important to respond to juvenile crime in ways that do not label or stigmatise young offenders – such that they perpetuate their criminal behaviour – but rather allow them to 'grow out of crime'.

The argument that many men grow out of crime is linked to the suggestion that there is a maturing process at work and that as long as young men do not become too heavily criminalised they stand a chance of leaving behind their deviant activity. Locking up young criminals is more likely to push them further into criminality, by reducing their prospects of doing something constructive, stigmatising them and rupturing their relations with non-criminal peers. This is confirmed by the fact that some 72 per cent of young men released from young offenders institutions are reconvicted of another crime within two years (Home Office 1996b). Consequently, people under the age of 18 are dealt with by a separate youth justice system which applies different assumptions, standards and principles to that of the adult process. While this limited interventionism has persistently informed policy and practice in relation to young people, it has also been subject to the vagaries produced by the winds of political change (see Pitts 1996).

However, according to recent Home Office research, young offenders – notably boys – no longer appear to be 'growing out of crime' as early in their lives (Graham and Bowling 1995). According to this new self-report research data, the peak in young men's criminal activity now forms a plateau between the years of 18 and their mid-20s. Girls appear to desist from crime at an earlier age and experience this transition more fully. However, the evidence in relation to boys suggests that the peak period is lengthening and the prospects of desistance are becoming more uncertain. Boys, it appears, are not growing out of crime, particularly property-related crime, although they may be shifting their criminality into less detectable offences.

This evidence seems to suggest that the juvenile justice system is not working: a view supported by the Audit Commission (1996) which concluded that the current system is both inefficient and expensive. It estimated that the cost of dealing with offending by young people to be around £1 billion a year. It recommended a greater shift to the prevention of youth criminality.

The self-report evidence appears to undermine any simple non-interventionist arguments which suggest that youths in less serious cases should be left alone to grow out of crime, rather than being labelled by the criminal justice system. Labelling theory arguments have been further undermined by recent research which suggests that some of the most serious and persistent young offenders have no criminal record and as such are unknown to the 'labelling' institutions (Graham and Bowling 1995).

Consequently, the task for crime prevention in relation to young people (largely male youths) generally has been twofold. The first task has been to identify the factors most likely to predispose certain youths to criminality in the hope that they can be prevented. The second task has been to identify factors that may encourage the desistance from crime among young people, in order to speed up the process by which youths 'grow out of crime'. We now consider the first of these but the second, as an aspect of tertiary crime prevention, is not considered further.

Identifying 'risk factors'

Research into youth delinquency has tended to concentrate on looking into the backgrounds, circumstances and attitudes of offenders and then identifying the characteristics which differentiate them from 'non-delinquents'. On this basis it has sought to explain why some young people become involved in crime and persist in their criminal careers, by identifying 'risk factors' which cluster among groups of known delinquents. In this regard 'persistent young offenders' have been the subject of particular attention (Hagell and Newburn 1994). Thus, criminologists have sought to identify variables which coincide with high levels of criminality and to draw out from them the implication that these are 'causal factors' which, if corrected, removed or lessened, will reduce crime. This is a classic positivist approach to the study of crime and social variables. As a result, criminologists have identified an ever-growing list of 'risk factors' that suggest a greater likelihood of involvement in crime.

The most obvious, but often ignored, risk factor associated with offending is gender: boys are considerably more likely to offend than girls. Other identified variables include:

- *individual personality and behavioural factors*, such as hyperactive behaviour in early childhood, impulsiveness and restlessness
- *family influences*, such as social class, family size, family poverty, lone-parenting, inadequate parenting, physical abuse, parental conflict and separation
- *living conditions*, such as poor housing and unstable living conditions

- *school influences*, such as poor schooling, bullying, poor educational achievement, truancy and exclusion from school
- *peer group pressure*: delinquents tend to have friends also involved in delinquent activities
- *employment opportunities*, such as lack of training and employment.

Clearly some 'risk factors' are more amenable to policy intervention than others. Reducing risk factors has largely focused on identifying the different developmental stages at which intervention may be possible – early childhood, primary school years and adolescence – and the different locations for programme targeting – family, school, peer group and community. However, research tends to suggest that *multiple* risk factors interact cumulatively to produce greater levels of risk. The implication is that interventions should seek to address multiple risk factors and the interactions between different sites of risk, thus confounding the task of policy-makers.

Following the insights of control theory, research evidence suggests that the school and the family play an important part in explaining why young people get involved in crime (West and Farrington 1973; Riley and Shaw 1985; Farrington 1992, 1994). In this context, recent Home Office research has suggested that a number of 'adverse factors' combine to increase the likelihood of criminality. For boys, the five key indicators of youths at risk of offending are poor parental supervision, truancy, delinquent peers, family in trouble with the law (delinquent siblings) and exclusion from school. Eighty-one per cent of the boys in a self-report study who were exposed to either four or five of these key risks were offenders (Graham and Bowling 1995: 47). The findings were slightly different for girls for whom the five key indicators include the same first three as boys – namely poor parental supervision, truancy and delinquent peers – but also include weak attachment to family and school. Sixty-one per cent of girls in the self-report study with four or five of these indicators were offenders (Graham and Bowling 1995: 48).

Within the literature there is now an emphasis on identifying ever-greater numbers of 'risk factors', as well as refining what are often blunt measurements for them (Farrington 1994; Tremblay and Craig 1995). Implicitly this raises the questions: what is meant by, for example, socially disruptive behaviour, cognitive deficits or poor parenting? How do we measure them? Can they be isolated from other, wider factors and relations? It is often accepted within research literature that positive results are more likely when interventions are aimed at more than one risk factor. And yet we cannot assume that by addressing more than one risk factor, as part of a packaged programme, we are actually addressing the interactive relations between those risk factors.

One of the problems of this kind of approach is that it can be very difficult to separate cause from effect. For example, while the research evidence shows that young delinquents tend to have delinquent friends and peers, it is not clear whether such acquaintances and peer groups lead to offending or whether delinquents merely gravitate towards each other's company. Specific 'risk factors' may actually be (indirect) indicators of other factors. For example, poor parenting as an indicator of risk may be a product of the stress and environmental adversities faced by socially disadvantaged families, rather than a direct cause in its own right. 'Risk factors' may tell us more about the processes of criminalisation for specific groups of people than they do about the crimes they commit.

A danger of 'risk factors' is that – particularly in political discourse – they may become seen in isolation, rather than as elements within a complex interactive process, or even as symptoms of much deeper social problems, such as poverty and inequality. James (1995) has produced powerful evidence of links between increasing inequality, struggling families and increasing violence against the person within what he describes as a 'winner–loser' culture. In so doing, he rejects many of the single-cause explanations which have often resulted in blaming certain kinds of families for crime, as a result of moral fecklessness or the inadequacies of lone-parent families which have only managed to reinforce and give credibility to the notion of the 'pathological family' (see Campbell 1994).

Preventing the onset of offending

While a considerable amount of criminological attention has been paid to identifying 'risk factors', comparatively less thought has been given to determining the factors that may protect young people against offending. We might refer to these as 'protective factors', which, research suggests, evolve at different stages of development between childhood and adulthood, with the implication that different forms of intervention are likely to be more or less effective with different age groups. As children grow older so the relative influence of school and peer group supersede those of the family. Graham and Bowling (1995) suggest the following six types of preventive intervention.

1. Strengthening families and supporting good parenting

Utting *et al.* (1993) suggest that this can be delivered through a three-tiered approach, broadly reflecting the targets of the public health analogy to crime prevention:

- 'universal services' for everyone
- 'neighbourhood services' for areas of high social disadvantage and crime
- 'preservation services' aimed at those families in difficulty, who have come to the attention of social services.

As with other aspects of crime prevention, 'universal services' have the advantage of not stigmatising those who receive the service. However, they also have the disadvantage of being the most expensive. 'Preservation services', on the other hand, may be the most focused form of intervention, but yet have the potential for being the most stigmatising. While this kind of crisis intervention may arrive too late in the process, it may also prevent children being taken into care, with all the financial implications and the link between care and crime. According to Utting *et al.* (1993) projects which report success in working with families most 'in difficulty' tend to emphasise the need to raise parental self-esteem and build on existing strengths within the specific family. The most optimistic scenario is that services to support good parenting will set in train a virtuous circle in which the social skills imparted to one generation of children feed into their own parenting when raising the next generation.

Under the Children Act 1989, local authorities have a statutory responsibility to provide services for families and children in need, as well as a duty (under Schedule 2) to take reasonable steps to encourage children not to commit criminal offences. Despite the preventive philosophy of the 1989 Act an Audit Commission Report (1994) suggests that social services departments have found it difficult to move from a reactive 'social policing role', which focuses on child protection cases, towards a more pro-active role which supports families. Furthermore, research shows that the services available remain targeted on families where children are registered 'at risk', limiting work to crisis intervention with suspected child abuse cases (Utting 1995). Many 'preservation services', such as Home-Start – which uses experienced parents as volunteers to visit the homes of families, with pre-school children, who are under stress (see Frost *et al.* 1996) – are more concerned with preventing breakdown and with health, psychological and emotional benefits, rather than the prevention of criminality. There is no real data on such schemes' impact on the prevention of later offending.

2. Strengthening and improving parental supervision

In their self-report study Graham and Bowling (1995: 38) found that while girls aged 14 to 15 were more closely supervised than their male counterparts, for both boys and girls the level of supervision was strongly related to offending. Thirty-two per cent of males and 14 per cent of females who were closely supervised admitted offending, as compared with 53 per cent and 30 per cent respectively of those who were not. They conclude that poor relationships between parents and children can have implications 'which extend beyond the four walls of their homes' (1995: 87). While new parents are provided with preparation for and assistance in the birthing process (through ante-natal classes) there is no mainstream preparation for parenting itself. As Graham and Utting (1996) note, there have been few attempts to develop parent skills education programmes in the UK. Family 'preservation services' intervene where relations between parent and child are already strained. They are in this sense 'eleventh hour' interventions offered on the assumption that the cost will be lower than allowing the next crisis point to be reached (Utting 1996). For example, NEWPIN, which developed from Home-Start, helps parents under stress to feel less isolated by providing local support networks for up to a year. It seeks to alleviate maternal depression and other mental distress while focusing on parent-child relationships and the prevention of emotional abuse.

3. Strengthening schools

Graham (1988) suggests that schools, through their capacity to motivate, to integrate and to offer pupils a sense of achievement regardless of ability, can have a considerable influence on whether or not pupils get involved in crime. Strengthening schools may involve interventions targeted at the 'whole school' and which entail significant organisational change or may be concerned solely with targeting individuals within schools. Various recent government initiatives have sought to address the question of discipline in schools, most notably the Elton Committee which reported in 1989. This led to a government circular on 'Pupil Behaviour and Discipline' (Department of Education circular 8/1994) which has encouraged a 'whole school' approach to behaviour and discipline. However, in practice there have been few attempts to set up and evaluate 'whole school' initiatives in the UK (see the case studies below).

4. Reducing truancy

Research shows that persistent truants are particularly likely to offend. Truancy rates vary widely between individual schools, but it is difficult to determine whether these variations are the product of the schools themselves or their different pupil intakes. In 1993/4 the Department of Education funded more than 80 projects for reducing truancy. Some projects are designed to improve attendance at specific schools as well as to identify good practice. Other projects have focused on improving the technology of registration. However, it seems clear that the involvement of parents in anti-truancy schemes is crucial particularly given the role that parents play in authorised absenteeism and its relationship with unauthorised truancy, as well as the importance of parental supervision noted above.

5. Reducing school exclusions

Exclusion, like truancy, is a key indicator of what the Audit Commission described as 'trouble to come, if corrective action is not taken' (1996: 66). This is supported by the fact that 42 per cent of offenders of school age who are sentenced in the youth court have been excluded from school. The number of permanent exclusions from school increased almost threefold between the years 1991/92 and 1993/94 in the UK (Graham and Bowling 1995: 91). Ironically, the publication by the Department of Education of league tables setting out authorised and unauthorised absenteeism (as well as tables of exam results) intended to curb truancy may have increased pressure on schools to expel children permanently.

6. Family–school partnerships

It is recognised that while the family and the school may have independent influences on propensities towards crime, an integrated approach that links the two major forms of socialisation needs to be developed and sustained. Often a key impediment to closer links between schools and families is apathy or lack of time on the part of parents and resistance to interference on the part of teachers.

Missing from Graham and Bowling's list of 'protective factors' is any mention of leisure and employment opportunities. Both these may have considerable implications for a young person's sense of their own self-worth and personal fulfilment, essential elements in providing a 'stake in conformity'. The absence or presence of such opportunities can also shape and influence peer group pressure – and hence the likelihood of offending. A limited number of such schemes which have been the subject of evaluation exist in Britain (see Utting 1996).

Recent government proposals

In March 1997 the Conservative government published a Green Paper on *Preventing Children Offending* (Home Office 1997c), the principal recommendations of which were widely endorsed and supported by the Labour Party. It was the product of the inter-ministerial Group on Juveniles and sets out a dual approach focusing on children 'at risk' and their parents. It proposed the establishment of 'child crime teams' with operational and supervisory functions, primarily to identify children at risk of offending and refer them to a suitable scheme which may reduce the risk. While it was envisaged that attendance should be voluntary, the consultation document proposed a new court power, a 'parental control order' which would be available in situations where a child, aged 16 and under, had demonstrated behaviour which was, at least, 'likely to lead to offending' (para. 88). The order would make attendance compulsory and a breach of the order would result in a criminal offence for which a non-custodial penalty would be available to the courts.

The current Labour government has taken on board some of the logic of these proposals in the Crime and Disorder Bill, but has shied away from setting up 'child crime teams' with a wholly preventive focus. The 'youth offending teams' (YOTs) which the Bill proposes are primarily concerned with 'desistance' from crime through the development of co-ordinated action plans, rather than the prevention of crime among 'at risk' youth. In the conceptual language the government has opted for 'tertiary prevention' as the essential aim of these teams, rather than 'secondary prevention'. Nevertheless, YOTs may have the scope to develop a more preventive orientation. The consultation document suggested that:

> Youth Offender Teams will, by the nature of their work, be well placed to provide advice and stimulus to the relevant agencies – including the local authority youth service – in respect of the kind of programmes needed to *prevent youth offending*, and perhaps to play some role in such preventative work.
>
> (Home Office 1997d: 8, para. 22, emphasis in original)

The proposed 'parenting orders' and 'child safety orders' do allow for significant secondary prevention to occur. The proposed 'child safety orders' will be available on application by the local authority to the civil court, if one or more of four conditions are satisfied:

- the child has done something that would constitute an offence if they were over ten
- the child's behaviour was such as to suggest they were at risk of offending
- the child's behaviour was disruptive and harassing to local residents
- the child has breached a local child curfew.

The 'child safety order' if established would place the child under the supervision of a responsible officer from the local authority social services department, normally for three months. The requirements of the order would be such as to support the child, protect them from the risk of being drawn into crime and ensure proper care and control. Consequently, the proposals in the Crime and Disorder Bill represent an important, yet tentative, step towards the institutionalisation and promotion of youth crime prevention for 'at risk' groups on a national basis. However, the precise ways in which the YOTs and child safety orders develop in practice remains uncertain.

Case studies of youth prevention

As we have seen policies and programmes have tended to focus on one or more sites of socialising influences: the family, school or peer group. The case studies reflect this.

High/Scope Perry Pre-School Project

One of the best-known American social crime prevention programmes is a long-standing scheme in a disadvantaged community in Ypsilanti,

Michigan. The Perry Pre-School Project sought early intervention for children at risk of impaired cognitive development and early failure in school through a special child care programme for children aged between three and five years old, who had been identified as 'at risk' of entering into criminality because of the situation of their parents. Originally it was started on an experimental basis when in 1962 the project randomly allocated 123 Black children from low socio-economic backgrounds, approximately half to a pre-school child development programme and the other half to a control group. The scheme ran in most cases for two years, operated by High/Scope, an educational charity. It involved the establishment of a highly structured pre-school educational programme which gave children more chance to choose their own activities (Berrueta-Clement *et al.* 1984). In addition to enrolling them for a few hours a day in a 'cognitive enrichment' programme, the project also visited the children's homes and worked with the parents on a variety of child-rearing and survival issues. The evaluation compared the long-term results of the group in the programme against the control group, following the children through to the age of 27. Adults who had been on the programme had significantly fewer arrests by the time they were 27. About 7 per cent had been arrested five times or more, a fifth of the rate of the control group (Schweinhart *et al.* 1993: 16). A similar percentage had been arrested for drug use or dealing as compared with 25 per cent of the control group. The evaluation also pointed to reductions in illiteracy, a failure to finish school and a reliance on welfare. Similarly, it identified significantly greater earning and home ownership among the programme group. The President of High/Scope commented on the apparent success of the project: 'we have almost a different social class emerging as a result of participation' (cited in Meikle 1993). The US senate has evaluated this to be a saving of $5 in welfare and criminal justice costs for every $1 invested in the programme. Although the Perry programme is only one study based on relatively small numbers, other Head Start projects from around America and elsewhere do appear to confirm the Perry findings.

Recently, the High/Scope approach has begun to be implemented in four pre-school sites in Britain through the Young Children First project (Santer 1996). However, some British commentators have doubted whether the Perry Pre-School programme would have the same impact on 'life chances' in the UK. It has also been suggested that there may have been contributing factors to produce such impressive outcomes, including the possibility of a 'continuity of interest' that the research maintained among families included in the experimental group (Graham and Utting 1996: 390).

Preventing bullying in schools

Bullying is seen as a problem in its own right within schools. It is also viewed as an indicator of wider problems, including an inadequate school culture, pupil–teacher mistrust and the existence of violent delinquent subcultures. Pitts and Smith (1995) report on an attempt to tackle bullying in four schools (two primary and two secondary) in two deprived inner-city areas of Liverpool and London, funded by the Home Office. The aims were to raise awareness about bullying, improve monitoring and supervision and maximise the support for victims and the involvement of those within and outside the school in the prevention of bullying. The programme adopted a 'whole school' approach. The target of the intervention was the organisational culture of the four schools. Hence, the specific strategies employed in each school varied slightly as each school had a different culture. The principal elements of the programme included:

- improved supervision and surveillance of play areas
- confidential contact for victims and others concerning bullying
- meetings about bullying between staff and parents
- class rules against bullying
- role-playing and literature to highlight the impact of bullying
- formal confrontations of pupils who bully
- encouragement of 'neutral' pupils to assist
- discussion groups for parents of pupils who bully or are bullied.

Within two years the levels of bullying had significantly decreased in three out of the four schools and had remained about the same in the fourth school. The programme appears to have had the most significant impact on the primary schools. In one of them, according to the researchers, the reduction in bullying seems to have been related to an increased willingness of teaching and ancillary staff to intervene in bullying incidents, whereas in the other it appears to have been the result of increased confidence to report bullying. Nevertheless, in both cases reductions seem to have been reliant on a shared perception by adults and children about the type of behaviour which should and should not be tolerated (Pitts and Smith 1995: 33).

The lack of a reduction in bullying in one of the secondary schools highlights a number of countervailing forces which may have undermined any benefit arising from the programme. These largely related to conflicts in the wider community spilling over into the school. Racial and group tensions which often 'demanded' allegiance infused the school environment. The implication is that schools reflect the wider culture and social conflicts which surround them. The school, rather like the family, does not exist in a vacuum. Prevention work therefore is forced to recognise and work with, or else be undermined by, these wider forces.

Dalston Youth Project

The Dalston Youth Project in east London draws on an American programme which was brought to England in 1990 by the 'Youth at Risk'

(YAR) organisation. The programme brings together young people, between the ages of 15 and 18, at serious risk of offending, as well as those who have embarked on a criminal career. The aim of YAR has been to allow young people to stop and see the direction in which their life is heading and to help them to turn around their lives towards positive goals to which they commit themselves. These goals are usually related to education, training and employment as well as personal development. The methodology of the programme involves:

- the recruitment of local 'volunteers' and young people 'at risk'
- an intensive week-long residential course, held outside the area, usually at a remote countryside location
- an education and training component to provide some skills
- matching individual youths with a volunteer 'mentor' to provide long-term support.

The Dalston Project, established in 1994, has supplemented the YAR approach through the addition of an 'educational' component. Youths are given an eight-week 'college taster'. In Dalston, the education and mentoring scheme is managed by Crime Concern in partnership with Hackney Council, the police and the probation service (Bright 1996). The idea is that the intensive residential course encourages the young people, both individually and collectively, to examine their own lives. Lecture-room work is supplemented by outdoor activities designed to develop mutual confidence, co-operation and trust. The young people are encouraged to commit themselves to 'goals' designed to improve their lives. The volunteer mentor helps the young person to monitor progress and discuss difficulties. The Dalston Project is currently the subject of research evaluation. Although it is still early days, initial indicators suggest that those who have experienced the programme had found it a useful experience and that a year after the Project's first cohort arrest figures had dropped by 61 per cent and more than half of the young people were in full-time education, employment or training (Burgin 1997). The initial evaluation judged the project to be cost-effective.

Criminality prevention – some issues

Early intervention – how early?

Crime prevention through early intervention into the development of young people, on the basis of identified 'risk factors', raises a number of issues. First, there is a logic within such an approach to seek ever earlier forms of intervention. Ideas of 'nipping it in the bud' push criminological concern further and further into child – and even foetal – development. This, in turn, leads to a second dynamic which is to identify ever more distant 'risk factors' which may (or may not) be linked through association with other 'risk factors'. Hence, researchers are encouraged to develop looser and looser 'chains' of 'risk factors', whereby, for example, A may lead to B which in turn is an indicator of C which is prevalent in a high percentage of known offenders. The impact of this logic is to extend the lens of criminological enquiry and to 'widen the net' of social control (Cohen 1985), as intervention is dispersed deeper and deeper into the social fabric. Third, as decades of criminological research have shown, early intervention carries with it the danger of labelling and stigmatisation (Becker 1963). Where individuals or groups are singled out for intervention they can become tainted by that very process. Moreover, stigmatisation and labelling can produce the seeds of a self-fulfilling prophecy. However, as Braithwaite (1989) has shown, sigmatisation is not an inevitable outcome of intervention and the degree of labelling may itself depend on the specific nature of the programme.

Finally, intervention with 'at risk' youths entails estimates of future behaviour on the basis of prediction. 'At risk' categories premised on 'aggregates' and 'statistical distributions' will always be inexact. Calculations of future risks can only ever involve probabilities. Hence, they will include individuals for whom prediction is inaccurate, euphemistically referred to as 'false positives'.[1] This raises certain ethical issues for early interventions which depend on the predictive accuracy of the factors identified. The broader and more inclusive an intervention, the probability is that it will include more 'false positives', with implications both for cost (the wider a service is spread the more it will cost) and stigmatisation (incorporating more people, albeit at a diluted level). If interventions are narrowly targeted there is an increased likelihood of stigmatisation as only specific individuals are singled out for special attention. Moreover, there may be an increased likelihood of programme failure, as the most extreme groups may be the most resistant to intervention and the hardest to turn around. If this is the case, there may be greater benefits to be had from deliberately not targeting the most in need. The difficult question, therefore, is how to intervene early, before risk factors or anti-social behaviour are too established or ingrained – but not too early so that risk factors are poor predictors of anti-social outcomes, thus producing more 'false positives' (Tonry and Farrington 1995a: 12). And yet early intervention may offer a means of targeting scarce resources at those who are most in need.

Crime and social policy

As we have seen, 'social crime prevention' remains particularly ill-defined. As a term it is essentially elastic. In some instances, it is taken to mean any activity or intervention into the social world which may improve people's quality of life or which may have some beneficial impact on the intended subjects, such that they may be less inclined to commit crime.

The exact mechanisms through which it is assumed that a particular intervention has such an impact are rarely specified. This is not to argue against social crime prevention *per se*, but rather to argue for clarity in policies and practice as to the causal relationships between interventions, their mechanisms and intended outcomes. Without this, crime prevention can become a metaphor for a variety of other social ills and practice can become enmeshed in a diversity of social issues. This poses two fundamental questions about the relationship between crime and social policy:

- where does, or should, one end and the other begin?
- is it appropriate to justify social policy by reference to its (potential) crime preventive qualities?

Some programmes referred to as 'social crime prevention' are more appropriately social welfare, education or health matters, albeit that they *may* have implications for crime and its prevention. In contemporary policy discourse crime prevention appears to have become a new reference through which to legitimise policies which otherwise would have had more limited but specific goals, such as improvements in employment opportunities and educational or health standards, or the reduction of inequality.

Consequently, there is a genuine anxiety that the high degree of influence given to *crime* prevention – as opposed to poverty prevention, for example – may result in social policy, its direction and funding being redefined in terms of its implications for crime. A potential consequence of according to crime a central place in the construction of social order is that fundamental public issues may become marginalised, except in so far as they are defined in terms of their crimogenic qualities. The danger is that, as a consequence, we may come to view poor housing, unemployment, poor schooling, the lack of youth leisure opportunities and so on as no longer important public issues in themselves. Rather, their importance may become increasingly seen to derive from the belief that they lead to crime and disorder. The fact that they may do so is no reason not to assert their importance in their own right. After all, there are other things which are more important than crime prevention. The fear is that social deficiencies may be redefined as 'crime problems' which need to be controlled and managed, rather than addressed in themselves. This would represent the ultimate 'criminalisation of social policy'. And yet, as the boundaries between social policy and crime prevention become more blurred, we could argue for the potential development of an inverse relationship – the 'socialisation of criminal policy' – whereby the traditional direction and funding of criminal policy is re-oriented towards proactive prevention through social welfare.

However, the experience of social crime prevention in Britain to date has been extremely limited. International experiences, from countries in which a greater emphasis has been placed on social crime prevention (see Chapter 7), suggest that crime prevention can either become so diffused within social policy – notably urban regeneration policy as in France – as to lose any distinctive identity, or it can begin to capture social policy such that it is dominated by criminological concerns. This tension imposes a considerable responsibility on central government to provide clear guidance as to the boundaries of, and relationship between, crime prevention activity and social policy. If this guidance is not forth-coming, then these dangers become more likely as government depart-ments as well as statutory and voluntary agencies scramble for their 'piece of the cake'. Hence, it falls to central government bodies to identify the responsibilities of different departments and organisations and to assess the resource implications.

Mainstream versus peripheral funding

The often quoted phrase that crime prevention and community safety work transcend the competency of any one particular organisation rep-resents an Achilles heel as well as an attraction. The danger is that dedicated crime prevention and community safety initiatives can be left to pick up the pieces that are no longer provided by mainstream services and funding. As a consequence, some programmes strive hard not to be dragged into the work which other agencies might otherwise have done and often for which schemes were not initially established. As organisa-tions are encouraged to focus on their 'core tasks', social prevention projects can be left to catch those that fall 'between the cracks', thus replacing mainstream services with often poorly funded, short-term or project-driven and peripheral services. Perversely, in order to secure fund-ing some schemes can be forced to take on board much harder (and more serious) cases than they were ever intended or designed to do. The intentions of 'early intervention' behind some prevention programmes can be undermined by external agencies dumping their hardest cases on such projects. Hence, they can get sucked deeper into the social control 'net'. Resisting such pressures can be difficult, particularly in the early life of a programme. This can have serious adverse implications for the evaluation and success of such projects.

Due to the fact that the responsibility for crime prevention is diffused throughout various organisations and agencies, the question of fund-ing has serious implications for the long-term viability and durability of social crime prevention. It appears less to be the case, in Britain as around the world, that there are not enough imaginative ideas and projects – on the contrary the notions behind many of the innovative projects have been around for some time – but rather that there is not the durable and long-term funding to sustain them beyond an initial phase of project work. In this light, what is the use of setting up a new crime prevention project, which may be shown to be highly effective, if the lessons of that initiative are not incorporated into mainstream organisational practice and hence long-term funding? This is demonstrably illustrated by the

High/Scope Pre-School Project. Why have the lessons of Perry not been taken up throughout the American educational system, instead of only affecting a few hundred individuals in limited areas of the USA? The answer, unsurprisingly, lies in and around issues of funding. If social policies are important because of their crime preventive implications then who, in the long-term, should be funding such projects as part of mainstream, everyday practice? If these policies are no longer to be justified solely in terms of their educational implication and importance, then why should the education system fund them? The crux of the problem is that in this new-found era of 'crime as everybody's problem', responsibility has become so diffused as to no longer reside anywhere in particular, with all the problems for funding to which that gives rise.

Social crime prevention in the US and UK

Given the relationship between social crime prevention programmes and the nature of, or inadequacies evident within, social policy, it is important to clarify some significant differences between the USA and British contexts. This is important both because the USA has been the origin and inspiration of many British social and developmental crime prevention initiatives and because of the very different constitutional, cultural, social and economic histories of the two countries. Social policy has a very different meaning in the USA, where the history of state welfarism is particularly limited compared to the European tradition which Britain shares. Hence, in the USA the relative lack of 'mainstream state provided' social services leaves a considerable vacuum to be filled by 'targeted programmes' such as those sometimes provided under the label of crime prevention.

The crime problem in Britain and the USA is significantly different in important respects. Anglo-American criminology is interwoven, sharing greater similarities than it does differences. The 'Americanisation of the British criminal justice policy' more generally has become an issue of significant importance in its own right, yet the two countries have very different homicide and incarceration rates. In relation to the former, the number of homicides in the city of Los Angeles (849 in 1995) is greater than the number throughout the whole of England and Wales (746 in 1995). The population of Los Angeles is 3.5 million as compared with over 50 million in England and Wales. The number of people in prison in the USA in 1993 was about 400 per 100 000 – this figure rises to 530 per 100 000 in Texas and the District of Columbia, excluding local jails – as compared to 89 per 100 000 in England and Wales (Home Office 1995b: 53). More significantly, this figure hides a dramatic concentration among particular social groups so that, for example, it is estimated that in any given year one in three Black men aged 20–29 is 'under the control' of the criminal justice system: in other words, in prison or jail, on probation or on parole (Mauer 1997). In California the figure is about four in ten. Black people now make up 50 per cent of the prison population compared to 20 per cent two decades ago. While the USA has been the home of some of the most interesting developments in crime prevention, it has become one of the world's most punitive nations, currently engaged in what can only be described as an extensive experiment in mass incarceration, the social impact of which is still unclear.

Community-focused preventive measures

One of the recurring critiques of individual-based preventive strategies is that through their individualistic focus they fail to address the wider communal or social context in which offending occurs and in which it is sustained. Criminological research has repeatedly shown that the crime rate within a given area – or 'community' – may be the result of something more than merely the sum total of individual criminal propensities. This suggests that there is something about a 'community' which itself shapes and influences rates of crime. This has focused attention on the level of 'community' as a potentially appropriate vehicle for crime prevention.

Weiss (1987), analysing latent assumptions about 'community' embodied in different forms of community safety and community-based crime prevention programmes,[2] identified the importance of two notions: first, the idea that community members be given a 'stake in conformity'; and second, the construction of 'informal control'. In a slightly different vein Graham and Bennett (1995) identify three distinctive approaches to community-based crime prevention: community organisation, community defence and community development. However, it is difficult to disentangle the first from the last. 'Community organisation' and 'community development', as we shall see, are often used interchangeably and are premised on similar assumptions. Hope (1995a), by contrast, suggests that over time the concept of 'community' in crime prevention has been informed by three different paradigms with their roots in different eras of urban development: the 'disorganised community' of the first half of this century; the 'disadvantaged community' of the 1960s and 1970s; and the 'frightened community' of the 1980s and 1990s. Drawing on all of these, I review community-based approaches under the following six headings:

* the mobilisation of individuals and resources
* community organisation
* community defence
* resident involvement
* intermediate institutions
* the political economy of community.

However, it is worth sounding an initial note of caution. Much that passes for community-based crime prevention is untheorised, ill-considered and inconsistent. Hence, as Hope notes, various forms of community crime prevention need to be interpreted 'not only as applications of criminological theory, but also as complex pieces of socio-political action that also have a defining ideological and ethical character' (1995a: 22). As a consequence, in presenting six discrete headings there is a danger of giving a false clarity and distinctiveness to the reality of practice which is often blurred and confused.

The mobilisation of individuals and resources

Much that passes for community crime prevention has very little to do with communities as collective entities, but rather is concerned with *aggregates* of individuals or households. This type of community strategy is really a form of 'collective individualism', often involving interventions or initiatives aimed at individuals but given the gloss of 'community' rhetoric. Hope and Shaw rightly note that while 'there is nothing intrinsically communal' about much crime prevention, 'its implementation often demands a focus upon residential communities' (1988b: 8). They go on to suggest that, for the purposes of the implementation of crime prevention, the concept of 'community' plays a dual role. First, it can be used to identify areas in which collective risks are perceived to be high, thus facilitating targeted action. Second, it is an appropriate level at which to encourage individual involvement. 'Involving communities,' they suggest, 'also seems a promising way of reaching ordinary people and encouraging them to adopt protective measures' (Hope and Shaw 1988a: 8). The kinds of advice offered may be concerned with protecting the individual from victimisation or with protecting the household from theft or damage. As such, it is aimed at affecting individual behaviour or securing specific alterations to property, but is not primarily concerned with transforming social or group relations. Reference to community level interventions does not necessarily imply a macrosociological perspective (Sampson 1987: 97). For example, the 'Communities that Care' programme which has recently been imported into the UK from the USA with the support of the Joseph Rowntree Foundation is in essence an individual 'risk and protection focused programme' which seeks to address aggregate risk within a given neighbourhood (see Farrington 1996).

In reality, therefore, 'community' often means little more than the sum total of individuals living within a given locality. Influenced by neo-liberal ideology, 'community' is often seen as merely the outcome of market processes, whereby individuals make reasoned decisions about whether to participate or not, premised on what is in their own private interests. Hence, the appropriate unit of analysis here is not the 'community' as an entity in itself, but rather individual actors and their rational choices. This model returns us to the ideological underpinnings of situational crime prevention as reviewed in the previous chapter.

Community crime prevention strategies may also be concerned with tapping the material and financial resources within a given neighbourhood. The logic here connects with neo-liberal critiques of the state. Such a perspective sets out from the premise that governments have overreached themselves in terms of what is possible and desirable, through programmes of social engineering. The state, it is argued, is not only a heavy financial burden on taxpayers, but is also an inefficient and insensitive tool of intervention. The modern welfare state has destroyed the conditions for the exercise of individual responsibility, while simultaneously undermining initiative and enterprise. It has also destroyed older forms of social support, such as voluntary associations, charities, churches, communities and even families (Dennis and Erdos 1992). In its place, the state has created a morally damaging 'culture of dependency' (Murray 1990) which has encouraged values of passivity and irresponsibility, as well as denying choice. The solution, for neo-liberal commentators, lies in the abandonment of overarching social and welfare programmes, the transfer of greater individual and collective responsibility for services traditionally provided by the state and the freeing of market forces in order to allow individuals and groups to exercise their responsibility.

Hence, for neo-liberals 'community' has become a metaphor for 'rolling back' the state and 'freeing up' collective voluntarism and entrepreneurship (Herrnstein and Murray 1994: 536–40). As social provisions are liberated to markets and forms of 'enterprise', so 'autonomy', 'self-help' and 'choice' are assumed to re-enter the spaces vacated by the state. The 'community' constitutes an acceptable collective imagery for activating and responsibilising individuals. Strategies which conform to this kind of analysis are often referred to in American literature as 'citizen' crime prevention, but might more accurately be described as 'consumerist' crime prevention.

Community organisation

Underlying policy initiatives around community crime prevention is the prevailing idea that crime results from a failure or breakdown of community life. This degeneration is traditionally associated with a failure of processes of communal socialisation and informal social control. The theoretical underpinnings of this approach owe much to Chicago School sociologists' notions of 'social disorganisation', particularly as developed by Clifford Shaw and Henry McKay. Drawing on rich (quantitative and qualitative) empirical data from Chicago in the 1930s, Shaw and McKay (1942) mapped the spatial and temporal relations of people within the city, as well as the residence of known delinquents. Urban development, they argued, is socially patterned. To explain this they drew on Burgess's 'zonal theory' (1928), in which he had suggested that cities tend to expand radially from the centre, such that the typical city could be seen as consisting of a series of concentric circles marked by five zones. At the centre lay the business district (or 'loop'), essentially a non-residential area. This was encircled by a 'zone in transition' which in turn was surrounded by a 'zone of working men's homes', then a 'residential zone' and finally a 'commuters' zone'. For Shaw and McKay this picture was confirmed by their research findings that recorded rates of delinquency, which follow broadly uniform patterns, are highest in the areas adjacent to the central business district and decrease with distance from the centre. High delinquency rates were found in the same areas over long periods of time despite the turnover of population. This led them to believe that the crimogenic factors must be located in the environment not the people, for as the people moved out to suburban areas so their delinquency rates declined. This led Shaw and McKay to ask: what is it about certain areas – notably the 'zone in transition' – which produces delinquency and allows it to be 'culturally transmitted' from one generation of occupants to the next?

Shaw and McKay turned to ecological theories for their explanation. It is within the 'zone in transition' that the processes of 'invasion, dominance and succession' are apparent, as new immigrants move into the cheapest residential areas of the city just outside the business district. As this occurs, older and more economically established residents migrate outwards. The process resembles the ripples created by dropping a stone into a still pond. The further out from the centre, the less the effects of this process of transition are felt and the more stable relations remain. The high turnover of residents in the 'zone in transition', particularly in a rapidly expanding city like Chicago in the 1920s and 1930s, produces economic mobility, constant population movements and hence instability. The constant turnover of residents restricted people from exerting informal social control over others in the area.

Social control here is taken to mean the ability of a community to realise common values, the lack of which is the underlying cause of delinquency. Social disorganisation as an explanation of delinquency points to the weakness within the structure and culture of a community, such that the community and allied institutions of informal social control are ineffective as 'socialising agents'. Thus, cultural heterogeneity and constant population movement were seen as processes which weaken family and communal ties that bind people together, resulting in social disorganisation. The weakening of social controls makes possible delinquent careers, as offenders could act with some degree of impunity. Thus social disorganisation is the absence or weakness of 'normal' social controls within 'natural' communities. Hence, Kornhauser (1978) concludes that Shaw and McKay's theory is basically a community-level 'control' theory.

For Shaw and McKay the implication of 'social disorganisation' meant that solutions lay in the physical renewal of community institutions and the regeneration of a 'sense of community'. Community reorganisation, from this viewpoint, acts to counter the processes which produce disorganisation, on the presupposition that it is an inherent capacity of communities to mobilise their own resources of social control. By strengthening community institutions, it was anticipated that the primacy of the normative law-abiding consensus of the community will be asserted. This was the aim of the Chicago Area Projects (CAP), founded in 1931, which were born directly out of the work of Shaw and McKay. Initiated by Shaw in a number of areas of Chicago, the CAP sought to work with residents to build a sense of pride and community and thus encourage people to stay within the areas and exert control over other residents, particularly the young. The CAP used a variety of methods including recreation for children, educational projects, outreach work with delinquent gang members and, more broadly, the generation of community support through the use of volunteers and existing neighbourhood institutions (Schlossman and Sedlak 1983). The CAP has been the model and inspiration for many of the 'community organisation' and 'community development' programmes ever since.

Criticisms of the Chicago School, in particular of Shaw and McKay, have been wide-ranging and varied (see Baldwin 1979; Heathcote 1981; Vold and Bernard 1986; Lilly *et al.* 1995). British 'areal studies' showed that British cities do not conform to the Chicago image of concentric zones (Bottoms 1994). The most significant criticisms have focused on the notion of an 'ecological fallacy', that it is wrong to assume there is any correspondence between the properties of areas and the properties of individuals or groups that live in an area. This raises the question, to what extent do slum areas produce delinquents, or on the other hand, do delinquents drift and gravitate towards such areas? The influence of ecological theory produced a deterministic bias which not only seemed to suggest that certain territorial places produce crime (a fore-runner of the architectural determinism we confronted in Chapter 3) but also appears to be overpredictive of crime. A further criticism relates to the failure of Shaw and McKay to significantly consider the role of powerful external forces which shape, and/or undermine the power of communities, notably big business and property interests (Snodgrass 1976) and the role of (local authority) housing allocation policies (Bottoms and Wiles 1986). These wider economic and political power relations can create slum areas or allow them to perpetuate. Criticisms have also pointed to the fact that their data relied on official statistics and was based on offender rates (i.e. the number of known offenders living within an area) rather than offence rates (i.e. the number of known offences committed within an area). Despite 50 years of the CAPs they have provided little evidence of 'success' (Schlossman and Sedlak 1983).

However, the most troubling and persistent problem with Chicago School theories of social disorganisation is the way in which it constructed and perpetuated the notion of the 'pathological community'. In criminological terms it represented a shift from individual pathology (associated with analytic individualism of early positivist theories) to communal or group pathology. It remained trapped in the Durkheimian embrace of separating out the 'normal' from the 'pathological'. It implies that disorganised communities are inhabited by immigrant residents who had failed to adjust to urban values. As a consequence, it inevitably touches on questions of family and race. Those who failed economically to move out of the 'zone in transition' to the more stable (and affluent) peripheries were seen to be trapped by their own cultural inadequacies.

It is assumed that what 'disorganised communities' need is more 'community'. Put another way, there is a relationship between a lack of 'community' and the existence of high levels of crime. However, there is much criminological evidence to suggest that 'organised communities' are crimogenic, such as the Mafia (noticeably absent from Chicago School theory despite its heightened activity caused by the prohibition in Chicago of the 1920s and 1930s), criminal gangs, football hooligans and deviant subcultures. And yet over half a century later, social disorganisation theories of the Chicago School maintain an enduring hold, both explicitly and implicitly, over community crime prevention (Sampson and Groves 1989).

What is more, as Hope (1995a: 22) rightly notes, any assessment of the development of community crime prevention needs to comprehend the changing nature of the crime problem in the urban environment. The current dominant process within cities, both in the USA and Britain, is not one of urbanisation and growth, as it was in Chicago in the 1930s, but is a fundamentally different process of 'de-urbanisation' or 'counter-urbanisation', through which cities are losing populations to more suburban and rural areas. The flight from Britain's metropolitan areas between 1981 and 1994 is estimated to be one and a quarter million more people leaving than arriving, equivalent to a net migration loss of 90 000 a year. For example, in inner London between 1990 and 1991 the population fell by 31 000 or 1.24 per cent because of migration (Champion *et al.* 1996). Shifts in community crime prevention paradigms reflect changes to, and perceptions of, crime problems within urban areas. De-urbanisation has tended to highlight the problem of the fragmentation and disintegration of the city, rather than the idea of the city as a united 'super-organism' in the throws of growth, on which the Chicago School's ideas of community organisation were premised.

Community defence: the 'broken windows' thesis

With the revival of interest in the relationship between areas and high offence rates, rather than high offender rates as had been the concern of the Chicago School, attention began to focus on places that seemed to attract a high degree of crime, particularly 'problem estates' and 'hot spots' of crime. As well as asking questions about architecture and environmental design, as reviewed in Chapter 3, criminologists began to ask, what is it about the social relations within particular places which may encourage crime? Why are some communities more crimogenic than others? Is there something intrinsic about a community or place which attracts criminality, or at least allows it to flourish? This led to further questioning about communities in terms of their perception and use by people. How do certain areas or estates gain a reputation for crime? Does the reputation gained have an 'amplifying' effect on the levels of crime? What are the 'tipping processes' involved in the production of high crime areas or estates?

In addressing these kinds of questions Wilson and Kelling (1982) developed their 'broken windows' thesis, implicitly reworking certain assumptions about social disorganisation. Wilson and Kelling's short paper outlining their theory has become one of the most widely cited and influential contributions to debates about communities, informal social control and crime prevention. In it they argue that minor incivilities – such as vandalism, graffiti, rowdy behaviour, drunkenness and begging – if unchecked and uncontrolled will set in train a series of linked social responses, as a result of which 'decent' and 'nice' neighbourhoods can 'tip' into fearful ghettos of crime. 'Untended' property and behaviour , they argue, produces a breakdown of community controls by a spiralling process which feeds off and reinforces itself, whereby incivilities lead to fear which leads to avoidance, withdrawal and flight by local residents. This in turn leads to reduced informal social control which results in more serious crime, which leads to increased fear and so on. As the neighbourhood declines, so disorder, fear and crime spiral upwards. As a consequence,

> [a] stable neighbourhood of families who care for their homes, mind each other's children, and confidently frown on unwanted intruders can change, in a few years or even a few months, to an inhospitable jungle. A piece of property is abandoned, weeds grow up, a window is smashed. Adults stop scolding rowdy children; the children, emboldened, become more rowdy. Families move out, unattached adults move in. Teenagers gather in front of the corner store. The merchant asks them to move; they refuse. Fights occur. Litter accumulates. People start drinking in front of the grocery; in time, an inebriate slumps to the sidewalk and is allowed to sleep it off.
> (Wilson and Kelling 1982: 31–2)

Here, Wilson and Kelling evocatively describe the important beginnings of the 'tipping' process. The pre-eminent indicator of decline, therefore, is the growth of incivilities, rather than crime itself. It is incivilities which act as the crucial catalyst. They represent signs of disorder and signify that 'no one cares', that the environment is 'uncontrolled and uncontrollable' and that 'anyone can invade it to do whatever damage and mischief the mind suggests' (1982: 33). Disorder, it is argued, violates a community's expectations of what constitutes appropriate civil behaviour (Kelling 1987: 90).

Wilson and Kelling's solution is to stop and reverse the 'cycle of decline' in its earliest stages by a focus on policing through 'order maintenance' and the aggressive policing of incivilities and other 'signs of crime'. What is deemed necessary, therefore, is for the community to reassert its 'natural forces' of authority and control, to show it 'cares' through early intervention in disorderly conduct. In support of this what is needed is to restore to the police the primary task of maintaining order rather than 'law enforcement' in a reactive mode. Hence, the police should not be judged solely on their ability as 'crime fighters', but rather priority should be given to their role in maintaining order.

> The essence of the police role in maintaining order is to reinforce the informal control mechanisms of the community itself. The police cannot, without committing extraordinary resources, provide a substitute for that informal control.
>
> (Wilson and Kelling 1982: 34)

The role of the police, therefore, is to support a community's political and moral authority. In order to do so, however, the police must accommodate those 'natural forces'. This should allow local residents to feel less fearful, as incivilities and signs of crime are removed, and enable the community to reassert its moral order and social control.

Social control here is understood both as forms of surveillance by residents over their environment which may lead to intervention by themselves or by calling in others and the idea of a community regulating its members and upholding its own norms of conduct. The focus of concern encourages a concentration of effort in communities and areas most prone to 'tipping' into spirals of disorder, where 'public order is deteriorating but not unreclaimable'. Where action is needed most, it appears, is where there is growing incivility but not yet high levels of crime. By implication high crime areas represent 'irredeemable' communities which can be written off as beyond salvation.

The main thrust of the 'broken windows' thesis is concerned with identifying the problem of urban decline, fear of crime and criminality. However, Wilson and Kelling's thesis has also found favour for its implied solutions. First, the need to allow and encourage communities to reassert their own moral order and shape behaviour has found favour among community activists and 'communitarians' such as Etzioni (1993, 1997), whose work has been highly influential on the British Labour leadership (see Crawford 1996). Second, the need to link informal and formal systems of control more coherently, such that the former supports and assists the latter, has been seen as confirming the arguments of supporters of community policing (Greene and Mastrofski 1988), as well as those arguing for greater police accountability (Kinsey et al. 1986). Third, the thesis implies that the police, through a focus on order maintenance, can 'make a difference'. As such it has found support among police officers and some police managers in search of a 'police solution', particularly in the modern era in which the inability of the police alone to solve the problems of crime has been continually asserted as the police have been encouraged into 'partnerships' with other agencies (see Chapter 5). Finally, it has a distinct commonsense appeal: it speaks to people's real experiences and concerns about crime, particularly those living in inner-city areas, in a way that takes them seriously. It also connects with the apparently insatiable demand of the public, identified in survey after survey, for more visible police patrols (Skogan 1996a).

Wilson and Kelling's thesis is essentially one of 'community defence' in that it envisages the community – its traditional moral authority – as under attack in a number of ways. First, it is under attack from values of 'disorder' which threaten to push it into a spiral of decline. Second, it is explicitly seen as under attack from 'outsiders'. In their article Wilson and Kelling deliberately distinguish between 'regulars' and 'strangers', and it is the latter which presents specific threats. Where disorder is represented by people living within the community they are presented as 'internal outsiders', notably unruly youths and marginal people who need to be cleared from public places. Hence, restoring order is in large part associated with defending community from external invasion. It assumes a definition of community as both a shared locality – in purely territorial terms – and a shared concern or 'sense of community'. It starts from the premise that mere proximity generates – or should generate – shared concern and goes on to propose that the combination of individual actions and behaviour, together with informal social processes of control to which those acts give rise, will help reconstitute and reassemble a 'sense of community'. And yet neighbourliness does not necessarily include sufficient control mechanisms to prevent crime or anti-social activity.

Despite its attractions, it is questionable whether the 'broken windows' thesis works empirically. The thesis assumes a causal relationship between incivilities, fear, a breakdown of informal social control – in other words a lack of 'community' – and the existence of high levels of crime. However, the existence of any of the various links is empirically dubious. For example, Taylor's (1997) research data from Minneapolis-St. Paul challenges the assumption that signs of incivility (particularly physical signs) influence crime and fear of crime in any simplistic manner. 'Broken windows' and incivilities do not necessarily have the same effects in different neighbourhoods. Contrary to Wilson and Kelling's model, crime does not have a uniform impact on community life. The way communities perceive crime and other social problems will often be mediated by the political and social resources available to that community (Lewis and Salem 1986). Much research also suggests that criminal victimisation is a better predictor of fear of crime than non-criminal incivilities (Maxfield 1987; Crawford et al. 1990).

Research into the relationship between crime, fear of crime and the inverse of urban degeneration, namely gentrification, provides a more complex picture. The 'broken window' thesis would suggest that gentrification – whereby more affluent residents move into an area – should occur in areas with low levels of incivilities, and that high levels of incivilities should be an impediment to gentrification. However, research seems to confound this assumption. For example, Taylor and Covington (1988) found that gentrifying areas suffer increasing violence during the process of change. It would appear that high levels of incivilities and crime are not a barrier to gentrification (McDonald 1986).

Within the 'broken window' thesis, community disorder and degeneration are identified as both the social cause and the effect of crime and the fear of crime. Crime is the product of disorderly communities and, at the same time, it is disorderly communities which create the conditions for crime to flourish. 'Order maintenance' is both a means to an end and an end in itself. In the seduction of this spiralling process, means and ends, as well as cause and effect, become badly confused. In this confusion, the 'pathological community' is reinvented in a more vicious guise. Communities that allow themselves to 'tip' into urban decline, by failing to show that 'someone cares', have only themselves to blame. The authors of disorder – the marginalised youths, beggars, vagrants, drug abusers and prostitutes – are identified as the architects of neighbourhood change and economic decline, rather than as its victims.

'Order maintenance' is controversial, a point which Kelling recognises (1987: 94–5), precisely because there are no clear and consistent definitions of what constitutes disorder and because the legal justification for police intervention is unclear. Many behaviours which may create disorder are not illegal and, by contrast, some incivilities are actually covered by criminal legislation. Hence, 'order maintenance', as Kinsey et al. (1986: 85) argue, is 'something of an ideological category'. The implication, they suggest, is that:

> By creating a false distinction, Wilson and Kelling take the pressure off criticism of the police for low crime clear-up, while at the same time justifying the extension of police control into any area of behaviour regarded as 'deviant' by the passing police officer.
>
> (1986: 86)

Wilson and Kelling also fail to acknowledge the absence of consensus about precisely what 'disorder' constitutes. This in turn raises the further crucial question: whose definition of 'order' should be accorded priority? The police officer's or the community's? And if the latter, which community or whose community? As Matthews (1992c: 35) notes, many of the communities where incivilities are common are marked by a general lack of consensus and in this context the police may have no unequivocal or clear mandate. Rather, they may come to be seen as acting on behalf of one section of the community and against others.

As far as Wilson and Kelling are concerned the moral argument – that community expectations of order are more fundamental than a liberal emphasis on due process and individual legal rights – should always triumph. As well as raising serious questions about civil liberties, this also poses fundamental concerns about the possible effectiveness of aggressive public order policing. The danger is that it will alienate precisely those sections of the community most likely to provide a 'flow of information' to the police about illegal activities. Paradoxically, as Kinsey *et al.* conclude, Wilson and Kelling's 'recipe for order would, in fact, increase disorder and disaffection from the law' (1986: 85).

Nevertheless, Wilson and Kelling's contentions about 'the link between order maintenance and crime prevention' (1982: 34) has assumed a powerful grip over contemporary community crime prevention. In so doing, they have successfully managed to revive interest in the 'community' as a specific unit of analysis and, more particularly, in its pivotal role in exerting moral authority. Hence, they have helped to re-orientate debate away from a sole focus on formal systems of control towards, first, the intrinsic power and dynamism of informal social control, and second, the relations between informal and formal forces of authority.

Communitarians such as Etzioni have developed on Wilson and Kelling's ideas, arguing for the need to revive the moral authority of communities and calling for a greater emphasis on social responsibilities rather than individual rights. A key aspect of 'community' as a form of informal social control, he argues, is its ability to transmit norms and regulate behaviour, in other words, to mould compliance through suasion.

> Communities speak to us in moral voices. They lay claims on their members. Indeed, they are the most important sustaining source of moral voices other than the inner self.
>
> (Etzioni 1993: 31)

Strong communities, it is argued, can speak to us in moral voices. Social control here consists of subtle, as well as some blunt, forms of persuasion (some might say 'coercion') involving rewards and sanctions to encourage conformity to the dominant values and standards of behaviour. Thus, strong communities allow the policing *by* communities rather than the policing *of* communities. Thus, 'the more viable communities are, the *less* the need for policing' (Etzioni 1993: ix–x, emphasis in original). Here is a virtuous circle, the inverse of Wilson and Kelling's vicious cycle, whereby 'more "community" equals less crime' (Crawford 1997a: 152). However, the problem for communitarians is that the ability of a community to bring social pressures to bear on its members is simultaneously both its enduring attraction and its abiding danger. For how do we know whether 'community suasion' is being used for good or bad ends? And if the latter, on what criteria do we judge this and seek to regulate it?

Resident involvement

Resident involvement connects aspects of social organisation with aspects of 'broken windows'. There is an 'organising' logic created through the structures of 'involvement'. There is also a concern with ensuring a smooth interface between formal and informal systems of control, as well as with addressing spirals of decline. However, the argument here is that 'adverse reputations' and 'tipping processes' can and should be responded to by offering residents a 'stake in conformity' through their involvement in decisions about the area in which they live and by investing in the 'human capital' of the estate or locality. A 'sense of community' can be constructed by offering residents some element of power or sway over their community. The problematic question, however, is how much power? The very notion of 'stakeholding' in this context suggests some kind of exchange, a new social contract in which powerful agencies and bodies *give up* a certain amount of control to local residents.

Resident involvement also connects with notions of 'problem-oriented' approaches to crime prevention, community safety and policing. In order to provide a service which is genuinely problem-oriented rather than premised on the basis of existing organisational goals, structures and working patterns, there is a need for good quality information about the nature of the problem (Goldstein 1979, 1990; Wilson and Kelling 1989). Resident involvement can be a useful way of providing data about crime and related social problems otherwise unavailable to agencies and actually changing the way organisations think about problems. Targeted strategies, it is argued, require a better understanding of local needs and problems. Information, as in the case of policing, may be a crucial aspect in efficient service delivery and it may be directly tied to public confidence and trust which 'resident involvement' is designed to enhance. Thus resident involvement should provide greater public confidence in the police, which should lead to greater information from the public which is a vital component of efficient policing – which in turn should produce greater confidence and trust, and so on. Hence, an important part of community involvement is often concerned with improving relations and effective communication between residents and formal agencies, notably the police. 'Problem-oriented' approaches are often linked to and associated with the decentralisation of decision-making and service delivery. The argument is that social problems such as crime are largely local issues and therefore agencies need to be sensitive to this local dimension through neighbourhood-based structures.

Resident involvement can act as a way of connecting formal systems of control with informal social control such that they support rather than conflict with each other. In Britain much effort has been put into tenant involvement in relation to local authority owned housing estates. This has been caused both by the extensive amount of public sector housing built in Britain in the post-war period and the fact that some housing estates suffer from particularly acute levels of crime. This has not been helped by the increasingly residualised nature of British public sector housing estates, especially in the aftermath of the 'right to buy' legislation of the early 1980s which led to the sale of a quarter of the national stock and which has concentrated some of the most socially disadvantaged populations in local authority housing.

The most innovative developments in this regard have come via NACRO, the Safe Neighbourhoods Unit (SNU) and the Priority Estates Project (PEP). The essential connection between resident involvement in estate management and crime prevention is thought to be that crime and incivility are affected by residents' ability to exert informal control over behaviour on their estate. The ability of residents to do so is thought to depend on communal self-confidence acquired through greater commitment to the estate, and consequently a greater concern with conditions and standards of behaviour within it.

However, 'resident involvement' can take on a variety of appearances, from active participation and community empowerment in the decision-making process, at one extreme, to weak forms of consultation and public relations exercises at the other. In reality, these are often top–down initiatives which are concerned with mobilising 'the public' in support of existing formal agencies. Such initiatives represent a form of 'responsibilisation strategy', whereby 'involvement' amounts to formal criminal justice agencies, such as the police, educating the public about their responsibilities and legitimate expectations. To an extent, this has been the experience of many of the Police Community Consultative Groups (PCCGs) set up as a result of recommendations by the Scarman Report in the early 1980s and given a limited legislative footing under section 106 of the Police and Criminal Evidence Act 1984 (now contained in section 96 of the Police Act 1996). Legitimisation becomes a key component of the exercise, *vis-à-vis* formal criminal justice agencies (Morgan 1989). Here responsibility is dispersed but power remains clearly vested in the hands of established professional bodies.

It is interesting that those individuals who get involved in such initiatives often have greater expectations and a different appreciation of their participation than do formal agencies. They see the relationship with formal agencies, such as the police, as providing them with a direct link into, and hence a means of influencing, the police or other criminal justice agency. This may explain why attendance and participation at such consultation arrangements tends to be sporadic and difficult to sustain. Hence, these kinds of initiatives often give rise to problematic questions about the nature and extent of participation, representation and accountability (considered in the next chapter).

Intermediate institutions

Recently, there has been a revived interest in the role of intermediate institutions in regulating behaviour. This has led to community crime prevention schemes whose function is the creation of intermediate institutions between the formal structures of policing, control and authority and the informal institutions of civil society such as the family, school, peer groups and community associations. While Shaw and McKay placed considerable emphasis on building social institutions within the community, for them the primary role of these institutions was as socialising agents. Where the new emphasis on 'intermediate institutions' departs from the Chicago School analysis is to see these institutions as primarily regulatory agencies in their own right. The aim is the creation and rebuilding of layers of intermediary bodies, within civil society, which stand between the state and the individual and which are capable of commanding suffi- cient authority to act as agents of social control. In other words, they are concerned with the self-regulation of crime and deviant behaviour within the community. Ideally these institutions should be able to do so without invoking the direct intervention of formal state agencies of authority. However, they operate within the 'shadow of the state' and therefore have a secondary function, where self-regulation fails or is insufficient, which is to act as a conduit into formal agencies of control. Some examples of intermediate institutions are community mediation schemes, concierges on housing estates and various forms of 'private policing' including secur- ity guards, citizens patrols and vigilante groups. Ironically, this revival of interest has manifest itself at a time when many intermediate institutions have been in decline. Many regulatory bodies, such as park keepers, bus conductors and station guards once familiar in public places, have all but disappeared.

Intermediate institutions, thus, in the first instance act as informal policing agents and/or informal modes of dispute resolution but may also act as referral agencies calling on the formal system when deemed necessary. However, relations between intermediate institutions and formal agencies should not be taken for granted. While they are usually co-operative and complementary – particularly where they are established or part-funded by the state – they may be conflictual and hostile. This has been further confounded by the phenomenal growth of a 'security market' and the expanding private sector involvement in policing. The research into private forms of policing has shown a complex set of inter- connections and social relations across the state/civil society divide, whereby intermediate institutions are neither always the 'junior partners' of the state nor part of 'one large disciplinary network', but rather con- stitute new 'hybrid' spheres with their own complex logic (Shearing and Stenning 1987b; Johnston 1992; Shearing 1992). The nature of how this logic is played out depends on various social, sectoral and ideological relations.

There is an important ideological divide about the arguments for and political implications of intermediate institutions. From a neo-liberal perspective the role of intermediate institutions connects with the rolling back of the state and the freeing up of individual and group enterprise. It is part of a privatisation ideology, in which the scope for voluntary action is expanded and advanced as the role of the state contracts. The Institute for Economic Affairs, an influential right-wing think-tank, has proposed tax incentives to encourage individuals and communities to purchase private policing (Pyle 1995: 61). From more radical perspectives, community institutions are seen as the home of grass-roots activism and a challenge to an unjust state. They represent a space in which to challenge structures of gender, race and class inequalities, as well as to support mutuality and self-empowerment. Somewhere between, and borrowing from, both these positions is the communitarian agenda, which argues that:

> rather than relying on the police to solve our crime problems society must take more responsibility itself. But that means creating effective intermediate institutions within civil society as well as links with the police which would allow more effective self-policing. One of the police's main roles should be to strengthen sources of authority within society, to strengthen society's ability to police itself.
>
> (Leadbeater 1996: 25)

There are unresolved questions about whether such 'intermediate institutions' actually reduce or increase the work of formal agencies through a process of 'netwidening' (Cohen 1985), whereby the formal system merely expands through informal institutions. There are also genuine concerns about the interests and purposes advanced by such 'intermediate institutions'. For if they are not 'public' bodies, but 'hybrid' or 'private' ones, to what extent might 'private' or 'community' interests conflict with the idea of a 'public purpose'? This raises profound questions about social – rather than local or private – justice (to which I return in Chapter 8).

The political economy of community

The central paradox of much community crime prevention, as Hope notes, stems from 'the problem of trying to build community institutions that control crime in the face of their powerlessness to withstand the pressures toward crime in the community, whose source, or the forces that sustain them, derive from the wider social structure' (1995a: 24). While the community organising approach of the CAP was designed to counteract the problems caused by dynamic growth, more recent research has sought to highlight the importance of changes in the dynamics of wider urban markets, be they stimulated by private or public sector policies and decisions (Taub *et al.* 1984; Bottoms *et al.* 1992). The importance of housing policy raises the question, what economic and social processes enable and encourage mobility within housing markets? Housing policy may influence and structure the desire and/or ability of residents to move to other estates. It can also influence the way in which adverse reputations of some estates and areas are created and maintained, through the processes of stigmatisation.

One of the ways in which notions of community crime prevention have been productively developed more recently by British and American criminologists is through the concept of 'community crime careers' (Bottoms and Wiles 1986; Reiss 1986). This concept shifts attention away from a focus on *more* or *less* 'community' as the key to criminality towards an understanding of a neighbourhood's crime patterns as a complex whole. A 'community crime career' is the totality of the consequences, whether intended or not, of the way in which a multitude of actors interact in an historical process (Bottoms and Wiles 1992: 25):

> in order to understand and explain offending behaviour by residents of particular areas, it is vital to consider who lives in those areas; how they came to live there in the first place; what kind of social life the residents have created; how outsiders (including official agencies) react to them; and why they remain in the areas and have not moved.
>
> (Bottoms *et al.* 1992: 122)

The notion of 'community crime careers' identifies the importance of an understanding of social relations within an area. More importantly, particularly in the light of the criticisms of the Chicago School, it also seeks to show how those relations are shaped by the wider socio-economic environment, most notably the urban market. Consequently, effective community-based crime prevention needs to be based on an understanding of the above interactive processes within a specific area.

This has caused commentators to consider the political economy of community prevention, which focuses on both the internal and external power relations and the way in which the latter mesh or conflict with the former. Hope (1995a) draws a useful distinction between *horizontal* and *vertical* dimensions of power. The horizontal dimension includes the 'social relations among individuals and groups sharing a common residential space' and refers to 'the often complex expressions of affection, loyalty, reciprocity, or dominance' (Hope 1995a: 24). The degree to which people within a community can relate to one another along these lines will greatly influence the effectiveness of any prevention programme. The vertical dimension, by contrast, refers to 'relations that connect local institutions to sources of power and resources in the wider civil society of which the locality is acknowledged to be a part'. It is this vertical dimension which much community crime prevention has neglected, and yet both dimensions need to be mutually supportive for crime prevention to be effective:

> While the principal mechanisms for maintaining local order may be expressed primarily through the horizontal dimension, the *strength* of this expression – and hence its effectiveness in controlling crime – derives, in large part, from the vertical connections that residents of localities have to extracommunal resources.
>
> (Hope 1995a: 24, emphasis in original)

Hope (1995a: 72) goes on to note that much community prevention has concentrated on the 'use values' of residential areas – including the benefits that stem from neighbourliness, informal support networks, a sense of identity, security and trust – but have ignored the dynamics of a neighbourhood's 'exchange value' – how properties are valued by prospective residents, investors and landlords. The important point is that the latter can serve to undermine or damage the former. While a focus on use values tends to direct attention towards the intrinsic qualities of particular neighbourhoods, with implications for pathologising them, exchange values direct attention to the position that a community has within the wider urban framework. It is toward the vertical power of local communities and the way in which this impacts on horizontal dynamics that the 'political economy of community' crime prevention research and analysis is directed.

Community crime prevention case studies

In the light of the above explanations of the relationship between 'community' and the prevention of crime, let us now consider some case studies which have sought to institutionalise aspects of these approaches.

Estate-based management – the Priority Estates Project

The Priority Estates Project (PEP) was set up in 1979 as a joint DoE and local authority experiment in an attempt to improve unpopular housing estates. PEP is a consultancy which works with local authorities and tenants to institute changes in the delivery of local housing services and management and to consult tenants about the running of their estates. The essential aims were (Power 1984):

- to establish a local management office
- to carry out meticulously the landlords' responsibility for rent, repairs, letting and monitoring the environment of the estate
- to give tenants a chance to exercise maximum control over their homes and neighbourhood.

This partnership between housing management and tenants has been translated into an established model with the following ten key elements: a local office, local repairs, localised lettings, local rent arrears control, an estate budget, resident caretaking, tenant participation, co-ordination and liaison with other services and agencies, monitoring of performance and training. This model places strong emphasis on regular consultation with tenants, as well as their participation in advisory or management groups. However, it should be noted that it constitutes an 'outline for action' which is highly dependent on how it is taken forward and adapted in each local situation.

Although PEP was not primarily intended to make an impact on crime, it seems to have had real consequences on crime rates. For example, between 1983 and 1985 on the Broadwater Farm estate in Haringey, a large estate with a population of around 3500, the burglary rate fell by 78 per cent, vehicle crime dropped by 61 per cent and major crime by 49 per cent. Despite the disturbance on the estate in 1985, crime continued to fall. In 1987 the estate was described by one senior police officer as 'probably the safest place in Tottenham' (cited in SNU 1993: 57). The estate accounted for 1 per cent of the area's crime despite housing 3.5 per cent of its population. As well as the basic PEP model, the project included an extensive job creation plan on the estate which created some 120 jobs by 1989. In 1995 the idea of 'joint management' was taken further with the signing of an 'estates agreement' between residents and the local council under which tenants' representatives meet senior council officials once a fortnight to discuss aspects of progress on a £33 million spending programme, which runs from 1993 to 2001. The estate is no longer 'difficult to let', with few vacant dwellings at any one time (Power 1997).

More broadly, of 20 PEP estates, nearly all considered to have high levels of crime and vandalism, it was estimated that vandalism and levels of insecurity declined on 15 estates following the introduction of estate-based management (Power 1987). After nearly 15 years, while crime remained a significant issue on the PEP estates, many of the problems have been reduced or are being contained, despite the greatly increased polarisation of the estates. As a result of a survey carried out in 1994, both managers and residents in a majority of estates thought that crime problems had reduced or at least got no worse over the preceding six years (Power and Tunstall 1995: 57).

Hope and Foster (1992) conducted a detailed study of two PEP estates in Hull and London using 'before and after' surveys of residents and ethnographic research methods. They found a number of examples of crime reduction on both estates, in contrast with two comparable 'control' estates. Burglary on one of the estates reduced over the period of the study, while they increased in the 'control' area. They concluded that 'these examples suggest that the PEP model does have a real potential for reducing crime' (Foster and Hope 1993: x). However, they go on to warn that all of the successes were only partial, in that they occurred in either one or the other of the experimental estates, or only for particular areas or groups of residents within each estate. They also found that the effect of management changes, together with environmental modifications and changes in tenant turnover and allocation to the PEP estate, served to alter the internal culture of the estates. On one estate, this produced an intensification of both social control *and* criminality – presented through the availability of criminal networks and a supporting culture which reinforced such networks. These 'conflicting forces' found expression in differences between parts of the estate and various groups of tenants. An essential ingredient in this was housing allocation policies. There had been an influx of young poor people on to the estate during the experimental period. Foster and Hope (1993: 88) note the difficulty for housing managers to attempt to use the allocation of prospective tenants in order to forestall the concentration of social problems, given their need to pursue a number of policies at the same time, in matching the supply of dwellings on an estate to the demand from prospective tenants, including trying to keep all dwellings occupied.

Concierge schemes in high rise blocks

The role of the concierge, or concierge-type personnel, remains considerably vague. At one level they are presumed to fulfil the function of an informal police officer or intermediate institution which combines a physical control over entrance, a surveillance capacity (more or less reliable than a CCTV) and a symbolic human presence, with the ability to intervene in problematic situations. At another level they may be seen as informal conflict negotiators resolving internal disputes, potentially extending to a low level 'community care' function. This lack of clarity is also a positive aspect of the concierge role as it is likely to alter given differences in local circumstances, as well as to change over time to meet new and differing expectations.

In 1992 the DoE commissioned the SNU to carry out an evaluation of a range of schemes involving concierges or controlled entry in a number of high rise blocks (Farr and Osborn 1997). This case study highlights the interesting inter-relationship between technological interventions and human interventions. The 15 schemes in the evaluation study were divided into three types:

- 'technology based' schemes, which relied on technology namely CCTV, rather than the presence of personnel in a concierge capacity
- 'intensive concierge' schemes, where personnel were based in each separate block
- 'dispersed concierge' schemes, where personnel were based in just one of a group of blocks linked by CCTV.

The research study, carried out between 1992 and 1995, sought to evaluate the impact of the interventions on levels of crime and concerns about crime, as well as the letability of dwellings, management and repair performance, levels of resident satisfaction and resident participation in 'community affairs'. The findings of the research highlight that schemes which rely on technology rather than the presence of personnel may only provide a satisfactory response where the population is relatively stable, where residents are generally mature or elderly and where there are few children. Where this equilibrium is disturbed the limitations of technological interventions become apparent. By contrast, the 'intensive concierge' schemes appeared to be consistently the most effective either in bringing about improvements in security, management and residential satisfaction in reasonably difficult circumstances or in containing problems in the most problematic circumstances. However, of the three the 'intensive concierge' schemes were the most expensive.

The 'dispersed concierge' schemes appeared to have had mixed fortunes. Improvements were most apparent in the 'control' block, where personnel were based rather than in 'satellite' blocks. The most effective of these schemes tended to be more staff-intensive, and therefore more expensive to operate. This would appear to call into question the justification that 'dispersed concierges' can operate as cheaper versions of 'intensive concierge' schemes.

In line with other research findings (Bottoms *et al.* 1992), the authors noted that the most successful schemes were those in which the introduction of concierges were supported by changes in housing allocation policies. Concierge schemes, the authors argue, do not of themselves appear to solve problems created by poor management performance or inappropriate allocation policies. However, they do seem to create the conditions in which improved management and allocations can be effective. Given the wide role designed for, or expected of, concierges the authors recommend that greater attention is paid to training needs, both in terms of human skills and technological skills, particularly where concierges are responsible for the operation of CCTV surveillance systems. The role of technology and its relationship with the function of the concierge remains a vexed issue. The authors conclude that:

> The purpose of technological aids needs to be questioned. For example, the purpose of CCTV cameras to monitor entrance halls and lifts appears to be clear where concierges or similar personnel are based in the blocks concerned. In these circumstances, the systems are clearly useful management aids but the scheme is not reliant on their operation. However, where such systems are used to extend the scope of personnel based in one of a series of blocks, they become substitutes for the presence of personnel and the scheme as conceived can no longer function if the equipment fails. Unfortunately, as the case studies showed the equipment does tend to fail because of design problems, poor maintenance or vandalism.
>
> (Farr and Osborn 1997)

A victim-led project

Following from the interest in repeat victimisation, there has been an awareness of the potential of community-based projects which seek to prevent crime from a victim's perspective. Consequently, some projects have sought to use victimisation as a means of targeting community support networks, in order to lessen the impact of victimisation, reduce the likelihood of repeat victimisation and fear of crime, and encourage self-help and networking between neighbours. One such project was set up by Victim Support and the Crime Prevention Unit on an inner-city estate with around 1000 dwellings. A notable proportion of residents suffered from interpersonal violence and threats. A survey had shown a high level of fear of crime on the estate, particularly among women, and a low level of formal social interaction between residents. A third of the residents had no friends living on the estate. Therefore the aim of the project was one of 'community development' through four practical strategies (Sampson and Farrell 1990):

- to convene an inter-agency working group
- to set up care watches – similar to the cocoon watches used on the Kirkholt estate project, where neighbours were asked to 'wrap round' a victim to protect them from further victimisation
- to establish a mothers' and toddlers' group
- to set up a community mediation scheme.

Two part-time project workers were employed to implement these strategies and later in the project added a fifth, a 'block watch' scheme. The workers sought to encourage self-referrals of crimes by victims or their neighbours so that they could provide support to all victims regardless of whether the incident was reported to the police.

The project is a good example of some of the problems associated with implementing community crime prevention schemes. Crime and the fear of crime were not significantly affected, although practical help was provided to victims to assist them with their emotional difficulties. The inter-agency group got bogged down with conflicts about autonomy, power and control (see Chapter 5). The 'care watches' were never implemented either because they were unacceptable to residents, largely because of the high level of distrust, or because the project workers were unable to 'sell' the idea and persuade neighbours to join. The 'block watches' suffered from similar problems. Residents tended to feel safe only in their own flats and were reluctant to engage in exchanges with others in communal areas. The experience of trying to set up the watches was that watching out for neighbours' flats did not in itself engender a sense of 'neighbourliness' or community spirit. The author of the research report concluded: 'These findings suggested communal security may be one prerequisite for increased neighbourliness since this would give residents a safe communal area within which to interact' (Sampson 1991: 24). The mothers' and toddlers' group was supposed to act as just such a place where residents could meet in a group setting. However, the group had a 'short and strife-ridden life'. There was conflict between the mothers and the project workers and there was tension within the tenants association (whose flat was used by the group) as to their support of the group. The history of the group demonstrated 'how crime prevention schemes can serve to increase social conflicts and provide a site for power struggles to be played out' (Sampson 1991: 30). Finally, community mediation was accepted as a worthwhile aim with the potential for reducing local conflicts and the associated unfriendliness that neighbourhood conflicts engender. It was pursued in conjunction with a local mediation service. However, few referrals to the scheme arose out of the estate.

Despite its lack of success there are important lessons to be learnt from such a project. It demonstrated the essential dilemma of 'implanting', from the outside, a crime prevention project on a community. It illustrated the fact that lack of any formal community infrastructure makes it difficult to develop community institutions. It also showed that intra-communal conflicts can serve to undermine crime prevention projects. On this estate, some of these conflicts reflected divisions between gender, race and age, while others related to divergent life-styles, disparate values and divisions over the use of space on the estate. Finally, it highlights the difficulty of engaging in crime prevention on an estate with multiple problems (there was no one overarching crime problem, unlike the Kirkholt estate) with insufficient and limited resources.

The San Francisco Community Board

Community mediation has been seen by advocates as a means of returning control over local disputes to communities themselves. It is premised on the belief that professionalised legal systems have 'stolen' conflicts from the parties themselves who are relegated to being passive observers in the processing of their dispute (Christie 1977). This 'theft' removes from the parties participation in what is seen as a socially constructive process: that of dispute resolution. Community mediation thus constitutes a pre-eminent intermediate institution designed to enable and facilitate community self-regulation, founded on a critique of formal systems of regulation. Schemes see their function as restoring to people the ability to resolve their own disputes and thus strengthen the informal bonds of community. As a consequence, they connect with a wider ideology of community empowerment and 'social transformation' (Harrington 1993).

The San Francisco Community Board (SFCB) has been the most prominent, well-funded and researched example of community mediation programmes. It was set up in 1977, the brainchild of Raymond Shonholtz, its charismatic founder until he retired in 1987. As with other schemes, it sought to apply conciliatory procedures to a range of neighbourhood problems as an alternative to the courts. These 'problems' may not involve technical breaches of the criminal law but they may have the potential to escalate into more serious matters. Thus, one of its central aims was early intervention and the reduction of anger and hostilities between people who know each other (Shonholtz 1993). Again like other schemes, they used community volunteers as mediators to act as a third party to facilitate communication between the two (or more) conflicting parties. The SFCB was founded on an understanding of communication in which conflicts of interests and rights are transformed into issues of feelings and relationships. It encouraged the parties to arrive at voluntary agreements themselves. The SFCB adopted a particularly antagonistic relationship to the formal state legal system, more so than many community mediation schemes (Shonholtz 1987).[3]

It is difficult to evaluate the impact of such schemes on local crime rates, particularly as they often deal with longstanding relations which may or may not have escalated into more serious matters. These are often the kinds of disputes which tend not to be reported to the police. Nevertheless, there is research evidence that schemes such as the SFCB have high satisfaction rates in terms of the parties' experience of the mediation process itself. Agreements reached by the parties through community mediation tend to be more enduring and respected by the parties than those ascertained through the formal courts (DuBow and McEwen 1993). However, research has also pointed to the incongruity between the rhetoric and practice of community mediation. The volume of cases that pass through community mediation remains very small and their impact on the wider community is marginal. The somewhat pessimistic conclusion reached by Yngvesson, in relation to the SFCB, was that community empowerment may be possible only for a privileged 'internal community' of volunteers rather than the external 'community of neighbours' (1993: 381). Despite the ideological critique of formal legal systems, community mediation tends to reproduce many of the symbols, rituals and procedures derived from state law. It tends to operate within the 'shadow of the court', frequently relying on formal agencies to refer cases or for funding support. The experience of community mediation has tended to be one of high ideals, pragmatic funding difficulties and thwarted aspirations. Nevertheless, many community-mediation schemes, inspired by the work of the SFCB, have been set up in the UK, such as the Southwark Mediation Centre, the Newham Conflict and Change Project and the Sandwell Mediation Scheme, which exist under the national umbrella organisation, Mediation UK.

Community policing

Many organisational initiatives have been called 'community policing' but there is little agreement as to what 'community policing' is. At one extreme 'community policing' may be merely anything which improves relations and trust between the police and local community. Essentially, it is a philosophy of policing which attempts to define a new kind of relationship between the police and the public, even if only at the level of rhetoric. As such, it embodies an implicit critique of traditional policing. This may explain why many experiments in community policing in both the UK and USA have never been fully implemented because of the passive resistance among the police themselves, particularly lower ranking officers, and institutional blockages (Rosenbaum 1994). In Britain, Fielding (1995) has highlighted the institutional barriers that exist within forces which tend to strangle community policing experiments in their early stages of development. Thus, translating the ideals into practice has proved problematic and despite the abundant references to 'community policing', there is little agreement about or evidence of effective work.

In reviewing the British experience Weatheritt (1993: 126) identifies three defining characteristics in much that passes for 'community policing':

- the greater use of foot patrols and the posting of officers to geographic areas for which they have continuing responsibility
- the development of partnerships in crime prevention
- the establishment of structures and processes for consulting local communities about their policing priorities and problems.

Certainly, the most popular organisational strategy for delivering these three elements of community policing is 'decentralisation', which in Britain has most often been referred to as 'sectoralisation', or 'sector policing' (Dixon and Stanko 1995) and 'problem-solving policing' (Leigh *et al.* 1996).

There is some evidence that the greater use of foot patrols and community constables allocated to a particular area are popular with the public. However, there is little evidence of an impact on levels of crime or even fear of crime. A study by Wycoff and Skogan (1994) of community policing in Madison showed that burglary rates dropped while robbery rates remained unchanged following the introduction of the programme, whereas a study of community policing in San Diego found no reduction in crime (Capowich and Roehl 1994). More extensive research in the USA showed that community policing had an impact on reducing fear of crime in five out of six research sites without any significant impact on crime (Skogan 1994). However, Bennett (1994) has shown that this effect is found less consistently in Britain.

The essential problems with assessing the effectiveness of community policing are twofold. The first relates to the lack of clarity about the specific mechanisms involved in community policing and how these are presumed to reduce crime. The second concerns the failure of many community policing strategies even to be implemented when they are the subject of evaluation research. As a consequence many commentators are cynical of much that passes under the name 'community policing', seeing it as little more than a rhetorical device (Bayley 1988; Weatheritt 1988). As Buerger concludes:

> For all the rhetoric about empowering the community . . . when it comes down to cases the police establishment assigns to the community a role that simply enhances the police response to crime and disorder.
>
> (1994b: 271)

Neighbourhood watch

Neighbourhood watch (NW) has been closely associated with the philosophy of community policing, and for some represents its most successful expression. The first NW schemes were set up in 1982 in Britain, although the earliest schemes in North America had appeared in the late 1960s. They were heavily promoted by senior police officers, most notably Sir Kenneth Newman, the Metropolitan Commissioner of Police in the early and mid-1980s. Between the years 1988 and 1992 the proportion of households where a scheme had been established rose from 18 to 28 per cent (Home Office 1994a). It is now claimed that there are more than 140 000 NW schemes covering 6 million households in England and Wales. Regardless of the exact figure, the quantitative growth and spread of NW has been extraordinarily rapid. NW was envisaged at its inception by Sir Kenneth Newman as a means of involving the public by encouraging community members to come together in neighbourhood groups assisted and advised by the police. The primary aim of NW is the reduction of crime, notably 'opportunistic crime' and residential burglary, although vehicle crime and criminal damage were seen as crimes which NW could do something about. A secondary set of aims related to reducing the fear of crime, encouraging awareness about crime prevention and improvements to domestic security, facilitating greater contact between neighbours and improving liaison between police and public. The principal mechanism for achieving these aims was for NW members actively to look out for suspicious behaviour: to become the 'eyes and ears' of the police.

Bennett's (1989, 1990) research into two experimental areas in London in the mid-1980s – in Acton and Wimbledon – is the most rigorous evaluation to date of the effectiveness of NW in England. The experimental areas were supplemented in the research by non-NW areas adjacent to the experimental areas in order to assess any displacement effect, and one non-NW area, some distance away from both of the schemes, to act as a 'control' area. The findings from Bennett's research showed that NW had no effect on reducing crime. In fact the prevalence of household victimisations increased in both the experimental areas, as well as in the displacement areas. Only in the control area did the prevalence of household crime decrease. Bennett did, however, identify a reduction in the fear of household victimisation, albeit that the decline was only statistically significant in one of the areas. There was also an increased satisfaction and sense of social cohesion in the same area. However, resident evaluation of police performance was mixed, reporting rates of incidents to the police broadly remained stable and there was no evidence that NW improved police detection rates. Bennett concluded that the effectiveness of public surveillance is likely to be very limited, as many households are unoccupied for most of the day and many residences are poorly located for surveillance purposes. Where there is a high turnover of residents it also becomes very difficult to identify strangers.

Evidence from the USA tends to confirm these pessimistic findings (Rosenbaum 1988b; Skogan 1990b). There is also some evidence from the USA which suggests that, rather than reducing fear, NW may actually heighten members' fear of crime, by providing them with greater information about local victimisation experiences. As Rosenbaum notes, 'small group discussions may even serve as a "consciousness raising" experience whereby participants leave feeling *more* (rather than less) helpless in the face of uncontrollable political and social forces' (1988b: 136, emphasis in original).

There is a question as to whether setting up NWs actually increases the workload of the police, rather than reducing it. One of the difficulties that the police have been confronted with is the task of having to service the expanding number of NW schemes, often with little or no extra manpower or resources. And yet research has shown that crucial to the survival of schemes is the assistance and support provided by the police (Hussain 1988). Despite or maybe because of this, researchers have noted that the level of activism is often restricted to putting a sticker in the window. Hence, McConville and Shepard concluded their research by stating that most schemes were characterised by 'low take up rates, weak community penetration and limping, dormant or stillborn schemes' (1992: 115). Research into the effect of other 'watch' schemes which have been spawned by the expansion of NW, such as 'vehicle watch', have also shown no conclusive impact on crime rates (Honess and Maguire 1993).

Using British Crime Survey data Hope (1988) has shown that there is support for NW where the risk of crime is thought to be high but where there is still satisfaction with the neighbourhood. By contrast, there is little support for NW in areas where the risk of crime is high and there is little sense of community and where the risk of crime is low and there is a strong sense of community. Research from North America confirms the fact that NW is easiest to establish in more affluent, suburban areas with low crime rates by people who hold favourable attitudes towards the police, rather than in inner-city, crime prone public sector housing estates with heterogeneous populations (Skogan 1990b).

If NW has no direct preventive effect for residents, why do schemes continue to flourish? One answer may lie in the fact that, increasingly, insurance companies have added a financial incentive to setting up and joining NW by giving insurance premium 'discounts' to members of NW schemes. In a different way NW may act as a kind of insurance policy, in that its members are privy to a 'club' with the police whose unwritten constitution is interpreted as saying 'call us if you need us' on behalf of the police. This is borne out by research which suggests that NW members are more likely than non-members to report suspicious incidents to the police (Dowds and Mayhew 1994). As a consequence, NW acts as a kind of formal link into the local police, and given that the police remain, by and large, a reactive force they will usually respond to calls made on them. Hence, in two different ways NW directs police resources to those areas where NW schemes are established: first, in terms of the time and resources spent setting up and servicing a NW scheme, and second, by responding to the increased reporting that NW indirectly produces. The problem that this highlights is that given the paradox that NW tends to exist where it is least needed, a by-product of NW may be to further distort police resources towards those areas and people most capable and least in need. NW thus may be more a 'club good' which benefits its members than a 'social good', which benefits society at large (Hope 1995a).

Street watches and citizen patrols

Some NW schemes have established 'street watches' involving patrols by local residents. In September 1994, this was given an impetus by the then Home Secretary Michael Howard when he suggested that NW schemes should be encouraged to include patrols of active citizens, who would 'walk with a purpose' in their local areas. However, these remain particularly contentious given their potential for vigilantism and the hostility of the police who may view such schemes as amounting to 'policing on the cheap'. A prominent example of 'street watch' was the scheme established in the Balsall Heath area of Birmingham to counter problems associated with prostitution and drugs. The street patrols involve residents logging information which they consider may be useful to the police, notably the vehicle registration numbers of suspected kerb-crawlers. It has been claimed that prostitution reduced dramatically during the period and that reductions in burglaries and violent crimes were also recorded. Supporters also claim that as a result of the scheme relations improved between the community and the police and city officials (Atkinson 1996). However, opponents of the scheme have said it has led to intimidation and harassment of prostitutes and women mistakenly assumed to be prostitutes (O'Kane 1994). Where schemes like this are successful in reducing a problem, it may just be that the problem is merely displaced to other areas.

One notable example of 'citizen patrols' in the USA (and to a lesser extent in the UK) has been the Guardian Angels. Pennell and colleagues (1989) found that the presence of Guardian Angels in San Diego did not reduce violent offences, for which they were primarily established, which declined by 22 per cent in the experimental area but declined by 42 per cent in the control area not patrolled by Guardian Angels (Pennell *et al.* 1989: 388). However, a community survey showed that residents believed that the Guardian Angels were effective in deterring crime and 60 per cent of the respondents who were aware that Guardian Angels patrolled in their neighbourhood said they felt safer as a result.

One of the principal problems with citizen patrols and street watch schemes relates to their accountability for their actions. To whom are they accountable and from where does their legitimacy derive? Unlike formal police bodies, their powers are not so clearly legally subscribed, nor are their members screened or given sufficient training. Here, the question as to the relationship between a patrol and the police has significant implications, whether it is envisaged as either an alternative or a complement to the established police. Interestingly, Marx's (1989) research in the USA suggests that the attitude of a group towards the police is not a necessary determinant of police attitudes towards the group. Hence, we need to examine both the extent to which a group sees itself as either 'adversarial' or 'supplemental' to the role of the police, as well as how the police, and other relevant organisations (such as local authorities), interpret that relationship. Given what we have already noted about the difficulty of sustaining citizen involvement in relation to crime issues, the life expectancy of patrols is usually limited (Yin *et al.* 1977). In order to survive, they may need to develop cordial relations with the police and other agencies as well as increasingly formalising their working practices, through guidelines and training, in order to establish some credibility and legitimacy.

Community patrols in Sedgefield

Community patrols differ from citizens patrols or watch patrols in their connection to, and relationship with, formal state agencies. The most notable example of community patrols is in Sedgefield, County Durham, where the District Council set up its own uniformed 'Community Force' to patrol the streets on a 24 hour basis (at an initial cost of £180 000). The Force came into operation in January 1994. It covers a geographical area (the district) of 85 square miles and a population of over 90 000 people. Although similar to a commercial security patrol, the Force is a department of the council, not a commercial company. It has its own control room and ten patrol officers, using mobile telephones, two-way radios and marked patrol cars. Its objectives are:

- to provide a community patrol which will increase public safety and reassure the public
- to consult with local residents about anti-social problems in their area
- to consult with local police about crime trends and problems and how the Community Force can assist in combating them
- to provide advice and information to local residents on crime prevention
- to adopt a non-confrontational policy of 'observe and report' (I'Anson and Wiles 1995: 3).

Thus the Force exists primarily to pass on information to the police rather than to take action and to regulate behaviour themselves. Officers have no police powers of arrest and they work on the assumption of not using their citizen's powers of arrest.

In its first year of operation the Force received 1284 calls from the public and a reduction in crime was recorded. However, it is unknown whether the Force had any bearing on this reduction in recorded crime. After six months operation, researchers noted high levels of awareness of the scheme: seven out of ten of a random sample of the population interviewed said they had seen vehicles belonging to the Force. Eighty-three per cent of respondents said they were happy to have the council employed Community Force patrols, albeit that a larger figure, 91 per cent, said they would be happy to have police specials or a new rank of 'police patroller' (I'Anson and Wiles 1995). A later survey of residents who had asked for assistance found they were highly appreciative of the service they had received. In comparing the survey findings with those of the 1994 British Crime Survey, the report concluded that, 'the public's satisfaction with direct contact with the Sedgefield Community Force is at least as good as that for police/public contacts nationally, and may even be better' (Wiles 1996: 4–5).

The survey also showed that most of the calls related to vandalism (39.4 per cent), anti-social behaviour (33.7 per cent) and general nuisances (39.4 per cent), with only a fifth (21.2 per cent) of calls concerning straightforward crime (the figures add up to more than 100 per cent because each call may have involved more than one type of problem). While satisfaction with the Force's response to problems is high, there was a lower level of satisfaction with how the Force resolved such problems. This is possibly as a result of the limited powers available to the Force. Some respondents saw the limited powers of the Force as a source of problem. At least one respondent commented that 'a couple of extra regular police officers' might be preferable (Wiles 1996: 9). However, the survey provides little by way of information as to exactly how the Force's officers actually go about resolving conflicts. Hence, the informal conflict resolution role of the Force, if any, is both undeclared and unknown.

Despite the Durham Constabulary's initial cautious attitude towards the Community Force, as an 'intermediate institution' it would appear to fulfil a co-operative 'junior partner' role in its relation to the established police service. It would appear that the Force is providing a service in precisely those areas – incivilities, vandalism and low level crime – which the public are often concerned about and yet where the police are often criticised for being inefficient or inactive. However, the extent to which the Force duplicates, complements or conflicts with the role of the established police force remains uncertain.

'Zero tolerance' policing in New York

Recently, Wilson and Kelling's ideas have had a considerable impact on debates about policing practice, most notably through the promotion of 'zero tolerance' strategies as a result of New York's experience. While the 'broken window' thesis was primarily concerned with identifying the nature of a complex phenomenon – the role of crime and fear of crime in urban degeneration and decline – 'zero tolerance' is concerned solely with offering a solution to that problem. In doing so, it draws out and focuses on only one element in that process. While 'zero tolerance' represents an attempt to operationalise aspects of the 'broken windows' thesis, they are slightly different creatures. 'Zero tolerance' promotes the confrontational policing of disorder and the 'signs of disorder', notably 'incivilities' such as youths hanging around street corners, drunks and even 'squeegee merchants'.

The New York experience was introduced by former New York Police Department Commissioner William Bratton who, between 1994 and 1996, presided over a sharp fall in recorded crime. The statistics are impressive. Between 1990 and the end of 1996 the number of murders in New York City plummeted from 2245 to 983, a drop of 56 per cent. The sharpest falls were in the years 1994 and 1995 (20 per cent and 24 per cent respectively). The 1996 figure represented the first time since 1968 that the number of murders in the capital had fallen below 1000. Burglaries declined over two years by a quarter and robberies by 40 per cent and the general crime rate fell by 37 per cent over the three years to the end of 1996 (Bratton 1997). The scheme has been hailed as an outstanding success, even though (and maybe because) it led to a dramatic increase in the number of people held in prison as a result of the aggressive policing policy. The city once synonymous with violent crime was recently ranked the 144th most dangerous city in a Federal Bureau of Investigation comparison of crime in America's 189 largest cities. Despite the fact that there has been no significant research evidence to suggest a link between the policing of disorder and the decrease in serious crime, Bratton (1997), with a touch of irony, has insisted that the credit lies with the 'zero tolerance' policing strategy: 'Crime is down in New York, blame it on the police'!

Nevertheless, there are other factors to be taken into consideration in assessing the New York experience. Crime has fallen in most big American cities, albeit less dramatically, like San Diego where very different methods have been used. The fall came upon the back of an incredibly steep rise in crime rates, particularly homicides, in the late 1980s and early 1990s, together with the waning of the crack cocaine epidemic which had fuelled this rise, and a general ageing of the population which resulted in fewer young men in their late teens (the group disproportionately likely to be involved in crime). Consequently, as Bowling suggests: 'By the time Bratton took office and unleashed the cops, much of the drug war had already been won and lost, and murder was on the decline' (1996: 11).

The dramatic fall may have been influenced by internal reorganisations in the police such as the introduction of innovative systems of crime monitoring, and new forms of accountability, whereby precinct commanders are held responsible for crime outbreaks in their area and are required to explain them at strategy meetings to senior officers. These twice weekly Compstat meetings (Bratton 1997: 38) introduced forms of confrontational accountability systems. This was combined with a decentralisation of power and responsibility for policing down to the precinct commander level. An extra 7000 police officers were also taken on in New York in 1990, where the existing ratio of police to public was already relatively high. It seems, therefore, that Bratton was able dramatically to improve the bad morale which had existed in the force, and restore a sense of purpose and self-worth.

It is the link between low level incivilities and violent or serious crime that is most problematic. Here the New York experience is unhelpful, as the policing of disorder associated with the 'zero tolerance' approach was also accompanied by a considerable effort to address the problem of guns and an attempt to get them off the streets. Hence, it may be that it was the success of the aggressive policing of guns rather than low-level incivilities which produced the decrease in violent and serious crime. If so, there are fewer lessons to be learned for Britain where gun crime is nothing like the proportion in the USA.[4]

The New York model of 'zero tolerance' policing is highly confrontational, and could well end up being counter-productive in a British context. It was after all a similar type of aggressive policing strategy, Swamp '81, which led to the Brixton riots in 1981 and away from which sensitive policing has sought to move. Those police officers willing to learn the lessons of police/community relations over the ensuing years have come to appreciate that the basis of effective policing is a sustained flow of information from the community to the police and which is dependent on public support and trust, including those groups of the population with whom the police have most contact. All these are placed in jeopardy and potentially undermined by aggressive and selective policing. Far from solving the problems of serious crime in Britain, aggressive order maintenance along the lines of New York's 'zero tolerance' may serve to exacerbate public confidence and police effectiveness, a consequence of which some senior police officers (Pollard 1997), if not politicians, are aware. Nevertheless, similar schemes have been implemented across Britain, most notably in West Hartlepool, Middlesborough, Kings Cross and Strathclyde (Chesshyre 1997; Dennis 1997). The concept of 'zero tolerance' has been endorsed and trumpeted by politicians of both major political parties and the Labour government has given its full support to 'zero tolerance' and is committed to promoting it (Labour Party 1997).

However, 'zero tolerance' may be more about policing the boundaries of increasingly fragmented social divisions within society. The implicit intention is to clear away, and thus hide, from certain symbolic locations the socially dispossessed. It has become a 'catch all' panacea, deployed by the police as a public relations exercise to give the semblance of doing something new and different. Increasingly different strategies have been subsumed within the phrase, far removed from the ideas of Wilson and Kelling's 'broken window' thesis. But this is often the consequence of the complex processes through which policies are translated into practice. There is a real danger that 'zero tolerance' strategies, as representing new departures in policing, may actually threaten some of the lessons of the 1980s and 1990s. As Bratton has stated about the New York experience: 'We have shown in New York City that police can change behaviour, can control behaviour and, most importantly, can prevent crime by their actions – independently of other factors' (1997: 41). This is a more assertive and independent image of police, well liked by many rank-and-file officers who have seen 'partnerships' limit the police's autonomy. However, by holding out the belief that the police alone can solve the problem of crime, this may serve to undermine the notion that the police need the support and trust of the local public and other agencies. The rhetoric and emotion underlying 'zero tolerance' is both confrontational and aggressive. This poses problematic implications for civil liberties, and the rights of certain marginalised groups of people.

The concept of 'zero tolerance' as a policing strategy is a misnomer. It does not entail the rigorous enforcement of all laws, which would be impossible let alone intolerable, but rather involves highly discriminatory enforcement against specific groups of people in certain symbolic locations. Where is the 'zero tolerance' of white collar crimes, business fraud, unlawful pollution and breaches of health and safety? In reality, the forms of policing conducted in the name of 'zero tolerance' would be more accurately described as strategies of 'selective intolerance'.

Yet as a rhetorical device 'zero tolerance' is sufficiently open-textured. It has been extended and used as a slogan with which to assert the case for the inclusion of often marginalised aspects of crime on to a crime prevention agenda. Domestic violence awareness campaigns around the theme of 'zero tolerance', such as those pioneered in Canada and Edinburgh, are one such example. The notion of 'zero tolerance' as a metaphor raises important questions about what should be tolerated, the quality of life and the local environment which some people endure and thus about the reality of relative deprivation.

A critique of community crime prevention

Despite the energy and effort put into community crime prevention there has been little sustainable success. This is partly caused by the pragmatic difficulties associated with implementation of sustaining community participation and involvement in crime prevention initiatives, which is considered in the next chapter. However, it also stems from many of the contradictory and ill-considered assumptions on which policies of community crime prevention are premised.

Contrary to the assumptions of many community crime prevention theories that crime is associated with a lack of informal control, Foster and Hope's research on two crime prone public sector housing estates in England (Foster 1995; Hope and Foster 1992) found that informal control mechanisms were not absent in all high crime areas. In contradiction with Wilson and Kelling's thesis, they found that on one of the estates the impact of crime was to a large degree contained, principally by local, mutual support networks. Crime, Foster concludes, is not always damaging *per se* so long as other mediating factors cushion its impact (1995: 580). More recent British research suggests that high crime areas can be both disorganised and 'differently organised' (Evans *et al.* 1996).

The idea of the 'pathological community' handed down from the Chicago School suggests that in order to 'cure' high crime communities a dose of medicine needs to be prescribed by 'outside experts'. Yet there is a central paradox in the idea of the regeneration of communities by 'external forces'. If communities are not strong enough internally, will any amount of external intervention ever be sufficient to create community cohesion? When that external intervention is withdrawn, will the community resort back to levels of sociability in existence prior to the intervention? This also raises the problem which many fieldworkers implementing community crime prevention measures face: how to gain the trust of a community, already marked by high crime and low sociability, in which distrust is likely to run high. The central assumption here is what Rosenbaum calls the 'implant hypothesis': the idea that 'informal social control and related processes can be "implanted" by collective citizen action in neighbourhoods where they are naturally weak or nonexistent' (1988a: 327) and that this can be conducted or initiated by outside agents.

Contemporary Western societies appear to exhibit changes which fly in the face of tight-knit geographical communities. Rather, we seem to be witnessing the erosion of the bonds and social interactions which sustain community. Modern social relations are increasingly becoming 'disembedded' from local contexts and dispersed across time and space (Giddens 1990). By focusing almost exclusively on territorial communities, theorists have tended to ignore the importance of non-territorial networks and relations which have replaced them.[5] Social trends and demographic projections within cities also suggest that there is and will continue to be declining opportunities for participation in 'community organisations'. This combines with a growth of what Lasch referred to as 'privatism' (1980: 25) – an introspective preoccupation with the care and development of the self – which finds expression in separation, privacy, political apathy, untamed consumerism and narcissism and results in forms of social and spatial withdrawal.

Low crime areas – most notably middle class suburbs – do not display the characteristics traditionally associated with 'community': intimacy, connectedness and mutual support. They do not rely on the types of informal social control mechanisms so beloved by disorganisation theorists. They are more likely to call rapidly on the intervention of formal control mechanisms. Middle class suburbs are both disorganised and orderly (Bottoms and Wiles 1996). Rather than resurrecting 'natural' communities, which may not be possible, we could look to the way in which order is maintained in middle class areas and to the ways in which people in these areas can mobilise regulatory mechanisms when deemed necessary.

The concept of 'community'

The concept of 'community', as used in much of the literature, often obscures as much as it enlightens about the given variable and social processes involved in the dynamics of crime prevention. One dominant assumption about 'community' is that it represents a set of shared attitudes. Consequently, reference is made to the importance of a 'sense of community' or a 'sense of belonging'. 'Community' in this light is seen in geographic terms as a location in which residents feel themselves to be bound together by shared interests or identity. Communities, thus defined, take much of their character from the way in which their members think about and 'imagine' themselves. Hence, 'community' exists 'in people's heads' and the (re)construction of 'community' merely involves a shift in attitudes by residents. However, this definition of social identity as a state of mind, while an important empirical aspect of 'community', fails sufficiently to explain the nature of a community's capacity for informal social control or its ability to address and organise around issues of crime and its prevention.

In order to illustrate the inadequacies of this understanding of community, Currie (1988) highlights two phases of community crime prevention development each with their own vision of what community means, as well as its relation to 'offenders'. In Phase 1, 'community' is understood in symbolic terms as a set of collective attitudes:

> Consequently, if you wish to improve community conditions you are in essence in the business of changing attitudes, or altering the symbols of community, in the hope that improved interpersonal relations will follow. In the ideal scenario you may thus start a benign cycle: improved attitudes lead to better behaviour, which in turn enhances people's conception of community.
>
> (1988: 280–1)

Phase 1 is most clearly typified by Wilson and Kelling's 'broken windows' model and by much situational crime prevention, particularly of the 'defensible space' type.

Currie suggests that this 'sense of identity' represents only a partial account of what a community is (1988: 281). More importantly, by itself it does not constitute the most significant element for the purpose of crime control. It lacks what Currie calls 'structural awareness'. This he illustrates by contrasting it with a Phase 2 vision. Here, 'community' is seen in 'much more structural, or institutional terms not just as a set of attitudes we can "implant" or mobilise, but as an interlocking set of long-standing institutions which in turn are deeply affected by larger social and economic forces' (1988: 282–3). The institutions to which he refers include work, family and kin, religious and communal associations, while the 'larger social and economic forces' include housing policy, urban markets and employment opportunities. This Phase 2 vision comes closer to what I have described as a 'political economy of community'.

Currie suggests that Phase 1 thinking fundamentally misunderstands the relationship between offenders and the community. Offenders are viewed primarily as 'outsiders' against whom the 'community' needs to defend itself. Hence, this vision tends to assume an 'us versus them' attitude. This is the archetypal 'community defence' model for whom crime and criminals are external 'others'. As Currie notes: 'There is no sense that these offenders against law and civility are *members* of a community – some community – like the rest of us' (1988: 281, emphasis in original). This thinking is explicit in the idea of neighbourhood watch, in which members of communities are expected to look out for 'strangers'. Given the failure of Phase 1 thinking to take into account this reality, it is hardly surprising that community crime prevention initiatives premised on it – such as NW – are hardest to establish in areas where there is intra-communal crime – i.e. deprived urban areas – and easiest to establish where the apparent threat is one 'from outsiders' – i.e. heterogeneous suburbia and small villages. More fundamentally, this assumption tends to blind community crime prevention from tackling forms of criminality which are genuinely intra-communal, or more specifically intra-familial. Hence, this kind of community crime prevention is virtually silent on issues of domestic violence, child abuse and workplace offences. Thus, the thinking that pervades Phase 1, as well as encouraging fortress communities, actually fails to address the nature of particularly important kinds of offending behaviour: notably that which occurs within and between family and community members.

What exactly is meant by 'community' remains elusive. As we have seen, crime prevention programmes draw on confused conceptions of 'community'. It is simultaneously seen as a means to an end, a way of reducing crime in that 'more community equals less crime', and as an end in itself, in that community is seen as an undeniable good. The 'good society' is equated with strong communities with moral voices, and the means of achieving the 'good society' is to strengthen communities.

Communities are often portrayed as the antithesis of violence and crime. On the contrary, however, the collective values of a community may serve to stimulate and sustain criminality. This is why the concept of 'community crime careers' is so useful: it deliberately destroys the hitherto criminological assumption that community is in all situations crime preventive. Research into criminal subcultures would suggest otherwise. Moreover, it is presupposed that community self-regulation and authority are havens from oppressive control. Community order is not necessarily peaceful or harmonious. An assertion of 'community' identity at a local level can be beautifully conciliatory and socially constructive but it can also be parochial, intolerant and punitive. It is also wrong to presume that community membership is freely embraced or that the ideal of unrestricted entry to and exit from a given community is unproblematic. Some people may feel trapped within their wider community and ill at ease with it. Compulsion to conform can be particularly powerful.

This in part stems from an assumed connection between conceptions of *community* and *consensus*. Notions of 'community' are often premised on the mythic image of the harmonious homogeneous group with shared values – the small village. And yet the reality in many urban areas is of a cosmopolitan mix of age groups, cultures, ethnicities and identities. Here lies the danger of 'moral authoritarianism', whereby one dominant group or interest seeks to impose its values on others and does so with little regard for individual rights. The empirical reality regarding the internal composition of existing communities is that they are not the Utopias of egalitarianism that some might wish, but are hierarchical formations, structured on lines of differential power relations, most notably as feminists have argued, on lines of gender, but also on lines of ethnicity, age, class and other personal attributes. Thus, the 'moral voice of a community' may come to be dominated and controlled by unrepresentative élites within communities.

Rebuilding communities as a set of shared beliefs is not, therefore, synonymous with the creation of social order. Rather than uniting communities, crime can undermine the capacity of communities in high crime areas to organise themselves collectively, as it can divide people as opposed to uniting them. Crime may be the least appropriate issue around which to regenerate communities, particularly if we are seeking open, tolerant and inclusive communities rather than ones which solidify around 'defensive exclusivity', which lies at the heart of the 'community defence' approach to crime prevention.

Yet the central paradox exposed by a century of research into community crime prevention remains that community responses to crime are easiest to generate in exactly those areas where they are least needed and hardest to establish in those where the need is greatest. As Buerger (1994a: 411) notes, it would seem as if the *sine qua non* of community organisation is an already organised community, while that for crime prevention is an area not already subject to significant crime.

In concluding his review of the North American literature on community crime prevention, Rosenbaum suggests,

> We are fooling ourselves if we think that small amounts of money for short periods of time are sufficient to make a difference in tough neighbourhoods where the crime problem is complex and deeply rooted . . . Also politicians must be disabused of the notion that community 'self-help' and 'volunteerism' are free.
>
> (1988b: 379)

Rather than over-exaggerating and idealising the role of 'community' in crime prevention we need to wrestle with the real question of what a 'community' is and what it can do within the constraints imposed on it by broader social and economic forces.

Conclusions

The development of social crime prevention in Britain has lagged significantly behind that of situational prevention. The long-term investment that such strategies require is often at odds with the short-term nature of much political thinking which tends to prioritise the 'immediacy of the question of power'. Nevertheless, it appears to have recently received new impetus with the elaboration of governmental strategies aimed at encouraging early intervention with young people at risk of offending and wider community safety programmes. However, the contribution of specific social programmes to the reduction of crime remains poorly defined and ill-tested. In this context the lessons to be learnt from programmes become less evident and the problems associated with the unintended consequences of given strategies remain a significant issue.

Social crime prevention is the subject of intense political debate. The nature of the relationship between crime and social policy, as well as that between community safety and social justice, remains largely unanswered. There is a clear danger that in the shift to a preventive paradigm, we may come to expect too much of social policy generally or communities specifically. Both may be ends in themselves which may become distorted if shackled around issues of crime and disorder. Of themselves they may be more important than crime prevention.

Notes

1. Interestingly, the usual explanation of such 'false positives' is that there is something about these people which made them resilient to the pressures of their 'risk factor' rather than to question the validity of the category of 'risk' itself (see Home Office 1997c: 13, para. 44).

2. Reference to the term 'community crime prevention' will be used to incorporate both 'community safety' strategies and 'community-based crime prevention' programmes, bearing in mind the concepts discussed in Chapter 1.

3. More recently, the SFCB has moved to a narrower vision of its purpose, which is more focused on providing a dispute resolution service and less committed to reshaping communities.

4. In 1990 New York had 12 times more murders compared to London. Even after the subsequent considerable drop in the murder rate in New York, by 1995 there were still 8 times as many murders compared with London.

5. A notable exception is the work of Braithwaite (1989, 1993) whose concept of 'communities of care' specifically transcends spatial boundaries.

Chapter 5

Implementation and the Partnership Approach

Only belatedly have issues concerned with the implementation and delivery of crime prevention risen to the fore in the criminological literature. In the naïveté of the early days of crime prevention it was as if all that was needed was a 'good idea' and the rest would take care of itself. However, researchers have highlighted the importance of the concept of 'programme failure' and a sensitivity to integral elements within a programme, its delivery and evaluation (Rosenbaum 1986; Ekblom and Pease 1995). More than a decade ago, Hope and Murphy (1983) concluded their evaluation of a Home Office demonstration project designed to combat vandalism in schools, by emphasising the importance of the 'quality' and extent of policy implementation. They found that the ineffectiveness of the measures was as much a consequence of 'implementation failure' as failure to influence the activities of offenders. Hence, they stated the timely warning that 'it is unwarranted to assume that implementation will *necessarily* proceed in a logical sequence towards the solutions suggested by research findings' (Hope and Murphy 1983: 47, emphasis in original). Similarly, Bennett (1990) concluded that problems associated with implementation lay behind the failure to reduce crime in the neighbourhood watch schemes he evaluated.

Crime prevention and community safety programmes embody three distinct, yet interdependent, levels of analysis – theory, implementation and measurement – all of which will determine any understanding of the outcome, impact or success of a given initiative. The previous two chapters have been primarily concerned with the former, the theoretical assumptions which inform given strategies, while the next chapter considers issues of measurement in the evaluation of programmes. This chapter concentrates on the intervening processes which constitute design and implementation and considers key aspects of the implementation process. It begins with a consideration of the dominant methodological approach to implementation and the importance of good quality information about the local context in devising appropriate strategies. This involves a review of different processes designed to elicit information. The chapter goes on to consider the issues raised by the 'multi-agency' or 'partnership' approach to crime prevention. This focuses on some of the difficulties associated with partnerships. In focusing on problems and tensions the intention is not to undermine or reject a partnership approach, but rather to highlight a number of critical issues, all-too-often ignored in policy and practice. It also considers some of the implications of community and private sector involvement in partnerships.

The focus primarily is on community safety initiatives, rather than generalised public awareness programmes or specific individual measures, for a number of related reasons. First, it is in regard to community safety, with its emphasis on locality, that an understanding of the context in which measures are to be implemented is so important. Crime is not uniformly or randomly distributed across the country, but is rather concentrated in specific locations and disproportionately affects groups of people. Furthermore, different crimes affect different areas at different times. Crime is not only socially, but also temporally and spatially distributed. In this light designing and implementing appropriate crime prevention strategies requires sensitivity to the nature of a specific local context. Second, community safety, through its emphasis on a broad approach to the problem of crime, suggests the importance of information which extends beyond reported crime statistics and the competence of the police and traditional criminal justice agencies. It suggests that such information needs to be supplemented by deeper and more sensitive, albeit potentially related, data. Third, it is in relation to community safety that discussions about a partnership approach have been most prominent.

Planning and information gathering

A problem-oriented methodology

Increasingly a consensus appears to have taken shape as to the suitable programmatic methods for preventing crime, the stages in the process of intervention and their appropriate sequence. This draws on a 'problem-oriented' approach, whereby the specific and often local nature of the crime problem is allocated a dominant role in determining the nature of the solution. Goldstein (1990) defines a 'problem' as 'a cluster of similar, related, or recurring incidents rather than a single incident'. The idea is that rather than transplant mechanisms developed elsewhere 'off the shelf', they should be tailored to fit the needs of the problems within the locality. Rather as the tailormade suit requires extensive prior measurement of the body it is made to fit, a problem-oriented approach to crime prevention requires extensive measurement and analysis of the nature of the problems within a given area. This approach involves at least the following five steps (see Ekblom 1987):

- detailed crime analysis
- selection of appropriate prevention strategies for the local problems in the light of the crime analysis
- a partnership between relevant agencies, including consultation with local residents or targeted population where appropriate
- implementation of the strategies
- evaluation of the effects.

Broadly speaking this methodology constitutes the framework for the statutory duty on local authorities and police to formulate and implement a community safety strategy under the Crime and Disorder Bill 1998.

Good quality information not only constitutes the basis for a 'problem-oriented' approach to crime within a given locality but also allows for a comprehensive backdrop against which to evaluate the success or otherwise of any subsequent intervention.

Various agencies routinely collect data about crime. The most obvious form of data is that held by the local police. However, police offence data on its own is unreliable because of the high levels of unreported and unrecorded crime. Reporting and recording rates vary according to the offence involved. Hence, not only does police crime data underestimate the extent of crime but it distorts it in relation to different types of crime and with regard to different groups of people as victims or witnesses. Victimisation surveys have shown that there are diverse and complex reasons why people do not report offences to the police (Jones *et al.* 1986; Mayhew *et al.* 1994; Mirrlees-Black *et al.* 1996). This may relate to people's perceived satisfaction with the police, whether they think the police will take their offence sufficiently seriously, or the perceived likelihood of effective police action. Nevertheless, the police do have other information which can be useful in the planning stage of crime prevention programmes. For example, information about calls from the public – both emergency and routine calls – can provide useful data about incidents which may not result in formal action but which may contribute to an understanding of overall crime patterns. Existing information can be improved to assist crime prevention strategies by requiring the collection of data – by 'scenes of crime' officers, for example – which may be of assistance at a later date. For instance, Farrell and Pease (1993) have argued for the need for the police to collect more information on the victims of crime which is sufficiently sensitive to identify and flag 'repeat victimisation'. Currently, it can be difficult to recognise repeat victims from police forces' own Crime Information System.

Crime analysis

In order to develop a localised and targeted approach, information can be used 'to break down the idea of "crime" into a more differentiated picture of exactly what crimes, against what kinds of targets, where, and by whom' (Shapland *et al.* 1994: 3). This is the aim of crime analysis. Crime analysis strategies encourage the police to obtain detailed information about local patterns of crime and devise prevention programmes appropriate to local problems in the light of this analysis. Crime analysis therefore involves two stages. The first comprises a summary of the data on offending and victimisation on the basis of which patterns and trends are sought. The second requires the interpretation of patterns of offending and victimisation in order to explain them (Ekblom 1988). Reed and Oldfield (1995) identify four overall patterns that may be sought through the analysis of local crime data:

- crime patterns – the nature and distribution of crime within an area
- crime trends – significant changes in an area's crime pattern over time
- crime clusters – groups of crimes linked through similar characteristics
- crime series – crimes with common offenders.

On the basis of these patterns, maps of local areas can be drawn up (with the use of sophisticated computer mapping programmes) which can identify particular crime 'hot spots', peak times in the day at which crimes occur, clusters of 'repeat victims' or other concentrations of offences, offenders or victims. These can be particularly useful in designing targeted crime prevention strategies.

Crime analysis has encouraged the police to use relevant data in a more systematic and rigorous manner. However, there is a danger that it prioritises certain kinds of data or reduces information to that which can be easily displayed on maps. There is also a concern that such information is used in a narrow way which excludes information not immediately or easily available to the police. Hope, for example, notes that 'local crime analysis ought not restrict itself to the examination of crime patterns and trends – important though this is – but should also seek to identify the opportunities and constraints which relevant bodies and organisations face in implementing crime prevention initiatives' (1985). And yet, as the Morgan Report concluded, cases where a strategic approach to crime prevention has been developed based on the 'factual analysis of problems' tend to be the exception. More often, however, 'problem identification is opportunistic and haphazard' (Morgan 1991: 21).

Local surveys

Given the limitations of official crime statistics, victimisation surveys have become a central component of many local crime prevention initiatives and a key element in the development of crime prevention policy. They give a more accurate representation of the nature and extent of crime, often obscured in official statistics by the 'dark figure' of unreported and/ or unrecorded crime. Consequently, they have become a central instrument with which to target and evaluate social strategies. They are also advocated by many practitioners as essential requirements for genuinely accountable and locally sensitive interventions. NACRO, for example, have argued that surveys provide 'the detailed information necessary for planning a local crime prevention strategy' (Osborn and Bright 1989: 10), whilst the Morgan Working Group Report concluded that;

> surveys of local people can provide further information [to supplement official statistics] which can be particularly useful in planning the detail of community safety initiatives. Obtaining the views and experiences of residents and young people can often give a different picture of criminal behaviour and indicate a different set of concerns.
>
> (Home Office 1991: para. 4.49)

Surveys, by mapping victimisation and associated social problems, allow crime prevention to be grounded on an assessment of local needs which goes beyond and may supplement official data. Crime surveys allow policy-makers to target need among those who suffer disproportionate levels of victimisation. Thus, 'multiple victims' can more easily be identified and targeted as the recipients of intervention (Forrester *et al.* 1990: 45). Surveys can provide data about the levels of crime against which crime prevention interventions can be evaluated at a later date. Consequently, the use of 'before and after' surveys has become an accepted model of evaluation (see Chapter 6). Surveys can provide important local information against which performance indicators can be constructed and measured. If sensitive to the dimensions of gender, age and ethnicity, surveys can help place otherwise neglected issues on the crime prevention agenda. By identifying much unreported crime, surveys can be used to move prevention away from traditional target-hardening approaches concerned with property crime to embrace crimes of the person against women, the young and ethnic minorities. It has been claimed that local victimisation surveys hold out the potential of being a 'democratic instrument' as they provide a map of consumer demand and satisfaction (Young 1992).

Nevertheless, it is important to acknowledge that the nature of local problems varies from one place to the next. Even within areas there is considerable variation in the concentration and mix of local problems. Some problems vary across time and may exhibit a seasonal pattern. Hence, surveys of large population samples covering wide areas tend to aggregate responses to the extent that they become almost meaningless and lack sensitivity to the highly localised nature (and experience) of much crime (Young 1988). There is therefore a need for local surveys with a large enough sample so as to identify the differences within and between areas and social groups.

However, there are complex methodological problems associated with crime surveys (see Chapter 6). Surveys are less able to tap certain forms of crime, particularly where there is no direct or clearly identifiable victim. As a consequence, it can be difficult to assert the place of corporate crime, for example, on local crime prevention agendas.[1] Locally based 'left realist' surveys have attempted to address this omission directly by extending the coverage of surveys to include commercial, and other white collar, crimes (Pearce 1990). Nevertheless, there are creative limits to the use of survey methods involving methodological problems, not all of which can be 'solved technically'. The requirement of surveys to use popularly meaningful definitions of crime inherently restricts the range of crimes covered in surveys.

One particularly acute general problem, as Skogan (1981) reminds us, is that crime surveys have an inherent 'events' orientation. This assumes that crimes are discrete incidents which can be isolated and measured. In relation to some crimes such as burglary, this may be unproblematic. However, in relation to crimes of violence and abuse this raises fundamental issues. Much research suggests that violence and abuse, rather than being an 'event' are better conceptualised as a 'process'. In some such situations violence may form part of a continuum of experience which is not exceptional but routine. This 'events' orientation is an inherent product of the need to quantify, central to the victimisation survey as a method of enquiry. Genn has highlighted the problematic implications of this 'events' orientation in relation to people who experience 'multiple victimisation' because of 'the demands of surveys that continuing states be conceptualised as individual events' (1988: 99).

This also suggests that the social and spatial focus of crime may affect the very conceptualisation of crime in terms of people's perceptions and definitions. Those social groups in the population who regularly experience particular types of victimisation come to perceive and define those acts in very different ways from those people who do not. They become part of their lived realities which only awkwardly translate into questionnaire responses. This can result in apparent anomalies like the higher levels of violence reported by White rather than Black people and middle class rather than poor respondents in a number of American surveys. Sparks (1981) explains this paradox in terms of an 'education effect' whereby those respondents with greater educational backgrounds are more likely to disclose evidence of violence in responding to surveys. This suggests that the cultural settings that people inhabit – their values, norms and perspectives – affect their sensitivity to, or tolerance of, violence.

There are also problems caused by the focus of victim surveys in that, at their most basic, they are about gathering data about events which respondents experience as victims, either directly or indirectly as a proxy. As I have argued:

> There is a danger that an over-reliance upon victimisation survey data
> by crime prevention policy makers will over-emphasise the attributes and

standpoint of the victim. This danger is evident in the tendency in much
crime prevention work to highlight the 'life style', 'situational' and
'opportunity' factors in the commission of crimes.

(Crawford 1997a: 252)

In attempting to address this problem, some crime prevention initiatives
have supplemented victim surveys with information from surveys of known
offenders (Forrester *et al.* 1988).

Finally, the use of surveys are limited by the type of questions asked
and the way in which they are framed, particularly in relation to questions about which individuals have little or no direct experience. As Skogan
concludes: 'Surveys are most appropriately a guide to policy when they
focus on things with which most people have had direct experience, but
for many of the general public this excludes important aspects of policing [and crime prevention]' (1996b: 81). Policy cannot be unambiguously read off from survey findings. The crime control needs of people
living within a given area will differ markedly. Surveys only represent an
aggregation of individual responses, not a collective response. While they
may tap previously unconsulted individual voices, it should not be presumed that those individuals collectively represent the 'community' or
even particular 'communities'. Surveys leave unresolved the difficult and
yet fundamental issue of their interpretation: how to negotiate between
the conflicting interests and demands to which they give rise. The
prioritisation of policies merely on the basis of numerical support or
majority consensus may lead to a form of majoritarianism in which
minorities' interests are ignored.

Consultation

In addition to surveys, other forms of consultation with local residents
can generate valuable data with which to inform the selection and targeting of prevention strategies. Moreover, consultation can serve to enhance
local ownership of a given crime prevention initiative, and consequently
increase its durability and effectiveness. A recent Home Office research
publication attempted to identify the aims of consultation for the purposes of policing, as well as to give an overview of different ways in which
this may be achieved (Elliot and Nicholls 1996). The report identified
seven aims of public consultation:

- reaching a broad and representative sample of the population
- identifying public priorities to influence annual policing plans
- identifying public priorities for immediate action
- providing the public with information on policing activity and
  initiatives
- developing partnerships with the public to prevent crime
- obtaining rapid police action on public concerns
- obtaining information from the police.

As the authors note, the last two are aims for policing from the public's perspective, while the first five are viewed from the perspective of the police and related organisations, such as the police authority. They imply that consultation arrangements which only meet the police's aims and not those of the public will fail to generate support for, and confidence in, the process of consultation itself. They go on to assess a number of mechanisms of consultation against these aims, including:

- police community consultation groups (PCCGs)
- social surveys
- focus groups
- consumer panels
- networking.

It is suggested that no single consultation mechanism can satisfy all seven aims, given their diversity. Consequently, the report's authors advocate a 'consultation package', the success of which should be evaluated as a whole.

What this ignores is that at the heart of consultation lies a tension, in that it blurs and confuses two potentially separate elements in the implementation process: information gathering and the selection or prioritisation of specific needs and strategies identified on the basis of the information gathered. The latter does not emerge unambiguously from the former, but rather the latter is concerned with political choices, and hence with policy-making. Forms of consultation differ in the extent to which those that are consulted are given a say in the policy-making process. Forms of consultation can be used to manage local expectations to 'test' support for particular strategies – which may or may not have been designed elsewhere – to give marginalised groups a stake in the process or to steer the direction of policy and own the initiative. Hence, consultation as a mechanism needs to be founded on an explicit understanding of why consultation occurs at all and what outcomes it seeks.

In addition to the channels of consultation identified by the Home Office report, some localities have experimented with 'citizen's juries' to help inform local initiatives (Stewart 1996). The process is designed to test local views on a variety of policies by exposing 'jurors' to evidence presented by various 'experts' and interested organisations. They can 'cross-examine' witnesses, while moderators assist them to draw up recommendations. However, despite the explicit policy-making role of citizen's juries the relationship between the jury and the body (often the local authority) which sets it up remains unclear. Are the recommendations to be binding? Do they supplement or inform the internal decision-making processes of the parent body? And if the latter, how and to what extent?

However, in practice it is often unclear exactly what the purpose of consultation is. There is often an ambivalence about consultation, which may amount to little more than a legitimisation exercise. Consultation can also be costly and time-consuming. It may uncover needs or concerns which cannot be addressed adequately by a crime prevention initiative and may raise expectations beyond that which can be delivered. Inherently, consultation embodies problematic concerns over inclusion and lines of representation: who should be included and what interests or whom do they represent? These are fundamentally important issues, particularly in the field of crime control and prevention where there are overt dangers of constructing policies *against* certain groups, resulting in their social exclusion.

As in other fields of public policy, 'consultative' mechanisms in crime prevention generally fail to confront questions about the (un)representativeness of community representatives. As Sampson *et al.* note, inclusion is bound up with powerful agency definitions of the 'respected' and 'respectable' (1988: 489), as a result of which 'troublesome' groups are often marginalised, ignored or overlooked. This is a common research finding and is frequently justified on the grounds that community safety partnerships are about consensus-building and that such 'troublesome' groups would merely disrupt any established accord. Most conspicuously, this affects young people who are often perceived to be potentially 'troublesome' and hence are largely absent from community crime prevention schemes. The question is how to get marginalised groups 'on side', particularly those with high representation within the criminal justice system. Some community safety groups appear to have tried to address these issues in more constructive ways than have others. With the considerable emphasis on 'youth at risk' in community safety strategies, there is a danger in constituting 'youth' as a problem. The crucial issue is how to incorporate youth interests into multi-agency structures and to ensure greater consultation with youth groups in order that their voices can be heard as constructive and not merely as 'problematic'. However, this can be fraught with difficulties, as 'youth' itself is not an homogenous social category.

The 'partnership' approach

The acceptance of the appropriateness and proliferation of a 'partnership' approach has been one of the most dramatic developments in crime control policy in the last decade, not only in Britain but also across Europe, North America and Australasia (Blumstein 1986; van Dijk 1995; Walters 1996). In Britain, ever since the 1984 inter-departmental circular 8/84, the development of crime prevention – community safety in particular – has become intimately bound up with the proliferation of a 'partnership approach'. The policy rhetoric is one in which various relevant agencies, organisations and the public are summoned into being active co-producers of crime prevention and public safety. This has been stimulated further by various financial incentives provided by central government which are available only on the basis of an explicit commitment to 'partnership' work. As a consequence, the development of 'partnerships' has become a pre-requisite for much public funding. The underlying justification for this is the belief that, as far as possible, social reactions to crime should reflect the nature of the phenomenon itself (Young 1992). Crime prevention and community safety lie beyond the competency of any one single agency. Crime by its nature is multi-faceted, both in its causes and effects. And yet the social response to crime is segmented and compartmentalised. Different agencies interact in divergent ways in relation to specific crime problems and they bring different expertise. A partnership approach allows the co-ordination of expertise and the pooling of information and resources. Most fundamentally, it affords an holistic approach to crime and associated issues which is 'problem-focused' rather than 'bureaucracy-premised'.

And yet a 'partnership' approach also embodies an implicit critique of traditional bureaucratic models of societal response and service delivery. It alludes to the lack of systemisation, co-ordination and integration which produce duplication, conflict, friction and institutional 'gaps'. Hence, the correction of these 'system failures' is in large part a managerial concern, as to how the system can be better administered. Consequently, it has become fashionable, in the United States and Britain, to describe criminal justice as a 'non-system' to emphasise this dysfunctionality.

However, the concept of a 'partnership' approach, while widely endorsed, has been the subject of little analysis or consideration. As recent practice has shown, achieving successful partnerships is by no means straightforward. While the advantages of multi-agency working are often rehearsed, the difficulties are seldom addressed. In order to do so it is worth beginning to specify the different forms that partnerships can take.

Types of partnerships

On the basis of its review of national developments, the Morgan Report (1991: 46) identified five basic models which reflect differences in co-ordination, structure and resourcing:

- the 'independent' model, with an independent co-ordinator
- the 'local authority based' model
- the 'police centred local' model
- the 'police centred headquarters' model
- the 'indeterminate' model, with no clear leader, co-ordinator or strategy.

To this list Liddle and Gelsthorpe have added a sixth, the 'corporate' model, with no 'lead agency' (1994a: 20). Here the co-ordination, decision-making and implementation of work are regarded for the most part as being the responsibility of the partnership group as a whole. The

Crime and Disorder Bill 1998 creates a slightly different model whereby the 'leadership' is shared between the police and local authority.

These models attempt to identify the existence or absence of a clear dominant party within a given partnership. This is important in itself for, as we shall see, power relations represent the central dynamic in the study of inter-agency relations. And yet, in doing so, these models tend merely to reflect the self-proclaimed image of a partnership and its organisational location rather than the more subtle nature of relations between the agencies. To some extent it is Liddle and Gelsthorpe's 'corporate' model to which most partnerships aspire, and yet in order to develop a nuanced understanding of how they operate we need to look behind the 'partnership' façade.

Some of the principal issues and differences within partnerships tend to revolve around a number of axis relating to:

- the nature of differential power relations between the parties and their implication for the management and negotiation of conflict
- the level of collaboration between agencies and the associated degree of loss of organisational autonomy
- the degree of formality or informality in the relations between the partners
- the level within an organisational hierarchy at which a partnership structure is located
- the existence or absence of a dedicated co-ordinator for the partnership.

Let us consider these in greater detail.

Inter-organisational conflict and differential power relations

Empirical research into the dynamics of partnership relations in crime prevention and community safety has highlighted the importance of inter-organisational conflicts and differential power relations between the parties (Blagg *et al.* 1988; Sampson *et al.* 1988; Pearson *et al.* 1992; Crawford and Jones 1995; Crawford 1997a). Research has shown that there are real conflicts and tensions between different agencies incorporated into partnership structures. Partnerships – especially within the field of crime control and criminal justice – by their nature draw together diverse organisations with very different cultures, ideologies and traditions, which pursue distinct aims through divergent structures, strategies and practices. Hence, deep structural conflicts exist between the parties that sit down together in partnerships. Criminal justice agencies have very different priorities and interests, as do other public sector organisations, voluntary bodies, the commercial sector and local community groups.

However, in the struggles over conflicting interests and ideologies not all agencies and groups are equally powerful. Organisations bring to crime problems competing claims to specialist knowledge and expertise, as well as differential access to both human and material resources. It is not surprising, therefore, that certain agencies tend to dominate the policy agenda. This allows for the capture of crime prevention by certain interests, and hence the prioritisation of certain forms of intervention against certain types of crime. In the field of crime prevention it is often the police who are in a dominant position. As Sampson *et al.* note:

> The police are often enthusiastic proponents of the multi-agency approach, but they tend to prefer to set the agendas and to dominate forum meetings, and then to ignore the multi-agency framework when it suits their own needs.
>
> (1988: 491)

However, this is not always the case as power relations, to some extent, are context specific. For example, in certain instances on estate-based projects, local authority housing departments often exert a dominant influence, while in other areas different local authority departments or the health service may occupy a more dominant position. Consequently, an understanding of the nature of differential power relations becomes a fundamental element in the study of inter-agency relations. As Sampson and colleagues suggest: 'It is power differentials running between different state agencies which influence other symptomatic forms of inter-agency conflict, such as struggles over confidentiality and privileged access information' (1991: 132).

Sampson and colleagues rightly note a distinction between these oppositions which are 'always latent' and 'surface level' relations (1988: 482). This points us towards examining a fundamental question for understanding partnership work: how do these oppositions and conflicts relate to, and how are they embedded in, routinised social action between the parties to a partnership? However, in their research Sampson *et al.* tend to concentrate on instances in which latent conflicts realise and express themselves in inter-agency tensions. While their research has been important in highlighting the nature of conflictual relations in partnership arrangements, it has tended to over-emphasise 'surface level' conflict and to ignore other strategies through which conflict is managed, suppressed or circumvented. They disregard the ways in which deeper level oppositions are negotiated in non-overtly conflictual interactions. Their research has marginalised the ways in which differential power relations express themselves through such strategies.

By contrast, Crawford and Jones (1995) have highlighted the significance of conflict avoidance in inter-agency relations, by which latent structural conflicts are side-stepped. On the basis of their empirical research findings, they suggest that what is most striking about partnership work, given the deep structural conflicts which exist between agencies and within communities, is the absence – rather than the presence – of overt conflict. This absence, they suggest, arises largely because inter-agency workers develop what are sometimes highly creative strategies for 'defining away' and circumventing conflict. Rather than being aired or resolved, conflict is avoided. Thus, for Crawford and Jones, unlike Sampson and colleagues, power differences produce conflict avoidance strategies as well as overt conflict. For them, power is understood as a creative and productive force – a means of getting things done – as well as a constraint upon action, expressed through conflict. However, they do not suggest that such strategies necessarily produce beneficial effects for partnership work. On the contrary, they associate conflict avoidance with a counterproductive dominant ethos within partnerships, an 'ideology of unity' (Crawford 1994a). This represents an ends-oriented rather than a means-oriented ideology, whereby conflict and dissensus are perceived to be the enemies of effective partnerships. Conflict is a necessary element of partnership work. Moreover, conflicts may exist for very good principled reasons. Criminal justice, after all, is concerned with balancing sometimes competing individual and group rights and embodies finely balanced tensions between the independence and inter-dependence of criminal justice agencies. Problematic issues such as confidentiality can easily be trampled in the stampede for 'unity'. A pervasive 'ideology of unity' tends to silence very real intra-community, as well as inter-organisational, conflicts by the dual processes of first, excluding 'non-consensual' voices and, second, through the working assumption that an homogeneity of interests actually exists.

Crawford (1997a: Chapter 4) points to two such strategies. The first, involves real conflicts being dispersed into other arenas, rather than being negotiated or resolved at formal multi-agency fora. Consequently, they are dealt with in informal or 'shadow' settings. In these settings differential power relations often become paramount in defining who is included and the ability of different organisations and actors to impose their definition of a situation on others, as well as to realise their strategic interests. Where structural oppositions, divergent values and professional missions exist, conflict may in fact be a desirable product of inter-agency work. Conflict may be the healthy expression of different interests. It is, therefore, important that these differences should not be ignored or defined away in the search for inter-agency consensus. Rather, they need to be recognised and addressed.

A second strategy is that of 'multiple aims'. This is common among community safety initiatives and takes the form of increasingly disparate aims or objectives being accorded a place on a partnership project's agenda. Rather than specifying clear and limited objectives, because of the conflict that this might provoke, some partnerships prefer to opt for vague and multiple aims. This is what we might prefer to call a 'Smögasbord' approach, in which something for everyone is placed on the menu (Crawford 1998a). While multiple aims enable crime prevention and community safety initiatives to draw on a wide and diverse audience for support, they also constitute their Achilles heel. In seeking to meet the divergent aims that they proclaim, these schemes are pulled in different, and often competing, directions as they attempt to satisfy the divergent demands of their different constituencies. Multiple aims increase confusion and ambiguity, which for some may be their explicit purpose. However, muddying the waters in the long-term is likely to damage trust, rather than enhance it. In the process, projects can find themselves signing up to such broad and sometimes confused aims as to be almost meaningless. The danger is that in the attempt to appease all interests, fundamental aims are not prioritised. This may lead to 'lowest common denominator' solutions and a lack of clarity and coherency. This also presents significant problems for evaluation, as it is unclear which criteria should be prioritised (for further discussion see Chapter 6).

In sum, Crawford and Jones (1995) suggest that conflict avoidance strategies are problematic for a number of reasons. First, differential power relations remain unaddressed, unregulated and unchallenged. As a consequence, powerful agencies will continue to dominate and to 'do their own thing'. What is more, weaker parties are likely to be excluded either directly by not being invited to participate in the shadow conversations that matter or by default in that their input is seen as increasingly irrelevant. Second, conflict is not negotiated or resolved in any socially constructive manner. As a consequence, real issues of principle or divergent interests are not confronted. In the long term this is likely to lead to false expectations and erode trust relations. Their research suggests that the mutual recognition of difference and the acknowledgement of the importance and limitations of different contributions by the divergent partners are fundamental for effective long-term partnerships. They represent a more preferable premise from which to set out in search of common interests in inter-agency relations than either an assumed consensus or an ends-oriented 'quest for unity'.

Levels of collaboration: inter-agency versus multi-agency work

In order to specify differences in levels of collaboration Crawford and Jones (1996) draw attention to, and begin to specify, differences between conceptions of 'partnership' work (understood as a generic term). They make a conceptual distinction between two different 'ideal types' of partnerships. They distinguish between, on the one hand, '*multi*-agency' relations and, on the other hand, '*inter*-agency' relations. These, they suggest, can be seen as two end points along a continuum which moves from simple co-operation to ever-greater levels of collaboration.

At one end of the continuum *multi-agency* partnerships involve the coming together of various agencies in relation to a given problem, without this significantly affecting or transforming the work they do. The same tasks are conducted in co-operation with others. The roles of the partners remain distinct. Key officers are called on to represent their organisation and to pool collective expertise and resources. Their core tasks remain largely unaltered, as multi-agency work is grafted on to existing practices, or those existing practices are redefined.

At the other end of the continuum *inter-agency* relations are those relations which interpenetrate and thus affect normal internal working relations. They entail some degree of fusion and melding of relations between agencies. They involve collaboration and interdependence. For example, inter-agency work may impact on the nature of mainstream service delivery within participating organisations. Often, new 'team' structures, identifiable units or forms of working, arise. These may be organisationally distinct from, and physically housed outside of, any of the participating agencies. One such example is the model pioneered by the Northamptonshire Diversion Units whereby the six participating agencies (probation, police, youth services, social services, education and health service) second at least one full-time worker to the Units for a period of between two and three years. The seconded workers perform broadly the same functions as part of a team, albeit drawing on their distinct skills, expertise and contacts. Here, team loyalties may replace or supersede parent organisational loyalties during the secondment period.

Actual initiatives lie somewhere between these polar types. While those which approximate more clearly to the 'inter-agency' model offer greater rewards in collaborative activities, as we shall see, they also present more acute problems for the management of the conflicts to which inter-organisational relations give rise. Importantly, both 'types' present participating agencies with different responsibilities and levels of involvement. This conceptual distinction points us towards the need for greater clarity and specification by the parties as to the desirable form to which a given partnership model should accord. It also identifies the fact that the more that a 'partnership' resembles a collaborative inter-agency approach, the more it is likely to blur the boundaries, as to roles and function, of the participating agencies – and the greater the loss of organisational autonomy. Partnerships, by their nature, blur the boundaries between the roles and functions of incorporated organisations. This can present difficulties for accountability and for the appropriate distribution of responsibilities. Hence, there is a need to maintain clarity of the divergent inputs and their collaborative objectives.

'Independence' and 'partnership' stand in a highly ambiguous relation to each other. For if, as Rock notes, it is the 'independent interdependence' between organisations which constitutes 'the weak force which binds the criminal justice system together' (1990: 39), what are the implications of partnerships for organisational autonomy? Given the tendency of partnerships (particularly of an 'inter-agency' type) to blur the organisational boundaries as to roles, tasks and purpose, difficult questions need to be asked about the independence and autonomy of the parties: how much autonomy is it necessary for each agency to lose for the sake of the corporate good? How much autonomy are agencies willing to forego? The answers to each of these questions will, in part, depend on the type of partnership relations envisaged.

Degrees of formality and informality

Partnerships vary considerably in their degree of formality from highly bureaucratic meetings, on the one hand, to interpersonal contacts or loose networks on the other. Many community safety practitioners prefer informal partnerships which prioritise action over formality. There is often a concern that formal meetings are unproductive and may become mere 'talking shops'. And yet informal partnerships are problematic as they are difficult to monitor or evaluate. The advantages of informal arrangements are that they allow greater flexibility and enable the parties to 'get on with the job' without formal arrangements hindering progress (Liddle and Gelsthorpe 1994a: 8). However, as a consequence of the important personal dimension to informal arrangements, they can be particularly susceptible to the negative impact of staff turnover. If partnerships are dependent on the nature of interpersonal relations alone, then any significant change in key personnel may have precarious effects.

Sampson and colleagues concluded their research recognising an important tension between formality and informality in partnerships:

> It must be frankly acknowledged, however, that there is a significant
> contradiction within our research evidence. On the one hand, informal
> systems of inter-agency working and information exchange are risky
> encounters which can endanger important confidentialities and might even
> sometimes constitute a threat to civil liberties. On the other hand, more
> informal and fluid systems of inter-agency relations seem to offer a more
> workable basis for communication and negotiation.
>
> (Pearson *et al.* 1992: 64–5)

This contradiction is particularly evident in their discussion of gender relations (Sampson *et al.* 1991). On the basis of their research they suggest that women's experiences of marginalisation and discrimination within their own organisations have a significant impact on inter-agency co-operation. Hence, gender relations, as well as producing sites of conflict between agencies, also constitute the locus of shared experiences and forms of allegiances across agency boundaries. They conclude that:

> These experiences mean not only that some forms of inter-agency work are
> severely limited by the avoiding action taken by women workers in order to
> minimise potentially discriminatory encounters, but also that as a means of
> countering their marginalisation women workers will establish different types
> of alliances with workers in other organisations.
>
> (Sampson *et al.* 1991: 115)

These networks may cut across structured power relations between agencies. Hence, there may be specific gender dimensions to the development of partnerships, particularly within organisations whose work is notably gendered, such as the police where 'real policing' is often associated with macho, male characteristics. Consequently, important inter-organisational trust relations which sustain partnerships may be formed around lines of gender.

However, Sampson and colleagues are right to highlight a tension in informal relations. For, while novel and creative informal networks may be made across organisational boundaries, they present problems as well as possibilities. As already noted, informal or hidden relations often may arise as a consequence of a strategy of conflict avoidance. This can lead to decisions being taken outside of formal and public processes. Often, important decisions are taken elsewhere, behind the scenes and in private settings. Such 'shadow' relations are hard to monitor and present problems for accountability. This can be, and often is, justified in terms of 'getting things done'. However, it runs counter to the spirit of transparency and often reinforces the power of the more dominant partners and, at the same time, undermines the role of weaker partners. Informal contexts may leave differential power relations unchecked, hide decision-making processes from review and remove them from any democratic input or control.

Questions of hierarchy

Formality may sometimes be wrongly conflated with questions of hierarchy, as Pearson *et al.* do (1992: 63). One important question often asked by practitioners about community safety partnerships is, what is the appropriate hierarchical level within organisations at which partnership structures should be located? There is often the problem that decisions struck at a senior level need to be renegotiated at a lower one. In many instances, the implementation of inter-agency co-operation requires the, often ongoing, renegotiation of any such agreements at various different organisational levels. The perceptions, attitudes and actions of 'ordinary' mainstream officers, therefore, are integral to an understanding of the way organisational change is fought over, negotiated and resolved. Some practitioners complain that partnerships are set too high within organisational structures and have little relevance for front-line workers. This tends to reinforce a 'top–down' approach to problems which runs counter to a 'problem-oriented' philosophy.

One option is to establish multi-tiered partnership structures. This necessitates good quality vertical communication between the structures. But as Liddle and Gelsthorpe note, there are difficulties involved in synchronising the strategic and practice levels in crime prevention structures (1994b: 3). Inter-agency relations and the influences that shape them can also vary across different hierarchical. A spirit of co-operation at one level might coexist with bitter disagreement at another. Ideally, effective partnerships need to be able to gain the commitment of senior officers and simultaneously affect front-line workers and make them feel involved.

The role of a co-ordinator

Co-ordination itself is a key feature of a competent partnership. The absence of co-ordination can be wasteful and ineffective, resulting in a situation in which the 'different interest groups pass each other like ships in the night' (Sampson *et al.* 1988: 488). Establishing a sense of local ownership of community safety problems among participating agencies can require a 'motivation for involvement' which co-ordinators are ideally well placed to promote (Liddle and Gelsthorpe 1994a: 18). Given these tensions and conflicts within partnerships, the role of an independent co-ordinator can be instrumental in negotiating conflicts and mediating power differences between the parties. Tilley (1992), in his review of the first phase Safer Cities Projects, identified the pivotal role of co-ordinators. The success or failure of some of the projects was in large part dependent on the ability of the co-ordinators, as well as the relationship that co-ordinators struck with their multi-agency steering committees. It would seem to follow, therefore, that the existence or absence of a dedicated co-ordinator will have considerable implications for the effectiveness of a specific initiative. However, co-ordination is both labour-intensive and time-consuming. Many crime prevention strategies are insufficiently large to be able to afford the cost of a co-ordinator. In this situation the function of a co-ordinator may have to be delegated, divided up or rotated.

Gilling (1994) suggests that the professional backgrounds of those working in multi-agency crime prevention may be an important influence on conceptions of what crime prevention is about, and hence the type of schemes prioritised. However, Sutton's (1996) analysis of Safer Cities co-ordinators suggests that there was no simple relationship between a co-ordinator's professional background and the proportion of money spent by a project on different types of crime prevention initiatives (be they situational or offender-oriented). Nevertheless, the influence of the steering committee and the co-ordinator's relationship with it remains a significant issue. On the basis of the experience of Safer Cities Projects, Sutton (1996) identifies three different types of relationship between steering committee and co-ordinator: 'dominant', 'consultative' and 'passive'.

Tilley (1992: 8) highlights the importance of a co-ordinator – acting as an 'honest broker' – in the process of overcoming initial suspicion, building trust between agencies and gaining local credibility. The co-ordinator, as a 'stranger', is in a good position to begin to ask for reciprocal co-operation in return for services and resources. In an ideal situation, he suggests: 'A virtuous circle sets in where trust leads to co-operation which leads to synergism which leads to successful outcomes which leads to resources which increases trust and so on' (*ibid.*). And yet Tilley also identifies one of the central tensions that a dedicated co-ordinator presents for crime prevention partnerships. Once co-ordination has been established there is the danger that the partnership agencies will become too reliant on the co-ordinator and devolve to them tasks and responsibilities which should rightfully be their own. In other words, there is a danger that the role of the co-ordinator can become counterproductive by acting as an alternative reference point which undermines the capacity of the partnership, as a collective entity, to solve its own problems. This is what Tilley calls the problem of the 'guest who stayed too long' (1992: 10).

The danger to which Tilley alludes is certainly a real one, particularly one which Safer Cities Projects experienced, as they were always envisaged to have a determinate lifespan. Safer Cities funding was provided for three years only, after which time they had to develop their own succession strategy which may or may not have involved a continuing role for a co-ordinator. However, Tilley's use of the analogy of the 'stranger' that comes to stay presupposes that co-ordination is a finite task. It assumes that trust, reciprocity and conflict negotiation once established can be maintained. It may be that the role of the co-ordinator, rather like that of the steering committee, changes over time as partnerships develop. However, the maintenance of trust and reciprocity, together with the ongoing negotiation of conflict, are tasks to which a dedicated co-ordinator could turn. As a consequence, some partnerships have found it necessary to design procedures which challenge and monitor inter-agency relations on an ongoing or periodic basis. Nevertheless, it is important to note that *co-ordination* by a dedicated (independent) party can get in the way of inter-agency *collaboration*.

Some further issues

Questions of trust

Trust has become acknowledged as a fundamental dynamic in inter-agency relations (Crawford 1997a). Research suggests that effective work across organisational boundaries requires the establishment and sustenance of trust relations. In the field of criminal justice this is not easy, particularly where there is a history of mistrust or misunderstanding. A crucial element in establishing trust relations is making people and institutions aware of the limitations of their own and other agencies' contribution, so that they neither try to 'do it all' nor do they have unrealistic expectations of what others can deliver. Hence, clarifying roles and responsibilities assists the development of trust as it mitigates the tensions caused by role confusions. Mistrust is often the product of stereotypes held by some agency workers regarding those who work in other agencies and with whom traditionally they have had little contact. Consequently, increased inter-agency contact itself, particularly in the form of joint or collective secondments, can help correct misunderstandings and unrealistic expectations as well as undermine stereotypes.

The importance of trust suggests a need to recognise that partnerships have an important temporal dimension, a 'lifespan' (Crawford 1998a). Partnerships develop and fluctuate over time as circumstances change. As trust develops and partnerships become more established, different ways of managing conflict may become more appropriate. However, trust relations are always fragile and need to be the subject of ongoing monitoring and nurturing. This may require the establishment of dynamics within inter-agency relations which continually or periodically seek to challenge and reinvigorate partnerships.

Research and practice suggest there is a need for mutual respect for different types of contributions. Here there is an important role for training in multi-agency relations and working dynamics which needs to be recognised, particularly in relation to designated staff performing link functions within partnership networks. Training can be one way of beginning to overcome the basis for misunderstandings and mistrust between agency workers.

Problems of accountability

Partnerships in crime prevention confront an ambiguity in organisational accountability. By their very nature there is no one identifiable agency or actor which is accountable for the outcomes of policy and its implementation. Rather, accountability is fragmented and dispersed. Joint and negotiated decisions tie the various parties into corporate policy and outcomes, but often fail to identify lines of responsibility. Institutional complexity further obscures who is accountable to whom, and for what. This gives rise to what Rhodes has identified as, ' "the problem of many hands" where so many people contribute that no one contribution can be identified; and if no one person can be held accountable after the event, then no one needs to behave responsibly beforehand' (1996: 663). As authority is 'shared' it becomes difficult to disentangle and can become almost illusive.

In the long term, the problems associated with organisational accountability are unlikely to disappear, but need to be addressed through openness about organisational roles, responsibilities and lines of representation. Problems of organisational accountability suggest the need to tie community safety structures to the local democratic structure, as the Morgan Report suggested (1991: 20), in order to establish some form of political legitimacy. However, partnerships do not derive their legitimacy at a *political* but at an *administrative* level: in claims to superior cumulative expertise and increased effectiveness of service provision. In practice, the involvement of elected representatives is rarely apparent. Liddle and Gelsthorpe warn that while this may increase 'local ownership' it can introduce a volatility into crime prevention work (1994a: 16). The danger of majoritarianism and the capture of community safety as a 'political football' should challenge local authorities to look to, and experiment with, other forms of democratisation, not instead of, but as supplements to, traditional channels of representation.

Inter-organisational and intra-organisational relations

As Pearson *et al.* note 'what often appear as *inter*-organisational conflicts are sometimes more appropriately understood as *intra*-organisational conflicts' (1992: 65). Managerial priorities, cultural perceptions and gender relations within specific organisations may all impact on the nature and ability of individuals and groups to work within and beyond organisational boundaries. Thus, partnerships not only confront structural conflicts between agencies but these are often compounded and confused by internal organisational conflicts. In other words, partnerships not only bring all the benefits offered by the inclusion of each partner, but are accompanied by the internal disputes and conflicts that sometimes rage within organisations. This can occur at an interpersonal as well as at a more structural level. For example, staff turnover, particularly of key link personnel or multi-agency co-ordinators, may undermine established trust relations or question the commitment of individuals or organisations to given partnerships.

Managerialism and partnerships

Recent government policy has seen a shift towards what (somewhat confusingly in that the name suggests a rupture with the past) is termed 'new public management' (NPM) reforms. These 'managerialist' reforms include hiving off certain traditional aspects of public service delivery to the private sector; the extensive use of internal performance measurement and management by outputs; disaggregating separable functions into quasi-contractual or quasi-market forms particularly by introducing purchaser/provider distinctions; and opening up provider roles to competition between agencies or between public agencies, private sector firms and voluntary sector bodies (Hood 1991; Stewart and Walsh 1992; McLaughlin and Muncie 1994). Many commentators have associated the rise of a partnership approach with the logic of managerialism in that it promotes the smooth administration of crime control and criminal justice in the name of the 3 Es of 'economy, efficiency and effectiveness' (Crawford 1994a: Bottoms 1995; Bottoms and Wiles 1996). Clearly, the development of a partnership approach has fed off managerialist assumptions that crime control needs to be better managed in order to reduce waste as well as limit duplication and friction. In their place a partnership approach appeals to 'coherence, co-ordination and synergy'. Nevertheless, there remain important incongruities between the logics of managerialism and the notion of genuine 'partnerships'. In a variety of ways managerialist reforms have served to exacerbate tensions between inter-organisational and intra-organisational dynamics.

NPM reforms encourage an *intra*-organisational focus that pays little attention to managing *inter*-organisational networks (Rhodes 1996). In this context, little attention has been given to negotiating shared purposes, particularly where there is no hierarchy of control. Hence, intra-organisational priorities can undermine, or run counter to, the needs of inter-organisational partnerships. The intra-organisational focus on 'outputs' can make agencies concentrate their energies on their core tasks and activities at the expense of peripheral ones. Community safety, by its very nature, is precisely one such peripheral function of diverse agencies. Perversely, NPM reforms may actually serve to push government departments and public sector agencies further into prioritising their own introspective needs at the expense of collaborative and inter-organisational commitments. The emphasis on intra-organisational performance measurement fails to recognise that partnerships inherently blur the boundaries between, and the roles of, the incorporated organisations, such that individual contributions cannot easily be separated off and disentangled from each other, without undermining the nature of that contribution.

NPM reforms by creating quasi-markets and injecting competition into community safety can also serve to produce new sites of conflict. This is exacerbated by the non-coterminous administrative boundaries of major service providers potentially involved in crime prevention and community safety partnerships. This can result in a nightmare of intra- and inter-organisational competition which may threaten co-operation, reciprocity and trust.

There are further concerns about the impact of the new-found emphasis, within NPM reforms, on 'outputs' as distinct from 'outcomes'. 'Outputs' often refer to internally defined organisational goals over which organisations have considerable control. These may depart significantly from 'outcomes': the effects of an output, or set of outputs, on the wider community. There is a danger that 'outputs' may take precedence over 'outcomes' and that the gulf between the two may grow larger, so that social goals are eclipsed by organisational goals. This can result in a form of 'measure fixation' whereby greater concentration is given to the measure, rather than the service which the measure is intended to signify. Concentration on output measurement can create a form of 'tunnel vision' among managers which neglects the unquantifiable aspects of a service and which may marginalise long-term thinking, so crucial to social crime prevention and community safety (see Tilley 1995).

The contractualisation of partnerships has been a hallmark of NPM reforms as some partnerships have been encouraged to conform to a purchaser/provider model of relations, often between public sector bodies and voluntary organisations, whereby the former purchases the services of the latter in order to provide some service. Recent governments have encouraged local authorities, social, health and probation services to enter into such contracts under the rhetoric of 'partnerships'. And yet these partnerships are more like contractual relations. For example, the partnerships envisioned within the government's proposals for the probation service appear to involve more the competitive contracting out of services, whereby the probation service purchases voluntary sector provision, than with a creative mutual negotiation over the service to be provided with all the parties contributing equally (Home Office 1992c). Peering through the rhetorical cracks, the underlying philosophy seems to be predominantly concerned with the construction of a 'mixed economy' in the provision of criminal justice. In this context, partnerships are associated with the privatisation of public services through a process of contracting out to the so-called 'independent sector': an amalgam of voluntary organisations, community associations and private companies. However, the primary concern is that as a consequence of this contractualisation the voluntary sector will lose its independence as it becomes increasingly linked to the pursuit of state sponsored initiatives.

Such partnerships, with their emphasis on contracts, audits and other 'rituals of verification' (Power 1997), involve a shift in the character of trust, from traditional trust in the 'professional' to trust in the purchaser and the auditor. However, the strict adherence to particular contractual specification is often antithetical to ongoing trust relations both in business and social interactions which are sustained over time (Macaulay 1963). Sustaining trust relations may require the overriding of contractual obligations. Consequently, the inflexibility of NPM reforms may serve to undermine the ability of partners to sustain trust over periods of time. There are also considerable difficulties in writing down complex services such as those involved in crime prevention and community safety in specifications such as contracts and output measurements. Experience from the UK suggests that 'contracts deal poorly with ambiguity in the policy process' (Deakin and Walsh 1996: 37–8). Such ambiguity is a fundamental reality of crime prevention and community safety work.

In many ways the focus of NPM reforms is unsuited for managing inter-organisational partnerships and may serve to undermine them. The effective management of inter-organisational networks requires appropriate conditions in which joint and collaborative action can be sustained. This requires policies which foster reciprocity and interdependence between organisations, not insularity and competition. The challenge for government is to enable partnerships and to seek out new forms of co-operation, rooted in inter-organisational trust.

The extent of 'partnerships'

In October 1994 Crime Concern claimed there to be over 200 genuine multi-agency crime prevention partnerships in England and Wales (Crime Concern 1994b: 2). A more recent survey of local authorities in England and Wales found that 62.6 per cent of authorities are involved in independent, multi-agency partnerships; 48.3 per cent are involved in local authority-based approaches and 44.9 per cent in facilitating approaches whereby the local authority 'signposts' and refers the public to community safety projects – such as crime prevention panels and neighbourhood watch – and encourages the public to take community safety measures (LGMB 1996: 10). It is clear that the proposed statutory duty on local authorities and the police to form community safety partnerships (Home Office 1997a) will significantly increase the number of such arrangements, as will developments elsewhere in criminal justice (Home Office 1997d). However, there is a need to be sceptical about the extent to which the rhetoric of partnerships is realised. There is a big gulf between the often-heard ideals of 'partnerships' and the reality of its practice. Many partnerships are mere 'talking shops' or are better described as 'paper partnerships', which exist merely for the purposes of satisfying funding requirements.

Making sense of 'partnerships'

In trying to understand partnerships Sampson and colleagues identify two dominant perspectives, which they term the 'benevolent' and 'conspiracy' approaches (1988: 479–80). The former, they argue, assumes an unproblematic consensus within and between both the local state and communities. It is promoted by those 'who advocate', and is essentially 'a justification for', the multi-agency approach. Thus, from within the 'benevolent' approach multi-agency is perceived as a benign development which can only assist in the prevention of crime through greater co-ordination, systemisation and efficiency. This perspective assumes consensus between the parties.

By contrast, the 'conspiracy' perspective emphasises the coercive nature of the local state and highlights a sinister interpretation of the multi-agency approach. From within this perspective multi-agency partnerships are seen as both the site of, and a set of social processes which facilitate, the expansion of disciplinary social control into new areas of social life. Through 'partnerships', social welfare and non-criminal justice agencies, as well as community groups, are co-opted into the disciplinary process (Gordon 1987; Brake and Hale 1992: 75–6). This perspective emphasises the conflicting interests of those parties in multi-agency arrangements and highlights the capture of social, welfare and health needs by criminal justice ones. Given the already mentioned importance of differential power relations the danger of certain agencies dominating the policy agenda and co-opting weaker agencies and interests remains a real one. However, from within this perspective, this is seen largely as an uni-directional process in which control moves outwards from the police and criminal justice complex into the social body. In this process the former invades and colonises the latter.

It is clear, as Sampson and colleagues suggest on the basis of their research findings, that examples of both of these perspectives are to be found in practice. And yet they are both only partial understandings, which fall into a trap of juxtaposing conflict with consensus and seeing partnerships as either a wholly good or bad thing. By contrast Crawford (1994a, 1997a) has sought to highlight the ways in which partnerships reflect corporatist tendencies within the capitalist state. In so doing, he has endeavoured to give prominence to the more nuanced 'centrafugal dynamic' and 'osmotic processes' within inter-agency relations and across the public/private sector divide. This approach attempts to avoid falling into an uni-directional understanding of power relations, while at the same time refusing to see parnerships as the outcome of pluralistic competition or equal bargaining. Rather, it highlights tendencies towards 'social closure' and 'monopolistic control' as dynamic processes within partnerships. These give prominence to questions about the processes of 'incorporation', which embody the power of exclusion as well as inclusion.

The idea of corporatism helps us to recognise the importance of a growing 'hybrid' sphere which links and invades the state and civil society (Johnston 1992). It identifies both the powerful privileges and the regulatory implications of incorporation into partnerships, whereby '"included" organisations are given a privileged "public" status which grants them certain powers – including access to policy-formation – while at the same time conferring on them responsibilities – in terms of ensuring the implementation of, and compliance with, public policy' (Crawford 1994a: 501). It highlights the dual processes whereby *private* access to *public* policy-formation is facilitated as is *public* access to *private* policy-making and implementation. In so far as private interests are incorporated into the policy-formation processes, they are granted a certain 'publicness'. It also involves a degree of external intervention in the processes of 'private' and intra-organisational decision-making. As such, it identifies an important element of, and questions for, a contemporary research agenda (Hughes 1996; Walters 1996).

> Corporatism highlights an organisation's capacity both to represent its members' interests and to discipline and control them as part of a negotiated interaction with other groups. This interaction focuses attention on the nature of the relationship between organised interests and the state. This is understood, however, not as a relationship in which the state merely directs the interest associations, nor is it one in which state agencies are 'captured' by private interests. Rather, corporatism implies certain weaknesses as well as strengths within the state.
>
> (Crawford 1994a: 502)

As a consequence it identifies the volatile and unresolved management of agencies' and the public's expectations of what can be delivered in the name of public safety. Importantly, this approach points towards the idea that partnerships represent new forms of 'governance at a distance' which may require different modes of regulation (see Chapter 8). There is a need, however, not to over-emphasise the novelty of these neo-corporatist arrangements. They may be better understood as representing new, but partial, elements within the existing political formation which coexist alongside other modes of administration and regulation.

Community participation and involvement

Almost all studies of local crime prevention activities identify a difficulty in sustaining participants' interest and enthusiasm over time, even in places where initial levels of awareness and participation were high (Rosenbaum 1987; Palumbo *et al.* 1997). Communities organised solely or primarily around concerns about crime are often short-lived (Podolefsky and Dubow 1981). As Skogan notes, 'concern about crime simply does not provide a basis for sustained individual participation' (1988: 49). Crime is a difficult issue around which to organise. In part, this stems from the tendency of crime to divide people, in terms of their values as to what is considered 'right' and 'wrong', in terms of their tolerance of certain forms of behaviour and in terms of the categorisation of people as either 'offenders' or 'victims' (reality is often more complex than that): those considered to be 'respectable' and those considered to be 'part of the problem'. The dynamics of incorporation and exclusion are particularly powerful in relation to 'community' participation and involvement. As we saw in Chapter 4, the notion of 'community' in community safety is often linked with ideas of shared homogenous values, whereby offenders are viewed primarily as 'outsiders' against which the 'community' needs to defend itself. Boundaries of inclusion are often constructed around insider/outsider distinctions which connect with local prejudices. Research has also shown that the ability of certain interest groups to organise around, and define, issues of crime is of paramount importance in attaining a voice (Crawford 1995). The unrepresentative nature of much 'community representation' is a recurring theme of much research (Sampson *et al.* 1988).

As Podolefsky and Dubow's research has shown, community workers are often aware that crime is a problematic issue around which to organise people precisely because it is difficult to produce demonstrable results and thereby gain the confidence of the community (1981: 226). This tends to mean that community crime prevention can unwittingly be pushed into prioritising situational forms of intervention because local people find it easier to identify with and organise around identifiable and tangible interventions in the physical world. This is often exacerbated by the fact that project workers are regularly under considerable pressure (notably from local politicians, the public and the media) to identify 'success stories'. This and analogous pressures often serve to prioritise interventions which produce short-term quantifiable results. The recognition of these real pressures should encourage policy-makers and project workers to consider the dissemination of information which may offer communities greater levels of confidence in their stake in long-term social crime prevention. As Walklate suggests, there is a need in community safety for 'a much clearer understanding of how and why some issues become "consumer issues" and others not' (1992: 114).

Commercial sector involvement

Throughout recent government policy statements – from circular 8/84, through the Morgan Report (1991) to the new Labour government's proposals (Home Office 1997a) – the business sector has been identified as a key element in a 'partnership approach'. Commercial sector involvement in crime prevention and community safety can broadly take a number of forms:

- crime prevention against the sector's own products or services, either at the design stage or some later one
- crime prevention against a business's own premises and staff
- contribution to local, or wider, community safety initiatives.

Each of these will have different implications for the benefits that may accrue to a given business. Governments have sought to encourage businesses to play a more active role in crime prevention in all three spheres (Home Office 1991: 37). Despite this, the recent experience of private sector involvement has been limited and patchy (Bright 1991). In large part, this is because it has been difficult to persuade businesses that it is in their economic best interests to do so, particularly as their primary concern remains the maximisation of profits.

As a consequence, it can be difficult to encourage a business to implement crime prevention measures at a design stage. For example, the motor car industry in Britain, despite producing a major object of criminality – the car – was reluctant to examine or move towards better security measures built into new vehicles. One reason for this is that the cost of vehicle crime traditionally has not been borne by car manufacturers. They could also be said to have benefited from the increased sales generated by crime. Individual manufacturers feared that the cost of introducing crime prevention measures might adversely affect their competitive position within the market place. The result of this competition between businesses within the car industry, together with the fact that the cost of crime did not seem to affect them directly, meant that little progress was made even when the government held meetings between government officials and motor manufacturers with the aim of encouraging the latter to consider preventive design measures (Laycock and Tilley 1995). These meetings failed to produce significant tangible results, largely because of the limited understanding of commercial consideration with which vehicle manufacturers operated.

This example illustrates some of the difficulties apparent in encouraging commercial sector involvement in the prevention of crime directed against their own products. These difficulties are often compounded in relation to commercial sector contribution to local community safety initiatives, where the benefits to business may seem less obvious. Two principal strategies have emerged in response to this reluctance (see Field and Hope 1990; Pease 1996). The first is the elaboration of a wider conception of 'commercial consideration' to encourage businesses to think about indirect, as well as direct, benefits. The second involves introducing cost incentives into the evaluation of commercial consideration by increasing the incentive to introduce prevention at the earliest possible stage in the manufacturing or service delivery process.

Encouraging a wider conception of commercial consideration

Commentators and groups such as 'Business in the Community' have sought to encourage private sector involvement in community safety by identifying a broader notion of commercial consideration. In so doing, they have drawn on an ideology of 'corporate community' investment which seeks to reorientate business objectives towards ones which identify businesses' stake in the wider community. The argument is that traditional narrow cost-benefit analyses fail to take into consideration the very real benefits that can be derived from a business contributing to the improvement of the wider community, not only through customer loyalty but also because improvements to a local community have indirect benefits for a business and its employees.

One way of illustrating this is by reference to 'game theory' models of behaviour. For example, the 'Prisoners' Dilemma' can be used to show a broader conception of self-interest, by which co-operation emerges out of mutual interests and behaviour on standards that no one individual or organisation can determine alone. The Prisoners' Dilemma is a non co-operative game involving the interaction of two players in which the 'rules of the game' are such that the players are not able to make binding agreements with each other but must act independently. In the Prisoners' Dilemma, two prisoners, let us call them A and B, have been arrested for illegal possession of a firearm, which it is suspected has been used in an armed robbery. The two prisoners are held in different police cells and, without knowing what the other prisoner will do, are given the choice either to remain silent or to confess. If they both remain silent they will both receive two years' imprisonment. If one of them confesses and the other remains silent, the one that confesses will go free, in exchange for his confession, while the other will receive 20 years' imprisonment. And finally, if both confess they will both receive 15 years' imprisonment

		B	
		Remain silent	*Confess*
A	**Remain silent**	**2**:*2*	**0**:*20*
	Confess	**20**:*0*	**15**:*15*

Figure 5.1 The Prisoners' Dilemma

		B	
		Co-operate	*Defect*
A	**Co-operate**	**2**:*2*	**4**:*1*
	Defect	**1**:*4*	**3**:*3*

Figure 5.2 Individual preferences in the Prisoners' Dilemma

(see Figure 5.1). As A cannot know what B will say, he is likely to confess for to do so would bring the least worse consequences, as will B for the same reason. Ironically, they are likely to opt for their third preferred outcome and the one which leads to the greatest cumulative time spent in prison: in other words, the worst collective cost to themselves as a 'community' (see Figure 5.2). The result is always mutual dissatisfaction. The game is designed to show that co-operation would be more beneficial to the parties. The provision of public goods and the conditions for participation in collective action, it is argued, are inescapably bound up with attempts to solve the Prisoners' Dilemma (Hargreaves Heap *et al.* 1992: 99 and 144–8).

The implications for community safety are that like the two prisoners, businesses have a choice of whether to co-operate or to defect from 'community' measures. If all businesses co-operate, they all benefit to some degree, albeit that this benefit comes at a price: the cost of co-operation and involvement. The problem is that individual businesses usually make individual decisions about their own specific costs and benefits, and hence may not participate because the cost of participation is higher than non-participation in the short term. However, there is the problem of the 'free rider' who operates in an area in which others co-operate, with costs to themselves, but from which the 'free rider' derives benefits. Hence, the 'free rider' has an incentive to gain from the efforts of others without suffering the costs of contributing themselves. This might give individual businesses a 'competitive edge', particularly in relation to other, co-operating businesses. The trouble is that other participants may defect, with the implications that co-operation may break down and no community safety benefits arise. The bottom line is that if everyone co-operates, everyone is better off than if everyone defects. However, the 'free rider', although a precarious position in the long term will remain the most attractive short-term strategy so far as maximising profits are concerned. The Prisoners' Dilemma points to the importance of co-operation and dialogue in identifying what is in the public or communal good rather than merely in the short-term interest of an individual business. It also highlights the significance of reciprocity and trust for long-term exchange relations between businesses and other agencies in partnership arrangements. As important as these insights are, the limitations of 'game theory' lie in the individualistic rational choice model of behaviour on which it is constructed.

Nevertheless, commercial sector involvement has been limited, particularly with regard to genuine community safety programmes where there is no direct benefit to businesses own security or to that of their staff. Some business commentators are even hostile to the idea of private sector involvement in community safety issues, which they see as 'an attempt to achieve public policy on the cheap and on the side' (Brittan 1993).

Cost incentives and the insurance industry

A number of commentators have suggested that the only real way to address the under-provision of crime prevention is to inject economic incentives into the crime prevention market both in relation to consumer demand and manufacturers' supply of products (Pease 1996). Here the insurance industry has had a large role to play. The relationship between the insurance industry and the market for crime prevention is a dynamic one. Some commentators have argued that the provision of insurance cover, for things such as domestic burglary and theft from and of a vehicle, has impeded the development of crime prevention by reducing the harmful impact of crime (Pease 1996). The market for insurance can produce what Field and Hope refer to as 'moral hazards' (1990: 92). These occur when people who are fully insured against a given risk have no incentive to reduce that risk in so far as it affects them. There is no financial pressure to prevent that risk from occurring, by purchasing expensive security measures for example. Consequently, burglars and car thieves, so it is argued, continue to operate in a context of little social restraint. Moreover, the cumulative effect of this results in at least two adverse social consequences: the crime rate rises and insurance premiums increase, albeit that this is thinly spread across a large number of people such that the effect is not significantly felt by any given individual. Hence, for Pease, it is the absence of incentives for the citizen to prevent crime which 'lies at the heart of the problem' (1996: 98). The remedy for this is for governments and the insurance industry in co-operation to 'promote self-protection against crime by individuals, companies and services, as well as providing subsidies for security improvements' (*ibid.*: 99).

Increasingly, however, insurance policies have built-in incentives to reduce crime risk. This has had implications both for consumers and manufacturers. For example, as we have seen, motor manufacturers for some time were able to ignore the vulnerability of their products to crime because of the blanket nature of insurance. However, more recently they are having to take an interest in questions of security against crime primarily because insurance premiums are beginning to influence consumer decisions. This has resulted in an engagement between insurers and motor manufacturers, in which insurers have targeted high risk performance cars for punitive premiums, while manufacturers have pushed for security hardware fitted during manufacturing to attract reduced premiums (Laycock and Tilley 1995: 557).

In relation to domestic burglary, insurance companies have encouraged, through financial discounts or conditions of cover, the spread of neighbourhood watch and the introduction of security hardware and alarm systems. Similarly, insurance has fuelled the dramatic expansion of CCTV cameras by cutting premiums where they are in operation. More significantly, the unequal geographic distribution of crime has led some insurance companies to penalise those who live in high crime areas, often on the basis of postcodes, as well as benefit those who live in low crime areas. According to a research report published by the Association of London Authorities (1994) residents of whole streets and estates in high crime areas are being refused cover by some insurance companies. So the role of insurance has added a powerful dynamic into the development of crime prevention and community safety.

Problems with private sector involvement in community safety

The experience from many Safer Cities Projects was that pursuing and persuading the private sector that community safety is their legitimate responsibility is both time-consuming and labour-intensive. One of the potential implications of significant commercial sector involvement may be that it influences the types of crime prevention measures prioritised and their location. In order to attract private sector involvement, projects may require 'tailoring' to the needs or interests of businesses (Crawford 1997a: 227). Thus businesses located within a city centre are more likely to be interested in the installation of city centre CCTV cameras, because it may have spin-offs for their business, than in work on high crime housing estates, located far from their premises. 'Tailoring' may also prioritise schemes with high visibility or public relations potential, from which businesses may benefit. Moreover, where businesses get involved in community safety for the public relations potential, they are generally interested in being associated with identifiable 'success stories'. Business people often have naïve expectations of success. This will tend to skew community crime prevention towards interventions which are easily quantifiable and subject to some kind of quantitative assessment of effectiveness. Private sector involvement, therefore, is often results-oriented and likely to favour interventions into the physical environment which are measurable.

Most problematically, as the Morgan Report (1991) noted, private sector sponsorship is likely to be short-term and project-driven which will generally exclude the long-term funding of 'problem-oriented' initiatives in high crime areas. Fluctuations in business performance and market benefits make businesses reluctant to commit themselves to long-term investments. And yet, as the Morgan working group noted, durability requires established resources. Furthermore, changes in the local economic climate can lead to the withdrawal of support for crime prevention initiatives by private sector sponsors, which in turn may lead to the collapse of an initiative. Hence, despite government's appeals to greater private and commercial sector involvement in community safety, this is by no means unproblematic nor are the implications inevitably beneficial.

Conclusions

Historically, insufficient attention has been given to the processes of planning and implementing crime prevention and community safety initiatives. This chapter has focused on two principal elements at the heart of contemporary implementation: the accumulation and analysis of information about crime and associated problems within a given area and the delivery of inter-agency partnerships. At first sight both these appear to be the most uncontentious elements of community safety in that they are the most widely accepted and endorsed. Few commentators argue against problem-oriented methodology or partnerships. Nevertheless, the issues to which they give rise are probably the least considered or understood. They are held up as ideal totems but rarely are practised in any rigorous or reflexive manner.

The very notion of community safety echoes the importance of locality. It stands in contrast to what Rosenbaum (1988a) referred to as an 'implant hypothesis' which underscores much crime prevention practice, whereby pre-packaged programmes are implanted into local social environments with little sensitivity to the specific local context in the implementation process. Rather than solutions being imposed on a local ecology, they should emerge out of the environment in which they will have to survive. As such, it connects with a problem-oriented methodology. It is precisely because action needs to be local that information about the nature of local 'problems' is so vital, but the use of information in practice tends to be *ad hoc* and ill-considered. So too with consultation which is the subject of rhetorical appeals but all-too-often brushed aside when complex issues arise. There is rarely clarity about the purposes or values underlying aims of consultation as there is little openness about the lines of representation in the consultative process. In the new order of things, diverse agencies and the public are to become co-producers of public safety. Yet the process of co-production is riddled with sites of conflict over values, purposes and priorities as well as considerable power imbalances between the parties incorporated into the co-production process.

This has produced a number of tensions. The pluralisation of sources of appropriate information and groups or interests with which to consult has raised the question of how to negotiate between the various potentially competing claims and priorities. Policy does not emerge unambiguously from the accumulation of data nor the process of consultation, but is concerned with political choices. Which sources of information are legitimate? Which groups should be incorporated into the process? And, by definition, which interests should be excluded? To what extent should specific interests be accorded a dominant position? To what extent should groups or organisations consulted be given an input into decision-making and policy-formation? Should the activity of formal state agencies – such as the police – be shaped or influenced by the values and standards of the locality or by universal norms? What is the appropriate relationship between local initiatives and the principles of equity? These questions are rendered ever-more complex by the fact that community safety and public order are inherently ambiguous.

Some of these issues have been considered in relation to a 'partnership' approach to implementation. In practice the process of partnership work is often given little thought as to its aims and methods. Lack of clarity and ambiguity cloud the process. This is compounded by uncertainties about accountability and confusions over the distribution of responsibilities and roles. Agreements struck in 'partnerships' often have to be renegotiated at rank-and-file levels within organisations where resistances abound.

This chapter has identified the centrality of conflict within partnerships and the need for conflicts to be managed and negotiated in an open and constructive manner in which there is a mutual recognition of different interests. The practice of conflict avoidance – associated with an assumed consensus or an ends-oriented 'quest for unity' – can encourage the development of exclusive and inward-looking partnerships dominated by specific sectional or organisational interests. Constructive and inclusive conflict negotiation, on the other hand, requires the recognition and appropriate compensation for power differentials between the parties. Conflict negotiation, conceptual clarity and the appropriate distribution of roles are of particular importance given the role of trust in inter-agency relations. It is clear that we have only begun to think through some of the implications and issues implicit in the realisation of a 'partnership' approach.

However, for a 'partnership' approach to be translated beyond the level of rhetoric into vibrant practice, policy-makers and practitioners will need to face some challenging and reflexive questions. Government will have to consider some of these implications, most notably how to foster the appropriate conditions for the development of inter-organisational trust and collaboration. Here we have identified important incongruities between the logics of managerialism – as expressed through NPM reforms – and the notion of genuine 'partnerships'. The intra-organisational focus of managerialist reforms and the contractualisation of relations may undermine inter-organisational partnerships. The fixation on a results-orientation incapacitates the need to address the nature and quality of conflict negotiation and the maintenance of trust relations over time.

Clearly the legitimacy of these inter-agency networks resides not at a political level but at an administrative one: in claims to greater cumulative expertise, smooth management and increased efficiency in the delivery of services. So many of the normative issues raised in this chapter tend to be sidelined from practice in the interests of administrative niceties and yet, if long-term legitimacy deficits are to be addressed and if genuine partnerships are to take root, these issues need to be faced at a political level. We have seen how partnerships as neo-corporatist arrangements have the potential to be highly disciplinary and authoritarian forms of administration. They raise important questions about the processes of inclusion and exclusion, conflict negotiation, agency domination of the policy agenda and accountability. The extent to which some of the fears and concerns raised in this chapter are realised is one of the central issues for the consideration of future research and practice.

Note

1. This was the experience of New Zealand where although corporate crime was identified as one of the seven key priorities for their national crime prevention strategy (New Zealand CPU 1994a), they have found it increasingly difficult to maintain interest at a local level (Crawford 1997b).

Chapter 6

Evaluating Crime Prevention and Community Safety

It is widely recognised that evaluation is the most deficient aspect of crime prevention and community safety practice (AMA 1990; Morgan 1991; Pease 1994). Methodologically rigorous research in the field of crime prevention is the exception rather than the norm. Many of the claims made by politicians and practitioners rest on flimsy methodological foundations. Rosenbaum concluded his overview of the state of Anglo-American crime prevention by declaring: 'The primary reason why we do not know what works in community crime prevention is the quality of the evaluation research' (1988a: 381). It was, therefore, of little surprise that the Morgan Working Group concluded its national review of crime prevention through the 'partnership' approach, in Britain, by stating that: 'evaluation and monitoring was the weakest element of most crime prevention programmes' (Home Office 1991: 22). Often evaluation research has been sought to justify previously taken policy decisions rather than as an aspect within a developmental process. Frequently, evaluation is tagged on to the end of a policy and given little consideration, as if it is an afterthought. Sometimes it has been ignored completely. For example, no proper research evaluation was built into the Five Towns Initiative by the Home Office. Only 2 per cent of Home Office money that is spent on crime prevention is specifically set aside for research. This contrasts with the Dutch Ministry of Justice which makes evaluation a requirement of any crime prevention funding and devotes about 10 per cent of all subsidies to research. Nevertheless, even the Dutch have recognised the 'disappointing quality of many evaluations' (Willemse 1994: 41).

This lack of evaluation leaves us with little knowledge about which forms of intervention 'work', under what conditions 'success' or 'failure' is determined and the possible transferability of initiatives across different social and demographic contexts. It also means that we fail to learn from others' experiences. Consequently, those engaged in crime prevention may be continually reinventing the wheel or, more problematically, embarking on wasteful and misconceived adventures.

However, rigorous evaluation is fraught with epistemological, methodological and conceptual debates and difficulties. Some forms of methodology are technically complicated (Ekblom 1992). Evaluation research is also costly and time-consuming. It can be disruptive to those trying to implement a given preventive measure. It can get in the way of inter-agency relations and can sharpen conflicts by forcing the prioritisation of evaluation criteria. The real pressures to show success can divert practitioners' attention away from the task of service delivery. Evaluation research can be threatening as it can expose inadequacies, conflicts and managerial incompetence.

This chapter considers some of the dominant means of approaching the task of evaluation research, both in regard to process evaluation and outcome evaluation. In relation to the latter the issue of measuring displacement is examined. The contribution of recent debates advancing a 'scientific realist' approach is outlined. The chapter explores the divergent evaluation criteria which have emerged in crime prevention and community safety as well as their implications for the definition and politics of 'success' and 'failure'. It concludes by proposing a number of questions for consideration in the evaluation process.

Outcome evaluation

Evaluations which have been built into crime prevention initiatives are still very much in their infancy. However, the primary focus of research interest has tended to concentrate on the impact or outcome of a given measure. At the heart of outcome evaluations lies the problem of disentangling the relation between *cause* and *effect*. In asking the question 'did it work?' we are striving to demonstrate an indisputable causal relationship between the intervention and the outcome. While this is no simple task, it is central to developing an understanding of crime prevention. As Rosenbaum notes: 'there is a compelling need to open up the "black box" of community crime prevention and test the many presumed causal links in our theoretical models' (1988a: 382). These causal links are not only internal ones but are also concerned with the relationships between internal assumptions and the context in which they are set. So we are not only concerned with the question of 'what works', but also with 'what works, for whom and under which conditions'? These questions are concerned with external validity and the generalisability of interventions across different settings, people, times and targets. Much evaluation research has been limited to concerns about establishing – as far as possible – internal validity.

Quasi-experimental methods

Experimental design is premised on positivist assumptions about knowledge and the testing of hypotheses (Campbell and Stanley 1966). It involves a process in which pre-test measurements are taken of the target group (or area) before the experimental intervention is implemented. This is followed up by post-test measurements after the intervention has had time to take effect. Pre-test and post-test measurements are also taken of a control group (or area) in relation to which no intervention has occurred. The implication is that if fluctuations in crime rates (either upward or downward) are repeated in the control group (or area), they are likely to be the product of general trends external to the given areas. On the other hand, differences between the experimental and control group (or area) are then attributed to the intervention, on the assumption that this is the only known difference between the groups (or areas). This methodological model is referred to by Pawson and Tilley (1994) as the 'OXO model' of evaluation (see Figure 6.1).

	Pre-test	Treatment applied	Post-test
Experimental group	O_1	X	O_2
Control group	O_1		O_2

Figure 6.1 The Classic Experimental Design
Source: R. Pawson and N. Tilley (1994) 'What Works in Evaluation Research?', *British Journal of Criminology*, 34, 293.
By permission of Oxford University Press, R. Pawson and N. Tilley.

However, full experimental methods are largely unavailable to researchers in the field of crime prevention. This is because in the social world the researcher cannot have full control over the conditions in which experiments or tests are conducted. The social world is continually in a process of change, in which numerous extraneous factors – some of which may be unknown or unknowable – may affect an intervention or its target. The social world is not a laboratory where such external factors can be kept to a minimum. Hence, criminologists have turned to quasi-experimental methods, which are premised on the investigation of the effects of an intervention *as if it were* an experiment. As the researcher cannot control the social world into which the intervention is inserted, quasi-experimental methods attempt to hold stable, or rule out, as many extraneous factors as possible.

Measuring outcomes

If crime prevention is defined as securing a 'non-event' the difficulties associated with measuring and evaluating the effectiveness of a given strategy become immediately apparent. How do we measure whether and to what extent something has *not* happened? The answer is that we cannot. What evaluators can do, however, is to measure the rates of crime at different points in time and to make assumptions about any reductions. However, successful outcomes in the prevention of crime may not produce reductions in crime rates. This can produce dangers of 'measurement failure' (Rosenbaum 1986). This is apparent within the evaluation enterprise, whereby evaluators fail to detect the real effect of a successful preventive intervention. There is also considerable uncertainty in crime prevention and a degree of uncontrollability of the future which makes planning crime prevention evaluation difficult.

Crime reduction is not the only criterion used to measure outcomes. Other criteria currently in use include reductions in the fear of crime, reductions in disorder, 'signs of crime' or incivilities, improvements to the quality of life for residents and local community support for specific measures or service delivery. This proliferation is associated with two developments. The first, notably in the discourse of 'community safety', is genuinely concerned with promoting wider criteria than the reduction of crime for the evaluation of outcomes. The second is connected with the conceptual obscurity that is to be found in much multi-agency crime prevention work which often results in a multiplicity of competing aims. The problem of 'multiple aims' for the purposes of evaluation is that there is little clarity about whether these outcome criteria are ends in themselves – irrespective of their relationship to crime – or means to an end: that they will foster change which is likely to impact on crime. If they are the latter, there is often little precision about the theoretical assumptions on which that relationship rests. For example, in relation to a given community safety project, is fear of crime an end in its own right or is it assumed that there is some causal relationship between fear reduction and crime reduction, as in the 'broken windows' thesis? Yet there is usually little precision in terms of the assumed relationship between criteria such as fear reduction and crime reduction. Fear reduction is often viewed as a 'consolation prize' to show to funders when crime has not been reduced. Regarding the relationship between crime reduction and the wider criteria for outcome evaluation Ekblom and Pease suggest that there are only three 'bottom line' positions which are defensible (1995: 598):

- that the aim of any initiative should be the prevention of crime and that any evaluation which does not reflect this is to be regarded as inadequate
- that quality-of-life measures are defensible as outcomes in their own right
- that quality-of-life measures are useful as short-term indicators for a longer-term measurement of crime reduction (and hence, that there is some acknowledged relationship between quality of life and crime reduction).

In many senses, this returns us to the conceptual debates about what crime prevention is, its boundaries and aims. The second of these positions is closely associated with the rise of 'community safety' as a distinct agenda to more narrowly defined crime prevention. Yet the central point here for many crime prevention initiatives which claim success by reference to wider criteria (of the third type) is the need for clarity about the presumed causal links between the various criteria.

Before-and-after surveys

The traditional measurement of crime through reported police statistics is the subject of significant methodological inadequacies. In this light victimisation surveys offer an important contribution to evaluative methodology which has become increasingly recognised in recent years. Surveys, while being resource intensive, have the advantage of being able to employ and collect a wide range of criteria for evaluation by measuring: (a) the increase/decrease in criminal victimisation within the target area, avoiding the unreliability of police crime records, particularly given the effect the initiative itself may have on the levels of reporting; (b) the impact on public assessment of their quality of life including the fear of crime; (c) public support for interventions and hence their credibility; and (d) public evaluation of the effectiveness of agencies in implementing policies and of the quality of service delivery. Allatt's (1984a, 1984b) evaluation of security improvements on a council housing estate was a pioneering example of the significant contribution crime surveys lend to methodologically rigorous evaluation. More recent British examples of evaluation surveys include Bennett's evaluation of two neighbourhood watch schemes in London (1989), and the evaluation of a 'package' of improvements to the Hilldrop estate in London (Lea et al. 1989).

One methodological development which allows greater sensitivity to the effect of interventions on local residents over time is the inclusion in the evaluation process of an 'embedded panel' element (Bennett 1989) within the 'after' survey. This involves dividing the sample in the 'after' survey into two groups. A sample of respondents from the initial 'before' survey is supplemented by a further random sample from the project area. This allows evaluation from two differing perspectives: the impact of the initiative on specified individuals and on the general residents as a group as well as the area as a location.

Some problems with pre-test/post-test quasi-experiments

One of the key problems in evaluating the impact of preventive interventions on crime are the 'natural' or 'random' fluctuations in levels of crime within a given area (Ekblom and Pease 1995). The more localised the intervention – and hence the evaluation in line with current community safety thinking – the greater the size of the problem. As crimes are relatively infrequent occurrences, there are bound to be considerable fluctuations over time in offending. Where numbers are particularly small, fluctuations will be greater. The implications are that it can be difficult to know whether changes in crime rates – either up or down – are the product of preventive intervention, of 'natural' fluctuations, or even a combination of the two. Hence, a small number of burglaries, for example, can have a dramatic effect on local crime rates.

Lurigio and Rosenbaum (1986) identify six threats to 'internal validity' which present themselves in attempts to demonstrate that outcome patterns are solely the product of specific crime prevention interventions:

- *History.* This refers to changes or events which occur between the pre-test and post-test measures. This may include increased police presence in the targeted area or developments by other agencies, such as the local authority or citizens, all of which may rival the specific crime prevention measure as an explanation of change
- *Testing.* Where the same group is used for pre-test and post-test measurement, the survey method may actually serve to affect the nature of what is being studied
- *Instrumentation.* This alludes to the effect of any inaccuracies or changes in measurement method between pre-test and post-test. This is particularly evident in relation to official police records where changes in reporting or recording behaviour may account for pre-test and post-test differences
- *Statistical regression.* This relates to the problem of 'random' variation discussed above. This is particularly evident if the crime prevention measure is administered in areas which exhibit notably high or low levels of the 'problem' of crime being studied. If the rate of crime within the areas is fluctuating over time and the intervention is implemented at a time of above or below 'normal' crime, change may merely be the product of 'regression to the mean'
- *Mortality.* This refers to the 'drop out' rate of participants between the pre-test and post-test measurements. If significant numbers of those who participated in the pre-test measurement are (for whatever reason) no longer part of the post-test measurement, the two groups are not strictly comparable
- *Selection.* This concerns the problems that arise if the participants in an evaluation are not representative of the target population, such that any changes may relate to some unrepresentative characteristics of the participants.

These dangers can compound each other or simply exert an independent influence on the evaluation process.

Several other problems present themselves in relation to evaluation through pre-test and post-test measurement of outcomes. First, researchers are confronted with the problem of isolating the multitude of influences which may impinge on the success or failure of the initiative. An estate or targeted area cannot be held in a vacuum and is continuously being shaped by social forces outside the control of researchers. This is exacerbated by the tendency in crime prevention to introduce not merely a single intervention but a 'package' of various social and situational interventions (Forrester *et al.* 1988; Lea *et al.* 1989) because such an approach provides a greater likelihood of success. It also meets principled and ethical objections to the use of people in high crime areas as 'human guinea pigs' for the sake of evaluators, when it is known that a number of interventions is more likely to produce beneficial results. However, this leaves evaluators in the difficult position of attempting to disentangle which intervention has had what effect. This dilemma was noted by the authors of the Kirkholt research evaluation:

> the adoption of a series of measures is likely to have much greater impact than simply taking one or two steps. Methodologically this is less attractive because it is scarcely ever practicable to tease out the relative contributions to crime prevention of the various measures, and the interactions between them.
>
> (Forrester *et al.* 1988: 11)

Second, there is the problem of time horizons. Pre-test/post-test interventions impose pressures of an artificial timespan on evaluation. The effects of some forms of prevention will have only been experienced after different periods of time. This is exacerbated in relation to a 'package' of crime prevention measures, where different measures may have different effects at different times. Politicians, for whom the 'immediacy of the question of power' is often paramount, tend to have short-time horizons. Consequently, there is much encouragement for interventions which are more easily monitored in the short term, rather than those which may be relevant to the longer-term social needs of the area. In practice these constraints are likely to mean the prioritisation of situational activities, which are amenable to easy quantitative measurement. This 'short-termism' of much evaluation is evident in the 'project-driven' approach which pervades British crime prevention and which largely mirrors the way crime prevention is funded. It assumes an end point to the process of evaluation, beyond which evaluators are little concerned with the effects of programmes as they move on to other initiatives. There are clear dangers that the use of before-and-after surveys merely perpetuates such an approach. If crime prevention is to be about the broader process of developing institutions and structures of 'community' (Currie 1988) and local empowerment, they will need to go beyond the pre-test/post-test model and involve residents in monitoring and evaluating effects on an ongoing basis.

Outcome pressures

The pressures for 'success stories' from the media, politicians and funding bodies are considerable (Lurigio and Rosenbaum 1986; Bottoms

1990). In the absence of 'success stories' or in the face of evaluation research which fails to identify positive findings, policy-makers tend to adopt one of two strategies. Either they distance themselves from the research findings by questioning their methodological assumptions, or they turn their backs on the preventive initiatives themselves. The former response was certainly the one that accompanied Bennett's (1989, 1990) evaluation of two neighbourhood watch schemes in the late 1980s. Yet rigorously researched negative – or 'no effect' – results can offer considerable lessons for crime prevention theory and practice. Research may help to identify whether the lack of success was the product of theory failure, implementation failure or measurement failure. As Ekblom and Pease note:

> Although theory failure is particularly frustrating to implementers and implementation failure particularly frustrating to impact evaluators, both are informative. If the worst happens, good evaluators will have placed themselves in a position to salvage much that is of use from the study beyond the bleak conclusion that the theory was wrong or the implementation was weak.
>
> (1995: 595–6)

Because of funding constraints, crime prevention programmes are often expected to deliver 'results' within an unrealistically short timespan. Funding constraints can also lead to the implementation of an insufficiently strong 'dosage' of a given measure. Limited resources may mean that interventions will make little difference and be harder to detect. An initiative may fail because not enough of it was implemented to be sufficiently detectable, which can compound 'implementation failure' with 'measurement failure'. In order to counteract this, Rosenbaum (1988a: 379) suggests that crime prevention programmes should narrow their focus to a few specific crimes or problems in a small target area, so as to maximise the impact and render measurement more discernible.

Another way of balancing evaluation needs against cost is the use of 'demonstration projects', which have significant inbuilt evaluation elements. Much of the rigorous evaluation research in the UK has arisen as a result of demonstration projects (see Hope and Murphy 1983; Hope 1985; Forrester *et al.* 1988, 1990). Demonstration projects focus resources into a particular example from which it is hoped that wider lessons can be drawn. However, by their very nature demonstration projects are time-limited. Little concern is given to the future of the initiative after the post-test measurement. Demonstration projects can inadvertently promote unrealistic expectations. Replications of 'successful' demonstration projects are rarely provided with the same kinds of resources pumped into the initial demonstration project (Crawford and Jones 1996). This can be very demoralising for project workers and can serve to undermine the value of initial demonstration project findings. In this sense, demonstration projects are inherently problematic, in that they may set others up merely to 'fail'.

A realist critique

Pawson and Tilley have recently made a number of important interventions into these debates (Pawson and Tilley 1994, 1997; Tilley 1993c),
in which they promote a paradigm shift away from quasi-experimental
approaches to a 'scientific realist' model of evaluations. They define this
as a 'theory driven' or 'explanatory evaluation' approach, involving the
specification and identification of key elements for the evaluation process – namely 'mechanisms', 'contexts' and 'outcomes' – as well as their
inter-relationships. The 'axiomatic base' on which realist explanation builds,
they argue, is as follows: 'Causal outcomes follow from mechanisms acting in contexts' (1997: 58). They define these essential ingredients as:

- *Outcome*: the product which is caused by a mechanism acting
  under particular conditions (O)
- *Mechanism*: the intervention with allows the reaction (M)
- *Context*: the conditions which allow a mechanism to come into
  operation (C).

The manner in which outcomes are the product of mechanisms in particular contexts is outlined in Figure 6.2. Importantly, the relationships
between the component elements – the manner in which a mechanism
seeks to bring about change and the conditions conducive to this – are
the subject of explicit theoretical assumptions. Thus 'realist' evaluators
inspect outcomes not merely to see if the programme 'worked', but 'to
discover if the conjectured mechanism/context theories are confirmed'
(Pawson and Tilley 1997: 217).

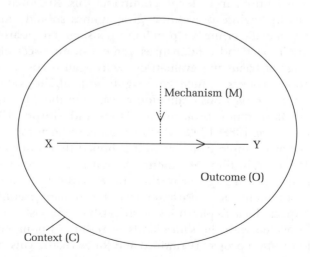

Figure 6.2   The Realist Experimental Design
Source: R. Pawson and N. Tilley (1994) 'What Works in Evaluation
Research?', *British Journal of Criminology*, 34, 300.
By permission of Oxford University Press, R. Pawson and N. Tilley.

Pawson and Tilley are highly critical of dominant quasi-experimental evaluations which ignore both mechanisms and their (social and physical) contexts. Experimental methods are only concerned with shifts over time between X and Y, which are recorded to see if they follow predicted 'regularity'. Quasi-experimental methods tell us about a mechanism likely to bring about this 'empirical regularity' (X–Y) and do so by trying to create a context which is believed to sustain the ideal conditions to bring the mechanisms into action (Pawson and Tilley 1997: 60). However, to do so experimental methods need to take place under a situation of 'control', which is highly problematic. This, they suggest, is 'neither feasible nor finalizable, and is, therefore, bound to end in the arbitrary evaluation of programmes' (Pawson and Tilley 1994: 294). Rather, they distinguish between two ways of considering causation (1994: 293). The first, which they call 'successionist', looks at causation 'externally': 'Cause simply describes constant conjunctions between events' (*ibid.*). This is the 'empirical regularity' referred to above. Quasi-experimentation embodies a successionist account of causation. The second conception of causation is 'generative', which sees causation internally and is built into the 'scientific realist' philosophy: 'Cause describes the *transformative potential* of phenomena' (*ibid.*, emphasis in original). Their contention is the belief that:

> Programmes cannot be considered as some kind of external, impinging 'force' to which subjects 'respond'. Rather, programmes 'work', *if subjects choose to make them work and are placed in the right conditions to enable them to do so.* This process of 'constrained choice' is at the heart of social and individual change to which all programmes aspire.
>
> (1994: 294, emphasis in original)

They suggest that quasi-experimentation is inadequate in that it is method-driven, rather than informed by theory. It fails to render explicit the implicit hypotheses which underscore the relationships between mechanisms, contexts and the resultant outcome patterns (Pawson and Tilley 1994: 297–8). 'Realist' evaluation, by contrast, places at the heart of the evaluation process certain hypotheses about the mechanisms (M) through which a programme seeks to bring about change, as well as an understanding of the conditions (C) most likely to foster it. Hence, mechanisms are always 'causal', i.e. they produce – or should be conceptualised as seeking to produce – specific ends. This is explicit in Tilley's definition of 'context' as 'the conditions necessary for a causal mechanism to be triggered to produce a particular outcome pattern' (Tilley 1993c: 13).

Pawson and Tilley (1994) illustrate their arguments with reference to Bennett's (1991) evaluation of police contact patrols, which were intended to reduce the fear of crime and enhance police–public communications. They do so because Bennett's work represents an example of 'good', rather than 'poor quality', quasi-experimental research, in that it is 'technically proficient' and 'statistically sophisticated'. Despite this, they accuse Bennett of failing to expose the 'black box' of relations between mechanisms, context and outcomes, a failure produced by the quasi-experimental method to which he is wedded. They suggest this leads to a failure to specify the 'mechanisms' – i.e. what is meant by 'contact' – and how it is assumed that this will cause change – i.e. the theory of causation. They also suggest that the design ignores contextual factors intrinsic to the success or otherwise of the programmes (but see Bennett 1996a).

The debates raised by Pawson and Tilley are fundamentally important to the development of crime prevention and its evaluation because they force the theorisation of the various mechanisms embedded within a given programme. It should oblige practitioners to substantiate and clarify the mechanisms to be deployed and the underlying conjectures about their relations to outcomes. However, the 'scientific realist' approach need not be seen as a rejection of all aspects of quasi-experimental designs. *Testing* mechanisms fired within specified contexts remains the dominant ethos. So it also has to contend with many of the pitfalls identified in relation to quasi-experiments, most notably the difficulty of disentangling the cause-and-effect relations of multiple mechanisms which have become the dominant approach of practitioners in the name of 'community safety'. As Ekblom and Pease note:

> The key practical ingredient in implementing a scientific realist approach to evaluation is whether it will prove possible to convince practitioners, collaborators, or administrators, as commissioners of research, of the value of repeated trials, evaluations, and adjustments focusing on a particular method and mechanism, instead of pursuing an unconsolidated conquest of virgin territory through a series of unrelated one-shot studies.
>
> (1995: 631)

This will require a significant cultural change on behalf of many and may well be unpalatable to some.

Process evaluation

The emphasis on outcome evaluation has meant that there has been a tendency to ignore the task of process evaluation. Yet it is a criminological truism that any outcome will in large part be determined by the policy-formation and implementation processes. There is no clear or logical linear progression from policy-making to implementation. Increasingly, it is being realised that 'implementation failure' is as likely as anything to be the cause of unsuccessful crime prevention programmes (Hope and Murphy 1983). This draws to our attention the importance of process evaluation in order to make sense of outcomes. Process evaluation needs to consider exactly what has happened over the life of the implementation, with a view to highlighting any difficulties and pitfalls encountered along the way. As such, process evaluation asks a number of related questions. Who was involved? What decisions were taken? How were they arrived at? How did the various parties relate to each other? Did the parties do what was planned or did they do something else? Did any unforeseen events arise? Thus, an understanding of the structure and decision-making processes of an initiative, the nature and extent of inter-agency involvement, the nature or extent of 'community' participation and the extent of implementation may all be important aspects of evaluating the social processes that constitute a crime prevention initiative. (Many of the problems and issues related to the implementation process, partnerships in particular, were covered in Chapter 5.)

However, there are some methodological issues raised by the lack of research into process evaluation. In part, this lacuna stems from a much broader reluctance among many researchers to use qualitative research methods in evaluative research. In our quest for 'scientific' and 'object-ive' data which can be statistically displayed and defended, there is a tendency towards what Rock (1988) has called a 'self-censorship' of other forms of data. In a plea for more 'detailed observational and ethnographic work on the social processes of housing estates' Rock (1988: 110) has rightly criticised this dominant over-emphasis on quantitative research in crime prevention evaluation:

> A whole area of knowledge is systematically suppressed by the limitations of prevailing research methods . . . What has been 'banned' consists in the main of evidence that is thought to be too personal, subjective and qualitative.
>
> (Rock 1988: 110–11)

There is a need to supplement quantitative methodologies with more qualitative research in the evaluation process. Hope and Foster's (1992) work evaluating the impact of the Priority Estates Project is an interesting example of the combination of victimisation survey research with other more qualitative methods. They used ethnographic studies to supplement before-and-after surveys, conducted with a three-year interval, of two 'problem estates' in London and Hull. The ethnographic work helped to explain apparently conflicting outcomes identified by the survey data by capturing some of the 'internal dynamics of community change'. It also helped to explain 'how external changes – in design, management quality or tenant allocation – affect the internal "culture" of an estate in such a way as to amplify or suppress tendencies towards offending on the estate' (Hope and Foster 1992: 489). In this combination of methodologies they added to a quasi-experimental design such that they were able to monitor the process of implementation and assess its impact. It is hoped that this example points the way forward for evaluative methodologies to combine quantitative and qualitative research methods.

Pawson and Tilley's 'scientific realist' approach produces certain problems in relation to process evaluation as it is concerned only with mechanisms which are 'outcome-oriented'. They fail sufficiently to develop an understanding of the interactive relationship between mechanisms and contexts. Some mechanisms may be specifically aimed not at directly producing outcomes but rather at altering the context. Such 'processual mechanisms' (Crawford and Jones 1996: 23) as key elements of interventions are reasonably common in crime prevention and community safety. They include, for example, 'multi-agency co-operation' and 'community consultation' which may not be causal in a direct manner but which may influence the social context, notably decision-making, modes of communication, conflict management and negotiation. They may not 'cause' a successful outcome but their absence may reduce the likelihood of attaining successful outcomes. As such, they may represent desirable ends in themselves. For example, the presence of constructive conflict negotiation in multi-agency partnerships will not cause the reduction of crime in any direct sense. However, it may well prove to create conditions which foster the success of other mechanisms. In Pawson and Tilley's (1997) terms, the conceptual boundaries between 'mechanisms' and 'contexts' become blurred. This is particularly so with community safety initiatives in which the community itself – i.e. the context – is a major element in the mechanisms of change. The evaluation of these mechanisms would focus on the intrinsic quality and efficacy of the policy-formation and implementation processes. By reducing everything to its causal relationship to outcomes, Pawson and Tilley produce blind spots with regard to process evaluation. They unduly over-prioritise outcomes at the expense of the processes of policy-formation and implementation.

Replication

The replication of initiatives is an important contribution to evaluation knowledge in crime prevention and community safety. It allows researchers to cross-check assumptions originated in initial programmes and to develop further theories. However, it needs to be realised from the outset that the same crime prevention programme can have different outcomes when implemented in different contexts. This can also be demonstrated by parallel comparative studies (i.e. Foster and Hope 1993). The problems of replication, however, are particularly acute in relation to 'demonstration projects', partly because these are intended as templates of crime prevention initiatives, the lessons from which are to be transferred to other areas and hence should be generalisable. In many senses, demonstration projects by their very nature encourage evaluators to leave out reference to the 'context' in which crime prevention measures are situated and to ignore its potential impact or influence on outcomes. For example, throughout the published reports of the Kirkholt Anti-Burglary project (Forrester *et al.* 1988, 1990) there is only limited information on the socio-economic context in which the project was situated (this example is used because in all other regards it is an example of high quality evaluation research). We know little about the nature of the social relations on the estate, the local economy and the history of inter- or even intra-organisational relations within the area. The authors of the Safe Neighbourhoods Unit report on 'Crime Prevention on Housing Estates' appear justified in their criticisms of the manner in which the Kirkholt researchers discounted the influence of the local authority's environmental improvements programme on the estate (SNU 1993: 110). This is symptomatic of a general trend in writing up crime prevention initiatives in which projects are abstracted from the specific local contexts which shape the resultant findings. In the search for tangible causal relationships between interventions and outcomes, researchers are often too hasty to exclude that which is not immediately tangible and quantifiable.

'Demonstration projects' also tend to encourage a top–down 'implant', as well as a project-oriented approach to crime prevention. This is why Crawford and Jones (1996) argue against the use of the term *replication*, as strict replication in the experimental sense is unrealisable. Instead they advocate the use of a concept of *transferability*, which acknowledges the importance of contexts. This builds on 'realist' insights (see Tilley 1993c: 11–15) and highlights context sensitivity without slipping into relativism. This requires evaluators to identify relevant contextual elements which may have influenced the success or otherwise of a given crime prevention mechanism. Failure to do so renders it very difficult for those who attempt to transfer these mechanisms into new contexts as they will not know if they are comparing equivalents.

Tilley (1993c) applies the 'scientific realist' approach to address some of the questions and issues raised by transferring crime reduction 'success stories'. He analyses three 'replication' projects of the original Kirkholt initiative and uses them to 'raise a number of theoretical and practical problems in relation to the business of replication'. He suggests that 'many of the root difficulties are not so much technical as conceptual' (Tilley 1993c: 2). Consequently, he berates evaluation research – which indicates only that a change has occurred without considering what brought it about – as of little value. Conjectures about the cause of change need to be made explicit and the evidence for them spelt out (*ibid*.: 19). He refers to the term 'replication failure' to identify situations in which the same measures are transferred to different contexts in which the conditions conducive to fostering change are not present, and hence do not yield the same outcomes.

Displacement

A crime prevention or community safety initiative may prove to be highly 'successful' in reducing crime within the confines of its own boundaries, but this does not necessarily mean that it has reduced crime or associated harm *per se*. There remains the complex issue of displacement which can take a number of forms – spatial, temporal, tactical, target and type of crime – all of which have implications for the evaluation of crime prevention initiatives. To date, the empirical evidence about displacement, its nature and extent, is relatively weak. As Gabor has noted, a major problem lies in the identification and operationalisation of the displacement phenomenon (1990: 48). The apparent absence of displacement may be camouflaged underneath a variety of forms of appearance as well as an over-abundance of extraneous influences. The empirical evidence about displacement tends to derive from one of two principal sources. First, there are crime prevention evaluations which monitor changes in the levels of crime – either measured through official statistics or surveys – both in the targeted area where the interventions are introduced and in adjacent or neighbouring areas. The introduction of 'adjacent' areas where crime prevention measures are not introduced allows for the potential monitoring of any spatial displacement effect. Evaluators may seek to measure any changes in the 'test' and 'adjacent' areas against a 'control' area, as Bennett (1989, 1990) did in his study of neighbourhood watch. This allows evaluators to monitor general trends external to the given neighbouring 'test' and 'adjacent' areas. The use of 'adjacent' areas should also enable evaluators to assess any 'diffusion' of benefits which might percolate from the 'test' area into the 'adjacent' area. However, the study of displacement through pre-test and post-test measurement is subject to the same concerns about internal validity, already discussed. It is possible that other factors unrelated to the crime prevention measures may have produced particular changes or differences in crime rates across the areas. This method also begs the question, how far afield should evaluators monitor for spatial displacement? In other words, what should be the scope of 'adjacent' areas?

Displacement can be more complex than just a spillover effect. Detecting for tactical, target or type of crime displacement will require assumptions to be made by evaluators as to the possible or likely new forms, targets or types of crime to which offenders will turn their attention as a result of displacement.

> If, in truth, displacement is complete, some displaced crime will probably fall outside the areas and types of crime being studied or be so dispersed as to be masked by background variation. In such an event, the optimist would speculate about why the unmeasured areas or types of crime probably escaped displaced crime, while the pessimist would speculate about why they probably did not. No research study, however massive, is likely to resolve the issue. The wider the scope of the study in terms of types of crime and places, the thinner the patina of displaced crime could be spread across them; thus disappearing into the realm of measurement error.
>
> (Barr and Pease 1990: 293)

So it needs to be accepted that the issue of displacement cannot always or simply be resolved empirically. It will require recourse to theoretical hypotheses and arguments about the likelihood and extent of displacement.

For example, Mayhew *et al.* (1989) in their study of the reduction of motorcycle thefts and its relation to the introduction of legislation requiring helmet wearing, arrived at the theoretically informed judgement about the scope of displacement by seeking to understand the 'choice structuring properties' (Cornish and Clarke 1987) of motorcycle theft. Cornish and Clarke (1990) have suggested that for alternative opportunities to be genuinely viable they must share the same 'choice-structuring properties' as the original offence from which the offender turned away. Hence, they argue, displacement will only occur when 'crimes serve the same needs at similar costs' (Cornish and Clarke 1990: 104).

Following this line of thinking, Mayhew *et al.* (1989) reasoned that motorcycles were stolen either for financial gain and extended personal use or for temporary use, notably 'joyriding'. They then hypothesised that those stealing for personal use and gain would think of carrying a helmet in preparation for the crime and therefore not be subject to the situational effects of the compulsory legislation. They concluded that 'helmet legislation might be expected to have its greatest effect on the more opportunistic offences of joyriding and theft for temporary transportation' (Mayhew *et al.* 1989: 4). So displacement would be restricted to those types of crime which might provide the same kind of 'joyriding' experience, which the opportunistic motorcycle thief would probably be seeking. As a consequence, their search for displacement was confined to car and bicycle theft. Whether this assumption about 'choice structuring properties' is justified or not is open to debate (see Gabor 1990) but at least it is a reasoned one. As such it is in line with realist aims of opening up the 'black box' of crime prevention. This example demonstrates that considerable inference is necessary in any evaluation of the presence or absence of displacement. This inference and theorisation is a task which evaluators need to be ready to confront.

The process of inferring the possible decision-making processes of potential offenders has been assisted by a second source of data about displacement. This arises from in-depth interviews with known offenders about their motivation and decision-making processes in the light of crime prevention. Such interviews usually focus on past events or hypothetical scenarios. They are often conducted with convicted offenders in prison as this is convenient (Bennett and Wright 1984), although the development of self-report studies means that this is not necessarily the only method of collecting such data. Some initiatives have combined information from both victim surveys and offender surveys in order to tailor the mechanisms implemented (Forrester *et al.* 1988).

Bennett and Wright's (1984) work is a good example of this kind of research which has helped to inform an understanding of the phenomenon of displacement. They interviewed 128 offenders imprisoned for domestic burglary and asked them what course of action they take if unable to complete a burglary. Nearly half of the respondents said that they had never experienced a situation in which they could not complete their burglaries. Of the remaining respondents, 43 per cent said that they committed their crimes elsewhere, thereby displacing crime. A similar study conducted in Holland concluded that 72 per cent of burglars said that when faced with blocked opportunities to commit domestic burglary they chose another target (van Burik and Overbeeke, cited in Hesseling 1994: 215). When asked the hypothetical question what they would do if unable to complete a burglary, two-thirds responded with statements which could be classified as some form of displacement, with 36 per cent indicating that they would resort to other crimes, 30 per cent saying that they would find other targets, 25 per cent responding that they would use different methods, and only 4 per cent stating that they would desist altogether.

However, it is not only incumbent on those who promote crime prevention measures as having little adverse effects to theorise the displacement process. Those who argue that displacement is an inevitable product of crime prevention also need to speculate about why and how this occurs. One of a combination of the following explanations is usually offered:

- that offenders' motivation for offending is predetermined and will not be overridden by blocked opportunities
- that offenders are sufficiently flexible to refocus or re-orient their offending
- that there are sufficient alternative targets and opportunities for their offending elsewhere.

These assumptions should also be the subject of evaluative research, as should the possibility of the 'diffusion' of benefits from a crime prevention initiative. Displacement is not necessarily an undesirable consequence of social intervention: it may be a legitimate policy choice, particularly in its benign, rather than malign, forms (Barr and Pease 1990).

Who should do evaluation?

One question which has become increasingly relevant is, who should be entrusted with the task of evaluation? Ekblom and Pease suggest that the growing government drive on 'value for money' in the form of the Financial Management Initiative has produced a shift from a situation in which 'evaluators were able to "parachute in" and conduct an evaluation on their own terms to one where they are increasingly "shackled together" with administrators and practitioners and are jointly responsible for arriving at an answer' (1995: 631). This is often referred to as 'action research'. However, rather like multi-agency relations, this 'shackling' can produce new, unresolved conflicts of interest, method and purpose. Ekblom and Pease go on to capture some of these by humorously caricaturing the three primary parties (1995: 632–4):

- '*The Practitioner: Never mind the quality, feel the width.*' The problem for practitioners is the lack of any professional culture of self-evaluation in the criminal justice agencies, coupled with a lack of evaluation expertise
- '*The Administrator: Bring me solutions yesterday!*' The problem for administrators is that they want 'speed, certainty and economy' all at the same time
- '*The Evaluator: If you're not part of the solution, you're part of the problem.*' Evaluators have themselves encouraged a 'nothing works' pessimism by their unwillingness to take risks with research findings, ensuring that only the most reliable and valid findings are disseminated to their own peers in the academic world. However, practitioners and administrators are unwilling to settle for 'don't know' as an answer.

There is much truth in these caricatures and they point to the need for each of the parties to begin to understand the limitations and constraints of the others. As Ekblom and Pease suggest, all those involved in the evaluation process 'should move towards the willingness to fail and the readiness to learn from failure' (1995: 636). However, the reality is that the administrators remain the dominant party in the evaluation process, as they control the purse strings. Nevertheless, there is a particular need to disseminate evaluation skills to practitioners and to routinise forms of data collection without it interfering with practice. This, as Ekblom and Pease imply, will require a change of culture on behalf of practitioners, such that every crime prevention initiative or programme should at least be willing to be evaluated.

Cost-benefit analysis

The development of cost-benefit analysis in community safety – which seeks to evaluate and balance the costs of crime prevention against the benefits produced by it in terms of crime and associated (social) costs – is relatively recent (Forrester *et al.* 1990). It has been constrained by the limited information available, particularly as regards the full costs of crime. Nevertheless, crime audits have been conducted, albeit in relation to large geographic areas (Shapland *et al.* 1995). These are likely to grow in their importance as the power of auditing grows (Power 1997) and could become periodic measurements of change. However, like evaluation research, audits are costly and complex. NACRO and SNU have floated the proposal in the UK of making evaluation a condition of access to funds for estate-improvement programmes (DoE 1993). They have promoted a broad definition of 'success' which includes a cost-benefit analysis of non-monetary matters, such as reduced fear of crime and increased resident and staff satisfaction. These kinds of benefits, the report argues, are likely to be the key to final judgements about the balance of costs and benefits.

The dangers of cost-benefit calculations lie in the nature and extent of the criteria that they include or exclude from consideration. There are hazards in emphasising the quantifiable, while neglecting the unquantifiable costs and benefits. There is also the problem that some benefits (or costs) may only come to light after a considerable period of time. There are difficulties associated with costing preventive action, especially where numerous agencies are involved. If cost-benefits arise in initiatives delivered in partnerships, this can give rise to new sources of conflict: who should get the benefits and how are these to be transferred across departments and between participating agencies? There is also the danger that cost-benefit analysis may become a substitute for, rather than a supplement to, a broader based evaluation of the relation between intentions and outcomes.

Redefining success and failure

We need to place evaluation within a broader political framework. Debates about 'what works?' only reveal that the politics of success and failure are often struggles about the status of criteria, which can rarely be reduced to 'any universally accepted scale of efficiency' (O'Malley 1992: 263). It is not a coincidence that the emergence of the shift to prevention in Britain as elsewhere connects with a crisis of criminological confidence. The rise of crime prevention has been associated with a process of 'adapting to failure' (Garland 1996: 455). As a consequence, there has been not only a pluralisation of those responsible for failure (see Chapter 8), but also a pluralisation of the criteria of success. Where once the crime rate stood as the test of successful criminal justice policy, now a multiplicity of emerging criteria jostle for prominence. In part this has been due to the criminological critiques of sources of information about crime rates, the complex processes through which official records are socially constructed and the problems of measuring crime displacement. Nevertheless, the methodologies utilised in the collection of alternative criteria are also often the subject of intense criminological debate. In some cases these alternative criteria have become viewed as on an equal footing with, or sometimes more important than, the impact on crime. Pre-eminent among these are measurements of 'fear of crime', 'multi-agency co-ordination' and 'customer relations'. These have become ends in, and of, themselves. 'Fear of crime' has attained such a significant place within policy discourse (Home Office 1989) that 'fear reduction' strategies have become legitimate policy aims in their own right (see Bennett 1991). Even if levels of crime do not fall, an initiative could be defined as successful if it were to reduce people's 'fear of crime' in some quantifiable way.

This is not meant to suggest that these alternative criteria are not important or legitimate aims of policy, but rather that their proliferation and prominence are representative of political struggles over success and failure. To some considerable degree, this debate has been set by the rise in dominance of 'the new criminologies of everyday life', such as 'rational choice' theory and 'routine activity' theory which underpin situational and environmental crime prevention. These have relinquished the ideal of the crime-free society and in its place have assumed that crime is a normal part of social interaction, to be better managed and controlled. These criminologies carry with them the 'normalisation' of high levels of crime. In this context, a reduction in people's 'fear of crime', greater 'multi-agency co-ordination' or improved 'consumer relations' appear to offer tangible success stories.

'Managerialism' has also highlighted 'system' characteristics and aspects of management as legitimate criteria of success. 'Performance indicators' against which an organisation's activities can be assessed have become central elements in the evaluation and monitoring processes. And yet this can lead to a focus on organisationally defined goals as criteria for success, rather than social goals. This is particularly likely where the 'outputs' measured by performance indicators – often restricted to internally defined organisational goals – differ significantly from 'outcomes' – the actual impact of an 'output' on the wider community. Managerialist pressures have tended to dissolve this distinction and focus on outputs, while abandoning the causal demands of outcome-based measures.

As some commentators have noted, the managerialist emphasis on defining and institutionalising 'auditable performance' may serve to reduce *evaluation* to *auditing* (Power 1997: 119). While the former is concerned with gathering empirical knowledge and addressing complex cause-and-effect issues, the latter focuses on 'verification' and the correspondence between an operation or activity and standards to which it should conform. As such, audit acts as a normative check on performance. In so doing, however, it departs from the social scientific reasoning which underlies evaluation research and substitutes the 'administrative objectivity of auditable measures of performance which are replicable and consistent even if they are essentially arbitrary' (*ibid.*). Herein lies the attraction of audit: it replaces ambiguity and qualifications with certification. However, it tells us little about cause and effect or the outcomes of particular programmes. There has also been considerable governmental resistance to the notion that managerialist reforms themselves should be the subject of evaluation – broad enough to consider any side effects and unintended consequences – as opposed to mere auditing (Broadbent and Laughlin 1997). As Power suggests, the power of auditing is itself one of the institutional barriers to the 'evaluation of audit' (1997: 121).

Conclusions

There are a number of flaws in much evaluation research. Evaluators, administrators and practitioners have much to learn about the evaluation process. The aims and objectives of many initiatives are often poorly articulated and clouded in obscurity, as is any realistically theorised notion of the timespan over which effects and outcomes may be produced and sustained. There is often little understanding of the relationship between mechanisms, contexts and outcome patterns or conception of the processes through which these are produced. These are issues programme implementers need to address in order to assist the evaluation process. But this does not absolve evaluators from greater efforts. The measurement of outcomes is often unreliable. Evaluators need to look beyond simple before-and-after experimentation to examine the implementation process itself. They need to develop more sophisticated ways of understanding and analysing the phenomenon of displacement. The transferability of 'successful' initiatives is largely unknown because of the lack of data about the contexts in which mechanisms produce given outcomes. So reported successes should be carefully scrutinised before extending the initiatives to other contexts or locations (Lurigio and Rosenbaum 1986: 42).

The paucity of knowledge about the transferability of crime prevention initiatives across social, cultural, spatial and temporal contexts leaves us with little challenge to a dominant framework which (a) prioritises the physical and the tangible; (b) emphasises an 'implant approach' to crime prevention; (c) prioritises outcome evaluation at the expense of the evaluation of social processes; and (d) emphasises a short-term project orientation rather than a longer-term strategic approach to crime prevention. By abstracting crime prevention projects from their specific social circumstances we are in danger of reifying crime prevention to the level of a false science. In the quest for quick technological fixes we have become blind to the complex social relations which are embedded in, and help determine the direction of, a given crime prevention initiative. In this light, policy-makers and funders need to be wary of pre-packaged programmes which are not tailored to the needs of a given locality.

However, evaluation research is neither easy nor cheap. It involves inherent difficulties. And yet improvements in the quality of evaluation research are attainable through the adoption of more rigorous approaches to measurement and analysis. In this regard, evaluation studies should address the following questions:

1. Was the initiative implemented as planned and what factors influenced implementation? (*the process*)
2. Did the initiative make a difference to, or alter the size of, the problem? (*the outcome*)
3. What did the initiative do which impacted on the problem and how was the problem affected by the initiative? (*the relation between the mechanism and outcome*)
4. In what ways did the context in which the mechanism was set encourage or undermine the impact of the initiative? (*the relation between the mechanism, outcome and context*)

5. What else resulted from the initiative as well as the impact on the problem? (*the unintended consequences or side effects*)
6. Did the benefits and/or side effects last? (*the temporal durability*)
7. Were the benefits greater than the costs? (*the cost-benefit*)
8. How, where and for whom could the effects be replicated? (*the transferability*)
9. What more do we know at the end of the evaluation about the patterns of outcome effectiveness of the initiative, and what else do we need to know? (*future evaluation*)

These questions should help evaluators develop greater knowledge about what works, where, in what circumstances and for whom. Unrealistic expectations of what crime prevention can deliver, and the timespan in which outcomes can be achieved, present a particular problem. There is a danger that because of the inherent difficulties of evaluation, crime prevention and community safety may fall victim to the pessimism of the 'nothing works' philosophy which infused debates about the treatment of offenders in the 1970s (Martinson 1974; Broady 1976). In posing these questions, evaluation needs to become an intrinsic part of the process of programme design and implementation.

Evaluators need to look to innovative and different methodologies which will help reveal the important processes in crime prevention which have hitherto remained hidden. They need to make their findings accessible to practitioners and policy-makers alike. They need to provide the information, particularly about the context in which initiatives are set, to allow for the transferability of good practice. Knowledge of techniques, as Ekblom and Pease conclude, may be less important than the possession of a clear conceptual framework covering the key questions posed in the evaluation process (1995: 642). Clarity about the theoretical assumptions on which mechanisms are premised – and their relation to contexts and outcome patterns – is the fundamental challenge to contemporary evaluation research. As Rosenbaum concludes: 'We are past the point of wanting to report that crime prevention does or does not work, and now are interested in specifying the conditions under which particular outcomes are observed' (1988a: 382). Rigorous evaluation can significantly assist our knowledge about the complex social processes and relations which make up specific prevention measures. However, it will not solve the political questions about crime prevention as a collective good, to which we return in Chapter 8.

Chapter 7

Some Comparative Experiences

In most industrialised countries the numbers of recorded interpersonal crimes have doubled approximately every 12 to 14 years, while the likelihood of a person being the victim of a crime has doubled or trebled in the last three decades (Waller 1991: 15). The fear of crime appears to be increasing around the world. The current levels of victimisation and concerns about crime are also reflected in the findings of the International Crime Surveys (van Dijk *et al.* 1990; del Frate 1997). In this context, governments are increasingly turning to forms of crime prevention and community safety in search of a panacea to the crises confronted by most criminal justice systems. Yet what this means in practice is not always the same thing. Societies' reactions to crime are not always the same: they reflect differences in socio-cultural and legal background. Crime prevention in industrialised societies around the world differs considerably according to political and cultural traditions. The ideas that inform crime prevention strategies vary, as do the policies to which they give rise, the means of implementation and the ways in which programmes are evaluated.

Nevertheless, a certain degree of information sharing and cross-fertilisation of programmes has developed as governments look to learn from the experiences of others. At a European level a number of developments have occurred which have begun to co-ordinate the divergent evolution of crime prevention (van Dijk 1991). The Council of Europe established a *Committee on Crime Problems*, which examined the issue of crime prevention through a series of international conferences under the auspices of its standing committee of Local and Regional Authorities, set up in 1985. Out of this the Council of Europe (1988) has published a report on the ways in which Western European countries organise and administer crime prevention. This has been followed by the establishment in Paris of a European Forum for Urban Safety, acting as a central agency for the exchange of information on crime prevention across Western Europe (Joutsen 1995). It has also participated in drawing up plans for an International Centre for the Prevention of Crime in Montreal, Canada.

However, the strategies and delivery structures of crime prevention and community safety across the world differ significantly, particularly with regard to the ideological and institutional assumptions that underlie them. This chapter is not a comprehensive review of international crime prevention developments, but rather offers the reader a selection of particular comparative examples, which raise salient questions about the nature of crime prevention strategies, their structure, implementation and impact. The focus is on four industrialised societies – Sweden, France, The Netherlands and Japan – whose experiences have either informed comparative debates or significantly influenced policies elsewhere. It is anticipated that the comparative examples will help to provide insights into different models, perspectives and understandings in order to stimulate a critical self-questioning of many of the taken-for-granted assumptions on which the British (and US) approaches to crime prevention are premised. These comparative insights should enable a better understanding of the ways in which certain approaches to prevention arise out of, and reflect, wider social relations within different legal, as well as political, cultures. It is hoped that these can help us to look at our own experiences afresh, on a broader horizon and through slightly different eyes.

Sweden – a national strategy

In 1974 the Swedish parliament passed a law to create the first National Crime Prevention Council (NCPC) in the world. Its aim was to promote and co-ordinate crime prevention initiatives throughout the country. From the outset it was concerned with the question of how to support local crime prevention initiatives in a systematic way through a national approach, and hence how to adapt models and strategies of crime prevention to local social conditions. The initial legislation required an important focus on measuring and analysing the causes of crime, as well as disseminating the results of this work. It did this primarily through research, monitoring and evaluation (Graham 1993).

As a consequence, much of the concern of the NCPC lay in establishing a clear and systematic structure for the dissemination and implementation of crime prevention programmes. It has developed a philosophy which emphasises a multiple approach, combining short-term and long-term strategies with situational and social prevention, delivered through programmes that target offenders, victims, at risk groups, the general population or particular places. Essential to this philosophy has been that all programmes should be implemented by those relevant people at the local level in accordance with a specific methodological model. This model involves four discrete, yet fundamentally connected, stages:

- the detailed mapping of crime and existing crime prevention activities within a given locality, as well as an assessment of the resources available
- on the basis of this, the relevant parties co-ordinate the planning of measures to be taken
- these measures are then implemented by and through those working locally
- the measures are then evaluated.

Sweden was the first country to develop a clear national policy on crime prevention. The organisation and structure of crime prevention which resulted from the establishment of the NCPC and its legislative framework has given crime prevention a particularly prominent formal status in the policy process. It has made it a permanent feature of government programmes with obligations for action and funding. It requires government to ensure that national, regional and local agencies are encouraged to plan, implement and improve programmes, to work in co-ordination with each other, to collect information on prevention and promote training programmes.

This structure has created an important degree of strategic oversight and stability which encourages and facilitates long-term thinking and planning. It recognises the important role that central government has in identifying and clarifying the responsibilities of different central government departments, the relationship between them and between central government and local bodies. Most notably, it seems to accept that there is a responsibility on central government to provide clear guidance on the boundaries of, and relationship between, crime prevention activity and social policy – an issue which is all too often left unclarified. It also places the responsibility for assessing the resource implications and monitoring progress squarely on the central structure. It seems to accept that if local institutions are to be accorded a genuine degree of local control, they will need central government to foster the conditions under which local action can be fully exercised and enhanced. Consequently, this structure has subsequently been adopted, with national variations, in at least Belgium, Denmark, Finland, Norway and France, albeit with different degrees of success.

France – social crime prevention

Traditionally French law and procedure has reflected the fact that punishment is regarded as the central object of the criminal law. This is culturally enshrined in the very terminology of *droit pénal* (penal law). This has been reflected in the traditional separation of 'welfare' policies, particularly those aimed at young people, and policies of *répression* (repression). In France, the latter is interpreted as meaning the 'strict enforcement of the criminal code by the police and the judiciary and the widespread use of imprisonment as a punishment' (de Liège 1991: 125). However, in the past 10 to 15 years France has seen the emergence of an increasingly coherent crime prevention policy separate from the administrative structure of the criminal justice system.

The beginnings were laid by the Peyrefitte Commission (set up in 1976) whose recommendations led to the decree of 28 February 1978 which established the National Council on the Prevention of Violence (*Comité National de Prévention de la Violence et de la Criminalité* – CNPVC) as well as 'departmental' (regional) councils. The latter were, however, of little effect, largely because they were 'expert led'. It took the arrival to power of the Socialist government in May 1981 to provide the engine for change. The new government had been highly critical of their predecessor's repressive and preventive policies. It also coincided with a perceived 'crime wave' and extensive rioting in several major cities, notably Lyon, during the summer of 1981 (de Liège 1988). Hence, a national commission was set up by the new government against a background of public anxiety over the handling of the growing 'crime problem' (Robert 1985). Chaired by Gilbert Bonnemaison, the Committee's Report (1983) *Face à la Délinquance, Prévention, Répression, Solidarité*, (*Confronting Crime: Prevention, Repression and Solidarity*) has had a major impact on the subsequent development of crime prevention policy and practice in France.

It embodied a number of key themes around three concepts: 'solidarity', 'integration' and 'locality'. First, it suggested that the causes of crime are rooted in deep and complex social factors, including living conditions, employment conditions, changes in the organisation of family life, the lack of social controls in people's relationships with one another, poverty and the exclusion from mainstream social life of certain categories of people. In response, it argued, the state should promote strategies of 'integration', by which those groups and individuals perceived to be at the margins of the bonds of social *solidarité* (solidarity) are deemed to require (re-)incorporation. Social isolation and the exclusion of certain groups, notably disaffected youths, immigrants and the unemployed, were seen by the Bonnemaison Report as the central problem affecting French society (Delatte and Dolé 1987).

Second, the report emphasised *prévention* as distinct from *répression*. Although repression and punishment through the criminal justice system were identified as essential elements in crime control, they were not seen as capable of addressing the fundamental causes of crime. Therefore, it was contended that prevention requires a separate and new administrative structure outside the criminal justice system, without the repressive and authoritarian aspects associated with the police and the courts. Crime should be attacked separately on both the preventive and the repressive fronts. In relation to prevention, Bonnemaison stressed that the key decision-making should not be assigned to the traditional criminal justice system. It should be included without being given a dominant position.

Third, the Bonnemaison Report emphasised the local dimension of such a new administrative structure. To be effective, policy should be flexible and capable of adapting to local circumstances. To this end, it stressed the need for 'horizontal' solutions to make communities safer from crime and bring together people with different expertise in local partnerships. The policy-formation process should be inclusive, linking all the relevant local partners, including local elected representatives, trade union officials, social services and non-profit organisations. The aim was to break down bureaucratic barriers through local inter-agency co-operation. The multi-party membership of the local institutional structures assumed that the correct composition of partnerships would be the key to their success (Lazerges 1995).

The Bonnemaison Report set the agenda for a specifically *social* approach to crime prevention in France which, despite the various subsequent changes in political leadership, remains largely intact today. A number of specific initiatives, both in the form (or administrative structure) and content (or substantive policies) of crime prevention arose as a direct consequence of the Bonnemaison Report and the particular preventive climate to which it gave rise.

Local crime prevention councils

The implementation of the Bonnemaison recommendations was elaborated through a tiered process of decentralisation, grafted on what had traditionally been a highly centralised state bureaucracy. An elaborate three-tier administrative structure was set up at national, departmental[1] and local levels under the decree of 8 June 1983. This involved, first, the creation of a National Council on the Prevention of Crime – *Conseil National de Prévention de la Délinquance* (CNPD) – chaired by the Prime Minister and attended by the majority of town mayors and representatives from relevant government ministries, with a total membership of nearly 80 people. Second, at the regional level, Departmental Councils for the Prevention of Crime were established, chaired by the Chief Administrator for the region and with the Chief Judicial Officer as vice-chair. Third, all cities and large towns were encouraged to set up Local Councils for Prevention of Crime – *Conseils Communaux de Prévention de la Délinquance* (CCPD). These became a major means of delivering city or town-wide crime prevention strategies. The three tiers of administration deliberately embody elements of institutional overlap, in order to mitigate conflicts and limit friction. This particularly takes the form of personnel overlap, a practice known as *cumul des mandats* (the accumulation of interests) by which an individual may simultaneously be a local mayor, a representative of the regional authority and/or a member of central government.[2]

This was part of a wider process of decentralising the state administration introduced by the Socialists in the 1980s in an attempt to move away from 'vertical' structures, whereby individual agencies determine policy in terms of their own hierarchical organisational needs, towards a 'horizontal' structure whereby local policy initiatives are established and co-ordinated between agencies acting in 'partnership'. The broad intention of this political initiative was to revitalise a sense of 'citizenship' within the institutions of the Fifth Republic. At each level the Councils draw on representatives from three principal sectors of society: elected officials, the judicial administration and citizen groups. Chaired by the elected mayor, they bring together representatives of a variety of ministries – justice, youth and sport, education, welfare – along with those working in the 'field', such as social workers and representatives of local associations such as voluntary organisations and trade unions, to set local policies on crime prevention and to co-ordinate fund-raising and resource allocation to various local agencies and projects. The explicit aims of the Councils are:

- to co-ordinate preventive action at the local level
- to define the local aims about the nature of co-operative action with particular regard to the aid of victims
- to monitor implementation.

They created a participatory and democratically informed structure through which local crime prevention policy as a 'third way' between traditional welfare and punishment took root.

This policy was administratively reorganised in late 1980s and early 1990s in which the focus moved to structures concerned with the re-generation of cities, with the creation of the *Conseil National de la Ville* (National Council for Cities) to replace the earlier CNPD. This shift was reinforced in 1990 when responsibility for crime prevention was handed to the new Minister of State for Cities. This is supported by the *Comité Interministériel des Villes*, a commission of ministers presided over by the prime minister (Lazerges 1995: 213–16). An important element of the new structure is the 'prevention action contract' (*Contrat d'Action de Prévention*) established in order to formalise and systematise plans of action between the local parties, either at regional or city levels, about the strategy of approach to be adopted. The contracts are signed between the central government and local representatives. The *Délégation Interministérielle à la Ville* is the operational structure established for implementing the action plans. The aims of the contracts are to fight social exclusion and urban segregation, as well as to increase the efficiency of public interventions through a co-ordinated approach. They do so by creating a consultation process involving local and national representation which constitutes the basis of the binding contracts between local and central government. In order to facilitate medium- and longer-term planning, the contracts, since 1990, have set out commitments for a period of three years.

There are about 700 local crime prevention Councils located in almost all the large and medium-sized French cities (Faget and Wyvekens 1996: 65). Research conducted into the implementation of the contracts has found that even in practice a central place has been accorded to the reintegration of deprived areas within the city as a whole and to improve the quality of life of the city generally (Lazerges 1995: 237). In all this the locality – particularly those comprised of 'at risk' populations, such as peripheral housing estates with marginalised youths particularly those of North African descent – has emerged as a new target of social action.

On a more critical note researchers have found that, in practice, a considerable proportion of funding has been directed towards generalised and rather vaguely defined projects targeted at the 'population at large', and that they were not being successfully targeted on those identified 'at risk' groups (Lazerges 1995: 229). In addition to the 'prevention action contracts' are two other strands of action: 'city contracts' (*Contrat de Villes*) and 'urban projects', also arranged between local and central government and involving only partial funding from the centre. The 'city contracts', of which there were 224 in 1995 extending to cover 750 municipalities and 1300 districts, have the dual aims of fighting social exclusion and efficiently co-ordinating public interventions through partnerships at the city level (Faget and Wyvekens 1996: 66). They are funded on a five-year basis in order to encourage long-term activity. The urban projects, of which there are 12, involve large-scale interventions into areas with deprived public housing, and require considerable financial support from the central state.

This complex structure does create some confusion but, importantly, it produces a necessary overlap whereby the actions at one level feed into the next and are checked by it. Yet one of the problems of the complex structure is that the voluntary and private sectors have experienced considerable difficulty in participating within it. The use of the 'contracts' has tended to reinforce, rather than disrupt, the traditional French approach to partnerships as remaining largely within the public sector (French terminology still largely defines partnerships as such). This deficit was recognised when the Praderie report, published in 1981 and entitled *Enterprise and Neighbourhoods*, concluded that greater efforts were needed to bring the private sector into multi-sectoral partnerships.

Summer camps – *étés jeunes*

One of the better known examples of the French social approach to crime prevention was the so-called *anti été chaud* (anti-hot summer) programmes, also referred to as the *étés jeunes* (youth summers), first set up in 1982. These programmes (now referred to as 'summer prevention initiatives' – *Opérations Prévention Eté* (OPE)) actually preceded the Bonnemaison

Report but embodied much of its wider philosophy. Originally they were established as an immediate response to the threat of urban disorder the summer after the 1981 disturbances, but soon became a major part of a general strategy. In line with the integrationist approach the programme was targeted at groups 'at risk' because of their social marginalisation. The programme took underprivileged youths (under 18 years old) from deprived areas at risk of outbreaks of disorder out of the cities on structured holiday camps and provided those who remained with a wide variety of activities over the summer months. In its first full year of operation 10 000 young people were given holidays, while a further 100 000 participated in some form of organised summer activity (King 1988: 9–10). Like their later counterparts the programmes were funded by a combination of central government, regional government and local voluntary organisations. Within the general philosophy of according sufficient space for local initiative and the participation of youths themselves, the activities varied widely.

The programme, it is claimed, cut the crime rate in central city areas, and also reduced the threat of urban disorder during the summer periods. In many ways the success of the *étés jeunes* was that it established the foundations for more permanent and enduring local projects. For example, it gave rise to a new breed of professional youth organisers known as *animateurs*. These youth workers who helped organise and run the local *étés jeunes* projects were drawn from young people of North African origin selected initially for their leadership qualities and the fact that they were held in high esteem by other youngsters. This was the result of a deliberate strategy aimed at 'penetrating' North African communities by eliciting support and co-operation of the young while at the same time providing paid employment for the most capable, and cooperative, of these young people. This had two important social implications: first, it gave those recruited employment and self-respect (even if only for the summer months). Second, these early recruits drew in other youths from among their family and friends. The 1987 programme for the first time included the involvement of girls from North African communities.

Continuing this theme of 'penetrating' and 'incorporating' marginal youths, a number of areas in France have established special reading programmes for children of North African origin and schemes to develop employment skills. Although in Britain this would be considered as a 'welfare' programme, in France it is viewed as long-term crime prevention in the battle against social exclusion, in that they will increase self-esteem, cement greater social cohesion and reduce crime over a number of years. Yet in many cases the activities are more concerned with improving social and racial integration rather than crime prevention (Graham and Bennett 1995: 33). There have also been some suggestions that most programmes no longer contain activities explicitly aimed at preventing crime.

Specialist crime prevention teams

It was out of the experience and development of the *étés jeunes* projects
that a new breed of social worker specialising in crime prevention emerged
in France during the 1980s. The deployment of teams of social workers
specialising in crime prevention has become an important element of
the national crime prevention strategy. These specialists have no direct
British equivalent and are distinct from other types of French social
workers (including generic and judicial social workers and probation
officers). They operate outside the criminal justice system. Their aim is
to integrate or reintegrate disaffected young people into mainstream social
institutions, so they seek to identify those individuals and groups who
may be slipping away from the control of family and school and into
truancy and offending. The teams work with the consent of the young
people rather than under a court order. It is normal for no information
to be passed on to other agencies or to the family without the young
person's permission (Walden Jones 1993: 8). This helps the workers
develop relationships of trust with the young people. As a consequence,
the workers often act as advocates for the youths in their dealings with
other agencies, as well as acting as mediators between youths and
between them and their families or community. The actual work that crime
prevention teams engage in varies around the central aim of reintegration,
dependent on local circumstances and priorities.

Les Missions Locales

One of the ways in which the local crime prevention Councils sought to
facilitate the integration of marginal youths has been through an extensive co-ordination and national network of Youth Centres (*Missions Locales*)
in more than 100 towns and cities. These centres attempt to bridge the
transition between school and work for the unemployed and unqualified
(aged 16 to 25) by offering youth training as well as advice and assistance
on a variety of matters such as finding accommodation, financial management, literacy and assisting the unemployed in setting up their own
projects. According to some commentators, one of the most important
aspects of the network of *Mission Locales* has been the way in which they
link youth workers with other agencies, enabling them to act as 'intermediaries' between young people and the formal institutions of society
from which they feel marginalised (Graham 1993: 135). An example of
the kind of innovative projects which have become established through
these youth centres are those that have employed and trained young adults
to assist teaching staff in schools. After a basic six month training period,
these 'recruits', as they are known, act as intermediaries between pupils
and teachers, sometimes helping to resolve conflicts and sometimes

assisting school staff in supervision roles. They can also act as role models or 'mentors' for estranged youths. Some research suggests that schools which have used these schemes have reported significant reductions in violence, as well as improvements in the relations between teachers and pupils (King 1988).

Discussion

As a package the Bonnemaison initiative managed to halt and reverse the steady increase in recorded crime in France. The national rate of crime per capita went down in 1985, 1986 and 1987, the drop of 8 per cent in 1986 being higher than any year since 1972. Comparisons between areas with a community crime prevention Council and those without showed that, for a range of common crimes, there were larger reductions in crime (by about 10 per cent) where a Council existed, even though the latter tended to have higher rates of crime. However, the distinct lack of sufficient French evaluation research makes it difficult to conclude that the reductions in crime were caused by the various Bonnemaison initiatives. Nevertheless, during the 1980s, while crime rates soared in Britain – most notably in the poorest neighbourhoods – they actually declined in France and, more importantly, the fall was most marked in deprived areas. The 'struggle against social exclusion' remains a firm rallying cry of such social interventions. The dominant political rhetoric in France is firmly committed to a social approach to crime prevention which has as its ultimate aim social cohesion rather than the punishment or deterrence of crime.

However, some commentators have tended to idealise this rhetoric (King 1991; Pitts 1997). It needs to be recognised that there is a clear gulf between the rhetoric or ideology of 'citizenship', 'solidarity' and 'social inclusion' which permeates French politics and life and the institutional practices and lived realities for people on peripheral housing estates. More recently, some French commentators have begun to question the viability of accepted strategies of 'integration' aimed at marginal youths, particularly those of North African origin (Wieviorka 1995). Nor did the crime prevention efforts stop rioting in some French cities in 1990. Some French commentators point to the growing presence on peripheral housing estates of youth subcultures, born of high levels of unemployment and social deprivation, which are antagonistic to the very notion of reinsertion into the dominant culture from which they feel locked out (Bailleau 1996). French notions of law and citizenship serve to deny cultural differences, producing a 'silence and blindness to French identity' (Wieviorka 1995). This dissonance between the imaginary and the real is an important element that frames French culture generally and French legal culture specifically (Garapon 1995). Yet this rhetoric, which the French often recognise as such, does have real strategic and institutional effects: that is to say, we should not confuse political rhetoric with reality. Nevertheless, the rhetoric remains the frame within which practice is cast: it both constitutes and is constituted by the idealised discourses.

As a result of the various structural and organisational changes crime prevention itself has been transformed. With the administrative focus firmly located at the city level, the prevention of delinquency as a specific target of enquiry has become blurred. It has become fused and confused within a more general notion of '*la politique de la ville*' – urban regeneration policy (Lazerges 1995). While, on the one hand this has emphasised the separateness of crime prevention from penal policy, on the other it has diluted any distinctiveness. As a consequence of the restructuring and new funding arrangements, interventions have become multi-institutional, rather than specialist. It has become increasingly difficult in France to distinguish crime prevention policy from social and economic policy. It has also raised the crucial question to what extent crime prevention policy has come to determine the nature of urban (social and economic) policy.

In summary the French experience highlights a number of notable features. The first is its structure for implementation, both in terms of its decentralised and yet overlapping tiers with a particular focus on the city, and its close connection to the state as a political entity. The state in French politics is considered as a 'moral unifier', a role which requires it to be strong and prominent for it to stand above and transcend particular interests, rather than as 'a vaguely threatening monolith' as in Britain (Prosser 1995: 510). Consequently, the responsibility for crime prevention and social integration lies firmly with the state, albeit at a local level and in conjunction with wider partners. However, it should be noted that civil society – in the form of voluntary, charitable and community associations – is relatively weaker than in Britain (Crawford 1998b). The structure established allows important 'horizontal' co-ordination and information exchange combined with 'vertical' co-ordination of neighbourhoods, particularly deprived peripheral estates, in the name of social cohesion. Second, the administrative structure is closely connected to and housed within the traditional process of political representation. The new structures do not circumvent established political institutions but are firmly linked to them. This approach resolutely recognises the political nature of crime prevention. Third, the separation of crime prevention, both in its content and delivery, from the criminal justice system, emphasises its social rather than penal attributes. This separation from the repressive criminal justice system has tended to limit the dominance of criminal justice agencies – notably the courts and the police – on the policy-making process within the local crime prevention Councils. The French approach places considerable emphasis on long-term solutions, which address the social causes of crime rooted in an understanding of crime as a complex, multi-layered phenomenon.

The Netherlands – a culture of tolerance?

There are similarities, and yet important differences, between the recent French experience and that of the Dutch. As in the UK, in The Netherlands, national crime prevention policy is primarily the responsibility of one Ministry, in this case the Ministry of Justice, albeit co-ordinated through an inter-ministerial committee. Yet, as in France, in The Netherlands a strategic vision of crime prevention concerned with focusing on the 'root causes' of crime was set out in a government document entitled 'Society and Crime' (*Samenleving en Criminaliteit*) published in 1985. It had been preceded by a committee of experts, the Roethof Committee, which in 1983 had recommended a new commitment to crime prevention drawing together all parts of society in co-operation at the local level. The Roethof Committee had concluded that petty crime is essentially the result of underlying social problems – notably the decreased attachment to institutions of social control like the school, the church and the family, for which the criminal law is not the appropriate mode of approach in the first instance (van Dijk and Junger-Tas 1988: 264). The focus of the Roethof Committee proposals was to stimulate a social approach to prevention by revitalising social control at the level of the school, the community and other associations.

The 'Society and Crime' document, which was subsequently adopted by the Dutch government, developed on this earlier insight. It begins by distinguishing between petty crime and more serious acts of criminality. In relation to the former, crime prevention is declared to be the principal focus, while the criminal justice system, it is argued, should be treated as a last resort. In regard to more serious crimes the traditional penal approach should be strengthened and intensified (Dutch Ministry of Justice 1985: 1). On the basis of this separation the plan asserts a corporate responsibility for crime prevention in which virtually the entire population should be involved. This is contrasted to the traditional one-sided emphasis of action against detected law-breakers (1985: 22). It goes on to identify three guiding principles of preventive policies:

- the strengthening of occupational surveillance of, and control over, potential offenders, by those who are particularly well placed to do so, for example bus drivers, janitors, shop staff, sports coaches and youth workers
- the development of urban and environmental planning which takes into account an attempt to limit the opportunities to commit crime

- the reinforcement of social integration, and particularly 'to strengthen the bonds of the coming generation with the rest of society' (through family, school, work and recreation).

Commentators, including some British ones, hailed the document as marking a 'radical redirection' in policy, in setting out a clear set of principles for crime prevention and criminal justice which 'stand in sharp contrast to the pragmatic and management oriented statements of criminal policy by British governments' (Bottomley 1986: 199).

To encourage implementation of the 'Society and Crime' proposals, the Dutch government set up an inter-departmental fund of 45 million guilders (approximately £17.5 million) for the period 1986–1990 to subsidise local authorities engaging in 'promising local initiatives'. Under the plan, local authorities were given a special responsibility to work together with local institutions, residents and voluntary groups to develop crime prevention. This new administrative structure brought together a process of trilateral consultation between the police, the Department of Public Prosecution and the local authority administrations, through the mayor. 'Scientific' evaluation was made a condition for receiving funding. In 1990 the funding was renewed and increased for another five years. The budget was equivalent to 1 per cent of the total annual expenditure on police, criminal justice and prisons (Waller 1991: 34). Compared to other countries, this stands as a high level of financial commitment to crime prevention. The programme continues to place a strong emphasis on research and evaluation with a commitment that at least 10 per cent of all crime prevention funds should be spent on evaluation.

During the experimental period more than 200 local projects were established. By 1990 all larger municipalities had appointed crime prevention co-ordinators and set up local crime prevention committees (van Dijk 1995: 8). To raise the profile of crime prevention among the media and public, since 1987 an annual award has been presented to the management of the most successful crime prevention project of the year. Some Dutch commentators have been critical of how the plan has been realised in practice. Beijerse and Swaaningen (1993) suggest that many of the crime prevention projects were merely a continuation of plans which practitioners and local politicians had already agreed on: a case of packaging 'old wine in new bottles'. They maintain that the standard of evaluation was generally poor and the results often ignored. According to the authors, many of the projects failed to develop any qualitative standards by which to judge their effects. They argue that the guiding principle concerned with the social integration of young people was unsatisfactorily institutionalised. After a detailed examination of the projects supported, they conclude that an 'integrative' approach to crime prevention 'can barely be distinguished' (Beijerse and Swaaningen 1993: 288). Nevertheless, the experiment was considered a success by the Dutch government and led to the establishment in 1989 of a Directorate for Crime

Prevention within the Ministry of Justice, on the same bureaucratic level as the directorates for prisons, the police and immigration. It has a permanent budget of about $12 million and has four main responsibilities (Willemse 1994: 43):

- promoting crime prevention among municipalities and business
- supporting police-based crime prevention
- co-ordinating victim policies
- regulating the private security industry.

Importantly, this broad ambit of responsibilities requires the directorate to consider the implications of crime prevention for wider issues of public policy, often ignored in other countries like the UK, most notably for victims and the role of the private sector.

The initiative has given rise to a number of particularly interesting crime prevention projects which have attempted to take forward the principles set out in the original 'Society and Crime' document.

An integrated youth policy

In 1994, a report on juvenile crime advocated a partnership approach to juvenile crime. Its recommendations are being implemented as part of the Dutch government's Major Cities Memorandum, which involves contracts, or 'agreements', signed between central government and the 19 largest cities in The Netherlands. The first four such agreements were drawn up between the government and the relevant authorities of Amsterdam, the Hague, Rotterdam and Utrecht and run for four years from the beginning of 1995. They cover four main areas of policy: education, employment, health/welfare and public safety. The government has set aside approximately £100 million over the four year period and a further £40 million per year thereafter to combat juvenile crime in all 19 cities (Bright 1997: 105). An additional £8 million has been allocated for tackling drug-related anti-social behaviour.

An inter-departmental group was set up to take the recommendations forward. This drew together representatives of the education, welfare, social affairs, interior and justice ministries. Rather like its French counterpart the idea is that responsibility should not rest solely with the justice ministry, nor should they be given a dominant position. To reflect this, the policy was given the broad title of 'Youth and Safety'. While there was some initial resistance to inter-agency co-operation, largely caused by uncertainties about the allocation of responsibilities (notably on the part of the education ministry), this was reduced by the fact that the initiative brought with it considerable new funds which ministries were keen to exploit. The negotiated contracts between central and local government in The Netherlands develop on their French counterparts in that they include commitments to meet specified crime prevention targets. Public Safety Plans identify the means of achieving these targets in each city.

For example, Rotterdam has undertaken to reduce the number of young people who get into trouble with the police by 30 per cent, to reduce the number of early school leavers by 35 per cent and to ensure that 90 per cent of school leavers get a job within a year of leaving school, all over a four year period (Bright 1997: 107). Although the signed agreements oblige each city to try to reach such targets, there is no compulsion to do so. The targets, however, do allow the public to assess the competence of city officials.

Safety, information and surveillance officers on public transport

Against the background of concerns over vandalism, aggressive behaviour and fare-dodging, a major prevention programme in Amsterdam, Rotterdam and the Hague was launched, initially for a three year experimental period. The public transport companies in the cities were authorised to take on 1200 unemployed young people to provide information and service to passengers on metros and trams and act in a surveillance capacity (van Andel 1989: 48). The boarding procedure for buses was also changed so that passengers were required to pass the bus driver and present a ticket. The logic behind the scheme was that since the 1960s the level of supervision over public transport had declined, most particularly with the disappearance of conductors as a result of economic pressures to save costs and the introduction of automatic machines to stamp tickets. Drivers were left with the unenviable and impossible task of control over the tram or metro, the safety of the passengers and the navigation of the vehicle along busy streets. The project clearly conformed with the aims of the 'Society and Crime' initiative in that it sought to tackle petty crime through a combined effort that would both strengthen occupational surveillance of, and control over, potential offenders and simultaneously reduce youth unemployment and open up employment opportunities for members of ethnic minorities and women. A sum of 33 million guilders was allocated to the project, although as van Andel notes this figure rises to 49 million guilders if the allowance for extra revenue for the public transport companies and the saving on the cost associated with vandalism are taken into account (1989: 48).

The official evaluation study reports a dramatic decline in fare-dodging in all three cities. For example, in Amsterdam after a year there was a sharp fall in the percentage of fare-dodgers on the tram, from 17.7 per cent to 9 per cent, and on the metro from 23.5 per cent to 6.5 per cent. The new boarding procedure on the buses also led to a substantial decline, from 9.2 per cent to 1.7 per cent (van Andel 1989: 50). Damage-repair specialists, passengers and staff all agreed that the initiative put a stop to the increasing trend in vandalism. The incidence of abuse against, and the number of attacks on, drivers also decreased as a result of the project and there was an increase in passenger satisfaction. However, increased staff presence did not reduce passengers' feelings of insecurity, although safety in a number of places did improve. After weighing up the social and financial costs and benefits of the project, van Andel concludes by highlighting the fact that:

> the measures have made an important contribution to cutting petty crime on the public transport system. This improves the quality of public transport . . . [the project] has created approximately 1200 new 32 hour-a-week jobs. Savings on unemployment benefits amount to some 21 million guilders per year. Many of the new jobs have been taken by young unemployed people, who thereby gain work experience and training.
>
> (1989: 55)

Hence, the project would appear to have met some of its deliberately social targets. However, the lack of formal legal powers was seen to be an impediment to officers' ability to impact on fare-dodging. Consequently, they were transformed into uniformed ticket inspectors, with the power to fine. Yet probably the most important success of the scheme was that it spawned a series of similar type initiatives.

City wardens

More recently the Dutch government has extended the concept of employing long-term unemployed people as surveillance and service personnel beyond the realm of public transport. In many city centres a number of *Stadswacht* – 'city warden' or 'city guard' – schemes have been introduced. The first started in 1989 in the city of Dordrecht. Young and long-term unemployed people are employed as city wardens to help visitors in the city centres feel safer, and provide information for them, as well as intervene if people litter the streets or engage in disorderly behaviour. They also report irregularities to the parking police and city authorities. They aim to provide a reassuring presence and act as 'ambassadors of the city'. Primarily, they have an order maintenance and regulatory function. The city wardens are unarmed, uniformed functionaries who patrol public areas, but without actual police powers. If necessary, the police provide a back-up service. Wardens carry radios, with their control room generally linked directly to the police control room. The training tends to differ somewhat between cities but in most programmes it is full-time and lasts about eight weeks. The wardens are expected to pass an examination after about a year, which gives them certain qualifications to work as private security guards. By 1994 there were approximately 650 city wardens spread over 26 cities in The Netherlands (Hofstra and Shapland 1997).

The research evidence (Hauber *et al.* 1996) suggests that the public were positively influenced by the presence of city wardens, who effected reductions in their feelings of insecurity. Some positive results in reducing some forms of crime were recorded, including bicycle theft and low level nuisances. In some cities, attaining a regular job after participation in the scheme has reached 100 per cent because these city wardens have a guaranteed job from the large private security companies. Elsewhere, obtaining a regular job varies from 33 per cent to 82 per cent, where city wardens are appointed for only one year, and from 16 per cent to 87 per cent in cities where wardens are appointed on a permanent basis (Hofstra and Shapland 1997: 275). Most city wardens find secure employment with private security firms within two years (van Dijk 1995: 9). It is suggested that the fact that the city wardens are 'ordinary people' seems to be an asset in dealing with the public in most instances. The funding for the schemes comes partly from state social security funds aimed at providing training opportunities for unemployed people. As the city warden schemes have become more established, the idea has been extended to residential areas (notably high-rise apartment blocks in Amsterdam), parking lots, recreational parks and other locations.

Truancy from school project

The Dutch Ministry of Justice believed that given the apparently strong correlation between truancy, school failure and delinquent behaviour, a focus on truancy offered crime prevention an opportunity of reaching youths at risk of sliding into delinquency in potentially non-stigmatising ways. A project was launched in three schools providing vocational instruction. The project introduced a number of related measures to address the problem of truancy in order to prevent it escalating and to try and reintegrate the youths back into school, while strengthening the bonds between school, parents and pupils (van Dijk and Junger-Tas 1988: 272–4).

- The first measure was a computerised truancy registration and warning scheme. This allowed parents to be called on the same day for the school to report the absence of their child. The aim was that this would increase the involvement of the parents and strengthen the bonds of parental control. It was particularly intended to discourage occasional truants
- This was supplemented by the appointment of a school counsellor responsible for identifying those at risk of dropping out, monitoring truancy and associated disciplinary problems. The counsellor notified teachers of those at risk and advised them of ways to handle the problems
- A special class for truants was made available, managed by teachers with particular remedial and technical skills. This lasted up to a maximum of three months and was designed to reintegrate the youths back into the curriculum as smoothly as possible.

Before the introduction of the project, the average hours per week of truancy per student in the participating schools stood at 1.4. This was halved to 0.7 hours per week after the introduction of the registration and warning scheme (Willemse 1994: 38). Some six months later, after all the measures had come into operation, the rate of truancy had declined further to 0.5 hours per student per week.

Discussion

Dutch criminal justice policy has been noted for its culture of tolerance (Downes 1988) which appears to have translated into the Dutch commitment to crime prevention and some of the innovative strategies developed. An important common theme which runs throughout these projects and initiatives is the attempt to use significant quantities of public money in a co-ordinated and well-evaluated manner. In addition to the designated initiatives mentioned above, 1 per cent of the criminal justice budget has been allocated for prevention. This compares with 0.37 per cent in the UK (Bright 1997: 108). In addition to the significant quantities of funding, the Dutch have sought to raise the profile of crime prevention by according to it an elevated institutional status in national politics, in the form of the Director of Prevention.

A further lesson from the Dutch experience lies in the attempt to reintroduce intermediate functionaries as crime prevention measures. The Dutch have experimented with initiatives to reinsert an element of human surveillance in public spaces. Paradoxically, in many cases this had been removed for short-term cost-efficiency reasons. In addition to 'city wardens', the perceived success of a social housing project in the city of Delft led the Ministry of Justice to commit itself over a period of three years towards contributing to the cost of employing 150 caretakers in local municipality high-rise flats experiencing serious social problems (Hesseling 1992). The caretakers spend on average 30 per cent of their time on cleaning, 25 per cent on general surveillance, 20 per cent on dealing with tenants and 20 per cent on repair work. Although there is no clear evidence that this more general policy has had a significant impact on serious crime, it has certainly reduced litter, vandalism and disorderliness, as well as having given the residents a greater sense of security and satisfaction (Willemse 1994: 40). Hence, it is argued that these measures produce social benefits which extend far beyond the narrower confines of crime. Importantly, these intermediaries act as crucial links between genuinely informal modes of social control and formal ones.

Japan – a culture of informal control?

At first glance Japan presents an anomaly for Western criminologists in that it is an affluent, mobile and urbanised society which enjoys possibly the lowest crime rate in the industrialised world. Japan appears to disprove the criminological assumption that high crime rates are automatically linked to industrialisation, urbanisation and consumerism, all of which are defining elements of Japanese society. It is unique in having crime rates that have dropped steadily in comparison with other countries (Waller 1991: 36). Between 1948 and 1976 the crime rate in Japan fell by 45 per cent. Since then, however, the rate has risen slightly. Nevertheless, the rate of crime in 1987 was the same as it was in 1966, while during the same period in the United States the rate for serious crime doubled – and more than doubled in Britain.

Most scholars appear to accept that one reason for Japan's low crime rate lies in its cultural emphasis on respect, mutuality and trust and its traditional reliance on informal group social control (Fenwick 1985; Moriyama 1993). The Japanese are enmeshed in tight-knit groups of well-known people who have the presumptive right to tell them how to behave and not behave (Bayley 1991: 177). The continuing endurance and strength of group and associational forms, despite its history of rapid economic growth in the post-war period, is a defining element in Japan's crime control. Thus high levels of interdependency in employment, neighbourhoods and families are believed to engender important moral and informal control mechanisms which prevent criminality.

However, also noteworthy is the fact that Japan's recent history has generally been one of low unemployment rates, low levels of poverty (particularly among children), coupled with less extremes between the wealthiest and the poorest people. It is therefore difficult to discuss Japanese crime prevention without addressing wide societal factors and issues of cultural difference (Miyazawa 1992). Hence, recent interest in Japan by Western criminologists has focused on the formal and informal system of policing in Japan and the notion of a specific Japanese 'culture of shaming' as fundamental to understanding its low crime rate and thus its distinctive approach to crime prevention.

Koban *and the system of policing*

Japanese policing is based on a unique system of fixed police posts or substations, referred to generically as *koban*. These 'posts' are one of two types: *Hashyutsujyo* are to be found in cities, while *chuzaisho* are located in rural areas. Personnel from a *koban* change each shift, after reporting for duty at a police station, while *chuzaisho* are residential. They both vary in shape and structure but are in essence decentralised, local mini-police stations. By the end of the 1980s there were about 6600 city-based *koban* and more than 9000 *chuzaisho* (Bayley 1991: 12). As four-fifths of the Japanese population live in cities, these *kobans* play the most prominent role in crime control. *Koban* may be situated anywhere accessible, for example on traffic islands, among shops or under railway bridges. They are usually in close proximity to the local population and each *koban* only covers a small geographical area. For example, in metropolitan Tokyo, there are approximately 1000 *koban* and the average area covered is about

0.22 square miles with a population of 8500 (Bayley 1991: 12). *Chuzaisho*, on the other hand, cover 3000 people on average and areas up to 18 square miles.

The central function of *koban* is to provide information to people about the area, addresses and locations, which is of particular importance given the complexity of Japanese streets, so *koban* officers need to have a deep and thorough knowledge of their area. According to a survey by the National Police Research Institute in Tokyo, more than one-third of the people who need police help seek it from a *koban*, either by telephone or in person (cited in Bayley 1991: 15).

The primary role of the Japanese police, as exemplified by *koban* officers, is crime prevention by enhancing groups' and communities' capacity to discipline themselves. For example, *koban* officers conduct twice-yearly home visits during which they distribute crime prevention material, raise the level of awareness about victimisation and offer security inspections (Bayley 1991: 183). They also gather low-level information and encourage people to report any suspicious activity in their locality. As a consequence, the clear up rate in Japan has consistently remained between 57 per cent and 60 per cent, as compared with just over 20 per cent in the USA and Britain. Hence, *koban* act as important informal links in the chain between the formal criminal justice system and the public and encourage the flow of information in both directions. Symptomatic of the importance of interpersonal trust relations which underlie Japanese culture is a police-run programme which allows anyone to go to a police station or *koban* and borrow a small amount of money at any time on the 'honour system'. This programme serves a useful purpose for those people who have lost their wallets or for some other reason need money. Almost all the money borrowed is quickly returned (Kristof 1995).

Crime prevention associations

In addition to the role of the formal police, every neighbourhood in Japan has a crime prevention association composed of resident volunteers who work closely with the police. There are some 1260 associations, mirroring the number of police stations around which they are organised (Bayley 1991: 88). The work of associations varies considerably: most supply residents with publicity and organise their own street patrols. Crime prevention associations join citizens with the police at the local level. In so doing, they connect with and draw on a traditional system of informal local government which reaches into every household.

The smallest unit of formal government in cities is the *ku* (township) and in rural areas the *buraku* (hamlet). Beneath these is a traditional network of informal government which incorporates the *han* and the *cho-kai*. A *han* comprises some 20 to 30 adjacent households, several of which form a *cho-kai* (Bayley 1991: 87–90). The *cho-kai* collects money for services not provided by formal government. Government information is often passed on to the community via the heads of *cho-kai*. Membership is taken for granted although the activity of the organisations differs between locality. Membership carries obligations, such as garbage collection and cleaning, as well as services and benefits. A household that fails in its duties to the community is called on to atone by sending a small gift to other houses. Through this system, community self-government is fostered. The heads of *cho-kai* also act as mediators in neighbourhood disputes.

The crime prevention associations connect this system of local government with policing. In many places the *cho-kai* contributes some of its resources to the local crime prevention association, as do local business enterprises and in some places local members directly. The local crime prevention associations are linked together at a national level to the All Japan Crime Prevention Association. In some metropolitan areas they are also linked at an intermediary level. It is difficult to calculate membership as, to some extent, everyone is affected by crime prevention associations, but it is clear that there are several hundred thousand people actively involved as leaders of crime prevention associations. Similarly, the impact of the associations on crime is difficult to gauge given their extensive spread throughout society, the low level of crime and the lack of significant Japanese research in the field.

Crime prevention associations supplement the local police who, as the dominant partners, view them as 'valuable instruments for developing a sense of neighbourhood identity, a need the police view as acute in the suburbs of modern Japanese cities' (Bayley 1991: 91). However, this relationship with the police has implications both for the type of membership attracted and the activities pursued. Consequently, the leaders and key members of the associations are inclined to be uncritical of local policing. Bayley notes that:

> Leaders of crime prevention associations tend to be elderly, male and conservative. Women and youth are seriously underrepresented . . . Retired people are the backbone of the associations. Leadership appears to be self-perpetuating, though the mechanisms are unclear. Social status as well as the ability to support activities financially are undoubtedly important elements. So too is an active sympathy for the police.
>
> (1991: 90)

In addition to crime prevention associations there is a wealth of other voluntary associations many of which have some potential impact on crime prevention, including traffic-safety associations, committees on juvenile delinquency, child welfare, violence and gas-main explosions (Thornton and Endo 1992). Importantly, the informal system of crime prevention is closely woven into the formal system. Hence, the primary function of the formal system is the informing, guiding and facilitating of voluntary and informal activity. For example, there are over 2000 police-school liaison councils, covering 90 per cent of all primary schools in Japan. Public Safety Commissions have appointed nearly 5000 juvenile 'guidance counsellors', who work with 57 000 volunteers offering advice and support to juveniles already in trouble with the law and at risk of further delinquency. These people patrol the streets and particular areas where youths congregate, usually accompanied by plainclothes crime prevention officers, in order to help and 'protect' juveniles (Bayley 1991: 186).

A culture of reintegrative shaming?

Recently, criminologists have sought to explain Japan's success at crime prevention with reference to its wider cultural and social formation. The most prominent explanation has been advanced by Braithwaite who has sought to show how Japanese culture, unlike that of more individualistic societies, fosters and nourishes forms of shaming conducive to preventing criminality. Japan is an example of what Braithwaite (1989: 61–5) calls a 'communitarian' society. This he defines as a society, or culture, in which:

> individuals are deeply enmeshed in interdependencies which have the special qualities of mutual help and trust. The interpedendencies have symbolic significance in the culture of group loyalties which take precedence over group interests . . . A communitarian culture rejects any pejorative connotation of dependency as threatening individual autonomy.
>
> (1989: 100)

In support of this view he points to the importance of the family, group affiliation and a culture of voluntarism which all constitute important elements in Japanese society. In Japan the obligations of belonging are accepted because in exchange, people in groups are nurtured, supported and cared for by the wider membership.

Braithwaite's contention is that criminology has tended to pose the wrong question. Rather than search for answers about why people commit crime, he contends we should be considering the question why people do not commit crime or, put another way, why people conform to social norms? He suggests that most people obey the law most of the time, not because they are deterred by the threat of official punishment, but because such acts are 'unthinkable' or they are deterred by informal controls, be they the potential of social disapproval that would greet an offending act or by pangs of conscience. These, he suggests, are real pressures to conform which express themselves both internally, through consciences, and externally, in the form of disapproval. Japan as a society nurtures pressures to conform through group interdependencies and the processes of shaming.

The key concept in his more general theory is that of *shame*. Braithwaite suggests there are two types of shame: 'stigmatising' (or disintegrative) shaming and 'reintegrative shaming'. On the one hand, stigmatisation, which Garfinkel (1956) earlier associated with 'degradation ceremonies', is shaming which creates outcasts, where 'criminal' becomes a master-status trait that drives out all other identities. Here bonds of respect with the offender are not sustained. No effort is made to reconcile the offender with the community. On the other hand, 'reintegrative shaming' is disapproval dispensed within an ongoing relationship with the offender based on respect. Here, shaming focuses on the evil of the deed rather than on the offender as an irremediable person. Shame occurs in the context of ceremonies to decertify deviance, where forgiveness, apology and repentance are culturally important. 'Shaming and reintegration do not occur simultaneously but sequentially, with reintegration occurring before deviance becomes a master status' (Braithwaite 1989: 101).

A fundamental condition for successful reintegration through shaming is the type of interdependency found in societies like Japan. 'Interdependencies must be attachments which invoke personal obligations to others within a community of concern' (Braithwaite 1989: 85). The formal criminal justice system in Western societies tends to stigmatise rather than reintegrate offenders. Braithwaite suggests that the role of 'shame' within close interpersonal relations acts as an important bond in the reproduction of conformity. This leads him to suggest that the 'uncoupling of shame and punishment manifested in a wide variety of ways in many Western countries is an important factor in explaining the rising crime rates in those countries' (Braithwaite 1989: 61, and see Braithwaite 1993). This leads Braithwaite to his central hypothesis that crime will be less in societies which shame offenders without stigmatising them; which denounce and reason with offenders over their crimes while maintaining the bonds of community and respect. Low crime societies are those that foster a sequence of shaming, forgiveness and repentance. They are societies that give relatively more prominence to moralising social control over stigmatising social control.

Japan has managed to retain a culturally important place for reintegrative shaming, both in its formal state system and in its wider society. For example, the apology has a central place in Japanese legal conflict (Bayley 1991: 126–8). Braithwaite notes that in Japan:

> ceremonies of restoration to signify the reestablishment of harmony between conflicting parties are culturally pivotal; the best way for this to occur is by mutual apology, where even a party who is relatively unblameworthy will find some way in which he contributed to the conflict to form the basis of his apology.
>
> (1989: 64)

Law enforcement authorities have also learnt to use and encourage confessions, remorse and victim compensation within the formal process. They have the flexibility to implement such procedures and their efforts are largely supported by the community (Haley 1995).

Clearly crime prevention in Japan is not something which is only the concern of the police or of certain agencies but transcends and informs both informal and formal local government, policing and the criminal justice system itself. A principle of the Japanese approach appears to be the use of formal structures and resources to support other informal sources of authority rather than to substitute for them.

Discussion

Some commentators have criticised as a 'myth' the idea that Japan is as safe and secure as some suggest. They point to the role of organised criminality as an essential element of Japanese society, which is not revealed by official statistics (Miyazawa 1992). In contrast to the rose-tinted image conjured up by Braithwaite, others have highlighted the size and role of subcultural formations such as gangs of street youths, *bosozoku* ('hot rodder' groups) and *yakuza* (networks of adult male criminal organisations) as significant and culturally visible phenomena (Kersten 1993). In 1991, it was estimated that there were more than 88 000 members of organised criminal groups (*yakuza*), which some commentators suggest are endorsed and encouraged to flourish by powerful sectors of Japanese society (Miyazawa 1992). According to police estimates, 6 per cent of murders, 16 per cent of robberies, 15 per cent of rapes and most drug and gun smuggling is committed by *yakuza* members (Bayley 1991: 168–9). Others suspect these figures to be considerable underestimates. There is also an increasing awareness in Japan of a link between organised crime and corporate crime:

> It seems that a culture like Japan can have both low rates of reported crime and (measured) victimisation and, on the other hand, an existence of subcultures of significant proportions dramatically overrepresented in crime statistics.
>
> (Kersten 1993: 293)

Japan's informal control mechanisms, its culture of shame and relations of interdependency, allow criminal gangs to coexist alongside orderliness. All this, Bayley suggests, 'raises questions about how this orderliness has been achieved and what the role of the police is in it' (1991: 169). It may be that Japanese culture, given the importance of close-knit informal social control, fosters conformity both to group norms which are law-abiding and those which are deviant.

It also needs to be recognised that Japan's relative safety from crime has been achieved at a cost, most notably in respect of the rights of the individual in criminal proceedings. Civil liberties are not given the same prominent place as in Western societies. The police have extensive powers, including the power to detain suspects for up to 21 days before a judicial hearing. Suspects have no 'right of silence' and are often pressurised into confessions. Conformity to authority is the product of intrusive communal pressures which enforce compliance. The power of formal and informal shaming can stifle diversity, oppress individuals and constitute a powerful tool in the hands of moral majorities. Group pressures to conform can be highly repressive, as well as produce orderliness.

The Japanese experience suggests that crime prevention, as with other forms of crime control and punishment, is connected to a society's cultural sensibilities. This means that specific models may not be easily transferable into very different cultural contexts. Yet it also allows us to question aspects of our own cultural assumptions which we often take for granted. For example, the cultural importance of interpersonal trust relations in Japanese society means there is a cultural opposition in Japan to forms of situational crime prevention, particularly of the target-hardening variety (Moriyama 1995). Human relationships are fundamentally based on the social structure of face-to-face interactions. These relationships and the trust that sustains them are fractured or destroyed by interventions such as intercommunication systems, protective glass, barriers and bars. So despite Japan's propensity toward technological advancements, they have been reluctant to adopt many Anglo-American developments in situational crime prevention. The lack of any real debate in Britain about the implications of target-hardening and situational crime prevention measures on interpersonal trust relations suggests that we may have failed to recognise their cultural importance.

In relation to the connection between culture and crime in Japan we need to recognise that it is embedded in a specific economic and social formation which is structural. Japanese economic performance is predicated on a corporate notion of wealth which does not allow the same kinds of relative deprivation that blight Western societies. Culture is not static but continually undergoing a process of change and adaptation. Thus, as Nelken suggests, we need 'to treat culture as a process of becoming and a point of departure as much as a functioning whole' (1995: 444). Japanese culture is not itself immune to the impact of globalisation, particularly through global communications and informational networks, which may have damaging effects on Japan's cultural approach to crime prevention. This may be beginning to show itself in Japan's growing recent concerns about criminality and violence.

Conclusions

Out of the preceding discussion we can select a number of insights which have significance for the British experience. First, the above overview identifies the important role of government, at the central, regional and local levels, in providing administrative structures which facilitate long-term strategic planning and funding. It identifies the role of the central state in promoting, monitoring and evaluating crime prevention strategies. Yet it also raises questions about the relationship between the role of the state, the private sector and 'civil society' (the community). In France, for example, the dominant role of the state can be seen as stifling the involvement of the other two dynamics. The different national structures through which crime prevention and community safety are delivered highlights the importance of 'process-focused' work as distinct from 'scheme-focused' work. Liddle and Gelsthorpe (1994c) define the former as work that creates structures and administrative arrangements which can deliver over the long term, since they are dependent on planned, strategic funding from within the existing mainstream budgets of agencies. This work requires links to local democratic structures as its development is dependent on ownership at the political level. By contrast, 'scheme-focused' work is driven by short-term goals on the back of one-off funding initiatives which lie outside agencies' mainstream funding. Crime prevention in Britain has almost exclusively followed this latter route. Other European experiences suggest that 'process-focused' work deserves a higher priority.

Second, the comparative experiences provide important insights into social crime prevention, traditionally weak in Britain and the USA. They also question the extent to which crime prevention strategies (seek to) embody a dynamic of social integration or exclusion. In other jurisdictions, attempts to fashion responses to questions of crime are directly connected to wider problems of social cohesion and the problems of social exclusion.

Third, the examples not only question the relative weight to be accorded to social rather than situational crime prevention, but also to the balance between technological and interpersonal control mechanisms. They highlight the human dynamic in social control. What is interesting about the Dutch experience of social crime prevention is its recognition of the importance of intermediate bodies or people as agents of social control in regulating social behaviour. Ironically, this appears to fly in the face of current British trends which prioritise technological 'quick fixes'. British cities have witnessed the removal and erosion of many traditional regulatory agents, such as park keepers, bus conductors and train-station guards, largely as a result of reduced local government finances and private competition. Public spaces – unlike private places such as shopping malls and entertainment centres where private security prevails – now have few regulatory links between informal and formal control mechanisms, hence leaving a regulatory vacuum. In this context, it is little wonder that the nature and use of public spaces has declined.

Yet some small-scale initiatives in reintroducing intermediaries as agents of social control have recently developed in the UK. For example, Glasgow has followed the Dutch 'city warden' schemes by introducing their own uniformed 'city centre reps' hired from the unemployment register. The scheme began in early 1996, the aim being to restore confidence, particularly among visitors, in the city centre. The scheme involves 28 'reps', 16 of whom will be on patrol, helping the public, greeting foreign tourists in their own language and alerting the council or police to maintenance and security problems (Meikle 1996). The remaining 12 will be 'clean up staff' removing fly-posters and graffiti and keeping signs clear. The number of 'reps' was due to be increased by a further ten in May 1996. The problem as ever is over the question of funding. To date the British government has been unwilling to step in with long-term funding for such schemes. The Glasgow experiment principally draws on European Union funds.

The European reintroduction of intermediate institutions, to establish social control mechanisms, links with the Japanese experience where such bodies exist in abundance. This reminds us that in Britain as a society we tend to employ what Leadbeater refers to as 'an outsourcing approach to crime', whereby we expect specialist institutions, such as the police, the courts and the prisons to solve most of our problems for us (1996: 1). A more plausible interpretation of history would suggest that these very institutions have appropriated, or 'stolen', people's conflicts and their legitimate role in the resolution of conflicts (Christie 1977). Nevertheless, what is clear is that the recent history of the relationship between the criminal justice system and the public in Britain has been one of the active, professional, specialist and bureaucratic 'expert' on the one side and the passive and ignorant lay recipient of a service on the other. Increasingly, the gulf between professionalism and self-help has widened. The importance of informal control until recently had been forgotten or taken for granted. Some of the experiences of social crime prevention in other countries highlight the neglect of a 'people dynamic' within British crime prevention. Unlike some of our European counterparts, we have tended not to utilise people as a resource and instead have turned too quickly to technology. Bottoms and Wiles (1992) suggest that this lack of a 'people dynamic' is more of a fundamental fault of Anglo-American criminology in general, and may even be a cultural artefact.

Cultural differences in approaches to crime prevention should warn us against any simple attempts to replicate successful experiences in different cultural contexts. Transferring models from one context to the next is by no means unproblematic. The connections between crime, prevention and culture are complex and nuanced. This is true when moving between localities within a specific society and is even more so across societies. At the same time, as in the Japanese example, experiences from elsewhere may warn us about the implications of forms of crime prevention for aspects of our own culture which we may take for granted or to which we may have been blind.

Notes

1. The administrative structure in France below the nation state has three tiers: (a) 22 regions (for which there is no crime prevention co-ordinating structure); (b) departments; and (c) *les villes*, towns or cities. These last two administrative levels have been used to co-ordinate the delivery of crime prevention.

2. This practice has led to accusations of the over-concentration of power in too few hands and of conflicting interests (Garapon 1997).

Chapter 8

The Politics of Crime Prevention and Community Safety

A central contention of this book has been that the last 20 to 30 years have witnessed the rise of crime prevention and community safety, accompanied by a host of new discourses, technologies, techniques and practices. This shift is not premised on a wholly coherent theoretical framework but a number of (sometimes) competing assumptions. Situational crime prevention sees crime as a routine aspect of everyday life to be avoided, discouraged and managed, and identifies criminals as essentially 'like us': no different from other rational actors. On the other hand, much social crime prevention remains premised on predispositional assumptions about crime causation, albeit less concerned with individual biologies than traditional criminology and more centred on identifying categories of 'at risk' populations. Yet in large part, the shift to crime prevention has its origin in failure and crisis within traditional criminal justice, which have engendered a search for legitimacy and identity. Both situational and social approaches look towards, and invest in, informal social control mechanisms, be they implicated in design, technological or human interactions. As such, under the banners of crime prevention and community safety, significant new dynamics have been introduced into the criminological enterprise.

Underlying this shift there has been a dispersal and pluralisation of policing and crime control. Diverse agencies, organisations, groups and individuals have become implicated in these tasks. The function of policing, in its broadest sense, is no longer the monopoly of the state and public police. It has become shared. The ensuing 'marketisation of crime control' has meant that security has become a commodity, to be purchased, owned and upgraded, giving rise to a new regime of individual and collective 'choice' into which people are situated. Yet 'choice' is socially circumscribed. Despite the rationalistic tones of much security discourse, 'security as a commodity' is intrinsically related to complex individual and collective sentiments of insecurity, anxiety and fear. These all connect with wider concerns about social (dis)order, as well as subjective, and non-rationalistic, elements of social identity and well-being.

Hence, in order to make sense of the shift to crime prevention we need to look behind the rationalistic and technological discourse in which much of the debate is couched. We need to scrutinise the fundamentally political nature of its origins and implications. Specific crime prevention techniques not only embody political assumptions and commitments to particular models of social explanation, they also imply a political context and have political consequences. Yet much of the discussion of crime prevention has been apolitical, with a focus on the needs of efficiency, administrative rationality and smooth management. O'Malley (1992) has correctly argued that we need to understand the spread of particular crime prevention technologies in relation to their alignment with specific political ideologies. In Chapter 3 we noted the convergence between the theoretical assumptions which underlie situational crime prevention – notably in the form of rational choice theory – and neo-liberal political ideology as embraced by the Thatcher and Reagan administrations and their successors. Furthermore, the importance of O'Malley's argument was illustrated by the discussions in Chapter 7, where we saw how the comparative reception and development of particular crime prevention technologies and strategies in different countries have been dependent on the local political and cultural contexts.

The aim of this chapter is to pull together some of the recurring themes which have been raised throughout the preceding discussions, while simultaneously attempting to make sense of the broad directions in which appeals to crime prevention and community safety are directing criminal justice. This will necessitate an engagement with wider social and political trends, in order to attempt to make sense of their implications for crime control and prevention. Hence, the first part of this chapter seeks to locate the growth of crime prevention within a socio-political context, which connects the preceding arguments with developments in political and social theory. In the second part, I consider a number of possible future scenarios for crime prevention as we near the millennium. The aim of this exercise is not merely to engage in crystal-ball gazing, but rather to extend and project the unfolding strands and tensions which remain embedded in the recent expansion of crime prevention. Underlying this will be a concern to address a number of related questions. Will a preventive approach to crime continue to spread and increase in the future? If so, what shape and form might it take? What might its implications be for social relations? In what ways are the responsibilities of individuals, communities and the state likely to be rearticulated by any such developments and with what effects?

We begin with a cautionary note by placing prevention in the wider context of current criminal justice. Despite its recent growth, the actual expenditure on crime prevention remains relatively small compared to that spent on the police, courts and prisons. In the UK, France, USA and Canada substantially less than 1 per cent of the total criminal justice budget goes to fund crime prevention (Waller 1991), and even in

Holland where crime prevention has secured a prominent place in criminal policy this figure is still less than 2 per cent (Willemse 1994: 44). So it needs to be emphasised that the developments outlined in this book are by no means the most quantitatively significant nor the most substantial aspects of current criminal justice and penal policy. Commentators such as Christie (1993) have rightly sought to highlight and focus attention on the massive expansion of incarceration across developed societies, most notably the USA and Russia. Despite the 'failure' of traditional modes of apprehending, sentencing and punishing offenders (Broady 1976; Clarke and Hough 1984) and the arrival of new 'experts' in crime prevention (Ericson 1994), there remains enormous vested interest in the formal criminal justice system. Hence, in spite of the evidence reviewed in this book, it is clearly too early to talk of the eclipse of the 'deterrent paradigm' by a 'preventive security paradigm', albeit that a 'mixed agenda' or 'plural order' appears to have emerged.

Responsibilisation strategies

A major recurring theme in discussions so far has been the extent to which the new-found interest in crime prevention represents an expression of the rearticulation of relations between the state, market and civil society. I have sought to show that appeals to prevention embody 'responsibilisation strategies', through which the state has attempted to redefine the legitimate expectations of the public in relation to crime control, as well as the criteria on which state performance should be judged. Hence, the new message is that the state alone, is not, and cannot effectively be, responsible for public safety and crime control. Now the public – as residents, property owners, parents, community-group members, manufacturers, consumers, business people, employers and individual citizens – has become firmly implicated in the tasks. As we saw in Chapter 4, the notion of 'community' has been deployed as the central motif around which the public are being mobilised to participate in crime prevention and to take on a greater share of responsibility for personal security and public safety. This dispersal of responsibility and the renegotiation of state functions is not limited to the field of crime control. Similar shifts have occurred in other sectors of social life, such as health care, social welfare and pensions. In many senses, crime control is following, rather than leading, trends set elsewhere, albeit in its own distinct fashion. As a consequence, the growth of crime prevention needs to be connected firmly to the spread of a neo-liberal political ideology which has sought to transform the modern state.

As we saw in Chapter 5 the private sector has been called on to play, and now plays, a significant role in crime prevention and control. Influenced by neo-liberal political ideology, successive governments have sought

to off-load certain state functions to the private sector in the name of increased competition and in the hope of increased efficiency. As such, we
have seen the 'privatisation' of crime control, which has taken a number
of broad forms.

1   The use of markets and the contracting out of service delivery

This most obvious form of 'privatisation' has seen the contracting out of
public services to the private sector, the use of special-purpose bodies
(such as quangos) and the marketising of public service delivery. This is
clearly a government-led initiative in which it has offered up certain state
functions to commercial interests, with varying degrees of incentive and
regulation. What has been transferred is the provision of services and
goods from public government to private corporations. However, in the
process, the boundaries between 'public' and 'private' have become
blurred, producing a 'hybrid' or 'grey' sphere in the administration and
delivery of key public goods (Johnston 1992).

2   The 'voluntarisation' of public services

A second governmental strategy has seen certain state functions handed
over to the 'voluntary', 'independent' or 'not-for-profit' sector. As discussed in Chapter 5 this has often occurred under the rhetoric of 'partnerships' whereby public sector agencies have purchased the services of
'voluntary bodies'. A somewhat different form of 'voluntarisation' has seen
the introduction of 'volunteers' to perform functions, some of which might
otherwise have been performed by state officials. A particularly notice-
able example has been successive governments' attempted expansion of
the special constabulary (Southgate *et al.* 1995).

3   The 'civilianisation' of public services

The civilianisation of public services has seen civilians replace state professionals in performing certain tasks. This process has been particularly
evident within the police, where various government enquiries have been
set up to identify 'ancillary' tasks appropriate for civilianisation. The Home
Office circular 105/1988 which identified 25 categories of work suitable
for civilianisation was followed up by an extensive review which has had
significant impact on the police service (Home Office 1994b).

4   Appeals to 'active citizenry'

Successive recent governments have sought to encourage 'active citizenship' and 'voluntary collective action' to assist in the provision of local
goods and services as the role of the state is withdrawn and redrawn.

Whether through national advertising campaigns or local initiatives, subjects are being constituted as active and responsible agents in their own security. The assumption is that the scope for voluntary action is expanded and advanced as the role of the state retracts, thus encouraging 'entrepreneurship' or 'communitarian support networks' (depending on your political standpoint) to fill these vacated spaces. This can take the form of 'private prudentialism' (O'Malley 1992) – whereby individuals manage their future life-styles through insurance against risk – or collective governance through community self-policing.

5   The expansion of the private security industry

As we saw in Chapter 2 the private security industry has boomed over the past two decades, although there is some debate as to when this expansion began and its size (see Jones and Newburn 1998). Nevertheless, 'security' has become a commodity which has produced a massive industry. In Britain the number of people employed within the private security sector is estimated to have outstripped the number of public police officers. In the USA it is estimated that there are about 2 million private security people as against 650 000 sworn police officers (Bayley and Shearing 1996: 587). What is clear is that the public police have lost their monopoly and their numerical supremacy. The market for crime prevention technology has also expanded dramatically.

6   The privatisation of public space and the growth of zones of private governance

The expansion of the security industry has been fostered and encouraged by the 'privatisation of public space' through the growth of 'mass private property', such as shopping malls, entertainment stadia, leisure centres and recreational grounds. 'Mass private property' refers to facilities that are owned privately but to which the public has access and use (Shearing 1992). As a consequence of the growth of 'mass private property', ever greater amounts of 'public places' are increasingly located on private property and policed by private security companies. This important societal development has transformed the relationship between social activity and public space (Shearing and Stenning 1987b). So the distinction between public and private spaces has become distinctly blurred. In this instance both the delivery and direction of security management and policing have been 'privatised'.

The ability of governments to advance and realise each of these strategies is variable and subject to limitations. Some of them are more easily performed by government alone, others are highly dependent on events which occur at some distance from the competence of government. For example, while the first three strategies require government merely to create appropriate conditions to attract private and voluntary sector interests, it is harder for governments to entice 'active citizenry'. The dynamic driving the last two strategies has lain more squarely within the private and commercial sector. This is not to suggest that government has not created a favourable climate for such expansion. British governments have provided this, notably through a lack of regulation of the private security industry and by encouraging or allowing the development of large out-of-town shopping malls (notably in the late 1980s and early 1990s).

Shearing (1996) has highlighted the differences between modes of 'privatisation' by differentiating two distinct processes of change. These he refers to as 'state rule at a distance' and 'private government'. The former (which approximates to the first four strategies identified above), he suggests, are state-initiated developments of 'rule at a distance'. The state maintains an important directing function and agenda-setting role, but hands over the performance and delivery to others. By contrast, in relation to 'private governments' (strategies five and six above) it is both the business and direction of policing which are privatised. Shearing's conceptual separation tends to simplify what are often interactive relations into either one or other of two processes of change. However, it is useful in its acknowledgement of the limitations as well as the strengths of state power in relation to this growing complex 'plural order' of policing, crime prevention and control.

Shearing also highlights the ways in which techniques developed within 'private governments' have influenced strategies of 'state rule'. With the expansion of private security and 'mass private property', Shearing has noted, 'policing changed as its location changed' (1992: 423). Thus, questions of location and control have implications for the nature and direction of policing policy itself. The strategies of private security are more concerned with loss prevention and risk reduction than with law enforcement or the detection and conviction of criminals. Hence, the concerns of policing here are more instrumental than moral (Shearing and Stenning 1987a). The regulation of these 'private spaces' is dominated by a future-oriented understanding of prevention and security. 'Private governments' in shopping malls and private security complexes are often more interested in plugging breaches of security and excluding those that pose a threat to order, rather than relying on the deterrent value of the formal criminal justice process and prosecution. The regulatory force of 'membership' and 'access' is a powerful mode of control. If the law is invoked it is often likely to be contract law, rather than the criminal law. The power of removal, dismissal, exclusion or termination to which such contracts may give rise are potent administrative instruments.

Importantly, the shift to supplement a 'preventive security paradigm for a deterrent one' – most prominent in mass private property – is increasingly influencing developments in 'public' policing and crime control. The private sector has, to some degree, set the agenda to which the public provision of security is turning its attention. For example, local authority town centre managers are increasingly looking towards modes of regulation and control deployed in privately owned out-of-town shopping centres, a development which has been described as the 'mallisation' of city centres and public spaces. Ericson and Haggerty (1997), drawing on Canadian research, have argued that more and more of the public police's time and resources are being deployed to service networks that have security rather than law enforcement as their principal concern. In this view, the police have increasingly become 'knowledge brokers, expert advisors and security managers to the public and other institutions' (Ericson 1994: 164). Multi-agency networks have enmeshed the police in 'communications policing' in which the police are primarily 'information brokers'. Here we see an example of the interactive nature of developments across the public–private divide. This reiterates the manner in which dynamics for change lie not wholly within the state but, on occasions, far from it.

Shifts in responsibility not only transfer the burden of cost but also relocate the weight of blame for failure. As suggested in Chapter 6 the pluralisation of policing has also fragmented and transformed the criteria of 'success'. However, 'failure' appears to have been moved out from formal criminal justice agencies into the public body. As the police no longer claim to be able to 'solve the crime problem alone' and now argue that they can only play a limited role in preventing crime, the shift to prevention has 'let the police off the hook' (Kinsey *et al.* 1986). The failure to stem the rising crime rate, so the new wisdom would have it, is no longer to be blamed on the state.[1] As crime prevention increasingly becomes the responsibility of the public, this burden has been shifted to potential victims. The victim – rather like the offender for the purposes of situational crime prevention – is cast in the clothes of the 'rational choice actor'. He or she is notionally free to make choices about what level of security is desired, by weighing up the costs and benefits. Victimisation, thus envisaged, becomes the outcome of rational choices – whether or not to purchase security devices, visit particular places or engage in certain 'life-styles' – for which the victim bares ultimate responsibility. In this logic 'carelessness' and 'irresponsibility' become the catchphrases of victim-blaming.

The shift to prevention outlined in this book implies crucial challenges to the state's claim to monopoly of public power and force, as it confronts its own limitations. Some 15 years ago the astute criminologist Stan Cohen commented:

> One need only pause for a minute to see that although in areas like mental illness the private sector might genuinely displace the state, this would be an impossible outcome in crime control. For the state to give up here would be to undercut its very claim to legitimacy.
>
> (1983: 117)

It is a testimony to how rapidly the face of crime control has changed that the 'impossible outcome' envisaged by Cohen now appears considerably more possible. In Britain, we now have a 'mixed economy' of social control. Yet Cohen is right to highlight the problems of legitimacy this may present. Privatisation, in all its guises, rather than resolving legitimacy deficits by attempting to alleviate the burden of the overloaded state has produced new problems of legitimacy. These have been dispersed into new social fields. The proliferation of 'private governments' and neo-corporate partnerships has raised questions about the nature of authority, accountability and civil rights. Pluralisation and responsibilisation have injected ambiguity into the power to define and deploy the legitimate use of force. Most notably, this has become apparent in struggles over the distinction between appropriate 'citizen action' and 'vigilantism' (Johnston 1996).

The reinvention of government?

If we turn our focus to the governmental reforms that constitute Shearing's 'state rule at a distance' we can identify a reasonably coherent political ideology infusing these strategies. This neo-liberalism is clearly set out in what has come to be seen as the 'Bible' of public sector reforms: Osborne and Gaebler's *Reinventing Government*, published in 1992. The book has become a highly influential text which has had considerable impact on public sector managers and politicians in the USA, the UK, Australia and New Zealand. In it, Osborne and Gaebler, two American commentators, seek to articulate a set of principles concerned with encouraging fundamental transformations in the scope and internal working of the public sector. Their aim of 'reinventing government' is described as little less than a political and management 'revolution'. In order to advance their argument Osborne and Gaebler (1992) use the analogy of a rowing boat to highlight what they perceive as the need to separate off the 'steering' activities of government from the 'rowing'. 'Steering' involves policy-formation – 'leading' and setting norms or agendas – as well as catalysing and facilitating change. 'Rowing', on the other hand, concerns policy implementation and service delivery: the 'doing' of things. Governments that 'steer' more, but 'do' less, are not weaker but stronger, they argue: 'After all, those who steer the boat have far more power over its destination than those who row it' (1992: 32). Hence, they advocate 'less government but more governance'. In this context, the term 'governance' is taken to signify a change in the process of governing involving new methods by which society is governed (see Rhodes 1996, 1997).

Bureaucracy, they argue, is defunct and counterproductive as a model for delivering 'rowing'. In its place, they identify ten tenets of 'entrepreneurial government':

Most entrepreneurial governments promote *competition* between service providers. They *empower* citizens by pushing control out of the bureaucracy, into the community. They measure the performance of their agencies, focusing not on inputs but on *outcomes*. They are driven by their goals – their *missions* – not by their rules and regulations. They redefine their clients as *customers* and offer them choices . . . They *prevent* problems before they emerge, rather than simply offering services afterwards. They put their energies into *earning* money, not simply spending it. They *decentralize* authority, embracing participatory management. They prefer *market* mechanisms to bureaucratic mechanisms. And they focus not simply on providing public services, but on *catalysing* all sectors – public, private and voluntary – into action to solve their community's problems.

(Osborne and Gaebler 1992: 20, emphasis in original)

The book is full of examples of 'entrepreneurial' public sector organisa-tions putting some or all of these principles into practice. In so doing, Osborne and Gaebler distil and articulate a philosophical case for 'new public management' (NPM) reforms and managerialism generally. This combines the 'responsibilisation' of the public (civil society) and the market to take on board traditional state functions, as well as the trans-formation of the state itself. In line with the 'reinvention of government', future modes of governance should be market-based, outcome-oriented, future-focused, prevention-concerned, mission-driven and customer-focused. They simultaneously entail processes of centralisation and decentralisa-tion: centralisation of policy and the setting of the parameters within which the system works and the decentralisation of operational management. They entail a rigorous attempt to separate off policy from administration or operational delivery. Hence, they necessitate processes of control and verification which allow those that 'steer' to monitor and correct the activities of those that 'row'. Contracts, performance indicators, audits and inspections are some of the practical tools used to deliver this rela-tionship of 'governing at a distance' (Power 1997). This 'revolution' in the relationship between state and civil society suggests a situation in which the former asserts a form of control through the setting of norms and the correction of deviations from them. Within the context of crime control 'state rule at a distance' gives birth to 'a system of rule that uncouples the "steering" from the "rowing" of policing and locates the responsibility for "steering" with the state and "rowing" with citizens' (Shearing 1996: 85).

The work of Osborne and Gaebler is useful both because of its direct influence on policy and because it articulates a coherent set of understandings which inform 'responsibilisation strategies', or at least those promoted by governments. The 'rowing' and 'steering' analogy seems to offer a simple catchphrase around which governmental solu-tions have been sought. It also appears to resonate with much of the new policy discourse that has accompanied the shift to prevention in criminal justice, and some of the associated institutional changes, over the past two decades or so. Yet commentators have tended to use Osborne and Gaebler's work – the rowing boat analogy in particular – as if it were unproblematic (Cope *et al.* 1995; Shearing 1996). Rather, it over-simplifies complex and controversial relations between the actors. Yet this is precisely why it is a useful starting point for our purposes. For this is also the case with NPM reforms. Hence, the inadequacies of the analogy assist in identifying and illustrating some of the complexities and tensions embodied within 'responsibilisation strategies' in the field of crime control.

First, unlike Osborne and Gaebler, we need to distinguish between *intention* and *effect*. After all, strategies have to be translated into practical processes, which may produce unintended consequences, resistance and conflict. As Giddens rightly warns, 'knowledge of social life transcends the intentions of those who apply it to transformative ends' (1990: 54). For example, Osborne and Gaebler's argument ignores the fact that 'street level bureaucrats' will inevitably exercise discretion (Lipsky 1980), which may thwart or undermine initial intentions. In other words, we need to differentiate between 'steering' as a process and 'directedness' as an out-come. Unlike many commentators who have sought to interpret and use Osborne and Gaebler's work, we should not assume but rather seek to problematise the effectiveness of such strategies.

Second, the capacity for governing and managing 'at a distance' through the monitoring of explicit standards is itself circumspect. There are difficulties implicit in observing effort and performance, as well as in obtaining information on which such monitoring may be based. While the person steering Osborne and Gaebler's rowing boat is able to see what the rowers are doing and where they are going, this is not true of the relationship between government and those charged with adminis-tering policy. The use of audits, inspections and contracts may assist in this process but they are still blunt instruments of verification which leave considerable blind spots. They also vest considerable control over the process in the hands of the administrators (or 'rowers') themselves. For example, objective setting works best in conditions of predictability and quantifiability. In areas of complexity and uncertainty – such as crime prevention and community safety – hard quantifiable pre-specification is not always possible and, if attempted, has a high potential to produce services that fail to support the desired policy goals. The use of contracts and performance specifications cannot reduce the uncertainty of the future.

The experience from the UK in health service reforms suggests that: 'The purchaser is often dependent on the provider for knowledge of what has been done, or even what should be done, so that information becomes a key battleground in service management' (Deakin and Walsh 1996: 37). The lesson is that delivery systems, once set up, have begun to exhibit a tendency to develop their own dynamic. In practice it is becoming harder to distinguish those who are 'rowing' from those who are 'steering', so issues of responsibility and accountability can become confused. In so far as they relate to the long-term legitimacy of institutions, these cannot simply be left to market logic to resolve.

Third, as a metaphor for the possible intentions of government policy the rowing boat analogy raises significant questions in the field of crime prevention for local community safety partnerships. For if these institutions occupy merely a 'rowing' function, this would appear to fly in the face of government rhetoric about the importance of 'local ownership' and the elaboration of a 'local vision'. What, therefore, is the policy-making role of local community safety partnerships? Are they merely rowing a boat, the direction of which is set by others, or are they themselves in charge of the direction? There seems to be a crucial tension between local control and central steering which government has not addressed. Even if steering is conceived of as only a limited process of setting boundaries within which local initiatives must operate, then the question remains: how constraining are these boundaries to be?

Fourth, we need to ask how appropriate Osborne and Gaebler's analogy is as a metaphor for contemporary organisational relations, particularly in the light of a 'partnership' approach. Inter-organisational relations mean, rather than one set of hands on the tiller, 'steering' the process, that there are now a multiplicity of 'steerers'. Extending the analogy even further, potentially there is a plurality of fragmented 'rowing boats'. As noted in Chapter 5, NPM reforms are primarily concerned with internal re-engineering and reorganisation. NPM may suit line bureaucracies but is largely inappropriate for managing inter-organisational networks. There are fundamental tensions between a 'partnership' approach and aspects of the intra-organisational focus of managerialist reforms. Where a 'partnership' approach envisages corporate decision-making on behalf of a number of actors, managerialism conceives of compartmentalised and independent responses coupled with an *intra*-organisational focus on objectives and results. Genuine 'partnerships' require trust, reciprocity, co-operation and interdependence, all of which may be undermined by the contractualisation, output measurement and competition fostered by NPM reforms. Despite its impact, this tension within managerialism has largely been ignored by criminological commentators.[2] However, if partnerships are to be taken seriously the debate needs to move beyond the 'reinvention of government' to the mechanisms for the integration of government within partnerships and the fostering of appropriate conditions under which partnerships will be able to flourish.

Risk, governmentality and power – the 'new penology'?

Throughout, we have come across reference to 'risk' as a dominant element in the shift to crime prevention. A number of commentators have connected this to a more fundamental social transformation which has been termed variously the rise of the 'risk society', 'actuarial justice' and the 'new penology' (Feeley and Simon 1992, 1994; Ericson 1994; Ericson and Haggerty 1997). Within this body of literature, it is suggested that the shift to crime prevention is an aspect of a wider movement from discourses of 'deviance' and 'control' to discourses of 'security' and 'risk'. The most obvious expressions of this are the proliferation of techniques for measuring 'predictors' and 'indicators' of risk, as well as the growth of 'community safety' strategies. Power in the 'new penology' is aimed at prevention and risk minimisation. The new discourses, it is argued, substitute the terminology of 'justice' and 'reform' with the terminology of 'safety' and the containment of 'dangerousness'. They point to the growth and elaboration of insurance-based and risk-based technologies, which bypass attempts to alter individual behaviour or motivation. In their place, it is argued, 'actuarial' techniques divide the population into statistical and behavioural categories organised around 'risk'. These techniques regulate groups as part of a 'strategy of managing danger'.

As Feeley and Simon note, this does not mean that individuals disappear in criminal justice, but rather increasingly are transformed: 'they are grasped not as coherent subjects, whether understood as moral, psychological or economic agents, but as members of particular subpopulations and the intersection of various categorical indicators' (1994: 178). Risk assessment and insurance disaggregate people by classifying them according to differences from others in a given population. They attempt to manage and 'manipulate the public as a demographic mass or aggregate'. As such, they 'radically reframe the issues, and target something very different, that is, the crime rate, understood as the distribution of behaviours in the population as a whole' (Feeley and Simon 1994: 175–8). In this emerging 'new penology', membership of risk categories or populations is increasingly becoming a defining criterion in configurations of social organisation (Simon 1988; Feeley and Simon 1992).

And yet, as Ericson and Haggerty note, 'risk assessment' embodies a 'logic of the norm' (1997: 92). Risk categories constitute population groups, and yet 'measurement is inexact, statistical probabilities are imprecise, and indeterminism, therefore, is everpresent'. Calculation of future risks – be they criminal victimisation, ill health, accident or unemployment – and the resultant risk groups which people are forced to inhabit, can never be an exact science. Consequently, 'deviation from the mean is in fact the norm' (*ibid.*). Even if we assume the accuracy of prediction, this strategy requires prevention to abstract 'at risk' individuals from their social context (O'Malley 1992). Consequently, there is no guarantee that individuals can be disaggregated from the social circumstances which may nourish their risk, nor that other people may not be drawn in to replace them.

A further aspect of this shift, according to Feeley and Simon, is the formation of new 'system objectives', criteria against which the success or failure of the criminal justice system is, or should be, evaluated. The new system objectives are concerned with 'smooth management', 'efficiency' and 'public safety', all of which resonate with echoes of multi-agency partnerships. As a consequence, 'justice is increasingly understood not as a rational system but through the rationality of the system' (Feeley and Simon 1994: 178).

This new form of governmental power is not located primarily within the state. Rose and Miller (1992) argue that power should be viewed as a matter of networks and alliances through which 'centres of calculation' exercise 'government at a distance'. Some commentators have argued that privatised risk-based technologies undermine state sovereignty (Simon 1988). Rose and Miller (1992) propose a rejection of the state/civil society dichotomy, as it fails to assist in the study of the new technologies of power and forms of 'governmentality' which are 'at once internal and external to the state' (Foucault 1991: 103). Their claim is that power is dispersed throughout society and that power operates through networks of action which transcend the divisions between the state and civil society. Their concern is with the exercise of power 'beyond the state', notably through the 'activities of expertise'. Rose (1996) argues that contemporary discourses of government have dispensed with the aim of 'governing through society': he calls this the 'death of the social'. Instead, he argues, they have focused on 'government through community':

> 'the social' may be giving way to 'the community' as a new territory for the administration of individual and collective existence, a new plane or surface upon which micro-moral relations among persons are conceptualized and administered.
>
> (Rose 1996: 331)

Commentators espousing the 'new penology' and 'governmentality', as understandings of contemporary change, have tended to suggest not only that new forms of risk-based governmental rationality have become a dominant mode of rule but, moreover, they are more effective means of control than earlier disciplinary forms (Simon 1988; Ewald 1991). This, they suggest, is because the management of aggregate risks – through the application of actuarial and other techniques – bypasses individuals (altering individual behaviour is difficult to achieve). Furthermore, risk-based technologies are more subtle and less likely to generate resistance.

The 'new penology' and 'governmentality' literature identifies an important field of investigation, enabling us to analyse alliances and unities within 'political rationalities' and 'governmental technologies' in institutions both within and outside the state. However, this approach tends to see these as overly unified, rational, intentional and instrumental. Accounts such as these tend to offer a totalising vision of regulation and leave little space for ambiguity and conflict. There is little concern for the actual realisation of programmes and the unintended consequences they often produce. There is also insufficient understanding of non-instrumental discourses, such as the emotional and morally toned elements of criminal justice policy (Garland 1997). They tend to imply a complete rupture with the past – a passing from the 'old' to the 'new' – rather than allowing for the coexistence of divergent rationalities. While policing and crime control represent pre-eminent and central symbols of state sovereignty, it would be wrong to assume the 'myth' of sovereign crime control as real. Although the history of private and non-state involvement in crime control has been uneven (South 1987; Johnston 1992), there has always been some degree of 'mixed economy'. To some extent the novelty lies in the fact that governments have only belatedly rediscovered (what others knew) the importance of the role that the public play in crime control and prevention and of informal social processes.

O'Malley, while accepting some of the insights provided by the 'new penology' and 'governmentality' literature, offers a more nuanced understanding:

> What influences the spread of technologies is most likely to be their appropriateness to particular ends, and this in large measure will be related to political struggles which establish programmes on the social agenda. The history of . . . actuarial techniques in crime prevention, this suggests, is not to be understood as the gradual encroachment of a more efficient technology of power, but the uneven and negotiated (and thus partial) implementation of a political programme and the consequent (equally partial) installation of the appropriate techniques.
>
> (1992: 258)

In pointing to the importance of political struggles O'Malley directs us towards important questions about the role and scope of the state as a site of political struggles and a locus of 'government'. These have tended to be reduced to the issue of whether current trends represent a weakening or a strengthening of state power.

Whither the state?

In line with Osborne and Gaebler, some commentators have suggested that current trends represent a strengthening of the role of the state as it refines and restructures its function (Jones 1993; Cope *et al.* 1995). As it attempts to 'steer' more and 'row' less the state authorises, licenses, audits and inspects the doings of others. Clearly, many of the changes inspired by NPM reforms have centralised considerable powers of standardisation and objective-setting which have enhanced the policy-making capacity of the state. Yet we have seen that both the shift to prevention and appeals to partnerships imply critiques of the state's role and its competency in crime control. In some senses these trends are 'anti-statist', as they look to individuals, communities and markets for solutions. Other commentators point to the 'hollowing out of the state' (Rhodes 1994; Bottoms and Wiles 1996), whereby the emergence of public–private partnerships, privatisation programmes, together with pressures of 'globalisation' and 'localisation', have eroded the state's capability to exercise political control. Moreover, forms of 'state rule at a distance' often leave unresolved legitimacy deficits and unanswered questions about accountability, increasing their fragility.

Both these positions provide an insight into current changes, and yet both are partial. We are witnessing weaknesses, as well as strengths, emerging as relations across the public and private divide are being reconfigured. The restructuring that is occurring is not only occurring within the state, but sometimes lies far outside its reach. Pluralisation has complex effects, which are neither uni-directional nor unambiguous. The central state's capacity in some spheres of operation is being diminished; in others it is being intensified; in still others it is being refashioned, often through new networks. Strategies and institutions of 'community safety' do not fit neatly into traditional hierarchical relations, but rather help to reconstitute them. Multi-agency 'partnerships', as we saw in Chapter 5, have further complicated state–civil society relations through the process of incorporation into arenas of policy-formation. They have problematised a number of traditional assumptions about the nature of relations within and between organisations and the public, particularly the basis of legitimacy, the premise of professional trust and the sources of authority and responsibility. Rather than 'smooth' orderings of 'systemisation' and synergy, these networks and partnerships have become what Charlesworth *et al.* (1996) evocatively refer to as 'tangled webs' effused with new tensions and sites of conflict.

This ambiguity has expressed itself in criminal justice policy through populist mood swings. Politicians in search of their own legitimation have fallen back on punitive rhetoric and the strong repressive state apparatus. This is witnessed by the recent (post-1993) *volte face* within the Home Office and has been encapsulated by the 'prison works' policy (Home Office 1996a), from which the present Labour government has not sought to depart or undermine. This 'punitive counter-tendency' has had important effects on penal and criminal justice practice, from reductions in the use of cautioning through to dramatic increases in the use of imprisonment (Bottoms 1995). This populism is an expression of the state confronting its very own weaknesses and discontents. Punitive populism and the responsibilisation associated with quests for crime prevention solutions are both rooted in 'political ambivalence'. It is almost as if they are, as Garland suggests, 'actually twinned, antithetical phenomena' in which one provokes the other (1997: 203). Yet at the heart of the populist tendency is a process of denial:

> A show of punitive force against individuals is used to repress any
> acknowledgement of the state's inability to control crime to acceptable
> levels. A willingness to deliver harsh punishments to convicted offenders
> magically compensates a failure to deliver security to the population at large.
>
> (Garland 1996: 460)

On this account, punitive rhetoric and policy are as much a product of
problems of state sovereignty and legitimation as a rational response to
the problems of crime. Consequently, as Garland argues, state sovereignty
over crime is simultaneously denied – as being 'beyond the state' – and
symbolically reasserted – through periodic episodes of hysterical and
populist denials of the state's limitations (1996: 462). Limitations of
traditional criminal justice – police and punishment – are recognised
in certain instances only to be discounted or ignored in others. This
dualistic denial and recognition produce volatile shifts in the state's
presentation of its own capacity for effective action in crime control.

Future visions

The purpose of the preceding discussion has been to highlight the connections between political developments and the rise of crime prevention. It has not been my intention to argue that the shift to prevention is
necessarily a product of neo-liberalism, although neo-liberal reforms have
served as a catalyst for certain trends within prevention. With this in mind
let us consider the potential future prospects of crime prevention in Britain. In so doing, we can identify a number of different scenarios in crime
control that represent an accentuation of particular current trends rather
than inevitable outcomes (see also Francis *et al.* 1997).

The eclipse of the 'prevention paradigm' and the growth of the punishment industry

The first scenario is that the recent shift to prevention is merely a short-
term trend or 'blip', which will recede with time leaving little by way of
enduring traces. The potential evidence for this lies in the recent 'punitive counter-tendency' as captured in the 'prison works' thesis advocated
by Michael Howard and apparently maintained by the new Labour government. It appears to have impacted on the judiciary as well as parliament. This logic maintains considerable hold over contemporary criminal
justice and has seen the prison population in England and Wales rise to
63 000 towards the end of 1997: a growth of well over 50 per cent since
the end of 1992 and over 10 per cent since the previous year (*Guardian*
21.11.97). It has also seen the proportion of those sentenced for indict-
able offences who are sentenced to custody increase from 16 per cent in
1992 to 23 per cent in 1996. At the Crown Court the proportion rose

from 46 per cent to 63 per cent while in the magistrates' courts it doubled from 5 per cent to 10 per cent. Consequently, three new prisons are set to become available and commentators are already warning of an impending capacity crisis by 1999. The logic behind penal expansion retains a belief in the ability and effectiveness of the formal systems of criminal justice, despite the empirical evidence to the contrary. More problematic in some ways – at least for government ministers that need to appease the Treasury – is the economic (not to mention the social) cost of mass incarceration. The average annual cost of prison per inmate at around £24 000 presents a heavy financial burden.

Nevertheless, it remains a powerful option, one which neo-conservative commentators continue to promote on both sides of the Atlantic (Murray 1997). Incarceration has also become an 'industry' in itself, fuelled by the rapid expansion in the number of private prisons in the UK and the USA. Several commentators have drawn attention to the rise of the powerful 'corrections-commercial complex' (Lilly and Knepper 1993) or 'penal-industrial complex' (Christie 1993). This refers to the increasingly international network of business and commercial interests which feed off the market-driven dimensions of the penal system, in much the same way that the global arms industry is sustained by fears of external security and warfare. With the use of imprisonment growing across much of the Western world, Christie has noted that there are 'no "natural limits" in the perception of what is a large prison population' (1993: 122). Thus the prison industry appears to have an unlimited potential for growth and injects an expansionist logic.

The scenario here is that the cost of mass incarceration will have social effects as authorities look to meet the financial burden of increased imprisonment by diverting public funds from other areas of public policy. The danger is that money which might otherwise have been spent on social policy will be increasingly diverted into the phenomenal cost of incarceration and incapacitation. More prisons result in less public money for education, health, training and social welfare, which leads to greater social 'fall out' in human terms, resulting in crime which, in turn, fans punitive measures of 'protecting the public' through incarceration. As this vicious cycle gains momentum, social policy becomes increasingly replaced by penal policy as a way of mopping up and containing its own consequences. This trend towards 'gulags western style' (Christie 1993) approximates to the 'authoritarian populism' of which British commentators such as Hall (1979) warned against nearly 20 years ago.

In many senses, this scenario appears to be the road on which the USA has embarked in a mood of 'penaholic' intolerance. In mid-1996 the total number of inmates in US prisons reached some 1.6 million people: one in every 118 men and one in every 1818 women were under the jurisdiction of correctional authorities (Currie 1996a). More worryingly, in the state of California more money is now spent on prisons than on schools. As many commentators have argued, the American experience should be regarded as a particularly compelling lesson in what should be avoided (Young 1997). However, this is not a warning that British politicians and policy-makers have been willing to heed. It is more often the punitive or technologically driven experiments in American criminal justice which have seen politicians from Britain rushing to cross the Atlantic, such as electronic tagging, private prisons and most recently California's so-called 'three strikes and you're out' legislation.

However, the rise of prevention and the punitive policies of incarceration are not necessarily mutually exclusive. The rise of one does not imply the decline of the other in any hydraulic sense. O'Malley goes so far as to suggest that 'there is no conflict between risk management *per se* and punitiveness' (1992: 266–7). On the contrary, he suggests that the same notions of individual responsibility and rational choice are to be found both in situational crime prevention and expanding punitiveness. Nevertheless, while crime prevention (beyond merely the situational kind) and punitiveness may well coexist, they do so in a somewhat ambiguous relationship. It is clear that they operate on distinct assumptions about offenders and the capacity of criminal justice interventions, which may be in conflict. They are also concerned with different aspects within the criminological enterprise, the 'passionate, morally toned desire to punish and the administrative, rationalistic, normalising concern to manage' (Garland 1990: 180). This tension is not a new phenomenon but rather is deeply embedded within the social processes of criminal justice and punishment. Yet the exact way in which the tensions between these key determinants of contemporary penal and criminal justice policy will be played out in the future is uncertain and unpredictable. The extent to which the 'corrections-commercial complex' does not restrict itself to the punishment industry but also straddles and penetrates the prevention and private security industries will become an important future area of study, with implications for the interrelations between the two. Nevertheless, the recent shift to a preventive paradigm does allow for a radical rethink of the appropriate social priorities as we enter the 21st century. It remains to be seen whether prevention and incarceration are genuinely alternative avenues or merely serve to reinforce each other.

Defended communities and ghettoisation

We have seen throughout this book, most notably in Chapter 4, that the rise of crime prevention – and of other 'responsibilisation strategies' – has been intimately bound up with appeals to community. 'Community self-governance', as well as embodying nostalgic and idealistic notions of real communities, also raises difficult issues about equity and social justice. Rendering communities responsible for their own safety, regardless of the context in which responsibility has to operate, fails to acknowledge the powerful dynamics created by the commodification of security or to address the relative distribution of social and economic disadvantage, including safety from crime. Communities, groups and individuals are not equally able to protect themselves against crime. Building community institutions that control crime is a complex task, particularly where the forces that sustain crime within a community derive from the wider social structure. Many communities may be powerless to withstand such pressures toward crime in the community. In this scenario it is the inequity in the distribution of 'security' and the resources it necessitates that constitute the fundamental dynamic in an increasingly fragmented and internally divided society. The concern is that growing social and spatial polarisation fundamentally undermine appeals to community as a force of *social* cohesion.

Despite the rhetoric of 'community' in crime prevention discourse which conjures up notions of shared sentiment, mutual connectedness and close-knit social bonds, the reality is more akin to forms of 'contractual communities' or 'collective individualism' (Crawford 1997a). It is the benefits that rational individuals derive from their place within 'communities' to which contemporary discourses appeal. Should the benefits decline over time, the rational individual – rather like the consumer in the supermarket – is placed in the position to 'choose' and move to alternative communities. In this regime of apparent choice, communities are primarily a means to an end, a response to insecurity and as such they operate within an individualistic framework. Neo-liberal, free market economies, rather than encouraging and sustaining self-regulating communities, are more likely to erode informal social support networks of care and foster the atomisation of communities (Currie 1997: 160), in that they promote a culture which exalts competition and consumption over social solidarity.

First, there are important exclusionary logics within 'community safety'. These can take an explicit form through defensive strategies such as neighbourhood watch, fortress-like security technology, 'defensible space' designs, CCTV, the use of evictions of disorderly tenants by housing authorities supported by court orders or the growing use of school exclusions. They can also be implicit in the parochialism, introspection and 'ideology of unity' often fostered by community safety partnerships. Community safety may thus be more a 'club good' which benefits its members rather than a 'social good' which benefits society at large.

Second, the geographic polarisation of rich and poor has been a marked feature of socio-economic change in Britain over the last 20 years (Hills 1995; Power and Tunstall 1995; Harker and Oppenheim 1996). Not only are wealth and poverty increasingly concentrated in certain areas and among specific groups of people, but so too is crime (Trickett *et al.* 1995). The spatial concentration of poverty has been exacerbated by the growing wealth of some within the population and the flight of people and capital out of certain localities. This 'market residualisation' is resulting in a growing social dislocation which is fundamentally spatial in nature. A particularly problematic aspect of these social divisions of wealth and power is the way they fuse with concerns about 'security' and the new-found sense of people's own responsibility to prevent or avoid risk. This adds a pernicious dimension to the process of social polarisation, in which 'security differentials' become defining characteristics of wealth, power and status. This polarisation is in danger of transforming the political agenda. With references to the notion of an 'underclass' it becomes increasingly easy to blame the plight of people who are trapped in high crime areas – either as victims or perpetrators – on their own inadequacies. They can come to be seen as the architects of neighbourhood change and economic decline, rather than as its victims.

This can produce 'spirals of ghettoisation' (Crawford 1997a: 280), whereby communities increasingly form themselves, and construct their boundaries, around concerns and anxieties about crime. There is an important defensive logic within many community crime prevention strategies. Hence, 'defensive exclusivity' can become a powerful dynamic in the formation and sustenance of communal existence, such that communities may increasingly come together less for what they share in common and more for what they fear. The 'public' police in this scenario will increasingly become a residual force which patrols the boundaries between the private 'security enclaves' and the surrounding residual public spaces and 'badlands' (Bottoms and Wiles 1995). The seeds for these developments are already in an advanced stage in North American cities such as Los Angeles (Davis 1990, 1992), and are becoming visible in Britain today. There are a number of identifiable elements in this possible dynamic that serve to widen existing 'security differentials'.

First, as crime is already differentially distributed, 'responsible' subjects will increasingly heed the warnings of government 'to protect themselves and their family from crime' or bow to the incentives of insurance companies and move to 'safer' locales.

Second, the power of the crime prevention industry may lead those communities and households that are able to afford preventive technologies and security devices to purchase them. The consequential displacement effects will adversely impact on those less able to protect themselves. The prevention industry, while fanning the quest for security, has little social concern but considerable social implications.

Third, the resources of the public police in Britain, already overstretched as they are required to respond to a wide range of problems and needs, may perversely be drawn away from high crime areas. This is because of the paradox of community crime prevention which, as noted in Chapter 4, means that community responses to crime are easiest to generate in exactly those areas where they are least needed and hardest to establish in those where the need is greatest. Hence, developments such as neighbourhood watch and citizens' patrols may actually skew police resources – to set up and service the demands generated by the schemes – towards those places which least need them and those people most capable of protecting themselves.

The most obvious expression of this dynamic is to be seen in relation to property and the housing markets. In the USA there has been a significant expansion of 'gated communities' – or 'private residential associations' – a generic term for planned residential developments regulated by a complex of land-use servitudes imposed in the deeds to all the individual lots within a development (Alexander 1997). Usually a homeowners' association is given enforcement powers in relation to these servitudes. Some, although not all, developments have physical perimeters and controlled access, often guarded and patrolled by private security police. It is estimated that over 30 million US citizens – nearly 15 per cent of the population – now live in some kind of planned, private residential association. It is expected that by the year 2000 this figure will have reached 50 million (cited in Alexander 1997: 223). Commentators have referred to this extensive development as 'a quiet revolution in the structure of community organisations, local government, land-use control, and neighbour relations' (Barton and Silverman 1994: xi).

In Britain the extent of such developments is less marked and less well-documented. What is clear, however, is that British cities are losing populations to more suburban and rural areas, a process in part driven by concerns about crime. The flight from Britain's metropolitan areas over the past 15 years has been marked. According to the authors of recent research, there is a 'marked trend for people to move progressively from larger to smaller settlements' (Champion *et al.* 1996). This has created a 'cascade effect' whereby each tier of the hierarchy receives net inflows from the tier above. In fact, the report's authors describe this as 'more of a downpour than a cascade'. The search for the rural idyll conjured up by the image of 'community' in England, free of crime and the fear of crime, is having real effects on the make-up and shape of the areas in and around British cities.

As the market increasingly comes to dominate the capacity of groups and individuals to police and manage crime, security derives from wealth and the ability to find sanctuary in secure zones, private guards, new technologies, architectural designs and defended spaces. This is a 'neo-medieval' vision of the future. Perversely, the acquisition of more and more 'security as commodity' may serve to undermine feelings of genuine 'security' by institutionalising anxiety. The 'anxiety market' may have an inexorable ratcheting effect because of the insatiability of security. In this context, 'security generates its own paranoid demand' (Davis 1990: 224). As I have argued:

> Strengthening communities is not always synonymous with the creation of social order and cohesion. An assertion of 'community' identity at a local level can be beautifully conciliatory, socially nuanced and constructive but it can also be parochial, intolerant, oppressive and unjust.
>
> (Crawford 1997a: 294)

This is particularly evident where the ideals of community collide with the commodification of security and the ravages of an increasingly polarised society in which the geographic concentration of poverty coincides with the concentration of crime.

Crime prevention and the 'risk society'

Crime prevention has developed alongside and encouraged the spread of 'risk assessment' and other actuarial techniques as described by the 'new penology' and 'governmentality' literature. In this scenario individuals at high risk of offending, or of becoming the victims of crime, are the focus of attention. They are seen as the 'cause' of epidemics of crime in communities, and thus the targets of intervention. The principal strategies would involve early intervention or 'inoculation' of 'at risk' individuals – either those likely to become offenders or those first time victims likely to be further victimised. Here, information and technology are the driving forces in the search for predictive techniques and modes of intervention premised on them. In this scenario the subject of intervention, be it the likely victim or offender, is cast in the role of the agent responsible for spreading the disease, in need of containment or incapacitation. This requires:

> the conceptual and practical disaggregation of communities – high crime areas are now just convenient locales in which prevention is to be concentrated. And there is no community effect, other than the processes of social selection that bring high risk groups together. Even then, the strategy depends upon its targeting efficiency, which in turn depends upon being able to predict high risk groups.
>
> (Hope 1997: 156)

Hence, this approach is less 'communal' and more 'categorical': concerned with targeting categories of people who – through life-style, location or some other attribute – are deemed to be 'at risk'.

Hope (1997) refers to this as the 'welfare solution' with its concern for doing something to, or for, 'at risk' individuals. Yet this is misleading. Although he is correct in that rather like individual welfare strategies, these developments hand considerable power to 'experts' and 'knowledge brokers', unlike welfare strategies the aim is not 'the alleviation and reduction of harm', but rather the 'management and control' of risk. The unequal society in which welfare strategies sought (as their ideal) the inclusion of all citizens is, in this scenario, increasingly being replaced by the 'risk society' (Beck 1992). Where welfarism sought to spread risks and to protect the most vulnerable through the distribution of material 'goods', the risk society is characterised by a negative logic, the distribution of 'bads' or dangers. People are increasingly united, or separated, included or excluded, on the basis of shared risk or a common interest in the distribution of risk. The concern with the universal citizen and the 'social' is giving way to an individualistic regime which extols 'choice'. Awareness of risk seeps into the actions of almost everyone as risk, and attempts at risk assessment, become fundamental to the 'colonising of the future' (Giddens 1991).

The assessment of risk forms the basis of preventive strategies like risk assessment measurement tools, criminal-profiling, risk of custody scales, dangerousness registers, selective incapacitation and preventive intervention with 'at risk' groups. Insurance and other actuarial assumptions have become central technologies in the proliferation of risk management. Insurance is instrumental to the 'rationalisation of risk' on the basis of 'probabalistic calculations' and 'statistical distributions'. As the role of the state is increasingly replaced by private insurance in the provision of welfare and health services, the identification and classification of those most 'at risk' become powerful dynamics in the constitution of future social relations. Knowledge of risk is not only a means of risk management but also a producer of new risks (Ericson and Haggerty 1997: 88). The quest for security and the control of risks drives the pursuit for greater and more superior knowledge of risk. This unquenched refinement of risk management, rather than producing peace of mind gives rise to new knowledge about insecurities. The concern with 'risk' connects with the managerialist trend in that it appears to offer little, or no, place for normative debates (Peters 1986).

An alternative future?

In a discussion about displacement Barr and Pease (1990) offer the interesting idea of the 'equal society' in which victimisation is 'shared around'. They suggest that the displacement of crime, produced by forms of prevention, could be used to redistribute the burden of victimisation in a more equal manner. This might involve, for example, displacing crime from high crime areas to areas with lower levels of crime as well as encouraging forms of benign displacement. However, as they note, the attraction of explicit policies of crime redistribution are likely to be difficult for politicians to promote publicly (1990: 312). Nevertheless, the importance of Barr and Pease's insights is that they illuminate the choices that constitute the current patterns of crime. They highlight that patterns of criminal activity and victimisation are not immutable but can be conceptualised as the outcome of 'conscious and unconscious decisions by the public, politicians and the police' (1990: 277).

This means that political choices exist about where society is willing to tolerate crime. As Barr and Pease suggest, we have tended to prefer to allow crime to be concentrated in high crime 'fuse' areas,[3] which may be easier to manage but which leave crime unequally distributed throughout the population. Moreover, individual choices by those who can afford to purchase 'security', or move to areas of lower victimisation, actually serve to further concentrate crime in 'fuse' areas. A political desire to move towards a more equal distribution of crime would consist in offering significant protection towards the most highly victimised individuals or areas. However, as Barr and Pease acknowledge the crucial question is whether the political will exists to address these problems (1990: 313).

It is clear from this discussion that to avoid the pitfalls of the other scenarios there is a need to think more normatively than before about the principles that should underpin the forms of crime prevention and the nature of 'partnerships' between communities and other organisations – be they private, public or 'hybrid'. In contrast to the 'marketisation' and 'privatisation' of everyday life, there is the need for a revival of a 'public sphere' and 'civic values'. These will require contemporary political struggles over notions of the 'public' as well as the 'private interest'. The role of the state as a 'power-container' in the public interest has become more vital rather than less so. This is particularly evident in relation to the regulation and control of the security industry. The massive expansion in surveillance technology necessitates the question of how to control the use to which technology is put. The task of government is to confront the realities of the complex mixture of modes of governance which are emerging and to use the state in its different forms to regulate developments in the interests of equity and social justice. This will require government to look to strategies of reintegration rather than social exclusion.

To ensure that security is conceived of as a 'public good', rather than a 'club good', the discourse of community safety should not be allowed to be captured by exclusionary politics or parochialism. The power of exclusion has become a significant social dynamic which needs to be confronted and regulated. If forms of surveillance and crime prevention technology are to be extensively introduced into public spaces we need to be clear about their purpose, use and consequences. If their aim is to keep 'troublesome youths' and 'unsightly people' away from 'citadels of consumption', we need to ask where are these people to go, what will they do there and what does this tell them about their place in a modern society? We also need to ask aetiological questions about the causes of the 'problem' they may present.

Community involvement needs to be seen as more than a means of managing and steering public expectations. If we are to hold back the dislocation of society articulated in the second of the above scenarios, there is an urgent need to reintegrate the inner-city 'islands of neglect' into the larger social fabric. Responsibilities for crime control and prevention should not be unduly shifted on to a community without first ensuring that that community is sufficiently empowered and accorded the capacity to perform the functions that are being expected of it. If local community safety initiatives are to be accorded a genuine degree of local control, they will need governments to foster the conditions under which responsibility, either collective or individual, can be exercised and enhanced. The development of community safety offers the potential to address issues of political economy which undermine the ability of many high crime communities to respond constructively to the severe problems they confront. It may present an opportunity to reconstruct the institutional bedrock of inner-city communities by assisting in building institutions of social solidarity (Currie 1988).

Conclusions

It is impossible accurately to predict the future. The purpose, here, has been to identify some of the themes and trends that characterise contemporary crime control and underlie the 'shift to prevention'. Against the background of a managerialist ethos dominated by administrative questions and in which ethical debates are eschewed, the need to hold normative deliberations about the shape of the future is as essential as ever. Questions about the direction and methods of crime control and prevention are inherently political and not purely technical or administrative. Yet some of the traditional expectations and modes of analysis of criminal justice and criminology may no longer be sufficient for the task. All of this presents considerable challenges to researchers, politicians and policy-makers alike.

In many ways the social value of crime prevention has been taken for granted and is rarely questioned. One of the central arguments of this book has been to assert the need to question, rather than assume, the social value of particular crime prevention strategies specifically, as well as the manner in which they connect with broader trends generally. To this extent, the wider view provided by the examination of cross-cultural differences in crime prevention (as discussed in Chapter 7) should warn of the need to question the long-term social and cultural implications of given measures. It should allow us to examine ourselves afresh – for crime prevention is both culturally embedded and has cultural effects. How do we explain the fact that Britain, more than any other country, has embraced CCTV cameras in public spaces and now seeks to locate more cameras in newer and different locations?[4] What does this tell us about our own sense of security and social values? Where will this expansion end – and with what cultural implications?

There are important social and ethical conflicts over the value of crime prevention as against other public goods which hitherto have not been sufficiently addressed. Is it more desirable that people have strong bars, doors and locks to keep intruders out or that in a crisis the fire brigade or other emergency services can gain easy access? If we could empirically evaluate the matter, how many prevented burglaries would outweigh a death or serious injury by fire? This may seem an extreme example but such issues infuse local conflicts between the police, the local authorities, landlords and the fire brigade as to the kinds of prevention advice to be given to the public and about which there is little agreement. Or, in a different context, if we knew that early intervention with certain 'at risk' four-year-olds would keep a number of those put on the programme out of crime but would adversely affect others, would this be a legitimate social policy? Crime prevention needs to be balanced against ethical issues as well as weighed against other social and human costs. Crime prevention was used as a powerful justification for the eugenics movement which led to extensive sterilisation programmes in the USA in the early part of this century. Technologically driven and administratively concerned measures may offer answers, particularly to short-term problems, but significantly they fail to tell us what the ethical and social questions are or may be. They tend to offer little or no place for normative debates.

By contrast, the ethics and social value of crime prevention need to be placed squarely on the policy agenda. There is also a need to develop a way of thinking about crime prevention which prioritises long-term needs. Crime prevention in Britain will fail to escape its situational embrace unless it is able to transcend the short-termism of much policy. This, as we saw in Chapter 6, will involve the development of evaluation criteria which accentuate long-term benefits. This will require the development of a dialogue between researchers, practitioners, politicians and the public. This must be premised on the understanding that crime prevention is a long-term agenda which is not reducible to a latest, quick-fix solution or 'golden bullet'. But it will also necessitate 'a much clearer understanding of how and why some issues become "consumer issues" and others not' (Walklate 1992: 114) as well as an engagement with public anxieties and concerns.

Investment in crime prevention offers a significant means of improving the quality of life for many people in society and simultaneously may allow for a substantial reduction in the extensive (economic and social) cost of the criminal justice and penal systems. Crime prevention is still very much in its infancy and we have much to learn about what works, where, and for whom. In facing this challenge, questions need to be asked about the rationale for much crime prevention activity and its implications for wider social relations. The technological, short-term and market-based dynamics which have driven much of the recent shift to crime prevention and community safety in Britain need to be contained. This will require new and challenging strategies of governance which straddle and transcend the public and private spheres. Crime prevention and community safety are complex phenomena which remain the subject of organisational and political struggles over meaning and direction. They offer fundamentally important new opportunities to consider the nature of social relations and social justice. If we are to avoid some of the distopian scenarios discussed above, normative questions need to be asked rather than brushed aside in the rush for 'security'. It remains to be seen whether the political will exists to address such issues.

Notes

1. Interestingly, this has produced internal resistance expressed in an unwilling-ness to accept this new logic by some in the police who believe that the new order of things, by acknowledging their limitations, has handicapped them from performing their essential tasks. Some in the police see 'partnerships' as having weakened the independence of the police and their ability to make an impact (Crawford 1994b). DCI Ray Mallon, a leading proponent of 'zero tolerance' policing, is an example of this kind of police officer seeking to restore the notion that the police alone can 'make a difference': 'When you pose the question "Can police reduce crime?", some police say "no". That's like a football team saying "we can't score goals"' (cited in Chesshyre 1997). For him, the fact that 'zero tolerance' involves the police in 'taking the gloves off', harks back to a pre-partnership age in which the police were judged on their ability to affect the crime rate.

2. Even Tony Bottoms (1995) in an otherwise perceptive essay on the philosophy and politics of sentencing in which he highlights three distinct aspects of managerialism within criminal justice – namely its systemic, its consumerist and its actuarial dimensions – does so without any real regard to the idea of significant tensions within and between these elements.

3. The analogy here is with an electric circuit in which a 'deliberately weak point, the fuse, is included so that a power surge will have quite minor consequences' (Barr and Pease 1990: 304). Similarly, with crime the concentration of victim-isation in one area, while inequitable, allows for those not living there to avoid it and for authorities to manage it.

4. Twenty-four hours a day CCTV schemes now operate in more than 450 towns across Britain (*Guardian* 9.1.1998). Three years ago, by contrast, there were only some 74 schemes.

Suggestions for Further Reading

General reading and Chapter 1: Conceptualising crime prevention and community safety

The literature on crime prevention, rather like the subject itself, is rapidly expanding. Since the completion of this manuscript a number of new texts have been published. A commendable student text is Gilling, D. (1997) *Crime Prevention: Theory, Policy and Politics*, London: UCL Press. Gilling offers the reader a good overview of the diverse criminological theories which have impacted on the development of crime prevention and traces significant institutional developments. Similarly, the recently updated, second edition of Maguire, M., Morgan, R., and Reiner, R. (1997) (eds) *The Oxford Handbook of Criminology*, Oxford: Oxford University Press, has a number of chapters which are useful sources of further reading, none more so than Ken Pease's aptly titled 'Crime Prevention'. An exhaustive American report, compiled by Lawrence Sherman and colleagues (1997), *Preventing Crime: What Works, What Doesn't, What's Promising* was prepared for the National Institute of Justice and submitted to the United States Congress. It draws together an impressive and wide range of research and evaluation and is currently available via the internet on the National Institute of Justice's home pages at: *http://www.ncjrs.org/works/index.htm*. Two recent collections of essays by leading contributors have also been published which contribute significantly to the literature. They both offer excellent detailed overviews and analysis of the theory and research in relation to various aspects of crime prevention. The first is Tonry, M. and Farrington, D.P. (eds) (1995) *Building a Safer Society: Crime and Justice a Review of Research, vol. 19*, Chicago: University of Chicago Press, which draws on British and American contributions. The second, Bennett, T. (ed.) (1996) *Preventing Crime and Disorder*, Cambridge: Institute of Criminology, focuses more specifically on Britain. The editors' introductions to both of these collections give helpful overviews of the general debates. The relevant chapters from each constitute commendable further reading in relation to the subject matter of specific chapters in this book (see below). A third collection of essays with some useful contributions is Lab, S.P. (ed.) (1997) *Crime Prevention at a Crossroads*, Cincinnati: Anderson Publishing. My own earlier book – Crawford, A. (1997) *The Local Governance of Crime: Appeals to Community and Partnerships*, Oxford: Clarendon Press – offers an examination of the wider theoretical debates supported by empirical research evidence. There is a good collection of essays aimed specifically at practitioners, Marlow, A. and Pitts, J. (eds) (1998) *Planning Safer Communities*, Lyme Regis: Russell House Publishing.

Chapter 2: The British experience

Jon Bright's overview of developments in the UK (1991) Crime Prevention: The British Experience, in Stenson, K. and Cowell, D. (eds) (1991) *The Politics of Crime Control*, London: Sage, 62–86, is useful, if a little dated. The relevant chapters (4–6) in Gilling's book have more contemporary information as does Chapter 1 in my own earlier book (see above).

Chapter 3: Situational and environmental strategies

There is a growing body of literature on situational and environmental crime prevention. The best recent overviews are to be found in Clarke, R.V. (1995) Situational Crime Prevention, in the Tonry and Farrington collection (see above), 91–150; Clarke, R.V. (ed.) (1992) *Situational Crime Prevention: Successful Case Studies*, Albany: Harrow and Heston; Heal, K. and Laycock, G. (eds) (1986) *Situational Crime Prevention: From Theory into Practice*, London: HMSO; and Coleman, A. (1985) *Utopia on Trial*, London: Hilary Shipman. Bottoms, A.E. and Wiles, P. (1997) Environmental Criminology, in Maguire *et al.* (see above), 305–59, provide an excellent overview of developments which they locate within a wider social and historical context.

Chapter 4: Social and communal strategies

On criminality prevention see Farrington, D.P. (1997) Human Development and Criminal Careers, in Maguire *et al.* (see above), 361–408; and Farrington, D.P. (1996) *Understanding and Preventing Youth Crime*, York: Joseph Rowntree Foundation. Graham and Bowling's research (1995) *Young People and Crime*, London: Home Office, has had a significant impact on policy debates in relation to crime prevention for young people, as has the Audit Commission's (1996) *Misspent Youth* report. A description of a sample of recent crime prevention programmes targeted at young people in the United Kingdom is to be found in Utting, D. (1996) *Reducing Criminality Among Young People*, London: Home Office. In relation to community-based crime prevention, see Hope, T. and Shaw, M. (eds) (1988) *Communities and Crime Reduction*, London: HMSO for an excellent collection of early recent developments. Rosenbaum, D.P. (1988) Community Crime Prevention: A Review and Synthesis of the Literature, *Justice Quarterly*, 5(3), 323–93 provides a good examination of the issues. More recent overviews are Hope, T. (1995) Community Crime Prevention, in the Tonry and Farrington collection (see above), 21–89; Chapter 5 in Crawford, A. (see above); and Bright, J. (1997) *Turning the Tide*, London: Demos.

Chapter 5: Implementation and the partnership approach

The literature on implementation is less well developed, although there are some useful chapters in the Marlow and Pitts collection of essays (see above). For a more analytically rigorous examination of the issues see Crawford, A. (see above), particularly Chapter 4. Chapter 7 in Gilling's *Crime Prevention*; and Hughes, G. (1996) Strategies of Multi-Agency Crime Prevention and Community Safety in Contemporary Britain, *Studies on Crime and Crime Prevention*, 221–44, both provide good reviews of the literature, as does Laycock and Tilley's contribution to the Tonry and Farrington collection of essays (see above) entitled, Implementing Crime Prevention, 535–84.

Chapter 6: Evaluating crime prevention and community safety

Pawson, R. and Tilley, N. (1997) *Realistic Evaluation*, London: Sage, gives a good introduction to the methodological issues and is full of examples from the crime prevention literature. Ekblom, P. and Pease, K. (1995) Evaluating Crime Prevention, in Tonry and Farrington (see above), 585–662, provides a useful source of further reading, as does the Sherman *et al.* collection (see above) and many chapters in Rosenbaum, D.P. (ed.) (1986) *Community Crime Prevention: Does It Work?*, Beverly Hills: Sage.

Chapter 7: Some comparative experiences

The best overview of international developments is Graham, J. and Bennett, T. (1995) *Crime Prevention Strategies in Europe and North America*, Helsinki: HEUNI. Shorter articles focusing on European developments are Graham, J. (1993) Crime Prevention Policies in Europe, *European Journal of Crime, Criminal Law and Criminal Justice*, 1(2), 126–42; and van Dijk, J. (1991) More than a Matter of Security: Trends in Crime Prevention in Europe, in Heidensohn, F. and Farrell, M. (eds) *Crime in Europe*, London: Routledge, 27–42. However, none of these really address the issues of comparison, which are considered by David Nelken in his chapter in *The Oxford Handbook of Criminology* (see above) entitled Understanding Criminal Justice Comparatively, 559–73.

Chapter 8: The politics of crime prevention and community safety

The politics of crime prevention, by its nature, draws on broad socio-political issues, and hence on developments in social theory. Two excellent introductions to some of these debates for students of crime prevention and criminology are Garland, D. (1996) The Limits of the Sovereign State: Strategies of Crime Control in Contemporary Society, *British Journal of Criminology*, 36(4), 445–71 and O'Malley, P. (1992) Risk, Power and Crime Prevention, *Economy and Society*, 21(3), 252–75. Chapter 6 in my own earlier book (see above) considers some of these insights with regard to crime prevention, as does Tim Hope's (1997) Inequality and the Future of Community Crime Prevention, in the Lab collection (see above), 143–58. Other worthwhile texts are Ericson, R. and Haggerty, K. (1997) *Policing the Risk Society*, Oxford: Clarendon Press; Feeley, M. and Simon, J. (1992) The New Penology, *Criminology*, 30(4), 449–74; as well as their later chapter (1994) Actuarial Justice: the Emerging New Criminal Law, in Nelken (ed.) *The Futures of Criminology*, London: Sage, 173–201. A powerful but disturbing insight into possible future directions in crime prevention is to be found in Davis, M. (1990) *City of Quartz: Excavating the Future in Los Angeles*, London: Verso.

Bibliography

Alexander, G.S. (1997) 'Civic Property', *Social and Legal Studies*, 6(2), 217–34.

Allat, P. (1984a) 'Residential Security: Containment and Displacement of Burglary', *Howard Journal*, 23(2), 99–116.

Allat, P. (1984b) 'Fear of Crime: The Effect of Improved Residential Security on a Difficult to Let Estate', *Howard Journal*, 23(3), 170–82.

Anderson, D., Chenery, S. and Pease, K. (1995) *Biting Back: Tackling Repeat Burglary and Car Crime*, Crime Detection and Prevention Paper 58, London: Home Office.

Association of Chief Officers of Probation (1988) *Crime Prevention and the Probation Service*, London: ACOP.

Association of Chief Officers of Probation (1993) *Working with Information for Crime Prevention*, London: ACOP.

Association of Chief Police Officers (1996) *Towards 2000 – A Crime Prevention Strategy for the Millennium*, Lancaster: ACPO.

Association of County Councils (1997a) *Crime – The Local Solution: Manifesto*, London: ACC/ADC/AMA.

Association of County Councils (1997b) *Crime – The Local Solution: Current Practice*, London: ACC/ADC/AMA/LGMB.

Association of District Councils (1996) *Crime – The Local Solution: Preventing Crime, Fear of Crime and Anti-Social Behaviour in Our Communities*, London: ADC/ACC/AMA.

Association of London Authorities (1994) *At a Premium*, London: ALA.

Association of Metropolitan Authorities (1990) *Crime Reduction: A Framework for the Nineties?*, London: AMA.

Atkins, S., Hussain, S. and Storey, A. (1991) *The Influence of Street Lighting on Crime and Fear of Crime*, CPU Paper 28, London: Home Office.

Atkinson, R. (1996) *Reclaiming the Streets: Building a Sustainable Community*, Birmingham: Phoenix.

Audit Commission (1993) *Helping with Enquiries: Tackling Crime Effectively*, London: Audit Commission.

Audit Commission (1994) *Seen But Not Heard*, London: Audit Commission.

Audit Commission (1996) *Misspent Youth: Young People and Crime*, London: Audit Commission.

Bailleau, F. (1996) *Les Jeunes Face à la Justice Pénale*, Paris: Syros.

Baldwin, J. (1979) 'Ecological and Areal Studies in Great Britain and the United States', in Morris, N. and Tonry, M. (eds) *Crime and Justice: An Annual Review of Research, vol. 1*, Chicago: University of Chicago Press, 29–66.

Barr, R. and Pease, K. (1990) 'Crime Placement, Displacement and Deflection', in Tonry, M. and Morris, N. (eds) *Crime and Justice a Review of Research: vol. 12*, Chicago: University of Chicago Press.

Barr, R. and Pease, K. (1992) 'A Place for Every Crime and Every Crime in its Place', in Evans *et al.* (1992), 196–216.

Barton, S.E. and Silverman, C.J. (eds) (1994) *Common Interest Communities: Private Governments and the Public Interest*, Berkeley: University of California Institute of Governmental Studies Press.

Bayley, D.H. (1988) 'Community Policing: A Report form the Devil's Advocate', in Greene and Mastrofski (1988), 225–37.

Bayley, D.H. (1991) *Forces of Order: Policing Modern Japan*, Berkeley: University of California Press.

Bayley, D.H. and Shearing, C. (1996) 'The Future of Policing', *Law and Society Review*, 30(3), 585–606.

Beck, U. (1992) *Risk Society: Towards a New Modernity*, London: Sage.

Becker, G.S. (1968) 'Crime and Punishment: An Economic Approach', *Journal of Political Economy*, 76, 169–217.

Becker, H.S. (1963) *Outsiders: Studies in the Sociology of Deviance*, New York: Free Press.

Beijerse, J. uit and Swaaningen, R. van (1993) 'Social Control as a Policy: Pragmatic Moralism with a Structural Deficit', *Social and Legal Studies*, 3(2), 281–302.

Bennett, T. (1989) 'The Neighbourhood Watch Experience', in Morgan and Smith (1989), 138–52.

Bennett, T. (1990) *Evaluating Neighbourhood Watch*, Aldershot: Gower.

Bennett, T. (1991) 'The Effectiveness of a Police Initiated Fear Reducing Strategy', *British Journal of Criminology*, 31, 1–14.

Bennett, T. (1994) 'Community Policing on the Ground: Developments in Britain', in Rosenbaum (1994), 224–46.

Bennett, T. (1996a) 'What's New in Evaluation Research? A Note on the Pawson and Tilley Article', *British Journal of Criminology*, 36(4), 567–73.

Bennett, T. (ed.) (1996b) *Preventing Crime and Disorder: Targeting Strategies and Responsibilities*, Cambridge: Institute of Criminology.

Bennett, T. and Wright, R. (1984) *Burglars on Burglary: Prevention and the Offender*, Aldershot: Gower.

Berrueta-Clement, J.R., Schweinhart, L.J., Barnett, W.S., Epstein, A.S. and Weikart, D.P. (1984) *Changed Lives*, Ypsilanti, Michigan: High/Scope.

Blagg, H., Pearson, G., Sampson, A., Smith, D. and Stubbs, P. (1988) 'Inter-Agency Co-operation: Rhetoric and Reality', in Hope and Shaw (1988a), 204–20.

Blumstein, A. (1986) 'Coherence, Coordination and Integration in the Administration of Criminal Justice', in van Dijk *et al.* (1986), 247–58.

Bonnemaison, G. (1983) *Face à la Délinquance, Prévention, Répression, Solidarité*, Paris: Documentation Française.

Bottomley, A.K. (1986) 'Blueprints for Criminal Justice: Reflections on a Policy Plan for The Netherlands', *Howard Journal*, 25, 199–215.

Bottoms, A.E. (1990) 'Crime Prevention Facing the 1990s', *Policing and Society*, 1(1), 3–22.

Bottoms, A.E. (1994) 'Environmental Criminology', in Maguire *et al.* (1994), 585–656.

Bottoms, A.E. (1995) 'The Philosophy and Politics of Punishment and Sentencing', in Clarkson, C. and Morgan, R. (eds) *The Politics of Sentencing Reform*, Oxford: Clarendon Press, 17–49.

Bottoms, A.E. and Wiles, P. (1986) 'Housing Tenure and Residential Community Crime Careers in Britain', in Reiss and Tonry (1986), 101–62.

Bottoms, A.E. and Wiles, P. (1992) 'Explanations of Crime and Place', in Evans *et al.* (1992), 11–35.

Bottoms, A.E. and Wiles, P. (1995) 'Crime and Insecurity in the City', in Fijnaut *et al.* (1995), 1–38.

Bottoms, A.E. and Wiles, P. (1996) 'Understanding Crime Prevention in Late Modern Societies', in Bennett (1996b), 1–42.

Bottoms, A.E., Claytor, A. and Wiles, P. (1992) 'Housing Markets and Residential Community Crime Careers: A Case Study from Sheffield', in Evans *et al.* (1992), 118–44.

Bowling, B. (1996) 'Zero Tolerance: Cracking Down on Crime in New York City', *Criminal Justice Matters*, 25, 11–12.

Braithwaite, J. (1989) *Crime, Shame and Reintegration*, Cambridge: Cambridge University Press.

Braithwaite, J. (1993) 'Shame and Modernity', *British Journal of Criminology*, 33(1), 1–18.

Brake, M. and Hale, C. (1992) *Public Order and Private Lives*, London: Routledge.

Brantingham, P.J. and Brantingham, P.L. (1997) 'Understanding and Controlling Crime and Fear of Crime', in Lab (1997), 43–60.

Brantingham, P.J. and Faust, L. (1976) 'A Conceptual Model of Crime Prevention', *Crime and Delinquency*, 22, 284–96.

Bratton W.J. (1997) 'Crime is Down in New York City: Blame the Police', in Dennis, N. (1997), 29–42.

Bright, J. (1991) 'Crime Prevention: The British Experience', in Stenson and Cowell (1991), 62–86.

Bright, J. (1996) 'Preventing Youth Crime in High Crime Areas', in Bennett (1996b), 365–83.

Bright, J. (1997) *Turning the Tide: Crime, Community and Prevention*, London: Demos.

Bright, J. and Petterssen, G. (1984) *Improving Council House Estates*, London: NACRO.

Brittan, S. (1993) 'Social Tasks of Business', *Financial Times*, 2 September.

Broadbent, J. and Laughlin, R. (1997) 'Evaluating the "New Public Management" Reforms in the UK: A Constitutional Possibility?', *Public Administration*, 75(3), 487–507.

Broady, S.R. (1976) *The Effectiveness of Sentencing: A Review of the Literature*, Home Office Research Study No. 35, London: Home Office.

Brown, B. (1995) *CCTV in Town Centres: Three Case Studies*, Crime Detection and Prevention Series Paper 68, London: Home Office.

Brownlee, I.D. (1998) *Community Punishment: A Critical Introduction*, Harlow: Addison Wesley Longman.

Bryant, M. (1989) *The Contribution of ACOP and Probation Services to Crime Prevention*, Wakefield: ACOP.

Buerger, M.E. (1994a) 'A Tale of Two Targets: Limitations of Community Anticrime Actions', *Crime and Delinquency*, 40(3), 411–36.

Buerger, M.E. (1994b) 'The Limits of Community', in Rosenbaum (1994), 270–3.

Burchell, G., Gordon, C. and Miller, P. (eds) (1991) *The Foucault Effect: Studies in Governmentality*, Hemel Hempstead: Harvester Wheatsheaf.

Burgess, E.W. (1928) 'The Growth of the City', in Park, R.E., Burgess, E.W. and McKenzie, R.D. (eds) *The City*, Chicago: University of Chicago Press.

Burgin, Y. (1997) 'The Panacea?', *Criminal Justice Matters*, 28, 11.

Burrows, J. (1980) 'Closed Circuit Television and Crime on the London Underground', in Clarke and Mayhew (1980), 75–83.

Campbell, B. (1993) *Goliath: Britain's Dangerous Places*, London: Methuen.

Campbell, B. (1994) 'The Underclass: Regressive Re-alignment', *Criminal Justice Matters*, 18, 18–19.

Campbell, B. (1996) 'Gender, Crisis and Community', in Kraemer, S. and Roberts, S. (eds) *The Politics of Attachment: Towards a Secure Society*, London: Free Association Books, 102–9.

Campbell, D.T. and Stanley, J.C. (1966) *Experimental and Quasi-Experimental Designs for Research*, Chicago: Rand McNally.

Capowich, G.E. and Roehl, J.A. (1994) 'Problem-Oriented Policing: Actions and Effectiveness in San Diego', in Rosenbaum (1994), 127–46.

Cassels Committee (1994) *Discussion Document*, London: Policy Studies Institute.

Cassels Committee (1996) *The Role and Responsibilities of the Police*, London: Policy Studies Institute.

Central Council of Probation Committees (1987) *Crime Prevention: A Role for Probation Committees*, London: CCPC.

Champion, T., Wong, C., Rooke, A., Dorling, D., Coombes, M. and Brundson, C. (1996) *The Population of Britain in the 1990s*, Oxford: Clarendon Press.

Charlesworth, J., Clarke, J. and Cochrane, A. (1996) 'Tangled Webs? Managing Local Mixed Economies of Care', *Public Administration*, 74, 67–88.

Chesshyre, R. (1997) 'Enough is Enough', *Telegraph Magazine*, 1 March, 20–6.

Christie, N. (1977) 'Conflicts as Property', *British Journal of Criminology*, 17(1), 1–15.

Christie, N. (1993) *Crime Control as Industry*, London: Routledge.

Citizen's Charter (1996) *Citizen's Charter*, London: HMSO.

Clarke, R.V. (1980a) 'Situational Crime Prevention: Theory and Practice', *British Journal of Criminology*, 20(2), 136–45.

Clarke, R.V. (1980b) 'Opportunity Based Crime Rates', *British Journal of Criminology*, 24, 74–83.

Clarke, R.V. (1983) 'Situational Crime Prevention: Its Theoretical Basis and Practical Scope', in Tonry, M. and Morris, N. (eds) *Crime and Justice: An Annual Review of Research, vol. 4*, Chicago: University of Chicago Press, 225–56.

Clarke, R.V. (ed.) (1992) *Situational Crime Prevention: Successful Case Studies*, Albany, NY: Harrow & Heston.

Clarke, R.V. (1995) 'Situational Crime Prevention', in Tonry and Farrington (1995b), 91–150.

Clarke, R.V. and Cornish, D.B. (1985) 'Modelling Offenders' Decisions: A Framework for Policy and Research', in Tonry, M. and Morris, N. (eds) *Crime and Justice: An Annual Review of Research, vol. 6*, Chicago: University of Chicago Press, 147–85.

Clarke, R.V. and Felson, M. (eds) (1993) *Routine Activity and Rational Choice: Advances in Criminological Theory*, New Brunswick, NJ: Transaction.

Clarke, R.V. and Harris, P.M. (1992) 'Auto Theft and Its Prevention', in Tonry, M. (ed.) *Crime and Justice: A Review of Research, vol. 16*, Chicago: University of Chicago Press, 1–54.

Clarke, R.V. and Hough, J.M. (eds) (1980) *The Effectiveness of Policing*, Farnborough: Gower.

Clarke, R.V. and Hough, J.M. (1984) *Crime and Police Effectiveness*, Home Office Study No. 79, London: HMSO.

Clarke, R.V. and Mayhew, P. (eds) (1980) *Designing Out Crime*, London: HMSO.

Clarke, R.V. and Mayhew, P. (1988) 'The British Gas Suicide Story and Its Criminological Implications', in Tonry, M. and Morris, N. (eds) *Crime and Justice: Review of Research, vol. 10*, Chicago: University of Chicago Press, 79–116.

Clarke, R.V. and Mayhew, P. (1989) 'Crime as Opportunity: A Note on Domestic Gas Suicide in Britain and The Netherlands', *British Journal of Criminology*, 29(1), 35–44.

Clarke, R.V. and Weisburd, D. (1994) 'Diffusion of Crime Control Benefits: Observations on the Reverse of Displacement', *Crime Prevention Studies*, 2, 165–83.

Cloward, R. and Ohlin, L. (1960) *Delinquency and Opportunity*, New York: Free Press.

Cohen, A.K. (1955) *Delinquent Boys*, New York: Free Press.

Cohen, L. and Felson, M. (1979) 'Social Change and Crime Rate Trends: A Routine Activity Approach', *American Sociological Reveiw*, 44, 588–608.

Cohen, S. (1983) 'Social Control Talk: Telling Stories about Correctional Change', in Garland, D. and Young, P. (eds) *The Power to Punish*, London: Heinemann, 101–29.

Cohen, S. (1985) *Visions of Social Control*, Cambridge: Polity Press.

Coleman, A. (1985) *Utopia on Trial*, London: Hilary Shipman.

Coleman, A. (1989) 'Disposition and Situation: Two Sides of the Same Crime', in Evans, D.J. and Herbert, D.T. (eds) *The Geography of Crime*, London: Routledge, 108–34.

Cope, S., Leishman, F. and Starie, P. (1995) 'Hollowing-Out and Hiving-Off: Reinventing Policing in Britain', in Lovenduski, J. and Stanyer, J. (eds) *Contemporary Political Studies 1995, vol. 2*, Belfast: Political Studies Association.

Cornish, D.B. and Clarke, R.V. (1986a) 'Situational Prevention, Displacement of Crime and Rational Choice Theory', in Heal and Laycock (1986), 1–16.

Cornish, D.B. and Clarke, R.V. (eds) (1986b) *The Reasoning Criminal: Rational Choice Perspectives on Offending*, Springer-Verlag: New York.

Cornish, D.B. and Clarke, R.V. (1987) 'Understanding Crime Displacement: An Application of Rational Choice Theory', *Criminology*, 25(4), 933–47.

Cornish, D.B. and Clarke, R.V. (1990) 'Crime Specialisation, Crime Displacement and Rational Choice', in Wegener, H., Losel, F. and Haisch, J. (eds) *Criminal Behaviour and the Criminal Justice System: Psychological Perspectives*, New York: Springer-Verlag.

Crawford, A. (1994a) 'The Partnership Approach: Corporatism at the Local Level?', *Social and Legal Studies*, 3(4), 497–519.

Crawford, A. (1994b) 'Social Values and Managerial Goals: Police and Probation Officers' Experiences and Views of Inter-Agency Co-operation', *Policing and Society*, 4(4), 323–39.

Crawford, A. (1995) 'Appeals to Community and Crime Prevention', *Crime, Law and Social Change*, 22, 97–126.

Crawford, A. (1996) 'The Spirit of Community: Rights, Responsibilities and the Communitarian Agenda', *Journal of Law and Society*, 23(2), 247–62.

Crawford, A. (1997a) *The Local Governance of Crime: Appeals to Community and Partnerships*, Oxford: Clarendon Press.

Crawford, A. (1997b) *A Report on the New Zealand Safer Community Councils*, Wellington, New Zealand: Ministry of Justice.

Crawford, A. (1998a) 'Delivering Multi-Agency Partnerships in Community Safety', in Marlow, A. and Pitts, J. (eds) (1998) *Planning Safer Communities*, Lyme Regis: Russell House Publishing, 213–22.

Crawford, A. (1998b) 'Contrasts in Victim/Offender Mediation and Appeals to Community in France and England', in Nelken, D. (ed.) *Contrasts in Criminal Justice*, Aldershot: Dartmouth.

Crawford, A. and Jones, M. (1995) 'Inter-Agency Co-operation and Community-Based Crime Prevention: Some Reflections on the Work of Pearson and Colleagues', *British Journal of Criminology*, 35(1), 17–33.

Crawford, A. and Jones, M. (1996) 'Kirkholt Revisited: Some Reflections on the Transferability of Crime Prevention Initiatives', *Howard Journal*, 35(1), 21–39.

Crawford, A., Jones, T., Woodhouse, T. and Young, J. (1990) *The Second Islington Crime Survey*, Enfield: Centre for Criminology, Middlesex Polytechnic.

Crime Concern (1994a) *Counting the Cost: A Briefing Paper on Financial Losses Arising from Crime*, Swindon: Crime Concern.

Crime Concern (1994b) *Crime Prevention Partnerships: A Review of Progress*, Briefing Paper 1, Swindon: Crime Concern.

Currie, E. (1988) 'Two Visions of Community Crime Prevention', in Hope and Shaw (1988a), 280–6.

Currie, E. (1996a) *Is America Really Winning the War on Crime and Should Britain Follow Its Example?*, London: NACRO.

Currie, E. (1996b) 'Social Crime Prevention Strategies in a Market Society', in Muncie *et al.* (eds) *Criminological Perspectives: A Reader*, London: Sage, 343–54.

Currie, E. (1997) 'Market, Crime and Community: Towards a Mid-Range Theory of Post-Industrial Violence', *Theoretical Criminology*, 1(2), 147–72.

Davies, S. (1996) *Big Brother*, London: Macmillan.

Davis, M. (1990) *City of Quartz: Excavating the Future in Los Angeles*, London: Verso.

Davis, M. (1992) *Beyond Blade Runner: Urban Control the Ecology of Fear*, Westfield, NJ: Open Magazine Pamphlet Series.

Deakin, N. and Walsh, K. (1996) 'The Enabling State: The Role of Markets and Contracts', *Public Administration*, 74, 33–48.

Delatte, J. and Dolé, P. (1987) *La Récomposition du Champ Sociale et des Pratiques de Prévention*, Paris: Ministère de la Justice.

del Frate, A.A. (1997) *Preventing Crime: Citizens' Experiences Across the World*, Rome: UNICRI.

de Liège, M-P. (1988) 'The Fight Against Crime and Fear: A New Initiative in France', in Hope and Shaw (1988a), 254–9.

de Liège, M-P. (1991) 'Social Developments and the Prevention of Crime in France', in Heidensohn, F. and Farrell, M. (eds) *Crime in Europe*, London: Routledge, 121–32.

Dennis, N. (ed.) (1997) *Zero Tolerance: Policing a Free Society*, London: Institute for Economic Affairs.

Dennis, N. and Erdos, G. (1992) *Families Without Fatherhood*, London: Institute for Economic Affairs.

Department of the Environment (1993) *Crime Prevention on Council Estates*, London: HMSO.

Department of the Environment (1994) *Planning Out Crime*, Circular 5/94, London: DoE.

Dixon, B. and Stanko, B. (1995) 'Sector Policing and Public Accountability', *Policing and Society*, 5, 171–83.

Dowds, L. and Mayhew, P. (1994) *Participation in Neighbourhood Watch: Findings from the 1992 British Crime Survey*, Research Findings No. 11, London: Home Office.

Downes, D. (1988) *Contrasts in Tolerance: Post-War Penal Policy in The Netherlands and England and Wales*, Oxford: Clarendon Press.

Downes, D. and Rock, P. (1988) *Understanding Deviance*, Oxford: Clarendon Press.

DuBow, F.L. and McEwen, C. (1993) 'Community Boards: An Analytic Profile', in Merry and Milner (1993), 125–68.

Dutch Ministry of Justice (1985) *Society and Crime: A Policy Plan for The Netherlands*, The Hague: Ministry of Justice.

Ekblom, P. (1987) *Getting the Best Out of Crime Analysis*, CPU Paper 10, London: Home Office.

Ekblom, P. (1988) 'Preventing Post Office Robberies in London: Effects and Side Effects', *Journal of Security Administration*, 11, 36–43.

Ekblom, P. (1992) 'The Safer Cities Programme Impact Evaluation: Problems and Progress', *Studies on Crime and Crime Prevention*, 1, 35–51.

Ekblom, P. (1994) 'Proximal Circumstances: A Mechanism-based Classification of Crime Prevention', *Crime Prevention Studies*, 2, 185–232.

Ekblom, P. (1995) 'Less Crime By Design', *The Annals*, 539, 114–29.

Ekblom, P. and Pease, K. (1995) 'Evaluating Crime Prevention', in Tonry and Farrington (1995b), 585–662.

Ekblom, P., Sutton, M. and Law, H. (1997) *Safer Cities and Residential Burglary: A Summary of Evaluation Results*, Home Office Research Study, No. 163, London: Home Office.

Ellingworth, D., Farrell, G. and Pease, K. (1995) 'A Victim is a Victim is a Victim?', *British Journal of Criminology*, 35(3), 360–5.

Elliot, R. and Nicholls, J. (1996) *It's Good to Talk: Lessons in Public Consultation and Feedback*, Police Research Paper 22, London: Home Office.

Empey, L.T. (1977) 'Crime Prevention: The Fugutive Utopia', in Inciardi, J.A. and Siegel, H.A. (eds) *Crime: Emerging Issues*, New York: Praeger.

Emsley, C. (1983) *Policing and Its Context 1750–1870*, London: Macmillan.

Ericson, R. (1994) 'The Division of Expert Knowledge in Policing and Security', *British Journal of Sociology*, 45(2), 149–75.

Ericson, R. and Haggerty, K. (1997) *Policing the Risk Society*, Oxford: Clarendon Press.

Etzioni, A. (1993) *The Spirit of Community*, New York: Simon & Schuster.

Etzioni, A. (1997) *The New Golden Rule: Community and Morality in a Democratic Society*, London: Profile.

Evans, D.J., Fyfe, N.R. and Herbert, D.T. (eds) (1992) *Crime, Policing and Place: Essays in Environmental Criminology*, London: Routledge.

Evans, K., Fraser, P. and Walklate, S. (1996) 'Whom can you Trust: The Politics of "Grassing" on an Inner City Housing Estate', *The Sociological Review*, 44(3), 361–80.

Ewald, F. (1991) 'Insurance and Risk', in Burchell *et al.* (1991), 197–210.

Faget, J. and Wyvekens, A. (1996) 'Urban Policy and Proximity Justice in France', *European Journal of Criminal Policy and Research*, 4(1), 64–73.

Farr, J. and Osborn, S. (1997) *High Hopes: Concierge, Controlled Entry and Similar Schemes for High Rise Blocks*, London: Department of the Environment.

Farrell, G. (1992) 'Multiple Victimisation: Its Extent and Significance', *International Review of Victimology*, 2, 85–102.

Farrell, G. (1995) 'Preventing Repeat Victimisation', in Tonry and Farrington (1995b), 469–534.

Farrell, G. and Pease, K. (1993) *Once Bitten, Twice Bitten: Repeat Victimisation and Its Implications for Crime Prevention*, CPU Paper 46, London: Home Office.

Farrington, D.P. (1992) 'Criminal Career Research in the United Kingdom', *British Journal of Criminology*, 32(4), 521–36.

Farrington, D.P. (1994) 'Human Development and Criminal Careers', in Maguire *et al.* (1994), 511–84.

Farrington, D.P. (1996) *Understanding and Preventing Youth Crime*, York: Joseph Rowntree Foundation.

Feeley, M. and Simon, J. (1992) 'The New Penology: Notes on the Emerging Strategy of Corrections and Its Implications', *Criminology*, 30(4), 449–74.

Feeley, M. and Simon, J. (1994) 'Actuarial Justice: the Emerging New Criminal Law', in Nelken (1994b), 173–201.

Felson, M. (1986) 'Linking Criminal Choices, Routine Activities, Informal Control, and Criminal Outcomes', in Cornish and Clarke (1986b), 119–28.

Felson, M. (1995) 'Those Who Discourage Crime', *Crime Prevention Studies*, 4, 53–66.

Fenwick, C.R. (1985) 'Culture, Philosophy and Crime: The Japanese Experience', *International Journal of Comparative and Applied Criminal Justice*, 9, 67–81.

Field, S. and Hope, T. (1990) 'Economics, The Consumer and Under-Provision in Crime Prevention', in Morgan, R. (ed.) *Policing Organised Crime and Crime Prevention*, Bristol: Bristol Centre for Criminal Justice, 87–99.

Fielding, N. (1995) *Community Policing*, Oxford: Clarendon Press.

Fijnaut, C., Goethals, J., Peters, T. and Walgrave, L. (eds) (1995) *Changes in Society, Crime and Criminal Justice, vol. 1, Crime and Insecurity in the City*, The Hague: Kluwer.

Forrester, D., Chatterton, M. and Pease, K. (1988) *The Kirkholt Burglary Prevention Project, Rochdale*, CPU Paper 13, London: Home Office.

Forrester, D., Frenz, S., O'Connell, M. and Pease, K. (1990) *The Kirkholt Burglary Project: Phase II*, CPU Paper 23, London: Home Office.

Foster, J. (1995) 'Informal Social Control and Community Crime Prevention', *British Journal of Criminology*, 35(4), 563–83.

Foster, J. and Hope, T. (1993) *Housing, Community and Crime: The Impact of the Priority Estates Project*, Home Office Research Study 131, London: HMSO.

Foucault, M. (1991) 'Governmentality', in Burchell *et al.* (1991), 87–104.

Francis, P., Davies, P. and Jupp, V. (eds) (1997) *Policing Futures*, London: Macmillan.

Frost, N., Johnston, L., Wallis, L. and Stein, M. (1996) *Negotiated Friendship: Home-Start and Family Support*, Leicester: Home-Start UK.

Gabor, T. (1990) 'Crime Displacement and Situational Prevention: Toward the Development of Some Principles', *Canadian Journal of Criminology*, 32(1), 41–73.

Gallagher, J. (1995) 'Anti-Social Security', *New Statesman and Society*, 31 March.

Garapon, A. (1995) 'French Legal Culture and the Shock of Globalization', *Social and Legal Studies*, 4(4), 493–506.

Garapon, A. (1997) *Bien Juger*, Paris: Odile Jacob.

Garfinkel, H. (1956) 'Conditions of Successful Degradation Ceremonies', *American Journal of Sociology*, 61, 420–4.

Garland, D. (1990) *Punishment and Modern Society*, Oxford: Clarendon Press.

Garland, D. (1992) 'Criminological Knowledge and Its Relation to Power: Foucault's Genealogy and Criminology Today', *British Journal of Criminology*, 32(4), 403–22.

Garland, D. (1994) 'Of Crimes and Criminals: The Development of British Criminology', in Maguire *et al.* (eds) *The Oxford Handbook of Criminology*, Oxford: Oxford Univeristy Press, 17–68.

Garland, D. (1996) 'The Limits of the Sovereign State: Strategies of Crime Control in Contemporary Society', *British Journal of Criminology*, 36(4), 445–71.

Garland, D. (1997) '"Governmentality" and the Problem of Crime: Foucault, Criminology, Sociology', *Theoretical Criminology*, 1(2), 173–214.

Genn, H. (1988) 'Multiple Victimization', in Maguire and Pointing (1988), 90–100.

Geraghty, J. (1991) *Probation Practice in Crime Prevention*, CPU Paper 24, London: Home Office.

Giddens, A. (1984) *The Constitution of Society*, Cambridge: Polity Press.

Giddens, A. (1990) *The Consequences of Modernity*, Cambridge: Polity Press.

Giddens, A. (1991) *Modernity and Self Identity*, Cambridge: Polity Press.

Gill, M. and Mawby, R. (1990) *Volunteers in the Criminal Justice System*, Milton Keynes: Open University Press.

Gilling, D. (1994) 'Multi-agency Crime Prevention: Some Barriers to Collaboration', *Howard Journal*, 33, 246–57.

Gilling, D. (1996) 'Crime Prevention', in May, T. and Vass, A.A. (eds) *Working with Offenders: Issues, Contexts and Outcomes*, London: Sage, 222–41.

Gladstone, F. (1980) *Co-ordinating Crime Prevention Efforts*, London: HMSO.

Goldstein, H. (1979) 'Policing: A Problem-Oriented Approach', *Crime and Delinquency*, 25, 236–58.

Goldstein, H. (1990) *Problem-Oriented Policing*, New York: McGraw-Hill.

Gordon, P. (1987) 'Community Policing: Towards the Local Police State?', in Scraton, P. (ed.) *Law, Order and the Authoritarian State*, Milton Keynes: Open University Press, 121–44.

Gottfredson, M.R. and Hirschi, T. (eds) (1987) *Positive Criminology*, London: Sage.

Gottfredson, M.R. and Hirschi, T. (1990) *A General Theory of Crime*, Stanford CA: Stanford University Press.

Graham, J. (1988) *Schools, Disruptive Behaviour and Delinquency*, Research Study 96, London: Home Office.

Graham, J. (1993) 'Crime Prevention Policies in Europe', *European Journal of Crime, Criminal Law and Criminal Justice*, 1(2), 126–42.

Graham, J. and Bennett, T. (1995) *Crime Prevention Strategies in Europe and North America*, Helsinki: HEUNI.

Graham, J. and Bowling, B. (1995) *Young People and Crime*, Home Office Research Study, 145, London: Home Office.

Graham, J. and Utting, D. (1996) 'Families, Schools and Criminality Prevention', in Bennett (1996b), 385–416.

Greene, J.R. and Mastrofski, S.D. (eds) (1988) *Community Policing: Rhetoric or Reality*, New York: Praeger.

Groombridge, N. and Murji, K. (1994) 'Obscured by Cameras?', *Criminal Justice Matters*, 17, 9.

Hagell, A. and Newburn, T. (1994) *Persistent Young Offenders*, London: PSI.

Hakim, S. and Rengert, G.F. (1981) *Crime Spillover*, Beverly Hills, CA: Sage.

Haley, J.O. (1995) 'Victim-Offender Mediation: Lessons from the Japanese Experience', *Mediation Quarterly*, 12(3) 233–48.

Hall, S. (1979) *Drifting Into a Law and Order Society*, London: Cobden Trust.

Hargreaves Heap, S., Hollis, M., Lyons, B., Sugden, R. and Weal, A. (eds) (1992) *The Theory of Choice: A Critical Guide*, Oxford: Blackwell.

Harker, L. and Oppenheim, C. (1996) *Poverty: The Facts*, London: Child Poverty Action Group.

Harrington, C.B. (1993) 'Community Organizing Through Conflict Resolution', in Merry and Milner (1993), 401–33.

Harvey, L., Grimshaw, P. and Pease, K. (1989) 'Crime Prevention Delivery: The Work of Crime Prevention Officers', in Morgan, R. and Smith, D.J. (eds) *Coming to Terms With Policing*, London: Routledge.

Hauber, A., Hofstra, B., Toornvliet, L. and Zandbergen, A. (1996) 'Some New Forms of Functional Social Control in The Netherlands and their Effects', *British Journal of Criminology*, 36(2), 199–219.

Heal, K. and Laycock, G. (eds) (1986) *Situational Crime Prevention: From Theory into Practice*, London: HMSO.

Heathcote, F. (1981) 'Social Disorganisation Theories', in Fitzgerald, M., McLennan, G. and Pawson, J. (eds) *Crime and Society*, London: Routledge, 341–70.

Her Majesty's Inspectorate of Constabulary (1998) *Beating Crime*, London: Home Office.

Herrnstein, R.J. and Murray, C. (1994) *The Bell Curve: Intelligence and Class Structure in American Life*, New York: Free Press.

Hesseling, R.B.P. (1992) *Social Caretakers and Preventing Crime on Public Housing Estates*, The Hague: Research and Documentation Centre.

Hesseling, R.B.P. (1994) 'Displacement: a Review of the Empirical Literature', *Crime Prevention Studies*, 3, 197–30.

Hillier, B. and Hanson, J. (1984) *The Social Logic of Space*, Cambridge: Cambridge University Press.

Hills, J. (1995) *Joseph Rowntree Foundation Inquiry into Income and Wealth, vol. 2*, York: Joseph Rowntree Foundation.

Hirschi, T. (1969) *Causes of Delinquency*, Berkeley, CA: University of California Press.

Hofstra, B. and Shapland, J. (1997) 'Who is in Control?', *Policing and Society*, 6, 265–81.

Home Office (1965) *Report of the Committee on the Prevention and Detection of Crime*, London: Home Office.

Home Office (1984) *Probation Service in England and Wales: Statement of National Objectives and Priorities*, London: HMSO.

Home Office (1989) *Report of the Working Group on the Fear of Crime*, Standing Conference on Crime Prevention, London: Home Office.

Home Office (1990) *Partnership in Crime Prevention*, London: HMSO.

Home Office (1991) *Practical Ways to Crack Crime*, 4th edn (first published 1989), London: Home Office.

Home Office (1992a) *Three-Year Plan for the Probation Service, 1993–96*, London: Home Office.

Home Office (1992b) *Home Office Response to the Report 'Safer Communities – The Local Delivery of Crime Prevention Through the Partnership Approach'*, London: Home Office.

Home Office (1992c) *Partnership in Dealing with Offenders in the Community: A Decision Document*, London: Home Office.

Home Office (1993) *Crime Prevention Statement*, London: Home Office.

Home Office (1994a) *Home Office Research Findings*, Home Office Research and Statistics Department, No. 11, London: Home Office.

Home Office (1994b) *Review of Police Core and Ancillary Tasks: Interim Report*, London: Home Office.

Home Office (1995a) *Home Office Annual Report 1995*, London: HMSO.

Home Office (1995b) *Information on the Criminal Justice System in England and Wales: Digest 3*, London: Home Office.

Home Office (1995c) *Close Circuit Television Challenge Competition 1996/97*, London: Home Office.

Home Office (1996a) *Protecting the Public*, Cmd 3190, London: HMSO.

Home Office (1996b) *Prison Statistics England and Wales 1994*, London: HMSO.

Home Office (1997a) *Getting to Grips with Crime: A New Framework for Local Action*, London: Home Office.

Home Office (1997b) *Tackling Youth Crime: A Consultation Paper*, London: Home Office.

Home Office (1997c) *Preventing Children Offending: A Consultation Document*, London: Home Office.

Home Office (1997d) *New National and Local Focus on Youth Crime: A Consultation Paper*, London: Home Office.

Home Office (1997e) *No More Excuses – A New Approach to Tackling Youth Crime in England and Wales*, London: HMSO.

Home Office (1997f) *Community Safety Order: A Consultation Paper*, London: Home Office.

Honess, T. and Charman, E. (1992) *Closed Circuit Television in Public Places*, CPU Paper 35, London: Home Office.

Honess, T. and Maguire, M. (1993) *Vehicle Watch and Car Theft: An Evaluation*, CPU Paper 50, London: Home Office.

Hood, C. (1991) 'A Public Management for all Seasons?', *Public Administration*, 69, 3–19.

Hope, T. (1985) *Implementing Crime Prevention Measures*, Home Office Research Study, No. 86, London: Home Office.

Hope, T. (1988) 'Support for Neighbourhood Watch: A British Crime Survey Analysis', in Hope and Shaw (1988a), 146–61.

Hope, T. (1995a) 'Community Crime Prevention', in Tonry and Farrington (1995b), 21–89.

Hope, T. (1995b) 'The Flux of Victimization', *British Journal of Criminology*, 35(3), 327–42.

Hope, T. (1997) 'Inequality and the Future of Community Crime Prevention', in Lab (1997), 143–58.

Hope, T. and Foster, J. (1992) 'Conflicting Forces: Changing the Dynamics of Crime and Community on a "Problem" Estate', *British Journal of Criminology*, 32(4), 488–504.

Hope, T. and Murphy, D.J.I. (1983) 'Problems of Implementing Crime Prevention: The Experience of a Demonstration Project', *Howard Journal*, 22(1), 38–50.

Hope, T. and Shaw, M. (eds) (1988a) *Communities and Crime Reduction*, London: HMSO.

Hope, T. and Shaw, M. (1988b) 'Community Approaches to Reducing Crime', in Hope and Shaw (1988a), 1–28.

Hough, M. (1987) 'Thinking About Effectiveness', *British Journal of Criminology*, 27(1), 70–9.

Hough, M. (1995) *Anxiety about Crime: Findings from the 1994 British Crime Survey*, Home Office Research Study, No. 147, London: Home Office.

Hough, M. (1996) 'The Police Patrol Function: What Research Can Tell Us', in Saulsbury *et al.* (1996), 60–71.

Hough, M. and Mayhew, P. (1983) *The British Crime Survey: First Report*, Home Office Research Study, No. 76, London: HMSO.

Hough, M., Clarke, R.V. and Mayhew, P. (1980) 'Introduction', in Clarke and Mayhew (1980), 1–17.

Howard, M. (1994) 'A Volunteer Army Awaiting the Call', *The Times*, 28 February.

Hughes, G. (1996) 'Strategies of Multi-Agency Crime Prevention and Community Safety in Contemporary Britain', *Studies on Crime and Crime Prevention*, 5, 221–44.

Hussain, S. (1988) *Neighbourhood Watch in England and Wales: A Locational Analysis*, CPU Paper 12, London: Home Office.

Iadicola, P. (1986) 'Community Crime Control Strategies', *Crime and Social Justice*, 25, 140–65.

I'Anson, J. and Wiles, P. (1995) *The Sedgefield Community Force*, Sheffield: Centre for Criminological and Legal Research, University of Sheffield.

Jacobs, J. (1961) *The Death and Life of Great American Cities*, New York: Vintage.

James, O. (1995) *Juvenile Violence in a Winner-Loser Culture*, London: Free Association Books.

Jeffery, C.R. (1971) *Crime Prevention Through Environmental Design*, California: Sage.

Johnston, L. (1992) *The Rebirth of Private Policing*, London: Routledge.

Johnston, L. (1996) 'What is Vigilantism?', *British Journal of Criminology*, 36(2), 220–36.

Johnston, V., Shapland, J. and Wiles, P. (1993) *Developing Police Crime Prevention: Management and Organisational Change*, CPU Paper 41, London: Home Office.

Jones, C. (1993) 'Auditing Criminal Justice', *British Journal of Criminology*, 33(3), 187–202.

Jones, T. and Newburn, T. (1995) 'How Big is the Private Security Sector?', *Policing and Society*, 5, 221–32.

Jones, T. and Newburn, T. (1998) *Private Security and Public Policing*, Oxford: Clarendon Press.

Jones, T., Maclean, B. and Young, J. (1986) *The Islington Crime Survey*, Aldershot: Gower.

Joutsen, M. (1995) 'The Emergence of United Nations Criminal Policy', *European Journal of Crime, Criminal Law and Criminal Justice*, 3, 294–304.

Keat, R. and Abercrombie, N. (eds) (1991) *Enterprise Culture*, London: Routledge.

Kelling, G. (1987) 'Acquiring a Taste for Order: The Community and Police', *Crime and Delinquency*, 33(1), 90–102.

Kelly, L. (1988) *Surviving Sexual Violence*, Cambridge: Polity Press.

Kersten, J. (1993) 'Street Youths, *Bosozoku*, and *Yakuza*: Subculture Formation and Societal Reaction in Japan', *Crime and Delinquency*, 39(3), 277–95.

King, M. (1988) *How to Make Social Crime Prevention Work: The French Experience*, London: NACRO.

King, M. (1991) 'The Political Construction of Crime Prevention', in Stenson and Cowell (1991), 87–108.

Kinsey, R., Lea, J. and Young, J. (1986) *Losing the Fight Against Crime*, Oxford: Blackwell.

Kornhauser, R.R. (1978) *Social Sources of Delinquency*, Chicago: University of Chicago Press.

Kristof, N.D. (1995) 'Japanese Say No to Crime: Tough Methods at a Price', *New York Times*, 14 May.

Lab, S.P. (ed.) (1997) *Crime Prevention at a Crossroads*, Cincinnati: Anderson Publishing.

Labour Party (1995) *A Quiet Life: Tough Action on Criminal Neighbours*, London: Labour Party.

Labour Party (1997) *Because Britain Deserves Better*, London: Labour Party.

Lasch, C. (1980) *The Culture of Narcissism*, London: Sphere Books.

Laycock, G. and Pease, K. (1985) 'Crime Prevention Within the Probation Service', *Probation Journal*, 32, 43–7.

Laycock, G. and Tilley, N. (1995) 'Implementing Crime Prevention', in Tonry and Farrington (1995b), 535–84.

Lazerges, C. (1995) 'De la Politique de Prévention de la Délinquance à la Politique de la Ville', in Fijnaut *et al.* (1995), 213–49.

Lea, J., Jones, T., Woodhouse, T. and Young, J. (1989) *Preventing Crime: The Hilldrop Environmental Improvement Survey*, Enfield: Centre for Criminology, Middlesex Polytechnic.

Leadbeater, C. (1996) *The Self-Policing Society*, London: Demos.

Leigh, A., Read, T. and Tilley, N. (1996) *Problem-Oriented Policing Brit Pop*, Crime Detection and Prevention Paper 75, London: Home Office.

Lejins, P.P. (1967) 'The field of prevention', in Amos, W.E. and Wellford, C.E. (eds) *Delinquency Prevention: Theory and Practice*, Englewood Cliffs: Prentice Hall.

Levitas, R. (ed.) (1986) *The Ideology of the New Right*, Cambridge: Polity.

Lewis, D. and Salem, G. (1986) *Fear of Crime: Incivility and the Production of a Social Problem*, New York: Transaction Books.

Liberal Democrat Party (1997) *Make the Difference: The Liberal Democrat Manifesto 1997*, London: Liberal Democrat Party.

Liddle, A.M. and Gelsthorpe, L.R. (1994a) *Inter-Agency Crime Prevention: Organising Local Delivery*, CPU Paper 52, London: Home Office.

Liddle, A.M. and Gelsthorpe, L.R. (1994b) *Crime Prevention and Inter-Agency Co-operation*, CPU Paper 53, London: Home Office.

Liddle, A.M. and Gelsthorpe, L.R. (1994c) *Inter-Agency Crime Prevention: Further Issues*, CPU Paper 53, London: Home Office.

Lilly, J.R. and Knepper, P. (1993) 'The Corrections-Commercial Complex', *Crime and Delinquency*, 39, 150–66.

Lilly, J.R., Cullen, F. and Ball, R. (1995) *Criminological Theory*, London: Sage.

Lipsky, M. (1980) *Street Level Bureaucracy*, New York: Russell Sage Foundation.

Lloyd, S., Farrell, G. and Pease, K. (1994) *Preventing Repeated Domestic Violence: A Demonstration Project on Merseyside*, CPU Paper 49, London: Home Office.

Local Government Management Board (1996) *Survey of Community Safety Activities in Local Government in England and Wales*, Luton: LGMB.

Lowman, J. (1992) 'Street Prostitution Control: Some Canadian Reflections on the Finsbury Park Experience', *British Journal of Criminology*, 32(1), 1–17.

Lurigio, A.J. and Rosenbaum, D.P. (1986) 'Evaluation Research in Community Crime Prevention: a Critical Look at the Field', in Rosenbaum (1986), 19–44.

Macaulay, S. (1963) 'Non-Contractual Relations in Business: A Preliminary Study', *American Sociological Review*, 28, 55–67.

Maguire, M. and John, T. (1996) 'Covert and Deceptive Policing in England and Wales: Issues in Regulation and Practice', *European Journal of Crime, Criminal Law and Criminal Justice*, 4(4), 316–34.

Maguire, M. and Pointing, J. (eds) (1988) *Victims of Crime: A New Deal?*, Milton Keynes: Open University Press.

Maguire, M., Morgan, R. and Reiner, R. (eds) (1994) *The Oxford Handbook of Criminology*, Oxford: Oxford University Press.

Manwaring-White, S. (1983) *The Policing Revolution*, Hemel Hempstead: Harvester Wheatsheaf.

Martinson, R. (1974) 'What Works? Questions and Answers About Prison Reform', *Public Interest*, 35, 22–54.

Marx, G. (1989) 'Commentary: Some Trends and Issues in Citizen Involvement in the Law Enforcement Process', *Crime and Delinquency*, 35(3), 500–19.

Matthews, R. (1986) *Policing Prostitution: A Multi-Agency Approach*, Enfield: Middlesex Polytechnic.

Matthews, R. (1992a) 'Regulating Street Prostitution and Kerb-Crawling: A Reply to John Lowman', *British Journal of Criminology*, 32(1), 18–22.

Matthews, R. (1992b) 'Developing More Effective Strategies for Curbing Prostitution', in Clarke (1992), 89–98.

Matthews, R. (1992c) 'Replacing Broken Windows: Crime, Incivilities and Urban Change', in Matthews and Young (1992), 19–50.

Matthews, R. (1993) *Kerb-Crawling, Prostitution and Multi-Agency Policing*, CPU Paper 43, London: Home Office.

Matthews, R. and Young, J. (eds) (1992) *Issues in Realist Criminology*, London: Sage.

Mauer, M. (1997) *Intended and Unintended Consequences: State Racial Disparaties in Imprisonment*, Washington DC: The Sentencing Project.

Mawby, R.I. (1977) 'Defensible Space: A Theoretical and Empirical Appraisal', *Urban Studies*, 14, 169–80.

Maxfield, M. (1987) *Explaining Fear of Crime: Evidence from the 1984 British Crime Survey*, London: Home Office.

May, T. and Vass, A.A. (eds) (1996) *Working With Offenders: Issues, Contexts and Outcomes*, London: Sage.

Mayhew, P. (1979) 'Defensible Space: The Current Status of a Crime Prevention Theory', *Howard Journal*, 150–9.

Mayhew, P. and Hough, M. (1988) 'The British Crime Survey: Origins and Impact', in Maguire and Pointing (1988), 156–63.

Mayhew, P., Clarke, R.V. and Elliot, D. (1989) 'Motorcycle Theft, Helmet Legislation and Displacement', *Howard Journal*, 28(1), 1–8.

Mayhew, P., Clarke, R.V. and Hough, M. (1976a) 'Steering Column Locks and Car Theft', in Mayhew *et al.* (1976), 19–30.

Mayhew, P., Clarke, R.V., Sturman, A. and Hough, M. (1976b) *Crime as Opportunity*, London: HMSO.

Mayhew, P., Mirrlees-Black, C. and Aye Maung, N. (1994) *Trends in Crime: Findings from the 1994 British Crime Survey*, London: Home Office.

McConville, M. and Shepard, D. (1992) *Watching Police Watching Communities*, London: Routledge.

McDonald, S. (1986) 'Does Gentrification Arrest Crime Rates?', in Reiss and Tonry (1986), 163–201.

McLaughlin, E. and Muncie, J. (1994) 'Managing the Criminal Justice System', in Clarke, J. (ed.) *Managing Social Policy*, Sage: London, 115–40.

Meikle, J. (1993) 'Nurseries to Join Fight Against Crime', *Guardian*, 22 April.

Meikle, J. (1996) ' "Have a Nice Day" Plan to Enhance Urban Living', *Guardian*, 20 April.

Merry, S.E. (1981) 'Defensible Space Undefended', *Urban Affairs Quarterly*, 16(4) 397–422.

Merry, S.E. and Milner, N. (eds) (1993) *The Possibility of Popular Justice*, Michigan: The University of Michigan Press.

Merton, R. (1938) 'Social structure and "Anomie" ', *American Sociological Review*, 3, 672–82.

Miers, D. (1992) 'The Responsibilities and Rights of Victims of Crime', *Modern Law Review*, 55, 482–505.

Mirrlees-Black, C., Mayhew, P. and Percy, A. (1996) *The 1996 British Crime Survey: England and Wales*, London: Home Office.

Miyazawa, S. (1992) *Policing in Japan: A Study on Making Crime*, Albany: State University of New York Press.

Morgan, J. (1991) *Safer Communities: The Local Delivery of Crime Prevention Through the Partnership Approach*, London: Home Office.

Morgan, R. (1989) 'Policing By Consent: Legitimating the Doctrine', in Morgan and Smith (1989), 217–34.

Morgan, R. and Newburn, T. (1997) *The Future of Policing*, Oxford: Oxford University Press.

Morgan, R. and Smith, D.J. (eds) (1989) *Coming to Terms with Policing*, London: Routledge.

Moriyama, T. (1993) 'Crime, Criminal Justice and Social Control: Why do We Enjoy a Low Crime Rate?', paper presented to the British Criminology Conference, University of Wales, Cardiff, 28–31 July.

Moriyama, T. (1995) 'The Possibilities of Situational Crime Prevention in Japan', paper presented to the British Criminology Conference, University of Loughborough, 18–21 July.

Murray, C. (1990) *The Emerging British Underclass*, London: Institute for Economic Affairs.

Murray, C. (1994) *Underclass: The Crisis Deepens*, London: Institute for Economic Affairs.

Murray, C. (1997) *Does Prison Work?*, London: Institute for Economic Affairs.

National Association of Probation Officers (1984) *Draft Policy Statement: Crime Prevention and Reduction Strategies*, London: NAPO.

National Board for Crime Prevention (1994) *Wise After the Event: Tackling Repeat Victimisation*, London: Home Office.

Nelken, D. (1994a) 'The Future of Comparative Criminology', in Nelken (1994b), 220–43.

Nelken, D. (ed.) (1994b) *The Futures of Criminology*, London: Sage.

Nelken, D. (1995) 'Disclosing/Invoking Legal Culture: An Introduction', *Social and Legal Studies*, 4(4), 435–52.

Nellis, M. (1995) 'Probation Values for the 1990s', *Howard Journal*, 34(1), 19–44.

Newburn, T. and Merry, S. (1990) *Keeping in Touch: Police–Victim Communication in Two Areas*, Home Office Research Study, No. 116, London: Home Office.

Newman, O. (1972) *Defensible Space: People and Design in the Violent City*, London: Architectural Press.

Newman, O. (1976) *Design Guidelines for Achieving Defensible Space*, National Institute of Law Enforcement and Criminal Justice, Washington DC: Government Printing Office.

New Zealand Crime Prevention Unit (1994a) *The New Zealand Crime Prevention Strategy*, Wellington: CPU.

New Zealand Crime Prevention Unit (1994b) *A Guide to Setting up a Safer Community Council*, Wellington: CPU.

Norris, C. and Armstrong, G. (1997a) *Categories of Control: The Social Construction of Suspicion and Intervention in CCTV Systems*, Hull: Centre for Criminology and Criminal Justice.

Norris, C. and Armstrong, G. (1997b) *The Unforgiving Eye: CCTV Surveillance in Public Space*, Hull: Centre for Criminology and Criminal Justice.

O'Kane, M. (1994) 'Cruising, Abusing or on the Game', *Guardian*, 23 July.

O'Malley, P. (1992) 'Risk, Power and Crime Prevention', *Economy and Society*, 21(3), 252–75.

Osborn, S. (1986) 'Phone Entry Systems and the South Acton Estate', *NACRO Neighbourhood News*, December.

Osborn, S. (1994) *Housing Safe Communities: An Evaluation of Recent Initiatives*, London: SNU.

Osborn, S. and Bright, J. (1989) *Crime Prevention and Community Safety: A Practical Guide for Local Authorities*, London: NACRO.

Osborne, D. and Gaebler, T. (1992) *Reinventing Government: How the Entrepreneurial Spirit is Transforming the Public Sector*, Reading, Massachusetts: Addison-Wesley.

Painter, K. (1988) *Lighting and Crime – The Edmonton Project*, Enfield: Middlesex Polytechnic.

Painter, K. (1989) *Crime Prevention and Public Lighting with Special Focus on Women and Elderly People*, Enfield: Middlesex Polytechnic.

Palumbo, D., Ferguson, J.L. and Stein, J. (1997) 'The Conditions Needed for Successful Community Crime Prevention', in Lab (1997), 79–98.

Pawson, R. and Tilley, N. (1994) 'What Works in Evaluation Research?', *British Journal of Criminology*, 34, 291–306.

Pawson, R. and Tilley, N. (1997) *Realistic Evaluation*, London: Sage.

Pearce, F. (1990) *Second Islington Crime Survey: Commercial and Conventional Crime in Islington*, Enfield: Centre for Criminology, Middlesex Polytechnic.

Pearson, G., Blagg, H., Smith, D., Sampson, A. and Stubbs, P. (1992) 'Crime, Community and Conflict: The Multi-Agency Approach', in Downes, D. (ed.) *Unravelling Criminal Justice*, London: Macmillan, 46–72.

Pease, K. (1991) 'The Kirkholt Project: Preventing Burglary on a British Public Housing Estate', *Security Journal*, 2(2), 73–7.

Pease, K. (1994) 'Crime Prevention', in Maguire, M. *et al.* (eds) *The Oxford Handbook of Criminology*, Oxford: Oxford University Press, 659–703.

Pease, K. (1996) 'Opportunities for Crime Prevention: The Need for Incentives', in Saulsbury *et al.* (1996), 96–104.

Pennell, S., Curtis, C., Henderson, J. and Tayman, J. (1989) 'Guardian Angels: A Unique Approach to Crime Prevention', *Crime and Delinquency*, 35(3), 378–400.

Peters, A.A.G. (1986) 'Main Currents in Criminal Law Theory', in van Dijk *et al.* (1986), 19–36.

Pitts, J. (1996) 'The Politics and Practice of Youth Justice', in McLaughlin, E. and Muncie, J. (eds) *Controlling Crime*, London: Sage, 249–91.

Pitts, J. (1997) 'Youth Crime, Social Change and Crime Control in Britain and France in the 1980s and 1990s', in Jones, H. (ed.) *Towards a Classless Society*, London: Routledge.

Pitts, J. and Smith, P. (1995) *Preventing School Bullying*, Crime Prevention Paper 63, London: Home Office.

Podolefsky, A. and Dubow, F. (1981) *Strategies for Community Crime Prevention*, Springfield, Il: Charles C. Thomas Publishers.

Pollard, C. (1997) 'Zero Tolerance: Short-term Fix, Long-term Liability?', in Dennis, N. (1997), 43–60.

Polvi, N., Looman, T., Humphries, C. and Pease, K. (1991) 'The Time Course of Repeat Burglary Victimisation', *British Journal of Criminology*, 31(4), 411–14.

Povey, K. (1997) Speech to the Local Government Association Conference, 'Crime: the Local Solution', 6 March.

Power, A. (1984) *Local Housing Management: A Priority Estates Project Survey*, London: DoE.

Power, A. (1989) 'Housing, Community and Crime', in Downes (ed.) *Crime and the City*, Basingstoke: Macmillan, 206–35.

Power, A. (1997) *Estates on the Edge*, Basingstoke: Macmillan.

Power, A. and Tunstall, R. (1995) *Swimming Against the Tide: Polarisation or Progress on 20 Unpopular Council Estates, 1980–1995*, York: Joseph Rowntree Foundation.

Poyner, B. (1992) 'Situational Crime Prevention in Two Parking Facilities', in Clarke (1992), 174–84.

Poyner, B. and Webb, B. (1992) *Crime Free Housing*, Oxford: Butterworths Architecture.

Prosser, T. (1995) 'The State, Constitutions and Implementing Economic Policy: Privatization and Regulation in the UK, France and the USA', *Social and Legal Studies*, 4(4), 507–16.

Pyle, D.J. (1995) *Cutting the Costs of Crime*, London: Institute for Economic Affairs.

Ramsay, M. (1991) *The Effect of Better Street Lighting on Crime and Fear: A Review*, CPU Paper 29, London: Home Office.

Reed, T. and Oldfield, D. (1995) *Local Crime Analysis*, CPU Paper 65, London: Home Office.

Reiner, R. (1992) *The Politics of the Police*, 2nd edn, Hemel Hempstead: Harvester Wheatsheaf.

Reiss, A.J. (1986) 'Why are Communities Important in Understanding Crime?', in Reiss and Tonry (1986), 1–33.

Reiss, A.J. and Tonry, M. (eds) (1986) *Communities and Crime: Crime and Justice: a Review of Research, vol. 8*, Chicago: University of Chicago Press.

Reppetto, T. (1976) 'Crime Prevention and the Displacement Phenomenon', *Crime and Delinquency*, 22, 166–77.

Rhodes, R. (1994) 'The Hollowing Out of the State: The Changing Nature of the Public Service in Britain', *Political Quarterly Review*, 65, 137–51.

Rhodes, R. (1996) 'The New Governance: Governing Without Government', *Political Studies*, 44, 652–67.

Rhodes (1997) *Understanding Governance: Policy Networks, Governance, Reflexivity, and Accountability*, Milton Keynes: Open University Press.

Rifai, M.Y. (1982) 'Methods of Measuring the Impact of Criminal Victimization through Victimization Surveys', in Schneider, H.J. (ed.) *The Victim in International Perspective*, New York: de Gruyter.

Riley, J. and Shaw, M. (1985) *Parental Supervision and Juvenile Delinquency*, Home Office Research Study, No. 83, London: HMSO.

Robert, P. (1985) 'Insécurité, Opinion Publique et Politique Criminelle', *Année Sociologique*, 35, 199–231.

Rock, P. (1988) 'Crime Reduction Initiatives on Problem Estates', in Hope and Shaw (1988a), 99–114.

Rock, P. (1990) *Helping Victims of Crime: The Home Office and the Rise of Victim Support in England and Wales*, Oxford: Oxford University Press.

Rose, N. (1996) ' "The Death of the Social?": Refiguring the Territory of Government', *Economy and Society*, 25(3), 327–56.

Rose, N. and Miller, P. (1992) 'Political Power Beyond the State: Problematics of Government', *British Journal of Sociology*, 43(2), 173–205.

Rosenbaum, D.P. (ed.) (1986) *Community Crime Prevention: Does It Work?*, Beverly Hills, CA: Sage.

Rosenbaum, D.P. (1987) 'The Theory and Research Behind Neighbourhood Watch: Is It a Fear and Crime Reduction Strategy?', *Crime and Delinquency*, 33(1), 103–35.

Rosenbaum, D.P. (1988a) 'Community Crime Prevention: A Review and Synthesis of the Literature', *Justice Quarterly*, 5(3), 323–93.

Rosenbaum, D.P. (1988b) 'A Critical Eye on Neighbourhood Watch: Does it Reduce Crime and Fear?', in Hope and Shaw (1988a), 126–45.

Rosenbaum, D.P. (ed.) (1994) *The Challenge of Community Policing: Testing the Promises*, London: Sage.

Safe Neighbourhoods Unit (1985) *After Entryphones – Improving Management and Security in Multi–Storey Blocks*, London: SNU.

Safe Neighbourhoods Unit (1993) *Crime Prevention on Council Estates*, Prepared for the Department of the Environment, London: HMSO.

Sainsbury, P. (1986) 'The Epidemiology of Suicide', in Roy, A. (ed.) *Suicide*, Baltimore: Williams and Wilkins.

Sampson, A. (1991) *Lessons from a Victim Support Crime Prevention Project*, CPU Paper 25, London: Home Office.

Sampson, A. and Farrell, G. (1990) *Victim Support and Crime Prevention in an Inner-City Setting*, CPU Paper 21, London: Home Office.

Sampson, A. and Phillips, C. (1992) *Multiple Victimisation: Racial Attacks on an East London Estate*, CPU Paper 36, London: Home Office.

Sampson, A. and Phillips, C. (1995) *Reducing Repeat Racial Victimisation on an East London Estate*, Crime Detection and Prevention Paper 67, London: Home Office.

Sampson, A. and Smith, D. (1992) 'Probation and Community Crime Prevention', *Howard Journal*, 31(2), 105–19.

Sampson, A., Smith, D., Pearson, G., Blagg, H. and Stubbs, P. (1991) 'Gender Issues in Inter-Agency Relations: Police, Probation and Social Services', in Abbott, P. and Wallace, C. (eds) *Gender, Power and Sexuality*, Basingstoke: Macmillan, 114–32.

Sampson, A., Stubbs, P., Smith, D., Pearson, G. and Blagg, H. (1988) 'Crime, Localities and the Multi-Agency Approach', *British Journal of Criminology*, 28, 478–93.

Sampson, R.J. (1987) 'Communities and Crime', in Gottfredson and Hirschi (1987), 91–114.

Sampson, R.J. and Groves, W.B. (1989) 'Community Structure and Crime: Testing Social Disorganisation Theory', *American Journal of Sociology*, 94, 774–802.

Santer, J. (1996) 'High/Scope – High Hopes: An Early Childhood Intervention Programme', in Bennett (1996b), 417–34.

Saulsbury, W., Mott, J. and Newburn, T. (eds) (1996) *Themes in Contemporary Policing*, London: PSI/Police Foundation.

Schlossman, S. and Sedlak, M. (1983) *The Chicago Area Project Revisited*, Santa Monica, CA: Rand.

Schweinhart, L.J., Barnes, H.V. and Weikart, D.P. (1993) *Significant Benefits: the High/Scope Perry Pre-school Study Through Age 27*, Ypsilanti, Michigan: High/Scope.

Shapland, J. and Vagg, J. (1988) *Policing by the Public*, London: Routledge.

Shapland, J., Wiles, P. and Wilcox, P. (1994) *Targeted Crime Reduction for Local Areas: Principles and Methods*, London: Home Office.

Shapland, J., Hibbert, J., I'Anson, J., Sorsby, A. and Wild, R. (1995) *Milton Keynes Criminal Justice Audit*, Sheffield: Institute for the Study of the Legal Profession, University of Sheffield.

Shaw, C. and McKay, H. (1942) *Juvenile Delinquency and Urban Areas*, Chicago: University of Chicago Press.

Shearing, C. (1992) 'The Relation Between Public and Private Policing', in Tonry, M. and Morris, N. (eds) *Crime and Justice: A Review of Research, vol. 15*, Chicago: University of Chicago Press, 399–434.

Shearing, C. (1996) 'Public and Private Policing', in Saulsbury *et al.* (1996), 83–95.

Shearing, C. and Stenning, P. (1987a) 'Reframing Policing', in Shearing and Stenning (1987b), 9–18.

Shearing, C. and Stenning, P. (eds) (1987b) *Private Policing*, London: Sage.

Sherman, L.W. (1995) 'Hot Spots of Crime and Criminal Careers of Places', *Crime Prevention Studies*, 4, 35–52.

Sherman, L.W., Gartin, P.R. and Buerger, M.E. (1989) 'Hot Spots of Predatory Crime: Routine Activities and the Criminology of Place', *Criminology*, 27(1), 27–55.

Shonholtz, R. (1987) 'The Citizens' Role in Justice: Building a Primary Justice and Prevention System at the Neighbourhood Level', *Annals of the American Academy of Political and Social Science*, 494, 42–52.

Shonholtz, R. (1993) 'Justice from Another Perspective: the Ideology and Developmental History of the Community Boards Program', in Merry and Milner (1993), 201–38.

Simon, J. (1988) 'The Ideological Effects of Actuarial Practices', *Law and Society Review*, 22, 772–800.

Skogan, W. (1981) *Issues in the Measurement of Victimization*, Washington, DC: Department of Justice.

Skogan, W. (1988) 'Community Organisations and Crime', in Morris, N. and Tonry, M. (eds) *Crime and Justice: An Annual Review of Research*, Chicago: University of Chicago Press, 39–78.

Skogan, W. (1990a) *The Police and Public in England and Wales: A British Crime Survey Report*, London: HMSO.

Skogan, W. (1990b) *Disorder and Decline*, New York: Free Press.

Skogan, W. (1994) 'The Impact of Community Policing on Neighbourhood Residents', in Rosenbaum (1994), 167–81.

Skogan, W. (1996a) 'Public Opinion and the Police', in Saulsbury *et al.* (1996), 72–82.

Skogan, W. (1996b) 'Partnerships for Prevention?', in Bennett (1996b), 225–52.

Skogan, W. and Maxfield, M.G. (1981) *Coping with Crime*, London: Sage.

Smith, S.J. (1986) 'Utopia on Trial: Visions and Reality in Planned Housing', *Urban Studies*, 23, 244–6.

Snodgrass, J. (1976) 'Shaw and McKay, Chicago Criminologists', *British Journal of Criminology*, 16, 1–19.

South, N. (1987) 'Law, Profit, and "Private Persons": Private and Public Policing in English History', in Shearing and Stenning (1987b), 72–109.

Southgate, P., Bucke, T. and Byron, C. (1995) *The Parish Special Constables Scheme*, Home Office Research Study, No. 143, London: Home Office.

Sparks, J.R. (1992) 'Reason and Unreason in "Left Realism": Some Problems in the Constitution of the Fear of Crime', in Matthews and Young (1992), 119–35.

Sparks, R. (1981) 'Multiple Victimisation: Evidence, Theory and Future Research', *Journal of Criminal Law and Criminology*, 72, 762–78.

Stanko, E.A. (1988) 'Hidden Violence Against Women', in Maguire and Pointing (1988), 40–6.

Stanko, E.A. (1990) *Everyday Violence*, London: Pandora.

Steedman, C. (1984) *Policing the Victorian Community: The Formation of the English Provincial Police Forces, 1956–80*, London: Routledge.

Stenson, K. and Cowell, D. (eds) (1991) *The Politics of Crime Control*, London: Sage.

Stewart, J. (1996) 'Innovation in Democratic Practice in Local Government', *Policy and Politics*, 24(1), 29–41.

Stewart, J. and Walsh, K. (1992) 'Change in the Management of Public Services', *Public Administration*, 70, 499–518.

Storch, R. (1975) '"The Plague of Blue Locusts": Police Reform and Popular Resistance in Northern England', 1840–57, *International Review of Social History*, 20, 61–90.

Storch, R. (1976) 'The Police as Domestic Missionary: Urban Discipline and Popular Culture in Northern England, 1850–80', *Journal of Social History*, 9, 481–509.

Sutton, M. (1996) *Implementing Crime Prevention Schemes in a Multi-Agency Setting: Aspects of Process in the Safer Cities Programme*, Research Study 160, London: Home Office.

Taub, R.P., Taylor, D.G. and Dunham, J.D. (1984) *Paths of Neighbourhood Change*, Chicago: University of Chicago Press.

Taylor, R.B. (1997) 'Crime, Grime, and Responses to Crime', in Lab (1997), 63–75.

Taylor, R.B. and Covington, J. (1988) 'Neighbourhood Changes in Ecology and Violence', *Criminology*, 26, 553–89.

Thornton, R.Y. and Endo, K. (1992) *Preventing Crime in America and Japan: A Comparative Study*, Armonk, NY: M.E. Sharpe.

Tilley, N. (1992) *Safer Cities and Community Safety Strategies*, CPU Paper 38, London: Home Office.

Tilley, N. (1993a) 'Crime Prevention and the Safer Cities Story', *Howard Journal*, 32, 40–57.

Tilley, N. (1993b) *Understanding Car Parks, Crime and CCTV: Evaluation Lessons from Safer Cities*, CPU Paper 42, London: Home Office.

Tilley, N. (1993c) *After Kirkholt – Theory, Method and Results of Replication Evaluation*, CPU Paper 47, London: Home Office.

Tilley, N. (1995) *Thinking About Crime Prevention Performance Indicators*, CPU Paper 57, London: Home Office.

Tonry, M. and Farrington, D.P. (1995a) 'Strategic Approaches to Crime Prevention', in Tonry and Farrington (1995b), 1–20.

Tonry, M. and Farrington, D.P. (eds) (1995b) *Building a Safer Society: Crime and Justice: a Review of Research, vol. 19*, Chicago: University of Chicago Press.

Trasler, G. (1986) 'Situational Crime Control and Rational Choice: A Critique', in Heal and Laycock (1986), 17–24.

Tremblay, R.E. and Craig, W.M. (1995) 'Developmental Crime Prevention', in Tonry and Farrington (1995), 151–237.

Trickett, A., Ellingworth, D., Farrell, G. and Pease, K. (1995) 'Crime Victimisation in the Eighties: Changes in Area and Regional Inequality', *British Journal of Criminology*, 35(3), 343–59.

Trickett, A., Osborn, D.K., Seymour, J. and Pease, K. (1992) 'What is Different About High Crime Areas?', *British Journal of Criminology*, 32(1), 81–9.

Tuck, M. (1988) 'Crime Prevention: A Shift in Concept', *Home Office Research and Planning Unit Research Bulletin, No. 24*, London: Home Office.

Utting, D. (1995) *Family and Parenthood: Supporting Families, Preventing Breakdown*, York: Joseph Rowntree Foundation.

Utting, D. (1996) *Reducing Criminality Among Young People: A Sample of Relevant Programmes in the United Kingdom*, Research Study 161, London: Home Office.

Utting, D., Bright, J. and Henricson, C. (1993) *Crime and the Family*, Occasional Paper No. 16, London: Family Policy Studies Centre.

van Andel, H. (1989) 'Crime Prevention that Works: The Case of Public Transport in The Netherlands', *British Journal of Criminology*, 29(1), 47–56.

van den Haag, E. (1982) 'Could Successful Rehabilitation Reduce the Crime Rate?', *Journal of Criminal Law and Criminology*, 73(3), 1022–35.

van Dijk, J. (1990) 'Crime Prevention Policy: Current State and Prospects', in Kaiser, G. and Albrecht, H-J. (eds) *Crime and Criminal Policy in Europe*, Criminological Research Report, vol. 43, Freiburg: Max Planck Institute, 205–20.

van Dijk, J. (1991) 'More than a Matter of Security: Trends in Crime Prevention in Europe', in Heidensohn, F. and Farrell, M. (eds) *Crime in Europe*, London: Routledge, 27–42.

van Dijk, J. (1995) 'In Search of Synergy: Coalition-Building Against Crime in The Netherlands', *Security Journal*, 6, 7–11.

van Dijk, J. and de Waard, J. (1991) 'A Two-Dimensional Typology of Crime Prevention Projects', *Criminal Justice Abstracts*, 23, 483–503.

van Dijk, J. and Junger-Tas, J. (1988) 'Trends in Crime Prevention in The Netherlands', in Hope and Shaw (1988a), 260–77.

van Dijk, J., Mayhew, P. and Killias, M. (1990) *Experiences of Crime Across the World*, Deventer: Kluwer.

van Dijk, J., Haffmans, C., Ruter, F. and Schutte, J. (eds) (1986) *Criminal Law in Action: An Overview of Current Issues in Western Societies*, Arnhem: Gouda Quint.

Vold, G. and Bernard, T. (1986) *Theoretical Criminology*, Oxford: Oxford University Press.

von Hirsch, A., Ashworth, A., Wasik, M., Smith, A.T.H., Morgan, R. and Gardner, J. (1995) 'Overtaking on the Right', *New Law Journal*, 1501–16.

Walden Jones, B. (1993) *Crime and Citizenship: Preventing Youth Crime in France through Social Integration*, London: NACRO.

Walklate, S. (1991) 'Victims, Crime Prevention and Social Control', in Reiner, R. and Cross, M. (eds) *Beyond Law and Order*, Basingstoke: Macmillan, 202–22.

Walklate, S. (1992) 'Appreciating the Victim: Conventional, Realist or Critical Criminology?', in Matthews and Young (1992), 102–18.

Walklate, S. (1997) 'Risk and Criminal Victimisation: A Modernist Dilemma?', *British Journal of Criminology*, 37(1), 35–45.

Waller, I. (1991) *Putting Crime Prevention on the Map*, Introductory Report to the International Conference on Urban Safety, Drugs and Crime Prevention, Paris: CNIT.

Walters, R. (1996) 'The "Dream" of Multi-Agency Crime Prevention: Pitfalls in Policy and Practice', *Crime Prevention Studies*, 5, 75–96.

Weatheritt, M. (1988) 'Community Policing: Rhetoric or Reality?', in Greene and Mastrofski (1988), 153–75.

Weatheritt, M. (1986) *Innovations in Policing*, London: Croom Helm.

Weatheritt, M. (1993) 'Community Policing', in Butcher, H., Glen, A., Henderson, P. and Smith, J. (eds) *Community and Public Policy*, London: Pluto Press, 124–38.

Weiss, R.P. (1987) 'The Community and Prevention', in Johnson, E.H. (ed.) *Handbook on Crime and Delinquency Prevention*, New York: Greenwood Press.

West, D. and Farrington, D.P. (1973) *Who Becomes Delinquent?*, London: Heinemann.

White, P. and Powar, I. (1998) *Revised Projections of Long-Term Trends in the Prison Population to 2005*, London: Home Office.

Widdecombe, A. (1997) Speech to the Local Government Association Conference, 'Crime – the Local Solution', 6 March.

Wieviorka, M. (1995) *The Arena of Racism*, London: Sage.

Wiles, P. (1996) *The Quality of Service of the Sedgefield Community Force*, Sheffield: Centre for Criminological and Legal Research, University of Sheffield.

Willemse, H.M. (1994) 'Developments in Dutch Crime Prevention', *Crime Prevention Studies*, 2, 33–47.

Wilson, J.Q. (1975) *Thinking About Crime*, New York: Vintage.

Wilson, J.Q. and Kelling, G. (1982) 'Broken Windows: The Police and Neighbourhood Safety', *The Atlantic Monthly*, March, 29–37.

Wilson, J.Q. and Kelling, G. (1989) 'Making Neighbourhoods Safe', *The Atlantic Monthly*, February, 46–52.

Worrall, A. (1997) *Punishment in the Community*, Harlow: Addison Wesley Longman.

Wycoff, M.A. and Skogan, W. (1994) 'Community Policing in Madison: An Analysis of Implementation and Impact', in Rosenbaum (1994), 75–91.

Yin, R.K., Vogel, M.E., Chaiken, J.M. and Both, D.R. (1977) *Citizen Patrol Projects*, Department of Justice, Washington DC: Government Printing Office.

Yngvesson, B. (1993) 'Local People, Local Problems, and Neighborhood Justice: The Discourse of "Community" in San Francisco Community Boards', in Merry and Milner (1993), 379–400.

Young, J. (1986) 'The Failure of Criminology', in Matthews, R. and Young, J. (eds) *Confronting Crime*, London: Sage, 4–30.

Young, J. (1988) 'Risk of Crime and Fear of Crime: A Realistic Critique of Survey-Based Assumptions', in Maguire and Pointing (1988), 164–76.

Young, J. (1992) 'Ten Points of Realism', in Young, J. and Matthews, R. (eds) *Rethinking Criminology: The Realist Debate*, London: Sage, 24–68.

Young, J. (1994) 'Incessant Chatter', in Maguire *et al.* (1994), 69–124.

Young, J. (1997) 'Charles Murray and the American Penal Experiment', in Murray (1997), 31–9.

Index

active citizenry, 248–9, 250
architectural design, crime
    prevention, 47, 51, 75, 76
Association of Chief Officers of
    Probation (ACOP), 46
Association of Chief Police Officers
    (ACPO), 33, 45
Association of Metropolitan
    Authorities (AMA), 9, 48, 54–5
Audit Commission, 44–5, 48, 59, 113

Barr, R.
    displacement, 81, 83–4, 85, 210,
        212
    equal society and victimisation,
        267–8
Bayley, D.H., 236, 237–8, 241
Bonnemaison Report, 1983 (France),
    221–4, 228
Braithwaite, J., 239–40
'broken windows' thesis, 130–4
bullying prevention, 117–18

Cassels Committee and Report, 48,
    101
CCTV cameras, 51, 67, 88–9, 142–3
    incentives and involvement, 41, 48,
        191, 192
Central Council of Probation
    Committee Report, 1987, 46
Chicago School, 66, 126, 128–9
citizen patrols, 150–1
civilianisation of public services, 248,
    249–50

Clarke, R.V.
    opportunity reduction model, 18
    rational choice, 73, 79, 82
    situational prevention, 36, 66, 69,
        74, 76, 85–6
classification of crime prevention
    measures and intended focus, 6,
        7, 13–14, 15–16, 18
    political models, 21–2
    proximal and distal mechanisms,
        19–21
    public health analogy, 14–17, 18, 19
    purposes and uses, 6–8
    situational and social prevention,
        17–19
commercial sector involvement
    forms of, 38, 50, 51, 187–8, 191
    game theory models of behaviour,
        188
    incentives, 41, 48, 190–1, 192
    'Prisoners' Dilemma', 188–90
    wider conception of, 188–90
commercial and social strategies,
    103–60
communitarianism, 131, 138, 239–40
communities, 'defended', 262–6
'community'
    collective attitudes, 157, 158, 159
    institutions and social/economic
        forces, 157–8
    meaning and, 9, 124, 125–6
    nature of, 157–60
community 'crime careers', 138–9,
    158

community crime prevention
  community defence, the 'broken
    windows' thesis, 124, 129–34
  community organisation, 124,
    126–9
  critique of, 155–60
  informal control, lack of, 155–6
  intermediate institutions, 124,
    136–8
  low crime areas, 156–7
  mobilisation of individuals and
    resources, 124, 125–6, 134–6
  political economy of community,
    124, 138–40
  resident involvement, 134–6
community crime prevention, case
  studies
  community patrols in Sedgefield,
    151–2
  community policing, 146–7
  concierge scheme in high rise
    blocks, 142–3
  mediation programmes, 145–6
  neighbourhood watch, 147–50
  Priority Estates Project (PEP),
    140–2
  San Francisco Community Board,
    145–6
  street watches and citizen patrols,
    150–1
  victim-led project, 143–5
  'zero tolerance' policing in New
    York, 152–5
community policing, 137, 146–7
community safety, 1, 5–28
  broader approach, 9, 10
  evaluating, 196–217
  'implant' hypothesis, 193
  local government, involvement,
    47–9
  locality emphasis, 9, 193
  partnership approach, 9–10
  politics of, 245–71
  private sector involvement, 162,
    191–2
  'reinvention of government' and,
    255
  'tailoring' incentive for private
    sector, 192
community self-governance, 262–3

comparative experiences and British
  perspective
  conflict resolution, institutionalised,
    244
  government role, importance,
    242–3
  intermediate functionaries, 243–4
  interpersonal and technological
    balance, 242, 243, 244
  wider social cohesion and
    exclusion, 243
concierge scheme in high rise block,
  142–3
Conservative government initiatives,
  40, 41, 48, 53, 54
  crime prevention, structural
    difficulties and, 54, 55, 62
consultation
  aims of, 167, 168–9
  citizen's juries, use of, 168
  forms of, 168, 208
  mechanisms and process, 168, 208
  package, 168
  unrepresentatives participants, 169
control theory, 105–6
Cornish, D.B., 73, 81, 82, 211
Cornish Committee on the
  Prevention and Detection of
  Crime, 33, 36, 42–3
corporate crime, 27, 166, 241
corporate sponsorship, 51
corporatism, 185–6
Council of Europe, European crime,
  and, 218
Crawford, A.
  community participation, 134, 186,
    262
  community crime prevention, 139,
    157, 158, 159, 263
  evaluation and research, 167, 203,
    208, 209
  organisation conflicts, 171, 172,
    173, 174
  spirals of ghettoisation, 264, 265
Crime and Disorder Bill 1997, xi
  assessment of, 61
  community safety strategy, 58–9
  orders, proposed, 59–60, 61, 115,
    116
  partnership model, 171

statutory duty and problem
oriented methodology, 163
youth justice reform, 60–1, 115,
116
Crime Concern, 40, 50–3, 57, 119
crime prevention
classifying, 13–22
conceptualising, 5–28
criminality prevention, 17
culture and transferability, 4, 218,
242, 244
evaluating, 196–217
fear of crime, 11–12
France, 220–9
future visions, 246, 260–9
history, British, 29–35
individuals at high risk, early
intervention, 120–2, 266
international variations, 55, 218,
219, 246–7
Japan, 235–42
key concepts, 3, 6–8, 27
models, 21–2
Morgan Report and, 38–40
market economies, effect, 137,
263–4
'marketisation', 51, 71, 245, 248,
249–50
Netherlands, The, 229–35
'new penology', 255–8
politics of, 245–71
public health analogy, 14–17
punitive policies, and, 262
shift in and loss of state power,
251–2
shifts to, 32–5, 246, 260
social and ethical conflicts with,
269–70
social value, 269
structure of responsibility, 38–40
Sweden, 219–20
victim-oriented prevention, 22–5
see also community crime
prevention, policing; situational
crime prevention; social crime
prevention; youth crime
prevention
Crime Prevention Through
Environmental Design (CPTED),
76

crime surveys, 1, 165–6, 167
criminal justice system
contemporary contradictions, 63–4
crime control, limitations of, 33,
34–5
crime prevention definitions,
10–11, 14
deterministic and voluntaristic
views, 101–2
dispositional bias of mainstream,
70–1
failure, origins of, 245
growth of, 31
Currie, E., 157, 158, 202–3, 263, 269

Dalston Youth Project, 118–19
'defended communities'
market economies, eroding effect,
263–4
spirals of ghettoisation, 264–6
'defensible space', 75–6
demonstration projects, 203, 208, 209
designing out crime, 74, 76
architectural design and, 75
design disadvantagement, 76–8
kerb crawling case study, 92–4
social control network, 75
desistance, 83, 93, 267
deterrence, 32, 69, 71
displacement
assumptions about crime, 81–2, 210
benign, 83, 93, 267
case study examples, 86, 87, 91, 93,
95
'choice structuring properties', 82,
85
crime control policy, as, 83–4
diffusion of benefits, 84, 88, 93, 95
evaluation and research, 81, 83,
210–12
forms of, 81, 83, 210
malign, 83
regressive, 87
routine activities theory, and, 82–3
situational control, criticism of, 80,
81–3, 99, 100–1

Ekblom, P.
crime prevention, defining, 10, 19
evaluation, 203, 206, 212–13, 217

methodology, 163, 164, 197,
199–200
proximal and distal mechanisms,
19–21, 73
environmental and situational
strategies, 66–102
environmental crime prevention
see architectural design crime
prevention; situational crime
prevention
estate-based situational prevention,
90–4
evaluation and research
before-and-after surveys, 165, 200
cause and effect, 9, 19–20, 197
conclusions on, 215–17, 270
costs, 203, 213–14
crime analysis, 8, 9, 12, 161, 164
crime audits, 213, 214, 215
crime prevention, of, 196–217
demonstration projects, 203, 208,
209
displacement, 210–12
fear of crime, 11, 34, 199, 214
France, in, 227
implementation, and failure of, 6,
7–8, 12, 161, 203, 206
internal validity threats, 201
interviews with convicted offenders,
73, 83, 211–12
local surveys, 164–6
measurements and measuring, 8,
198–203
neighbourhood watch, 148–9, 161,
203, 210
Netherlands, The, 230–1, 232–3,
233–4, 235
problems of, 165–7, 196–7, 201–2,
214, 215–16
process, questions on, 206–7
'processual mechanisms', 208
qualitative research, 207
quality, unsatisfactory, 196–7,
215–16
rational choice theory, and, 73,
215
scientific realist model, 204–6, 209
success and failure, 8, 214–15
transferability of prevention, 216,
242

victimisation surveys, 164–5, 166–7,
200
wider criteria, use of, 199, 214–15
see also outcome evaluation;
planning and information
gathering

fear of crime, 11–12, 34, 199, 214,
215
Feeley, M., 256–7
France, 220–9
Bonnemaison Report, 221, 222–4,
227, 228
crime prevention and social/
economic policy, distinguishing,
228
criminal law, separation from
welfare policies, 220–1, 228–9
cultural differences, 227–8
evaluation, 227
funding, 224
implementation structures, 38, 41,
221, 222–4, 228
local crime prevention councils,
222–4, 227
Praderie Report, 224
preventive action contracts, 223,
224
specialist crime prevention teams,
226
summer camps and initiatives,
224–5
Youth Centres, 226–7
funding
France, 224
international trend, 246–7
mainstream versus peripheral,
122–3
Netherlands, The, 230, 235
United Kingdom, 63–4
future visions, 246, 267–9
community involvement, 262,
268–9
defended communities and
ghettoisation, 262–6
'equal society', 267–8
governance, modes of, 253
prevention paradigm and
punishment industry, 260–2
public sphere and civic values, 268

reintegration strategies, 268
'risk society', 266–7

Garland, D.
  criminal justice system, 11, 63, 260
  criminology, 2, 31, 80
  penology, 34, 259, 260, 262
gender, 27–8, 110, 111, 176–7
Gladstone Report 1980, 35–6
Gottfredson, M.R., 105
governance, 249–50, 252, 253
governmentality, 255–6, 257, 266
  risk, 255–6, 257, 266
  state power, 257, 258–9

High/Scope Perry Pre-School Project,
    116–17, 123
Home Office
  initiatives, 33, 36–7, 40–1, 45–6, 52,
    196
  Research and Planning Unit, 66
  Standing Committee on Crime
    Prevention, 33, 36
Hope, T., 124, 125, 129, 139, 207
'hot spots' of crime, 79–80, 129, 164
Huddersfield Project, 96–7

implementation, 4, 161–2, 192–5
  failure, 161, 203, 206
  outcome and, 6, 7, 206–8
  partnership approach, 161–95
  planning and information
    gathering, 162–9
Inspectorate of Constabulary, H M,
    1988 Report, 45, 59
intermediate functionaries, use of
  Glasgow, 243–4
  Japan, 237–9, 244
  Netherlands, The, 232–4, 235, 243
inter-organisational conflict and
    power relations, 171–2
  agency domination, 172, 184
  collaboration, 174–6
  conflict avoidance, 172–3, 173, 174,
    194
  co-ordinator, role, 178–9
  formality and informality, degrees
    of, 176–7
  gender, 176–7
  hierarchy, questions of, 177

'ideology of unity', 173
trust, 179–80
  see also partnership approach
interpersonal and technological
  balance, 242, 243, 244
intervention, identification and focus,
  6, 7, 13–14

Japan, 235–42
  civil liberties in, 241–2
  'communitarian' society as, 239–40
  crime, corporate and organised,
    241
  crime prevention associations,
    237–9
  crime rates, 235–6, 241
  formal structures supporting
    informal, 238, 240–1
  informal group social control, 236,
    241
  intermediate functionaries, 237–9,
    244
  policing (*koban*), 236–7, 240–1
  re-integrative shaming, culture of,
    239–41

Kirkholt burglary project, 95–6,
    208–9

Liddle, A.M., 170–1, 176, 177, 178
local government, 38, 47, 48–9, 58–9
low crime areas, 156–7
Lurigio, A.J., 201, 202, 216

managerialism *see* new public
    management reforms
Mayhew, P., 35, 70, 86–7, 211
Morgan Report
  Crime and Disorder Bill 1997, 58–9
  evaluation and surveys, 164, 165,
    196
  impact statements, 108
  involvement, commercial,
    government and private, 54–5,
    56, 187, 192
  partnership approach, and, 38
  recommendations, 38–41
  structure of responsibility, 38–40
multi-agency approach *see* partnership
    approach

National Crime Prevention Agency, 25, 41, 55, 59
National Association for the Care and Resettlement of Offenders (NACRO)
  cost-benefit analysis, and, 213
  crime prevention, 36, 49, 165
  resident involvement, 136
  Safer Cities Programme, 53, 57
neighbourhood watch, 40, 51, 147–8
  evaluation and research, 148–9, 161, 203, 210
  police and, 149–50
  support for, 51, 149
Netherlands, The, 229–35
  city wardens, 233–4
  crime prevention, responsibility, 41, 229, 230–1
  evaluation, 230–1, 232–3, 233–4, 235
  funding provisions, 230, 235
  initiatives implemented, 231–5
  intermediate functionaries, 232–4, 235
  preventive policies, principles, 229–30
  public transport, initiative on, 232–3
  Roethof Committee, 1983, 229
  'Society and Crime' government document, 229, 230, 232
  truancy project, 234–5
  youth policy, integrated, 231–2
'new penology'
  power in, 256, 258
  problems of, 257–8
  risk reducing and prevention, 256–8, 267
new public management reforms, 181–3, 253–5
  see also managerialism
  evaluation: success or failure, in, 215
  'outcomes' and 'outputs' conflict, 182
  partnership contractualisation, 182–3, 194
  reinvention of government, 254, 255, 258

offender-oriented measures, 15, 16, 68, 71
opportunity reduction, 18, 66, 67–8
Osborne, D., 252–3, 254–5, 258

partnership approach, 162, 169–70, 184–6
  acceptance and extent, contemporary, 36–7, 45, 62, 169, 183–4
  accountability problems, 180–1
  collaboration levels, 174–6
  commercial sector involvement, 187–90
  community participation, 9–10, 186–7
  conflict avoidance, 172–3, 174, 175, 194
  conflicts, multiple aims, 173–4
  contractualisation, 182–3, 194
  co-ordinator in, 178–9
  corporatism, 185–6
  development of, 36–7, 45, 62, 169, 183–4
  financial incentives, 169–70, 190–1
  formality and informality, 176–7
  gender relations, 176–7
  'ideology of unity', 173
  implementation, 161–95
  independence, and, 175–6
  power relations, differential, 171–4
  process of work, 193–4
  public funding, pre-requisite, 170
  reinvention of government, and, 255
  roles and responsibilities, 180–1
  trust, 179–80, 183
  types of, 170–1, 174–6
Pawson, R., 198, 204–6, 207, 208
Pearson, G., 171, 176, 177, 181
planning and information gathering
  conclusions on, 192–5
  consultation, 167–9, 193
  crime data and analysis, 163–4, 165
  problem-oriented methodology, 161, 162–3
police
  annual plans, 49, 59
  Audit Commission and policy, 44

crime data, 163
foot patrol research, 42
Morgan Report proposals, 38,
    58–9
neighbourhood watch, 147–50
specialisation, 42–3, 44–5
Police Community Consultative
    Group, 136
political economy of community, 138
    power dimensions, 139, 140
    socio-economic environment, wider,
    139
Priority Estates Project (PEP), 50,
    108, 136, 140–2, 207
prison population, 33, 260–2
private sector, 50–2, 247–50
probation service, 45–7
problem-oriented approach, 162–3,
    192, 193
programmes failure, 161
proximal and distal mechanisms,
    19–20, 73
public health analogy, crime
    prevention
    families and good parenting,
    112–13
    primary, secondary and tertiary, 14,
    15, 16, 18, 19, 68
    situational and social, 18–19, 68
    van Dijk, J. and de Waard, J.,
    approach, 15

quasi-experimental method,
    evaluation, 198, 204–5

rational choice theory, 70–1
    choice structuring properties, 82,
    85
    criminality and criminal events,
    73–4
    criticisms, 72–3
    evaluation and research, 73, 215
    limited rationality model, 73, 74
'reintegrative shaming', 239–41
'reinvention of government'
    critique, 254–5
    'entrepreneurial government',
    252–3
    managerial reforms, 254, 255, 258
    public sector, transformation, 252

repeat victimisation, 23–4
    cause, potential explanations, 97–8
    crime prevention considered,
    96–8
    Huddersfield Project, 96–7
    insurance implications, 97
    intervention, 24–5, 96–7
    Kirkholt Project, 94–6
    research, 23, 24
replication, 208–9
research see evaluation and research
'responsibilisation strategies'
    'active citizenry', 248–9, 250
    civilianisation of public services,
    248, 249–50
    markets, contacting out, 249–50
    private governance, and, 249–50,
    251, 253
    state, dispersal of responsibilities,
    247
    voluntarism of public services, 248,
    249–50
'risk society', 256, 266–7
Rosenbaum, D.P.
    community, 146, 148–9, 159, 186,
    217
    evaluation, 196, 197, 199, 203
    implant hypothesis, 156, 193
routine activity theory, 26, 78–9
    displacement, 82–3
    evaluation: success and failure in,
    215
    generator and receptor places, 80
    'hot spots' of crime, 79–80

Safe Neighbourhoods Unit (SNU),
    49–50
    cost benefit analysis and, 213
    evaluation studies, 91, 142–3, 209
    resident involvement, 136
Safer Cities Programme, 37, 52–4,
    55–6
    assessment, 54, 57–8, 88–9, 178–9
    inter-organisational conflicts, 171,
    172, 173, 176, 177, 178
    partnerships, perspectives, 184–5,
    186
Sampson, A.
    strategic foresight, lack of, 56–7
    structure, 54–7

San Francisco Community Board, 145, 146
schools, 105, 114–15
scientific realist evaluation model
    essential ingredients, 204–6
    replication, 209
Shaw, C., 126, 127, 128
situational crime prevention, 3, 36, 65
    assessment, 69–70, 98–102
    definitions and hypotheses, 66–8, 69, 245
    'designing out' crime, 74–8
    deterrence and, 69, 71
    displacement, 80–4
    generator places, 80
    informal control, 34, 66, 236, 241
    multiple measures, assessment, 95–6
    neo-liberal ideology, convergence with, 72
    offender-oriented approach, 72, 86–8
    opportunistic crime, 69, 70, 73
    opportunity reduction, 18, 66–8
    rational choice theory, 69, 70–4
    receptor places, 80
    routine activity theory, 78–80
    theoretical background, 68–70
    see also community crime
        prevention; crime prevention;
        social crime prevention
situational crime prevention case
        studies, 84–5
    British Gas suicides, 85–6
    CCTV in car parks, 88–9
    'designing out' kerb crawling, 92–4
    Kirkholt Burglary Project, 94–6
    motorcycle theft, 86–7, 211
    phone entry systems, 91
    post office robberies, 89–90
    repeat victimisation, 94–6
    residential security, problem estate, 90–1
    steering column locks, 87–8
    street lighting, 91–2
Skogan, W., 132, 147, 148, 149
social crime prevention, 3, 17, 103–60, 245
    assumptions, 104–8
    broad social policies, 108
    conclusions on, 160
    control theory approach, 104–6
    individual, 104–24
    NACRO methodology, 49
    situational crime prevention, distinction, 17–19
    US and UK, differences, 123–4
    young people, 109–16
    see also community crime
        prevention; crime prevention;
        situational crime prevention
social disorganisation, 126, 127–8, 129, 130
social policy
    broad, 102, 108
    'community' concept, 157–60
    community-focused preventive measures, 124–40
    crime prevention and issues, 103–4, 108, 120–3
'spirals of ghettoisation', 264–6
'square of crime', 26–7
'stake in conformity', 104, 106–7
Standing Conference on Crime
        Prevention (Home Office), 10, 37–8, 39, 55, 56
strain theory, 106–7
street watches, 150–1
Sweden, 219–20
    National Crime Prevention Council, 41, 219

target hardening, 66, 68, 90
terminology, 5–6, 64
Tilley, N.
    Safer Cities Programme, 52, 56, 58, 88–9
    scientific realist model, 204, 205, 209
truancy, 114, 234–5

van Dijk, J.
    crime prevention definition, 10–11, 22, 23
    Netherlands, The, 229, 230, 234
victimisation, 11–12, 24–5, 72, 251
victimisation surveys, 164–5, 166–7, 200
victim-led project, a, 143–5
victim-oriented measures, 15, 16, 68

victim-oriented situational crime
    prevention, 22–5, 68
  case studies, 94–6
voluntary sector
  Morgan Report, 38
  NACRO, and, 49–50
  voluntarisation of services, 248,
    249–50

Weatheritt, M., 29–30, 147
Wilson, J.Q.
  'broken windows' thesis, 129–34
  crime prevention, 69–70, 71

Young, J., 26–7
young people and crime, 109
  case studies, 116–19
  'growing out of crime', 109–10
  in The Netherlands, 231–2
  prevention of offending, 38, 110,
    112–15
  risk factors, 110–12, 119–20

youth crime prevention
  families, parenting, 105, 110,
    112–13, 115
  government proposals, 58–61,
    115–16
  local authorities, 38, 39–40, 113
  orders, proposed, 59–60, 61, 115,
    116
  preventive intervention, 112–15,
    120
  protective factors, 112–15
  schools, 105, 114, 114–15
  truancy, reducing, 114, 234–5
youth justice system, 60–1, 109–10
youth offending teams (YOTs), 60–1,
    115–16

'zero tolerance' policing, New York,
    153–5
zonal theory, 126
'zone in transition', 127
zones of private governance, 249–50